Sacred Vessels

Sacred Vessels

The Cult of the Battleship
and the Rise of the U.S. Navy

Robert L. O'Connell

Westview Press

BOULDER • SAN FRANCISCO • OXFORD

To my mother and father,
Dorothea O'Connell and Robert J. O'Connell

Frontispiece photo courtesy of the U.S. Naval Institute.

Published in 1991 in the United States of America by Westview Press, Inc., 5500 Central Avenue, Boulder, Colorado 80301, and in the United Kingdom by Westview Press, 36 Lonsdale Road, Summertown, Oxford OX2 7EW

Library of Congress Cataloging-in-Publication Data
O'Connell, Robert L.
  Sacred vessels : the cult of the battleship and the rise of the
U.S. Navy / Robert L. O'Connell.
    p. cm.
  Includes bibliographical references and index.
  ISBN 0-8133-1116-0 (HC)
    1. Sea-power—United States—History—20th century.
2. Battleships—United States—History—20th century. 3. United
States Navy—History—20th century. 4. Battleships—History—20th
century. 5. Naval history, Modern—20th century. I. Title.
VA50.036 1991
359′.03′09730904—dc20   91-24527
                                                                   CIP

Printed and bound in the United States of America

The paper used in this publication meets the requirements
of the American National Standard for Permanence of Paper
for Printed Library Materials Z39.48-1984.

10   9   8   7   6   5   4   3   2   1

"The psychology of the Navy Department . . . frequently seemed to retire from the realm of logic into a dim religious world in which Neptune was God, Mahan his prophet, and the United States Navy the only true church."

—Henry L. Stimson

"It's almost idolatry for me to feel this way about a piece of metal."

—Former crew member speaking of the USS *Wisconsin* on NBC's *Today Show*, June 10, 1991

Contents

Contents

Illustrations

America's dreadnoughts, ca. 1936.

Preface

Writing critically about something you have come to regard with affection must provoke mixed emotions. As I learned more and more about the modern battleship's shortcomings, I found myself, like so many before me, falling under its spell. I have traveled hundreds of miles to visit these wonderful ships, reverently preserved like a necklace of talismans around our nation's coasts. I have stood in awe under the great guns, wondering what it must have been like to hear them fire. Perhaps it is true that their sound and fury signified very little in terms of actual destructive power. But most people thought they did, and that was and still is important. Besides, for the most part, we were proud of those ships. Now we live in a time of weapons so terrible that we must actually hide them—beneath the ground and below the surface of the sea. But, like battleships, they keep the peace precisely because of what others think they can do. All things being equal, who would not prefer the dreadnoughts?

Few books are written quickly, or without help. This one took a very long time and received much assistance from colleagues, friends, and family. First in line for thanks is Joe Kett, who poked this thing along from masters thesis, to doctoral dissertation, and finally . . . into print. I owe Joe a lot. Peter Kracht, my editor, literally dragged the manuscript out of my bedroom closet, breathed life into it, and set me on my way revising and expanding. Truly, there would be no *Sacred Vessels* without him. I will probably never write as well as John Casey or Norman Graebner, but I want to thank them for providing me with encouragement and personal standards of excellence.

We are all busy, and frequently middle-aged and farsighted. Thus reading even the best-typed manuscripts—mine wasn't—constitutes a true act of kindness. With this in mind I want to thank Peter Karsten, Dennis Evans, Alex Roland, Elting Morison, Whittle Johnston, Gordon Bowen, Carl Brandt, and William McNeill—all of whom, at one point or another, waded through my collected thoughts on battleships and provided valuable guidance.

The research for this book was done mostly at the Library of Congress and the Alderman Library of the University of Virginia. The excellent staffs of both institutions were extremely helpful and generous with their time. I also want to thank the staffs of the Operational Archives of the U.S. Navy's Naval History Division, the Library of the U.S. Department of State, and the U.S. National Archives. I am additionally very grateful for the meticulous editing of Marian Safran and the skilled coordination of Beverly LeSuer, Senior Project Editor at Westview Press, and her replacement (Bev has moved on to law school), Michelle Starika. Thanks also go to Stephen Eitelman at the Foreign Science and Technology Center, who provided computer support for my index.

Finally, I want to thank my wife, Benjie, and my daughters, Jessica and Lucy, for their love and generosity in giving me the time to write. They are far more important to me than any book.

Robert L. O'Connell

1

Introduction:
A Fatal Vision

I

One day in the spring of 1921 a battleship recently surrendered to the American Navy by the vanquished German High Seas Fleet swung placidly at anchor in the middle of Chesapeake Bay. Several smaller craft soon arrived on the scene and took stations around the great warship. Aboard those latecomers were a number of important observers, including the civilian head of the Navy Department, a former secretary of war, several influential senators and representatives, a large body of admirals and other high-ranking officers, and numerous members of the press. All attention was focused on the German dreadnought, stolid and defiant, bristling with guns, aesthetically the very epitome of belligerence. Squatting there in the water, it must have seemed to most of the gathered dignitaries virtually invulnerable.

This quiet scene was soon interrupted by the buzzing of airplanes. As the squadron appeared over the horizon and drew closer, it was revealed to be made up of a number of frail biplanes, looking and sounding a bit like a swarm of flying insects. Presently, the aircraft gathered above the dreadnought and one by one dove down to drop bombs upon it. At first these sorties must have seemed no more menacing than mosquitoes attacking a rhinoceros. But soon the battleship was revealed to have suffered heavily—her superstructure was in shambles and the stern of the ship was almost entirely submerged. Relentlessly the planes continued the assault, their bombs throwing huge spumes of water and assorted chunks of dreadnought high into the air. Finally, after two particularly ferocious

1

hits, the great ship stood nearly straight up in the water and then slipped quickly beneath the waves.

Among most of the observers, reactions ranged from shocked silence to scarcely concealed glee. But in one quarter the response was considerably more demonstrative. Aboard the USS *Henderson* a group of admirals gathered on the deck were reliably reported to have wept openly for the martyred Teutonic dreadnought—a remarkable reaction considering that the United States had been at war with Germany just two and a half years before. Certainly it was true that these officers had staked a considerable portion of their professional prestige on the battleship's ability to survive this airborne assault. Yet these were men trained practically from adolescence to maintain an iron grip over their emotions in the face of adversity—to carry on with friends of a lifetime lying dead at their feet. Consequently, it seems probable that something more was involved there than simply a public demonstration of bad judgment. The destruction of this ship must have cut very deep into the naval soul.

When I first heard of the test and the emotions it provoked, it struck me as strangely universal and archetypical. There was something archaic, almost medieval, implied in that twentieth-century trial of arms. It hearkened back to the days when not only ships but also cannon and swords had names, when weapons of all sorts were embellished with elaborate decorative motifs and anthropomorphized as a matter of course. Nevertheless, this was a serious test of two of the reputedly most potent weapons then in existence. The machines involved were products of considerable technological sophistication and not supposed to be the subject of much emotion. But that was obviously not true in the case of the weeping admirals. The atmosphere was more theatrical than empirical, a melodramatic combination of joust and stress analysis, with the emphasis on the former. The admirals were innocent and honest enough to betray their emotions, but otherwise the staging was not so very different from contemporary tests. It seemed to say a lot about the way we value technology—how we manipulate it and how it manipulates us. Yet it is more important to understand why, to explore the causes and origins of those attitudes.

II

The dreadnought sunk by the swarm of aircraft was as much a symbol as it was a warship, an armor-plated embodiment of the possibilities for compromise between technology and tradition. For beneath the metallic flanks of that and every modern battleship beat the heart of a sailing ship-of-the-line. For hundreds of years those noble wooden vessels had epitomized virtually every aspect of naval life—its rituals, its social structure, its conceptions of power, courage, and fighting etiquette. The sailing battleship was the linchpin of an entire way of life, an existence so stable that it seemed virtually immutable.

But the coming of steam propulsion and explosive-shell fire left the wooden warship hopelessly obsolete in a matter of a few decades. And as the sailing warship went, so went the skills of the professional naval officers, who were, after all, experts at harnessing the wind with ropes and canvas. So, overwhelmed by what amounted to a tidal wave of technological innovation, naval officers fell into a sort of torpor, watching passively as their ships metamorphosed beneath them, with barely an idea of what this new world might bring. Their lassitude would stretch out over three decades, until finally, inspired by the writings of a fellow officer–turned historian, naval leaders would take stock of the new environment and conclude, with profound relief, that nothing fundamental had changed. The new ships in which they rode were judged entirely amenable to the rules that had governed naval warfare for centuries. These supposedly revolutionary vessels were simply steam-powered, armor-plated equivalents of what had come before. To virtually all concerned, it seemed that technology had been tamed and the traditional world of the naval officer saved.

Unfortunately what appeared to be salvation was ultimately based on self-deception. The battleship concept was an exercise in tunnel vision. In fact, the possible applications of technology to naval warfare were far broader than those defined by the simple interaction of big guns, armor plate, and steam propulsion, so in wartime the fate of the battleship would be that of tactical underachiever and victim. Nonetheless, the dominant element of virtually all the world's navies resisted this reality with all of their strength. And it could hardly have been otherwise.

Their attitude was not simply a matter of stubbornness and blind conservatism. To those men the battleship was the single most important artifact of their professional existence: It symbolized everything that was acceptable and orderly about naval life. It was at once a place to live and work and a bulwark against technology-induced anarchy—a true vessel of culture. Put in this context it is easier to see why the battleship was passionately defended in the face of all logic, why American naval officers could weep over the sacrifice of a single German dreadnought.

All of this might be considered somewhat quaint and largely irrelevant to anything other than naval sociology, were it not for the fact that those ships were perceived to be the ultimate weapons of their day. They had their detractors. But among the states owning them, dreadnoughts were generally considered the final guarantee against seaborne aggression. And in spite of numerous wartime disasters that dragged thousands of men to their deaths, the battleship's reputation as terror of the high seas persisted long beyond the point that pure logic might have dictated. Plainly, naval officers did their best to promote and perpetuate battleships. But in America and most other modern states the influence of the uniformed military is far from absolute. Nonetheless, politicians and the public, with a much smaller stake in the arguments and the ships, went along with them. That seems to say something very basic and timeless about the way weapons are chosen.

We live in a time that is at once similar and far removed from the point at which the members of sailing navies found their world being transformed. In our case the specter of nuclear weapons has also raised the most fundamental questions about the relevance or irrelevance of past experience, particularly as it relates to weaponry. On the face of it, the impersonal forces of technology appear to have complete control, the life-and-death dictates of our own security environment mandating the most efficient weapons possible. Indeed, the course of the great Soviet-American arms race, having sent the potential destructiveness of strategic weapons spiraling upward beyond even comprehension, seems to be prima facie evidence that this is in fact the case—that the operational imperatives driving arms development are absolute and devoid of human content. Yet consider the case of the Reagan-era Pentagon graphic that featured side-by-side comparisons of very large Soviet ICBMs with the relatively puny U.S. Minuteman III and MX missiles, in an effort to demonstrate that the United States was lagging in this area. Although the comparison said almost nothing about relative capabilities, it spoke volumes about the way people ultimately value weapons and, still more fundamentally, how the course of technology might be influenced by human preconceptions.

III

At one level, of course, technology is immune to influences beyond those generated by its own internal logic; it is the equivalent of a mechanical mouse following the path dictated by the line of least resistance. In that sense technology is not just a product of reason; it is reason activated and externalized from the human, its creator. But if the step-by-step progression of technology must blindly follow only the laws of possibility, that explanation fails to account for the peculiarly human element in so much of our machinery, even the most sophisticated examples. Rather it seems that humans, although unable to manipulate the stages of a particular process other than in accordance with the rules of feasibility, are nevertheless able to exert a generalized influence over the entire process. The force behind technology remains distinctively human, as well as a matter of pure technique. The relationship, however, is one of coexistence, not integration—an eccentric interaction, like a cam gyrating first in one and then in another direction. Human effectiveness in modifying technology is generally maximized at the beginning or end of a developmental sequence. Once the choice is exercised, however, the course of any process is henceforth determined by rules inherent to the procedure itself. Therefore, although the results of a particular chain of events may be directly opposed to the purposes and desires of humans, it is nonetheless true that choice has been exerted—just as Mickey Mouse undeniably set the brooms in motion in *Fantasia*, though he might not have planned or liked the outcome.

Meanwhile, the manner in which people alter the course of technology is subtly influenced by a number of characteristically human preconceptions and conventions, which are themselves often irrelevant or even inefficient and whimsical. Historians have noted the persistent check that aesthetic values exerted upon the potential destructiveness of preindustrial warfare. Weapons makers were artisans, and the beauty of their products was frequently as important as their deadliness. Similarly the manifest sleekness of so many contemporary weapons might be used to question whether aesthetic preferences have entirely disappeared from their design. Another example of this general phenomenon is the persistent, almost instinctive, equation of size with power in spite of the fact that the opposite often tends to be the case. The desire to recreate one's own being at times profoundly conditioned the course of invention. The telephone, for instance, was the result of a calculated attempt to imitate the operations of the ear. To point to specific examples oversimplifies a state that is really a ferment of cultural and emotional values operating on all levels. Elting Morison captured that spirit of multifaceted valuation that people use to appraise machinery in his description of the modern era's archetypical mechanism:

Probably the machine that took human beings most into account and was the most fun to work with was the first serious prime mover, the steam engine. It was big enough to be imposing and small enough to be comprehended. The principal working parts were sufficiently exposed, not only to get at but to give a feeling for what was going on. It made perfectly wonderful noises and produced stimulating quantities of smoke, steam, and fire. It moved at majestic tempos and gave off a sense of mass and permanence.[1]

IV

Almost without exception those factors are ignored in the environment that generates and approves today's weaponry. The B-2 bomber will be built or canceled solely on the basis of cost and performance, not because it gives the U.S. Air Force's pilots something to fly, or because it is ominous looking, black, and resembles the Batplane. Should some responsible official make note of those characteristics at a congressional hearing, it is likely that such comments would be judged as frivolous or even absurd. Nonetheless, the B-2 does look like the Batplane, and that is not necessarily irrelevant to its true mission. Having negotiated the frightening landscape of the cold war, we would do well to remember that the success of nuclear deterrence was based in large measure on the symbolic and psychological impact of the weapons involved. And under the circumstances, it seems entirely more reasonable and appropriate to consider seriously the aesthetic and institutional paradigms around which weapons have traditionally evolved. Because of the peculiar ability of technical and emotive factors to coexist in mutually exclusive spheres, any weapons system, no matter how deadly, is still likely to be subject to many of the same cultural presumptions that determined the nature of its obsolete predecessors. Therefore, although an outmoded weapon may appear simple in terms of technological refinement, it is not without relevance. Weapons are always built to be taken seriously and therefore must be justified in pragmatic terms. But the defense of a particular weapon must inevitably reveal the cultural context from which it sprang, and this context, in turn, may be expected to have some significance for the problem of armaments in general.

The dreadnought battleship is a particularly appropriate candidate to be studied in that light, for its capabilities as an engine of destruction were far exceeded by its appeal. "That she survived so long in the world's armories," wrote Richard Hough, "was evidence of the dreadnought's power to inflame men's imaginations."[2] Granted, the state of technology in the late nineteenth and early twentieth centuries left a great deal more slack in the evaluation of weapons than would be encountered today. But naval officers were still obligated to champion the battleship, not in terms of likes and dislikes, but according to what they believed was the best and most up-to-date technical data available. Nevertheless, to the average naval officer before Pearl Harbor, a navy without battleships was no navy at all. Those ships represented a way of life, they were at the core of the naval soul, and for that reason their occupants clung to them with remarkable tenacity.

But ironically it is the dreadnought's very shortcomings as a weapon, its propensity for under-kill, that provide the prime basis for strategic comparison with our own nuclear arsenal. For each was very much better not used than used. In the case of our nuclear arsenal, that was always more or less understood; in the case of the battleship it was an accident of technology and resisted strenuously by its designated users. Nevertheless, the dreadnought represented, among other things, a groping prototype of deterrence, a weapon of last resort whose reputation underlay some very basic political relationships. For that reason alone, it is worth considering its peculiar history.

But even if that were not the case, the modern battleship would still warrant serious study. Today almost all weapons cost a great deal. In choosing them we must look at them skeptically and from every angle to ensure that we are getting what we pay for. In that regard the story of the dreadnought is a cautionary tale.

2

In the Beginning: Traditions of the Naval World

I

On a lonely ship in the middle of the Pacific Ocean on November 17, 1901, an obscure commander in the American Navy was taking the chance of his life. He was writing a letter to the president of the United States, reporting what he considered to be the gross inefficiency of the country's warships and crews. A friend wrote later, "It amount[ed] in effect to reporting everyone in Washington for neglect of duty."[1] Yet the outspoken commander felt that "things were in such a state that . . . I was persuaded that no military reform would be made without outside pressure." So he sent the letter to the newly installed occupant of the White House, Theodore Roosevelt. The president's background and his well-known ambition to greatly increase the size and efficiency of the American Navy ensured that the letter would receive the chief executive's close attention. What he read was hardly reassuring: "I have . . . been forced to the very serious conclusion that the protection and armament of even our most recent battleships are so glaringly inferior . . . that our marksmanship is so crushingly inferior . . . that one or more of our ships would, in their present condition, inevitably suffer humiliating defeat at the hands of equal numbers of an enemy's vessels."[2]

The commander then went on to describe the events that surrounded the latest target practice of the North Atlantic Squadron. Five battleships had fired at the hulk of the Rams Island lightship for five minutes at the short range of between 2,800 and 2,000 yards. The results were appalling: A total of two hits had been scored.[3] Roosevelt, when he finished reading the letter, was reported to have exploded with rage. But he was impressed with the courage and concern

9

of the writer and soon appointed him inspector of target practice. The incident began a long and significant friendship.[4]

The author of this naval exposé was William Sowden Sims. He was destined to become one of the most influential figures in modern U.S. naval history. His schemes and reforms would become a major factor in the determination of naval policy up to Pearl Harbor.

Sims was a remarkable man. Blessed with a tall, erect frame and a strikingly handsome face, he possessed a commanding presence that rarely failed to impress his contemporaries. "He was so goddamn good-looking," muttered one of his many adversaries.[5] His personality was positively magnetic, and he never lost his nearly spellbinding knack of drawing men to support one or another of his endless causes. His capacity for self-dramatization was immense. His energy seemed without limits. But for all his innate ability, Sims was very much a product of his environment.

He was first and foremost an officer in the United States Navy. An Anglo-Episcopalian from upper-middle-class background, Sims fit precisely the genteel mold of the early twentieth-century Navy. He never forgot he was a member of a profession with very definite ethics and standards of behavior, and he charted his course of reform so as to avoid, whenever possible, crossing the faint line that delineated what was considered honorable conduct by his brother officers. A disgruntled friend complained, "Willie S. Sims held the record for high kicking at the Naval Academy, but he so arranged the process afterward that the higher he kicked, the higher he kicked himself."[6] It was that ability to ascertain the limits of acceptable conduct that enabled him to maintain a critical attitude without jeopardizing his rise to rank and influence.

A second key theme in Sims's career was the need to come to grips with the series of mechanized contrivances that were revolutionizing modern naval warfare. Although not an engineer, Sims was fascinated by the possibilities of technology. His biographer noted, "In the world of ideas there are still entrepreneurs. Sims was one."[7]

With relentless zeal for more than thirty years, he promoted one or another innovation designed to improve the operation of Uncle Sam's fleet. Yet the fact that he never contributed an invention of his own is symptomatic of the manner in which he conceived of technology. Considering the fact that he specialized in death-dealing instruments, he had an almost childishly innocent belief in the ultimate benevolence of technology. To Sims, the concept of mechanization was infinitely applicable. In a good-natured sympathy note to fellow officer Henry C.

Admiral William Sowden Sims. (Courtesy of the U.S. National Archives)

Mustin, he wrote: "I heard for the first time that you are laid up for repairs. . . . This human machine of ours is a curious and complicated chemical proposition that is subject to disarrangement from various causes. . . . You've had the safety valve screwed down ever since I've known you."[8]

To such a mind technology was less a question of tangible devices than almost a magic wand whose wondrous properties enabled it to cut through the most tangled of problems. One of his apologists, C. V. Babcock, noted that Sims, throughout his career, "represented what might be called the more modern and up-to-date view . . . devoted to constant searching and ruthless examination of . . . methods with a view of ousting them root and branch . . . if they are blocking progress or if a more efficient means could be found."[9]

The use of the word "efficiency" is important. To Sims and his followers the term represented a sort of universal solvent. It was the common denominator of all naval procedure, the sole criterion of tactical and strategic expedience. The possibility that efficiency might prove to be a very relative thing was not apparent.

This fascination with efficiency does provide a clue to the larger relevance of Sims's outlook. That elusive term was also the byword of the elite group of civilian reformers who marched under the banner of "progressivism" and looked to Theodore Roosevelt for leadership. Indeed, the style and nature of this movement provided the third major theme in both Sims's career and the course of modern American naval policy.

The early years of this century brought forth a flowering of Progressive reform, and Sims epitomized its spirit and limitations. His methods were those of the insurgent, the same process of minute investigation, the same faith in publicity and public awareness, the same zeal and moral righteousness. For all its strident opposition to economic injustice and political corruption, progressivism seldom questioned the basic assumptions of liberal capitalism and democracy that underlie the national experience. It was presumed that if the obstacles of greed and reaction could only be removed, things would work smoothly and the country would thrive.

So it was with Sims. He approached nautical reform with a frenzied enthusiasm, but he was not inclined to probe deeply into the key postulates that formed the foundation of naval policy. In his quest for better means, he frequently lost track of ends. Once, while endeavoring to improve and simplify the code used by the Navy to communicate between warships, Sims was informed by Seaton Schroeder, commander in chief of the Atlantic Fleet, that he had "manifestly rendered public a portion of the Signal Book, the secrecy of which is the object of every precaution."[10] In the face of spectacular failure, Sims eventually became aware of the fallacies that gave rise to the "all-big-gun" battleship, but not before he had played a major role in the propagation of the mammoth warships.[11] Though friend and fellow naval insurgent Bradley Fiske was well aware of Sims's drive and talent, Fiske nevertheless wrote: "He [Sims] was not a very well-balanced man, or a very thoughtful man."[12] Neither was Fiske. Their importance lies in the fact that they both were early examples of a personality that would come to dominate the U.S. military establishment in the era of technological warfare. Just as the convergence of those three forces, professional naval tradition, technology, and progressivism, help to explain the motivation of William S. Sims, so do they also help to clarify the development of modern naval policy.

II

The United States Navy in the period from 1880 to 1941 was hardly a representative American institution. Dedicated to the defense of a society increasingly committed to the ideals of equality, democracy, pluralism, and irreverence for tradition, the Navy was aristocratic, hierarchical, exclusive, and rigid. If it could be said that American society did not always live up to its ideals, the Navy hardly ever deviated from its own. That divergence of spirit was due in part to the peculiar circumstances of naval life and in part to the organizational structure necessitated by those special conditions.

Central among the factors responsible for the uniqueness of nautical life was the ocean. Men sail upon the sea, but they are never a part of it. It is an alien world, hostile and overwhelming to the terrestrial creatures who traverse it. As Lieutenant Commander Charles B. Gary wrote, "The vast emptiness, the ceaseless rollers whelling monotonously from the other side of the world, make clear to man his essential solitude in the midst of an awesome and indifferent universe"[13]—an exaggerated response perhaps, but not atypical.

Paradoxically, this pervasive sense of isolation is contradicted by the sea's liquidity, enabling armadas from the opposite ends of the earth to meet on this common ground. Consequently, frequent socializing among the officers of the major maritime powers became an important and traditional aspect of naval life. Driven together by loneliness and mutual professional interests, officers were received by their counterparts with extreme courtesy, practically without regard for international affairs. Therefore, Admiral George Dewey's men thought it natural to exchange social calls with the Spanish naval officials they were about to replace in the Philippines—behavior reminiscent of the European military aristocracy during the ancien régime.[14] Nonetheless, the dictates of the machine age were not entirely forgotten. Therefore, although Admiral Yates Stirling conceded the importance of receiving prospective enemies such as the Japanese with respect, he worried about "making certain everything in any way considered secret on board ship was covered over to conceal them from prying eyes."[15] In actual fact an environment that favored the frequent contact between fleets of many nations could tolerate few secrets, and visits to foreign warships were relished by officers as excellent means of gaining information. Thus access to rival weaponry inevitably led to the kind of duplication that partially accounts for the remarkable homogeneity that characterized the shipbuilding policies of the major naval powers.

The culture of the sea was still more pervasive. It had its own traditions and history that influenced all sailors, no matter what their origin. And at the core of this nautical heritage was the remarkable success of the British Royal Navy for a period approaching three hundred years. It was a record unparalleled in naval annals, and it imparted an influence to British naval practice that is hard to exaggerate.[16] The Royal Navy was until 1919 the standard by which all other important fleets judged themselves. New naval contenders like the Germans and Japanese shamelessly aped the ships, the uniforms, even the aristocratic outlook and anachronistic customs of the Royal Navy. Whereas German officers "were accustomed from early times to regard the English ships as models, the external appearance of which alone produced the impression of perfection," the Japanese built for their naval academy at Etajuma a replica of the British Dartmouth (the Royal Naval College) and ceremoniously furnished it with a lock of Nelson's hair.[17] The very fact that the British pursued a certain course, regardless of its intrinsic merit, was a strong argument for its duplications by the admiralties of the world.

Nowhere was this respect for the Royal Navy stronger than in the American service between 1880 and 1920. That had not always been so. But after the American Civil War the two English-speaking nations had begun a gradually accelerating process of reconciliation that was paced and foreshadowed by steadily more intimate relations between British and U.S. naval officers. The British, for their part, began to perceive the Americans as potential junior partners in the naval Pax Britannica; whereas the Americans viewed the Royal Navy as the paragon of all things nautical and a guide to what they hoped to become. Thus

Alfred Mahan could write in 1894: "Indeed, naval officers of the United States should feel a peculiar sympathy with Englishmen, over and above which is felt by the mass of our fellow citizens, because by our education and our habits of thought we are brought in close sympathy and contact with the greatest of all British interests, the British Navy."[18]

Similarly, Admiral C. F. Sperry noted to his wife that compared to the U.S. fleet, "there was something grand in the display that England makes."[19] Indeed, the affinity sometimes led naval officers to race ahead of policy. Thus when William Sims told a London audience at the Guildhall in 1910 that Britons might count upon "every man, every ship, and every dollar from their kindred across the seas,"[20] he received a furious reprimand from President William Howard Taft. Yet the comments of his fellow officers made it clear that Sims was expressing the dominant opinion of the service. For example, Captain G. W. Steele, when he wrote Commander-in-Chief H. T. Mayo concerning American naval aviation, noted, "So many of our ideas of naval policy have been gained from the British that any discussion of the subject must consider their methods."[21]

Blatant Anglophilia and the peculiarity of the nautical environment were only contributing factors to the U.S. Navy's singularity; the Navy was, in the words of Elting Morison, "not unlike a society that had been placed under laboratory conditions."[22] Its activities were carried out within a narrow set of conditions, and random influences on its members were minimized. The result was something approaching a "naval personality," an orientation decidedly different from that of an average American.

The maintenance of a worldview so divergent from the norm required thorough indoctrination of the membership.[23] The process began at the United States Naval Academy at Annapolis.

Established in 1845 by James K. Polk's Jacksonian secretary of the Navy, George Bancroft, the academy came to occupy a key formative role in the Navy by 1880.[24] Until 1925 (almost every officer mentioned here would have graduated by that date) education at Annapolis was the sole means by which an aspiring navalist might be commissioned an officer of the line, thus making him eligible to command a warship.[25] An officer's record and reputation while attending the Naval Academy were the foundation of his later career.[26] Class rank, a number quickly forgotten by most degree holders, was a figure of the utmost importance to the graduates of Annapolis. It established permanently an officer's place in the naval queue of promotion and settled most questions of military etiquette.[27]

Captain Puleston may well have been right when he stated that "no other school in the world has such a complete control of a navy."[28]

Yet the most important effects of an Annapolis education were probably intangible: "What was far more significant was the loyalty to the service and the 'band of brothers' mentality that grew behind the Academy walls."[29] As in most military academies, the constant emphasis upon slogans, unwritten customs, and tradition tended to foster unity and an almost mystical sense of esprit de corps subtly. This four-year initiation into the "order of line" was the central event of a representative American naval career, so much so that the graduate truly deserved the appellation "Annapolite."

Prior to World War II even the manner in which young men were recruited for the academy tended to facilitate the desired homogeneity of the midshipmen. The fact that political patronage was necessary for appointment gave a decided advantage to influential families in obtaining places for their sons at Annapolis. When Woodrow Wilson's secretary of the Navy, Josephus Daniels, tried to make the procedure more democratic, the *Army-Navy Journal* reminded him of "the necessity of governing naval appointments in some measure by the rules prevailing in social clubs."[30] Biographical information on the parents of midshipmen provides a consistent picture of upper- or upper-middle-class origins, British ancestry, and Episcopalian religious affiliation.[31] Blacks, Jews, and candidates of Eastern or Southern European ancestry were, if not officially, then effectively, barred from admission. An example of the extent to which a policy of ethnic exclusivity was pursued is provided by a 1937 letter from F. A. Todd, commandant of midshipmen, to David Sellers, commander in chief of the U.S. fleet:

> After the [Black] Midshipman had been here about ten days or more, I was anxious for an opportunity to . . . talk with him. . . . I took the opportunity of telling him we would do everything we could officially to see that he had a square deal and sympathetic treatment while he was in the Naval Academy; also what he might expect after graduation. I explained that a successful life for a man must necessarily primarily depend on his having a congenial occupation, but I did not think he had chosen one. . . . At this stage of amalgamation of his race into general society, I thought he was rendering a disservice to his people by forcing himself on other young men. . . . The following Saturday he appeared in my office and to my utter amazement said that he had talked over the matter with his mother and they both agreed that he should resign.[32]

Yet the socioeconomic similarities of midshipmen were greatly reinforced by their course of study on the banks of the Severn. Academically, Annapolis was, after the mechanization of naval warfare, essentially an engineering school. The academy had not accepted the role of technical institute easily, and at least one prior attempt to introduce such a curriculum had failed.[33] One instructor noted that Annapolis was "the only technical school in the world where the students are allowed to believe that manual labor is undignified."[34] In addition to engineering, students were also given a fair quantity of liberal arts, along with subjects [generally classified as being] of a professional nature, such as gunnery, seamanship, navigation, and tactics.

Finally, there was sailing, a subject dear to the heart of any true mariner. It was (and still is) taught to midshipmen with enthusiasm, and a goodly share of each summer was spent as crew on one of the academy's full-rigged ships. The fact that steam had rendered this fine art largely irrelevant in warfare was not taken as a sign that its instruction could be dispensed with. Rather the opposite seemed true.

But what was learned at Annapolis was often less important than how it was learned. Instruction was not innovative. Learning by rote was emphasized, and the aspiring officer often found himself memorizing all the parts of a sailing ship in French or one of several hundred mathematical theorems whose derivation was ignored. Fleet Admiral E. J. King, who taught at the academy, felt that the tradition of military discipline stifled the spirit of free inquiry. He "remembered all too well the average midshipman, reluctant to admit his ignorance, would stand at the blackboard chewing chalk rather than ask a question."[35] Park Benjamin, one of the academy's historians, wrote, "this was not an environment which favors original thought or act, or even any material departure from the beaten track."[36] Instead, the midshipman was, in the words of Captain W. D. Puleston, encouraged "to stow his information away in an orderly manner so that it can easily be drawn upon; his mind should be neatly and completely furnished like his locker."[37]

Indeed every aspect of the environment inspired Annapolites to believe that all things had their own time and place. The cadet inevitably came to understand the importance of the minutely defined system of rank that was the soul of military procedure. Lieutenant Ridgely Hunt noted that midshipmen "surrendered the privileges of a birthright of equality in favor of a doctrine of an organization in which the knee must be bent in pagan-like adoration of a uniform worn by they know not whom."[38]

Meanwhile, midshipmen were carefully isolated from outside influences that might distract them from the academy's definition of proper and productive behavior. The school was segregated from the town of Annapolis by a high wall, and mingling with the general population was strictly prohibited. In 1933 the irrepressible Sims noted that for four of the key years of character formation the Annapolite was "practically isolated" from civilian life and therefore could not help but to emerge a rather "cut and dried" figure.[39]

Almost inevitably the Annapolite's later career tended to reinforce the conformity learned at the academy. Even more than the environment of other military officers, the insularity of the naval profession served to exaggerate homogeneity and unanimity of opinion. Even while ashore, the social contacts of the line officer were limited to fellow Annapolites or a small group of elite residents of coastal cities. Indeed, the high rate of intermarriage among the families of naval officers was a convenient index of their isolation.[40]

Aboard ship it was only natural to forget civilians. As Lieutenant Commander Gary noted, "Here within the steel walls of this living ship is a world within a world, in the world but not of it."[41] And the isolation of the officer at sea was simultaneously accompanied by an intensification of his professional environment. The ship's dimensions were the absolute barrier to movement and accommodations, for all but the captain were generally crowded. The warship was in fact a tightly organized floating society where assigned status dictated almost every personal relationship. Not only was the behavior of officers dominated by an ever-present awareness of rank, but also the rigid military barrier between officers and enlisted men was sanctified by hundreds of years aboard sail-driven vessels as critical to battle efficiency. The result aboard the battleship *California* to Seaman Theodore Mason "resembled a walled fortified medieval town with a rigid hierarchical structure of peasants, artisans, clergy, and nobility all answerable to the *seignior*, or lord of the manner."[42]

The prerogatives of command were absolute, not to be questioned, only passed on. As Park Benjamin noted: "The commodore bullied the captain, the captain bullied the lieutenant, the lieutenant bullied the midshipmen, the midshipmen bullied the petty officer, and so on down through all the ranks and ratings. . . . Thus the young officer of the Navy learned that discipline was merely the arbitrary enforcement of the will of an autocrat."[43] The importance of command aboard ship is hard to overestimate. It was the keystone of naval government, from which all authority must theoretically emanate. The symbolic investiture of ultimate authority in the person of one man often stifled the most constructive of criticism. Lieutenant Commander J. Odgen Hoffman's advice to young line officers was a typical manifestation of the naval reverence for command: "If the captain reproves you for something . . . that you know is absolutely right, just stand and take it and keep quiet unless you are asked."[44]

The roots of that obsession with discipline and blind obedience flowed from the days under sail. A full-rigged sailing vessel was probably the most complex and tightly organized of all purely human-operated mechanisms. The very large amount of sail and the precision required in bad weather or in battle demanded almost instantaneous obedience by very a large number of men. That factor, combined with the very long cruising ranges of such ships and attendant poor food, miserable living conditions, and absence of women, encouraged truly draconian discipline. But though the blind obedience had a pragmatic basis aboard the crowded and unpleasant sailing warship, the introduction of less-manpower-intensive steam propulsion scarcely dispelled the psychological climate of obedience that hung over warships.

As with most things naval, the Royal Navy led the way. The most notorious example of blind and mindless following of orders took place on the British battleship *Victoria* in 1893. The commander of the English fleet, Admiral Tryon, a noted martinet who particularly delighted in tactical drills, ordered the fleet to execute a maneuver that every officer on the bridge realized would result in collision. Yet not one of them could bring himself to inform the admiral of his folly. As a result the *Victoria* collided with the *Camperdown* and sank shortly thereafter.[45]

In keeping with the tradition of obedience, great ceremonial significance was attached to the concept of command in all major navies. Consequently, the ritual that accompanied the transferral of a ship's command was extremely elaborate, including the piping of pipes, the playing of bands, multigun salutes, and the formal reading of the departing and arriving captain's orders—all done, with the most minute attention to detail, for the presumed edification of the assembled crew.[46] Yet that rite, interpreted on a different level, was symptomatic of another characteristic feature of shipboard life, a fascination with ceremonialism itself. Ceremonialism extended even to the sphere of recreation. For instance, a ship's crossing of the equator inevitably was made the occasion of a rowdy dramatization that oddly resembled a medieval religious ritual. Morris Janowitz suggested that such elaborate forms of personal intercourse served to obscure both the harsh realities of military life and the boredom of endless routine.[47]

The repetitive nature of work aboard ship is certainly striking. Much of the work involved the proper maintenance of the vessel itself. In 1904 Lieutenant R. G. Turpin maintained that "almost without exception, the organization of the

"A *fascination with ceremonialism itself.*" The USS Texas, *ca. 1918. (Courtesy of the U.S. National Archives)*

ship's company is based on the facility with which the ship can be cleaned."[48] Although it is unquestionably true that ships at sea require very considerable maintenance, this endless cycle of scrubbing, scraping, polishing, and painting must have created a rhythm of somnambulance that would deaden the senses and extract sullen obedience from all but the most rebellious of enlisted men.

In that regard, ship cleaning acted as a seaborne analogue to relentless terrestrial small-arms drill, which was the key training institution of the firepower armies that dominated European politics during approximately the same period that sailing warships dominated the bounding main. But whereas small-arms drill was directly related to loading and firing the soldier's weapon, the cleaning of ships was basically unrelated to survival and success in battle.

Nonetheless, neatness and cleanliness were extolled by officers as indicative of the qualities necessary in war. As Admiral Mahan noted: "It is undoubtedly true that attention to minutiae is symptomatic of a much more important underlying spirit, one of exactness and precision running through all the management of a ship and affecting her efficiency. I concede that a thing so trifling as a button of a frock-coat may indicate a development and survival of the fittest."[49] Thus the diligence of Admiral Hugh Rodman, who "threw confusion into one of his own captains by finding dirt under a chest of drawers," although perhaps not typical, was not regarded as exaggerated.[50] The strongly positive overtones that naval officers habitually associated with "nautical housekeeping" are obvious in Admiral Gleaves's description of a morning's activities at sea: "Today was a field day and they began early to holy stone the deck over my head. However, I never mind real ship noises. . . . At noon the deck was as white as a shark's tooth and the white uniforms and polished bright work reminded me of old times in a frigate."[51]

Gleaves's nostalgia for sailing was understandable. The conversion to the sooty, belching steam engine presented an obstacle to cleanliness that must have been excruciating to many officers. "Coaling a steamer," one officer noted in the 1870s, "is one of the most disagreeable tasks; the dirt penetrating every corner. For this reason, I would prefer to cruise in the old sailing ships as in days gone by."[52] A former captain of E. J. King's, whose only comment after his first and last trip to his ship's engine room was, "It's too dirty down there," must have summarized the feelings of countless cohorts.

The days of sail were remembered as a golden era. "In a stiff breeze, when the ship is heeling over," wrote Admiral Mahan, "there is a wild sort of delight that I have not experienced before."[53] The exhilaration of sailing was sufficient

USS Alfred, *the first battleship commissioned by the United States. (Courtesy of the U.S. National Archives)*

to provide an outlet for the romantic impulses of what must be considered a very prosaic group of men. Admiral Henry Wiley's lyrical description of the sailing vessel *St. Mary's* was not unusual: "I liked her best when she labored under a full spread of canvas, close hauled in a good stiff breeze. Then she couldn't talk but she would sing and behave most like the beautiful creature she was. . . . If there is any inanimate object as human as a ship like this, I don't know what it is."[54] For seventy years after the introduction of steam, loyalty to the fond memory of happier days spent under billowing pure white sail would intimately affect the course of U.S. naval policy.

Under sail or steam, the success of a naval career was measured by an officer's ability to climb the rank hierarchy. As Commander W. W. Phelps noted, "To each of us, his naval title is the hallmark in life and after."[55] Therefore, the system of advancement employed by a navy was of major significance in shaping the values and attitudes of those who reached high command. Until the turn of the century, the U.S. Navy's system was based, in peacetime, strictly on seniority. Whereas most navies, including the British, placed heavy emphasis on time in grade (prompting Sir John Fisher's famous remark about risking the fleet just because it was Buggins's turn), that stress was virtually a fetish in the American service. There, an officer's progress in rank was subject to two factors only: relative place on the naval seniority list (determined by class rank at Annapolis) and the number of vacancies created ahead of him through death or retirement. With the passage of the Personnel Act of 1899, some element of selection by merit was introduced, but the U.S. Navy remained basically a gerontocracy.[56]

However, it cannot be said that most officers were particularly dissatisfied with the arrangement. If a man had the proper background to be chosen an officer, it was assumed he was innately capable of discharging increased responsibilities. Even Sims, a leading critic of the arrangement, was forced to admit that "all are in favor of promotion by seniority, because barring scandalous conduct or very gross incompetence, all will reach higher grade."[57] Nonetheless, it seems apparent that the effects of the seniority system upon the U.S. Navy were generally injurious. The system presupposed an ideal conception of the appropriate sequence of assignments and, as a result, standardized experience and further enforced conformity among officers. An unorthodox career implied some predisposition toward innovation and a capacity for criticism, which was not to be encouraged.

The relative antiquity of the officers who emerged at the end of the naval conveyer belt was an even more serious consequence of the system. In 1906 the youngest captain in the U.S. Navy was fifty-five years old, or twenty years the senior of his youngest European counterpart.[58] Promotion to rear admiral before the age of sixty was considered unusual. Because of a mandatory retirement age of sixty-two, that meant that the high command of the U.S. Navy was less experienced than that of almost any other comparable force. It was also more fragile. During the famous world cruise of the battle fleet in 1908, a 50 percent casualty rate was sustained by a high command not subjected to a single shot of hostile fire.[59]

Despite numerous protests, things hardly improved. In 1941, 94 percent of the thirty-one top-ranking naval commanders were still over sixty.[60] This general superannuation of officers at the highest level must have been a strong force in the perpetuation of conservatism in a profession not ordinarily predisposed toward a progressive outlook.

In effect, the many peculiar conditions and requirements of a naval career combined to create an environment so isolated from extraneous influence, of such intense professionalism, and so conducive to conformity that the single most significant characteristic of any officer became his association with the United States Navy. Under the circumstances, it is understandable that the average naval officer emerged a relatively pure personality type, whose thoughts and actions tended to echo those of his brothers. As Peter Karsten noted: "Obviously not every officer thought and behaved like every other officer. . . . But all things considered, I still maintain that this virtually timeless ideal type of officer actually existed."[61] Moreover, the perpetuation of what amounted to a homogeneous "naval aristocracy" was of particular significance in a country like the United States. For it virtually ensured that in an age of intense social and technological change, the reactions and accommodations of such an elite would be distinctive and in many ways at odds with those of the nation as a whole.

At the core of what can be termed the American nautical personality was a profound suspicion of all things and beings not within the United States Navy. In a sense that was natural enough, since the Navy was the cutting edge of the republic, occupying a point at which the conflicting interests of nations became overwhelmingly obvious. Consequently, in spite of their personal affinity for the members of other navies, officers were almost universally inclined toward an intensely pessimistic estimation of the motives of possible international adversaries.

Concomitant with this distrust of the world at large was an expectation of aggression and resultant belligerence toward outsiders—again, not necessarily inappropriate in a profession ultimately dedicated to organized violence. Naval autobiographies are replete with youthful incidents of physical confrontation, the unoffending officer-to-be reacting only after serious provocation from what were often characterized as bullies.[62] The tendency to conceptualize the world in terms of strife and competition, although characteristic of the age, was pronounced in American line officers, who persisted in applying evolutionary jargon, describing the United States as locked in an eternal struggle for survival. For Admiral William L. Rodgers and his brother officers the fight "for a favorable position is a law of nature. We see it not only among men but among animals as well. This is the reason we cannot trust the good will of other nations."[63] Prudent perhaps for European navies—whose members saw the world in very similar terms—but more than a bit exaggerated for representatives of a nation separated by entire oceans from its principal competitors.

Nonetheless, the possibility that international competition would inevitably escalate into real warfare was accepted as part of the natural order of things. Bradley Fiske undoubtedly enunciated the feelings of a majority of his profession when he answered the rhetorical question, "Is there any change toward peaceful methods now?" with a resounding "no, on the contrary, war is recognized as the most potent method still, the prominence of military matters is greater than ever before."[64] Nor were these naval officers necessarily alone in this overall judgment. The period between 1890 and World War I was an increasingly militaristic one, with war coming to be perceived by many as both an economic stimulus and an antidote to the enervating tendencies of urban and industrial life. What separated Annapolites from their fellow citizens and even Army officers was the degree to which naval technology and their own largely bloodless experience with combat allowed them to abstract it and then romanticize it. Thus to Admiral William Fullam and his generation, "there was a certain delight in war."[65] Of course, when the real came into contact with the ideal the effect could be devastating. "What became of the knights of our childhood?" wondered William Leahy after learning that a Philippine priest had been tortured to death by American soldiers.[66] Yet such occurrences were rare.

War and fighting remained "delightful" largely because naval officers remained free to view them largely on their own terms. And those terms were based primarily on a heroic tradition that stretched back to Homer and before and that clearly dominated naval history under sail. Essentially, combat was viewed as a confrontational and highly ritualized act in which major combatants, assuming an importance far greater than their numbers, ideally met each other in what amounted to decisive actions. Fighting was thus perceived as ordered, individualized, and aristocratic in its essence. Lesser units might play some initial role, but the largest and the best armed remained the ultimate focal points and the keys to victory. Conversely, tactics and weapons that went against this grain—small, furtive devices relying on surprise—were not only disdained but also considered in a very real sense unethical. More than anything, those themes would mark the tempo of naval warfare and ensure the dominance of the battleship until Pearl Harbor.

Related to the naval officer's conception of violence was another major facet of his personality—an emphasis upon order. It is axiomatic among military men that the confusion and immense danger of panic in battle necessitates a degree of discipline much greater than what would ordinarily be necessary in a more pacific environment. Yet there was in most U.S. naval officers (and presumably those elsewhere) an obsessive fascination with "order" and "control" that went beyond tactical considerations. The ritualized nature of virtually all shipboard activities, the preoccupation with cleaning the vessel, the constant drill and formal assembly of the crew, and the extreme uniformity of behavior and outlook among officers are all symptomatic of what amounts to compulsive orderliness. Conversely, disorder was habitually identified with anarchy and helplessness, conditions to be avoided at all costs.

To the representative officer, "order" was often synonymous with "hierarchy." Rank was a positive good precisely because it organized men in the most reasonable fashion, one above the other. An officer's rank gave him an absolute definition of his identity, it simplified relations with his peers, it provided a neatly prefabricated channel for future ambition. This remains applicable to almost any military organization, rank being the key factor in virtually all of them. What distinguished and intensified the naval conception of rank was the close quarters and length of time spent aboard ship, making it particularly important to define social relationships as unambiguously as possible. To maintain order in such an environment it was vital that every man literally "knew his place." Thus rank was revered in the naval context particularly to the degree that it dispelled ambivalence and preserved order.

Psychologically, the relentless drive to maximize the control exerted over any and all situations represents a total cognitive defense against doubt and uncertainty, among the worst fears of a military man. It implied that there was a "right" and a "wrong" approach to every problem. By prescribing a specific procedure to be followed in the face of difficulty, it facilitated the kind of decisiveness preferred in military men. Yet such a stable frame of reference often lacks the flexibility needed to deal successfully with changing conditions.

Annapolites were prone to make decisions in accordance with their own frame of reference rather than by what the situation itself demanded—to keep unacceptable information out of the level of consciousness—for they occupied a world quite literally narrower and more abstract than that of most men.

American naval officers were not necessarily anti-intellectual. Quite the contrary, many spent considerable time reading and thinking about their profession. Yet there was always a tendency toward abstraction and tunnel vision. They were creatures of their environment, and theirs was a narrow—almost hermetically sealed—one, populated by men largely like themselves. In an era of technology and change, such rigidity and homogeneity were bound to produce distortions, and their dreadnought fetish was merely the most spectacular.

The U.S. Navy and its passion for battleships were hardly isolated phenomena. They were integral parts of a larger world of navies born of the same environment and dominated by similar frames of reference. In such a world nautical orthodoxy was contagious, traditions mutually reinforcing. If American naval thinking impressed its citizens as hidebound and divorced from reality, Annapolites had only to point to the rest of the naval world.

There was some variation—the German Navy was less aristocratic, the French more iconoclastic. Yet those were aberrations, largely the product of institutional youth or defeat. The standard bearer of the naval world was Britain's Royal Navy. Its organizational profile was conservative, hierachical, authoritarian, and mired in centuries of tradition. Moreover, as much or more than any other member of the naval world, the Royal Navy was wed to the sailing battleship-of-the-line.

III

Change came slowly to war at sea, more slowly than to any other form of organized combat. Until 1850 the naval world had known only two capital ships—the oar-powered ram of ancient and medieval times and the gun-based sailing battleship. In part because of the length of their respective reigns, both types would exert a continuing influence on the evolution of military naval architecture long after their time as effective weapons had passed. Naval designers almost instinctively resurrected the ram with the introduction of steam propulsion, just as they based virtually the entire rationale behind the modern armored battleship on the nature and tactical characteristics of the sailing ship-of-the-line. Indeed, the thinking that eventually brought forth the steam battleship's ultimate manifestation, the dreadnought, goes back hundreds of years to a time when the Royal Navy first reached for greatness.

The naval world of 1588 was a very different place than it had been just a half century before. During the early years of the sixteenth century the Arsenal of Venice had combined full-ship's rigging, heavily reinforced internal construction, and a low-hull form dedicated to the optimal placement of guns, producing the galleon, the first real challenger to the supremacy of the oared galley in almost three thousand years. The oared warship's structural incompatibility with heavy guns and fragility in the face of their fire ensured that the dominance of the galley would not survive much beyond its last great victory at Lepanto in 1571.[67] Nor would Venice, whose Arsenal had blown up the year before, retain the mantle of seapower.

Instead, it would migrate northward, from its ancient seat in the Mediterranean to the states facing the North Atlantic—Catholic Portugal and Spain on one side and Protestant Holland and England on the other. It was upon oceanic waters that sailing vessels would truly prove themselves, enabling the powers possessing them to project firepower unheard-of distances to create world-girding empires. But in doing so those vessels would also help to generate colossal rivalries and the bitterest of enemies.

Spain had gone to sea with motives typical of an imperial land power. The ocean was seen not primarily as a means of commerce but as an avenue to its enemies and a conduit for colonial tribute. And in pursuit of the landlubber goals, Spain would be preyed upon by those who plied the waves as a birthright. The English, and in particular a group of privateers known as "sea dogs," played havoc with Spanish lines of communications and bullion shipments from the New World. Of these privateers none was more successful than Sir Francis Drake, or simply "El Draque" to the terrified Spaniards who were his victims as he intercepted plate ship after plate ship, so that by 1586 not a single bar of Mexican or Peruvian silver made it safely across the Atlantic.[68] The next year Drake went so far as to attack the Spanish naval base in the Bay of Cadiz, demonstrating in the process the complete superiority, even in sheltered waters, of sailing gunships over the galleys that had attempted to mount a defense.[69]

Philip of Spain was far from admitting defeat at sea. Instead, he sought his revenge by overawing the English in their home waters, with a fleet assembled for him by the Marquis de Santa Cruz, the victor of Lepanto who bore the revealing title: captain general of the Ocean Sea.

The Spanish Armada, like other subsequent pretender navies manufactured by ambitious land powers—the French, the Germans, the Russians—was the product of one outstanding individual, in this case Santa Cruz—the Spanish Tirpitz, the Iberian Gorshkov. Like his spiritual successors, Santa Cruz did a good job with equipment. The fleet he put together was basically a modern one, with a core of stoutly built galleons. Naval scholar Michael Lewis dismissed the popular conception of the two opposing fleets' being radically different—huge Spanish vessels versus tiny English ones—as having little basis in fact.[70] The representative ship types were basically similar.

But there were some very significant differences. The chief architect of the English anti-Armada was John Hawkins, apart from Drake the most famous of the "sea dogs," and the first major innovator in galleon design since their introduction. Like his nautical reembodiment, Sir John Fisher, the force behind the HMS *Dreadnought*, Hawkins was transfixed by the possibilities of speed and big guns. So he lengthened and narrowed his galleons (subsequently described as "race built"), allowing them to sail faster and closer to the wind and providing more room along the sides for armament. Moreover, fore and aft castles were cut down dramatically, not just to add stability, but because they were able to mount only light secondary armament. Big guns belonged at or near the waterline and were fired through hinged ports. And increasingly Hawkins replaced the previous stubby, short-range armament of English galleons with long-barreled culverins capable of casting an eight- or nine-pound shot up to 1,000 yards with at least a pretense of accuracy. Perhaps of equal, though less obvious, importance, the guns were mounted on four-wheel naval carriages, allowing them to be retracted and loaded inboard.[71]

What emerged was a pure artillery ship. Unlike previous English galleons and those of the Spanish, which were oriented toward close-in fighting and boarding, Hawkins's "race built" vessels were designed to overcome their adversaries strictly through stand-off firepower. Moreover, Hawkins's innovations brought with them the promise of invulnerability—not only were they faster and more maneuverable in all weather, but also their armament would enable them to engage the Spanish at ranges from which the latter could not retaliate. It was the very logic that would cause the HMS *Dreadnought* to steam forth 320 years later. It did not work well then, nor would it prove effective against the Armada.

Fortunately for those Elizabethan proto-dreadnoughts, their shortcomings were outweighed by still-greater weaknesses in the armament of the Armada. Archaeological evidence has revealed that the large Spanish guns capable of inflicting significant structural damage were mounted on two-wheeled, nonretractable carriages, an arrangement that effectively prevented them from being loaded more often than twice a day.[72]

Yet as the two fleets drew together off Plymouth, it was impossible to be certain what would happen. Garrett Mattingly explained:

> Fleets like these were new thing in the world. . . . Nobody knew what the new weapons would do, or what tactics would make them most effective. This was the beginning of a new era of naval warfare, of the long day in which the ship-of-the-line, wooden-walled, sail driven, and armed with smooth bore cannon, was to be queen of battles, and for which the armor plated steam-powered battleship with rifled cannon merely marked the evening.[73]

True enough, but the dawn of the gun-based battleship would prove no more decisive than its sunset at Jutland. In a series of running engagements up the English Channel, approximately 200,000 rounds would be fired, testifying both to the acceptance of naval firepower and to its inability to do decisive damage when employed as the two contestants had initially intended. The Spanish failed utterly in their plan to close, rake their adversaries with secondary armament, and then board, while the English galleons sorely lacked the accuracy to inflict serious damage at long range with heavy guns. Tactics proved rudimentary, with the ships sailing into range in clumps and crescents, thereby bringing relatively few guns to bear on their targets. Only at Gravelines, when the English cast aside their overambitious approach to gunnery and closed to point-blank range, were they able to do significant structural damage.[74] Their advantage in that case was gained largely because their big guns could be reloaded and those of the Spanish could not. Even so, it was the bad weather of the North Atlantic, not firepower, that brought about the final undoing of Philip's Armada.[75]

For all its indecisiveness, the defeat of the Spanish Armada marked a major milestone in naval history. The English had retained command of the sea and would not relinquish it until the first half of the twentieth century. Although the Royal Navy had existed before, the flame and fury of the Armada campaign fused it into a self-conscious entity. Britannia would be challenged again and again, but from this point it ruled the waves and did so primarily with battleships.

However, it was true that the Armada campaign revealed several key tactical limitations of sailing battleships. The next four-score years would see the abandonment of long-range naval gunnery and a continuing search for battle formations that would deliver the maximum firepower at the minimum range.

Nevertheless, strategically, the sailing gunship demonstrated remarkable potential. The very fact that a fleet like the Armada could threaten a whole country was telling. Powered by inexhaustable supplies of wind and guided by precision navigation instruments (themselves among the hallmarks of European technical supremacy), the reach of those vessels was limited only by the availability of sufficient water to float them. Rather suddenly, northern Europeans and particularly the English found themselves in possession of a unique and formidable instrument of coercion, which might be brought virtually anywhere with a coastline, transporting very considerable quantities of men and equipment. Imperial implements par excellence, key factors in the expansion and triumph of European technology and economics, sailing warships were, in the words of anthropologist Marvin Harris, the "forerunners of spacecraft."[76]

As such, they presented special problems to a power like England, seeking to dominate at sea. First and foremost there was the difficulty of coming to grips with far-ranging adversaries. As John Keegan noted, "the depths of the ocean . . . remained no man's lands, which fleets might beat almost in perpetuity without getting glimpse of each other."[77] Thus it was no accident that with the exception of the Glorious First of June in 1794, all the major engagements in the Age of Sail took place virtually within sight of land.[78] The key was to pin down a rival fleet before it had a chance to disappear into the vastness of the sea. The best way to accomplish that was to bottle up the rival in its home base. So it was that blockade became the most useful—if also the most arduous—tool in the Royal Navy's strategic arsenal.[79]

Because success in that effort would necessarily strip an enemy's seaborne commerce of protection, blockade always had economic implications—the slow strangulation of overseas trade that Alfred Thayer Mahan focused upon in the *Influence of Seapower upon History: 1660–1783*. Yet blockade was also pursued for its own sake as a distinctly military measure.

Blockade as habitually employed by the Royal Navy in the Age of Sail encompassed a variety of activities.[80] Yet its basis was the physical interposition of the heaviest fleet units athwart the opponent's lines of trade and communications.[81]

The "heavy units," as they would come to evolve out of the galleon, were the great triple-masted, square-rigged ships-of-the-line. High, ungainly craft generally displacing around two thousand tons, a representative sailing battleship "rated" approximately 74 guns. "Rating" was purely quantitative. From the reign of Charles I to the 1850s, British warships customarily were subdivided into six classes, based upon the number of guns that were carried. A First Rate ship had 100 guns or more, a Second Rate carried 90, a Third Rate mounted from 60 to 90 guns, Fourth Rate ships had around 50 guns, and Fifth Rate ships carried about 24.[82] All Third Rate ships and above were considered fit to "stand in line" (join the main battle formation). Vessels of the First and Second Rate were rare, however, having been used only as flagships.[83]

Although the wooden ship-of-the-line was the largest and most complicated machine produced in eighteenth-century Europe,[84] its evolution had been extremely slow. To some degree, that was the result of the traditionalism surrounding the craft of shipbuilding. Sailing ships were dependent upon six thousand years of slowly gathered experience as to what timbers hard and soft, aged for what periods, joined by what cuts, at what angles, would resist best the ravages of wind, water, and rot. David Howarth noted that by the seventeenth century many European countries, England included, possessed mathematicians who might have made significant improvements to the rules by which hulls were formed.[85] Nonetheless, shipbuilding remained wed to the rule of thumb, a craft monopolized by artisans ruled by the limited possibilities of wood structures and wind propulsion. This orientation, combined with the subtle but nonetheless effective moratorium on all weapons technology during the eighteenth century, worked to ensure that every British capital ship built until 1850 was similar in all but detail to the *Sovereign of the Seas*, launched in 1637 and the first sailing warship with three gun decks. Despite their archaic design, such ships were extraordinarily well adapted to naval warfare and therefore remained impressive even in the mid-nineteenth century, when John Ruskin remarked: "Taken all in all, a ship-of-the-line is the most honorable thing that man, as a gregarious animal, has produced."[86]

Although the maintenance of a blockade ultimately depended upon these oaken juggernauts, they were too slow to ensure its enforcement. That was left to smaller, swifter craft of the Fifth and Sixth Rates called frigates and lesser vessels such as corvettes and sloops of war.[87] The duties of these "cruisers" consisted of capturing blockade runners and protecting British commerce on the high seas from depredations by enemy frigates.

That form of commercial guerrilla warfare, or *guerre de course*, was conceived by the French as an alternative to the destruction of the blockading battle fleet and was premised upon the vulnerability that necessarily accompanied Great Britain's preeminence as an overseas trader. Although *guerre de course* proved to be a dangerous menace and was often successful in inflicting severe losses upon British cargo carriers, it never seemed to win wars. Because *guerre de course* was fundamentally incapable of loosening the fetters of blockade, its successes were seldom directly beneficial to the suffocating homeland.[88] So at the most fundamental level of naval belief it came to be accepted that in the long run war could only be won by the physical removal of the blockading battle fleet. That necessitated a direct confrontation between the besieged power and the British battleships. Yet in most cases during the pivotal eighteenth century, the besieged were represented by the French who, unlike the Dutch, avoided such a decisive engagement except as a desperate expedient, justified in terms of some ulterior motive.[89]

That orientation was reflected in Gallic tactics. Uncertain sailors, the French usually adopted a leeward, or downwind, position and attempted to destroy their adversary's mobility by crippling its rigging with relatively long range cannon fire. Such a plan was essentially defensive and oriented toward preventing an opponent from closing to a more decisive range while at the same time preserving the French ability to retreat.[90]

The British were much more aggressive. In the long series of battles with its Spanish, Dutch, and French adversaries, the Royal Navy invariably attempted to press home a crushing attack from the windward gauge. When the British were successful in this objective, the circumstances of the resulting encounters were in large measure determined by the configuration of the sailing battleship itself. As French naval historian J. Charbaud-Arnault noted:

> Since the disappearance of galleys, almost all the artillery is found upon the sides of a ship of war. Hence, it is the beam that must necessarily and always be turned toward the enemy. On the other hand, it is necessary that the sight of the latter must never be interrupted by a friendly ship. Only one formation allows the ships of the same fleet to satisfy fully these conditions. That formation is line ahead.[91]

This may seem rather obvious, but it took nearly eighty years from the defeat of the Armada for the line-ahead formation to evolve.[92] It was finally perfected at the Four Days' Battle in 1666 where, as an observer (de Guiche) noted: "Nothing

Action off Cuddalore, 1783. Painting by August Louis de Rossi de Cerci. (Courtesy of the directors of the Musée de la Marine, Palais de Chaillot)

equalled the beautiful order of the English at sea. Never was a line drawn straighter than that formed by their ships; thus, they bring all their fire to bear upon those who draw near them . . . whereas the Dutch advanced like cavalry whose squadron leave their ranks and come separately to the charge."[93]

The dogmatic adherence to that tactical scheme eventually all but robbed the Royal Navy of flexibility. The insistence of the so-called Formalists upon the maintenance of a strict line-ahead arrangement so as to maximize order and control had the effect of eroding individual initiative to the point that numerous opportunities for decisive engagement were missed because of the need to maintain the proper formation.[94] No wonder—after Admiral Byng failed to follow the permanent fighting instructions at Minorca in 1756, he was court-martialed and shot. Only Horatio Nelson, by charging straight into the French line first at Aboukir Bay in 1798 and then at Trafalgar in 1805, was able through sheer aggression and favorable results to break the grip of line-ahead momentarily. Yet his death in the latter action, along with the fact that Trafalgar was the last major and truly decisive naval action for nearly a century, minimized the impact of the precedent.[95]

Therefore, tactics remained ossified, with parallel engagements the norm, the ultimate objective being to surge ahead sufficiently to cross an enemy's line of bearing. If that could be accomplished—and it was far from easy—the file of ships as it passed in front of the adversary line could concentrate the entirety of their broadsides, one after another, upon targets that could reply with only a few bow guns. Crossing the T, as this was called, was a particularly effective maneuver since a sailing warship's bow was relatively fragile, and fire, if it did not strike there, would carry down the entire length of the deck, maximizing the possibilities of hitting something or someone.[96]

It had long been clear that in order for such maneuvers to be truly effective, they had to take place at very close range. Rather quickly after the Armada campaign that situation led to a wholesale abandonment of long-range naval gunnery; therefore, by 1622 John Hawkins's son Richard could observe, "How much nearer, so much the better." And that maxim would remain relevant well into the nineteenth century, for it was based on the fundamental inaccuracy of the guns carried aboard sailing warships. The heavy cast-iron muzzle-loaders had an effective range of at most around 200 yards, or less than a tenth of their extreme carry.[97] The explanation lay partly in the necessity of allowing for "windage" (the difference between the gun's bore and the diameter of the ball) in order that the gun might be loaded quickly by ramming the projectile down the barrel. Consequently, the ball bounded from side to side as it was fired, the ultimate direction it took being determined by the last place it touched the barrel. The error created by this "angle of deflection" multiplied with every yard of extra distance that a shot traveled. Aiming at long ranges was irrelevant; only at close range could a hit be ensured.

The projectile itself was a solid, roughly cast iron ball. Because it did not burst, the destructive effect of a shot was directly proportional to its kinetic energy upon striking, which was maximized at short ranges. Although its lateral area of destruction was strictly limited, the razor-sharp splinters created as the ball struck or passed through the ship's wooden structures, splinters that flew off in all directions, were capable of inflicting horrible wounds.[98]

As John Keagan has demonstrated, sailing battleships, in spite of their numerous guns and prevalent short firing ranges, remained essentially man killers, really capable of inflicting ship-destroying structural damage only under special conditions when multiple broadsides might be delivered.[99] Thus most decisive close encounters were decided by sheer butchery. That was somewhat paradoxical, however. For although casualties were frequently high relative to the number of crew members, sea battles in the Age of Sail, because they were often fleeting and because even defeated ships did not usually sink, generally accounted for much smaller absolute numbers of dead than those on land. Nonetheless, the perception of so many men dying, often horribly, in such a small space, had the effect of imparting an especially bloody tone to that type of war at sea.

In strictly conceptual terms, fights between sailing warships were analogous to those of Homer's heroes on the plains of Ilion. For both, standards of courage and effectiveness were defined by a willingness to engage at the closest possible range in the most confrontational way. The results were gory rites of manhood, stand-up-and-fight, blood-and-guts encounters, where the weak-willed were bound to perish or be disgraced. It called forth the virtues of blunt aggressiveness, blind courage, and staunchness. Trickery was disdained. Under such circumstances, the traditional training and personalities of naval officers were supremely relevant.

This was no free-for-all. Just as with Homer's sword fighters, sailing warships generally fought only their equals.[100] Yet upon the sea that was as much a matter of physics as it was of choice. The character of naval warfare in the Age of Sail was regulated and articulated to an astonishing degree by three absolute factors: the basic similarity of the armament that the vessels of all rates or classes carried, the strength limitations of wood, and the nature of wind as a means of propulsion.

Because the solid-shot-firing muzzle-loading gun was basically the only ship's weapon, all military vessels of the period differed in lethality by degree rather than kind.[101] Not only did the development of those guns remain essentially static for two and a half centuries after the Armada, but their size also became more or less standardized throughout all the classes of the major fleets.[102] Therefore, the offensive power of a vessel was in direct proportion to the number of guns it carried.

Yet structural factors determined how the armament would be mounted: All ships were built of wood, and in the vast majority of cases major structural members were made solely of oak. This material had very definite strength limitations that uniformly prevented the construction of wooden ships measuring much more than 200 feet in length, lest they be in danger of "hogging"—of drooping at the ends.[103] Since guns were mounted at regular intervals on either side of a ship, only a finite quantity could be carried per deck. Therefore, if armament was to be increased beyond a certain number, it became necessary to pile gun decks one upon the other. Since all six rates were square-riggers of the same basic configuration, each making use of a common power source, the breeze, vessels with numerous cannon piled in lofty tiers were bound to be slower than their more lightly armed cousins.

The consequence was an absolute segregation of function in naval warfare under sail.[104] Naval battles took place with Homeric selectivity and decorum. Disregarding lesser prey, equals naturally sought each other out to do what generally amounted to individual combat, for the numerous guns that rendered larger rates substantially more powerful than their smaller relatives ensured that the larger rates could not catch the smaller ones. In practice, it was understood that frigates were not to be used in fleet actions except as signal-repeating ships.[105] An extreme, but nonetheless instructive, example of what happened to disrespectful frigate commanders who had the temerity to attack a battleship was provided by the unfortunate case of Nicholas Biddle. While cruising in the thirty-two-gun *Randolph* off Barbados in March 1777, he allowed the British ship-of-the-line *Yarmouth* to approach within range. After a thirty-minute running battle, the *Randolph* took a hit in the magazine, causing her to explode, with the loss of all but 4 of her crew of 315.[106] The same principles applied between frigates and lesser categories of warships. Indeed, sound rules of engagement could be summed up in two simple phrases: A small ship could never beat a bigger ship, and a big ship could never catch a smaller ship.

The configuration of the sailing warship even influenced the order in which the events of a naval campaign unfolded, imparting a curiously theatrical pace to the struggle. Ideally, swifter, lighter rates made contact first and fought the preliminary bouts, while the more ponderous heavyweights were saved for the exciting finale. Relentlessly, the tension mounted toward a climax worthy of the *Iliad*, with the opposing lines of sailing behemoths deciding at last who commanded the sea.

Even given the brutality of the climactic struggle, it amounted to a highly satisfactory and orderly way of fighting. For the rigid articulation and structure imposed by factors of wood, wind, and water predisposed officers to believe there was but one way of combat at sea. The conditioning did not end there. Of particular interest was the manner in which the structure of human command was paralleled and therefore reinforced by the nature of the weaponry—a hierarchy of ships supporting a hierarchy of people and vice versa. Thus, an admiral aboard his flagship might command a line of battleships, each directed by a captain, surrounded by a screen of progressively smaller ships controlled by a descending scale of officers. Given such a sociological-technological pyramid, the idea of a smaller ship attacking a larger one was not just imprudent, it was fundamentally insubordinate. The scheme was not simply structurally stable, it was stable in time. Thus warfare under sail was a key component of the

Enlightenment military mechanism dedicated to controlling the gun and the overall destructiveness of warfare. So for hundreds of years naval technology was suspended, tactics and strategy remained basically unchanged, and the world of navies must have seemed as immutable as the sea itself.

Meanwhile, Britain grew stronger and stronger, for a general shortage of materials strongly favored the Royal Navy. The construction of one seventy-four-gun battleship required two thousand oak trees. Nelson's *Victory* alone contained 300,000 cubic feet of timber, or the yield of one hundred acres of woodland.[107] In deforested Western Europe, an aspiring naval power had to base its calculations upon the most thrifty possible use of a limited quantity of oaks. Immediate and rapid construction of a fleet necessarily meant a future shortage of trees. Moreover, experience dictated that wooden ships built too rapidly out of less than thoroughly seasoned wood began rotting almost immediately.[108] However, the life expectancy of a properly constructed sailing warship was likely to be long. Whereas the frozen state of naval architecture ensured against obsolescence, proper maintenance of a wooden vessel enabled it to retain its structural integrity for upwards of a hundred years. Consequently, *Sovereign of the Seas* was still a flagship at Barfleur at age fifty-six, just as *Victory* was forty years old when she served as the principal flagship at Trafalgar.[109]

The whole system favored the slow accumulation of warships and placed great importance upon the number of battle-ready ships available. Britain, which pursued a fairly consistent construction policy, was bound to have a great advantage. During the period between 1689 and 1713 the Royal Navy's fleet grew steadily, and by 1727 the Admiralty could count 84 ships-of-the-line on the books. By 1763, the figure had risen to 141. The wars with France, Spain, and Holland that began with the American Revolution further inflated the naval lists. By 1783, there were 174 battleships in the Royal Navy, though many of them were unfit for service. Finally, at the close of the Napoleonic Wars in 1814, an all-time peak was reached with 100 battleships actually in commission and a force of 60 fully seaworthy craft held in reserve.[110] Such accumulated bulk could hardly have been encouraging to its naval rivals. Yet Britannia's dreams of enduring supremacy resting upon its horde of oaken retainers was to be rudely interrupted by the arrival of a hissing iron monster.

3

Upon This Rock:
The Technological Revolution
and the Prophet Mahan

I

The advent of the reciprocating steam engine as a practical means of propulsion for vessels upon the water initiated a chain reaction that revolutionized naval warfare.[1] This fundamental sequence of innovation provided the components from which the modern battleship would grow and be perfected. Like so many strings of technology, each step in the progression logically followed its predecessor; the whole process had a superficial air of inevitability that obscured alternatives.

Although the era of self-propelled ships began in 1807 with Robert Fulton's successful trip up the Hudson, it was almost forty years later before steam was adopted on a large scale by the world's navies.[2] Beside simple prejudice and conservatism, there were several very practical reasons why the major admiralties hesitated. First, the early steam engine was a cumbersome and inefficient device, producing less horsepower per pound than a sail rig.[3] In addition, reciprocating steam machinery was notoriously subject to breakdowns. But most important was the early steamboat's vulnerability to gunfire. The first steam vessels were driven by massive paddle wheels whose high axis of rotation demanded that all machinery be located well above the waterline. Not only did the position of wheel and engine make them obvious targets, but also those massive contrivances left little room for armament.[4]

Despite those undeniable drawbacks, the steam engine's potential for military application was great. Wind was theoretically inexhaustible, but navies under sail had always been vassals to its caprice, traversing the seas at its sufferance. Though predictable in certain seasons and locations and imparting enormous range to sailing fleets, countless times the breeze had either abandoned commanders at critical moments or exceeded the point at which gun ports might safely be opened and firing begun. Mechanical propulsion promised a solution, a means of going anywhere on the sea at any time, subject to the limits imposed by the size of coal bunkers. The latter factor would necessarily complicate questions of endurance and set off a scramble for overseas coaling stations. But for a profession whose ultimate logistical objective had always been the provision of the maximum number of heavy units at a particular time and place, steam's increased potential for coordinated and precise strategic and tactical movement was impossible to ignore. Consequently, the progress of steam propulsion was closely followed by the world's navies.

In the civilian sphere the pace of improvement was breathtaking. Just thirty years after Fulton's little boat had chugged up the Hudson, the *Sirius* managed to cross the Atlantic, driven by an engine rated at 600 horsepower. Barely twenty years after that, steam engines with a combined total of 11,500 horsepower propelled the 27,000-ton, 690-foot *Great Eastern* at nearly fifteen knots.[5] Yet these ships were paddle wheelers, and the basic military drawback of steam remained to be overcome.

The solution presented itself in the form of a screw propeller, based on principles first described by Swiss mathematician Daniel Bernoulli. In 1842 and 1843, Swedish inventor John Ericsson, under the patronage of the energetic Captain Robert F. Stockton, built the first propeller-driven warship in the world, the USS *Princeton*.[6] The ship's screw propeller, besides being considerably more efficient than the paddle wheel, allowed most of the steam equipment to operate out of harm's way below the waterline, thus clearing an increased portion of the deck for armament.[7] Consequently, the *Princeton* proved itself to be a suitable warship and paved the way for a general, though grudging, naval acceptance of steam power.[8]

After the initial breakthrough, the military career of the reciprocating steam engine for over sixty years involved continuous modification and improvement. Once the thermodynamics of steam were better understood, it became clear that to improve efficiency a simple expansion motor required considerably greater quantities of the gas (about 30 pounds pressure) than had previously been thought necessary.[9] To increase the supply of steam, engineers began constructing larger boilers. However, the enlarged vaporizing capacity allowed the boilers to produce a great deal more steam than could efficiently be used by simple expansion engines. That led to the development of the compound engine, which, because it expanded the gas in two stages, could handle higher pressures (around 60 pounds) economically.[10] Improved motors then led to boilers with corrugated steel furnaces (130 pounds), evaporators (155 pounds), and large and small tube condensers (250 pounds).[11] The quantum jump in pressure was predictably followed by the triple-expansion engine, the last major development in reciprocating steam power.[12] The significance of the series of improvements lay in the momentum it built—both in terms of facilitating power-consuming developments in other areas and in breaking down resistance to each successive change.

Steam propulsion also had important repercussions in the sphere of armament. Although the propeller system eased the crush, the increasingly bulky machinery associated with reciprocating steam power still occupied space that had been once reserved inside the ship for guns. Although early auxiliary-steam-powered warships were able to preserve the basic broadside configuration, technological logic pointed in the opposite direction.

That in turn would lead down two separate paths. The first of these was an aberration, the subordination of the gun to the resurrected ram. If machinery left less room for guns, then steam-powered vessels would revert back to what they had been for three thousand oar-powered years—floating projectiles. The logic could not have been more revealing. In what amounted to an astonishing affirmation of traditionalism, the major navies sedulously equipped virtually every capital ship prior to the HMS *Dreadnought* with rams, conveniently ignoring the fact that they proved virtually useless in combat and turned several peacetime collisions, most notably that of the *Grosser Kurfürst* in 1878 and *Victoria* in 1893, into ship-destroying and man-killing disasters.[13]

A far more realistic response and one destined to chart the primary course of naval armament in the future was a reliance on a smaller number of guns of greatly increased size and power. The first step in the deadly metamorphosis of the naval gun was the replacement of its traditional solid ammunition with explosive shells. Though such shells, shot from high-trajectory mortars, had long been employed on land, they had been ignored at sea, where a ship's rocking motion made anything other than a flat-shooting gun virtually impossible to aim.[14] Consequently, it was not until 1824 when Henri Paixhans demonstrated the feasibility of horizontal shell fire that the major navies began to consider seriously the possibilities of the exploding missile. Yet the importance of this innovation continued to be universally underestimated until 30 November 1853, when a large Turkish squadron and three hundred years of naval history were blown out of the water at Sinope by shell-firing Russians.[15]

Besides demonstrating the vulnerability of the wooden warship, the greatly augmented power of the individual shell was a tremendous stimulus for further ordnance development and caused a decisive shift in emphasis from quantity of armament to quality. Because the shell was hollow, it was considerably lighter than its solid predecessor. Therefore, it could be used in larger calibers, which, of course, meant bigger guns.[16] However, the strains created by the shell's increased dimensions soon surpassed the strength limitations of the primitive cast-iron muzzle-loaders, a fact that quickly led to an intensive effort to make guns stronger.[17] The problem proved to be in the crystalline structure of metal itself, which cracked no matter how thick it was cast.

A solution first dawned on a British manufacturer of hydraulic equipment, William Armstrong, in 1854, as he read an account of the Battle of Inkerman in the Crimea, during which British troops were barely able to wrestle their ponderous smooth-bore artillery into firing position. Exclaiming that it was "time military engineering was brought up to the level of current engineering practice," Armstrong promptly roughed out plans for a revolutionary compound gun barrel built up from a core of metal strips (later cable) wound around an inner tube and then sheathed with a heated steel sleeve, which, when allowed to cool, applied tremendous pressure inward.[18] The resulting tube was not only enormously stronger than any homogeneous barrel, but it also allowed for a rapid increase in gun size because it had become possible to fabricate artillery in pieces and assemble them into a unit of far greater bore and caliber than any cast in one piece.[19]

Meanwhile, the increased speeds at which the larger, less-dense shells traveled favored the elongation of the projectile itself for the purposes of streamlining. However, such missiles, when thrown by smooth-bore guns, tended to tumble end-over-end in flight, thereby compounding the inaccuracies imparted by the "windage" necessary for muzzle-loading. Those erratic flight characteristics were eventually eliminated in 1855 by "rifling" the bore of the barrel with a twisting series of parallel grooves that imparted rotation around the long axis of the shell and made it potentially accurate at ranges far beyond the capabilities of traditional naval guns.[20]

By 1870 the great durability of the reinforced gun permitted the introduction of slower-burning propellant. This powder, when used in conjunction with lengthened gun barrels, permitted slower but longer projectile acceleration and higher terminal velocities capable of greatly extending ranges. But muzzle-loading was not well suited to the new conditions. The tight projectile/barrel seal necessitated by rifling and the stretching of the tubes to take advantage of slower-burning powder made it extraordinarily slow and difficult to ram a shell home from the muzzle. The adoption of breech-loading was a foregone conclusion, postponed by the lack of a reliable mechanism capable of withstanding the extreme pressures generated during firing. Finally, the evolution of the modern naval rifle was completed in 1880 with the general acceptance of the French interrupted-screw breech lock.[21]

The product of this spurt of technology was a gun infinitely larger and more deadly than its simple ancestor, the thirty-two pounder of only sixty years past. With each increase in size and power, the naval rifle wrenched tactics and ship design a bit its way. Guns became fewer; the space within which battle lines might potentially score hits grew wider. In addition, the expectation of longer ranges, combined with the growing consequences of a single hit, raised the possibility of transforming the character of naval tactics from those of a Homeric brawl to a duel between distant adversaries, where death might be sudden and unexpected.

Of course, the means of defense could hardly be ignored, and the bursting effect of the shell suggested its own antidote, armor. Since shells tended to burst on contact with water, only surfaces exposed to the air required protection. Therefore, a high degree of invulnerability to shell bursts at first seemed contingent only upon the possession of armor of sufficient stoutness and impenetrability. Moreover, this conclusion was reinforced by a military tradition of armoring key combatants that stretches back at least 4,500 years to the Sumerians and constitutes one of the strongest and most persistent historical paradigms of weapons development. Consequently, it is not surprising that the simple logic of this classic confrontation between offense and defense charted the course of military naval architecture for virtually the entire life span of the modern battleship.

Yet from a qualitative and metallurgical standpoint, the first forty years proved critical. From 1855 to the mid-1870s, protection consisted of countering each escalation in gun power with a proportionately thicker slab of relatively soft, but tough and malleable, wrought iron. But unacceptable increases in weight, manufacturing difficulties, and the invention of case-hardened projectiles that cut through wrought iron like a knife slicing butter eventually made further endeavors in that direction appear futile.[22]

Technology's response to the apparent cul de sac was an intensive search for more adamantine substances. The efforts did not long go unrewarded. By 1877, armorers had begun facing their wrought-iron plates with a layer of hard but brittle steel, hoping to combine the best qualities of both metals. The problem of joining the two layers was never really solved, and by the mid-1880s metallurgists were producing all-steel armor superior in every respect to the compound variety.[23] In the early 1890s further improvements were made in the elastic qualities of steel by the addition of small quantities of nickel and chromium. That advance was, however, overshadowed later in the decade by the final step in the development of the armor that was to shield the modern battleship, the selective tempering processes of Harvey and Krupp, which allowed steel plate all the advantages of the compound principles without sacrifice to solidity.[24]

That led to the development during the 1890s of fuses that retarded the detonation of the projectile's explosive filling until it had pierced the armor and entered the vitals of the ship, thereby completing the transformation of the naval gun from bludgeon to rapier, in theory at least. Only the Germans actually perfected a truly reliable armor-piercing shell prior to World War I.[25]

As technology exhausted the means by which ferrous metals might be made more impervious to shell, the idea of invulnerability became increasingly more relative.[26] Ordnance experts had consistently and successfully responded to the challenge of penetrating the hardest armor available.[27] In addition, the enormous weight of protection aboard vessels that, after all, were meant to float, forced engineers of the defense to the unavoidable conclusion that only a small portion of a ship's exposed surfaces could be shielded with armor thick enough to prevent damage. This realization did not, however, lead to the repudiation of the principle of armor protection. For the central task of the armorer, the protection of a warship's offensive capability, was actually simplified by the decisive trend in ordnance development toward a smaller number of greatly enlarged guns. To achieve a fair degree of invulnerability against shell fire, it was only necessary to consolidate a vessel's relatively few artillery pieces behind a single armored casement of sufficient thickness to be impenetrable. Such ironclads came to be known as central-battery ships.

However, the reduction in the number of large guns put a premium on giving each one the greatest possible arc of fire. The man-of-war's guns, then, very naturally had to be further concentrated, this time into revolving armored citadels from which they could be trained in all directions. Turrets, as the devices were called, appeared for the first time in the 1860s and soon became the standard housing for naval ordnance as well as a characteristic feature of all future armored battleships. Once the basic configuration of the turret was established, its development was limited to increases in size and thickness and the addition of an armored stem below to protect the magazines and loading mechanisms. Meanwhile, it was the mast's interference with the training of naval rifles in turrets, as much as further developments in steam propulsion, that led to the abandonment of sail as an auxiliary means of power.[28] That and sheer weight.

For despite the relative compactness of the turret itself, the armor it used and the guns it contained, along with the rest of the ship's machinery, were all enormously heavy—far too heavy for either the continued use of sails or, more pressing still, oak construction. To accommodate all the accoutrements of the naval-technological revolution, it became rather quickly apparent that hulls of vastly increased strength had to be developed.

Although the idea of building vessels out of a substance heavier than water seemed at first "contrary to nature," the enormous advantage to be gained by substituting ferrous metals for trees quickly silenced conservative opposition. Thus by the early 1860s, with the appearance of the revolutionary iron-hulled British Warrior, the day of the wooden capital ship had definitely passed.[29]

The consequences of the change were quite literally enormous. The use of iron, and later steel, in the hulls of warships obliterated two of the most important stabilizing factors in naval technology. First, those metals were so much stronger than wood that it became almost immediately apparent that the traditional limits on the size and weight of warships were no longer relevant.[30] Suddenly vessels with dimensions exceeding the wildest dreams of traditional shipwrights became not only feasible but also practically inevitable. And if that was not enough, contemporaneous advances in the mining, manufacturing, and forming of ferrous metals promised a cheap and plentiful supply of the key materials needed to build ships. Technology's bounty wiped out in a stroke the perennial shortage of timber that had for so long prevented the rapid buildup of any one of Britain's naval rivals. For a power with a well-developed steel industry and a coastline, a battle fleet was now largely a matter of will.

The rapid evolution of those four components (steam propulsion, naval ordnance, armor plate, and ferrous-metal hulls) and their trial-and-error combination as integral parts of a single fighting unit characterized the early life of the

"*The emergence of a sort of primitive, generalized battleship.*" USS Massachusetts, 1893. *(Courtesy of the U.S. Naval Institute)*

modern capital ship.[31] During the final decade of the nineteenth century, this process of development resulted in the emergence of a sort of primitive, generalized battleship displacing between 10,000 and 15,000 tons, carrying turret-mounted, breech-loading heavy ordnance of mixed caliber, clad in a fairly thick and extensive coat of selectively tempered armor, and containing triple-expansion steam engines capable of driving it at something over fifteen knots.[32] With the exception of improved sighting devices, all the basic elements necessary for the final development of the species were available in one form or another and awaited only a better interrelationship of parts—and the removal of the ram. Once the importance of speed and long-range accuracy became critical in the eyes of naval theorists, the dreadnought would be born.

One thing about the armored capital ship was clear from the beginning. It was bound to grow. Indeed, growth was to be the hallmark of the battleship, and it seemed at times as if it could do little else.

All manner of physical laws, technological contingencies, and psychological factors conspired to promote the relentless enlargement of the modern ship-of-the-line. To begin the spiral, a peculiarity of fluid dynamics dictated that a long ship was inherently a fast ship. In fact a vessel 81 feet in length, moving at nine knots, required proportionately as much power as did a ship 900 feet long being propelled at thirty knots.[33] Given the strength and availability of steel, the temptation of naval architects to elongate their creations proved all but irresistible. However, the greater bending stresses to which longer craft were subject logically required stronger and heavier construction. That conclusion was driven home by the general proposition that the strength of a vessel was in an inverse relationship to its length and directly proportional to its width and the square of its depth. Consequently, any stretching of the battleship was most prudently accompanied by a corresponding increase in its girth.[34] This chronic swelling of the capital ship's exterior dimensions was further encouraged by the superior seaworthiness and steadiness that large ships usually demonstrated as gun platforms.[35]

However, the propagation of long, swift warships encountered a number of vexing complications. Because water resistance varied approximately according to the cube of velocity, any augmentation of a vessel's top speed above about fifteen knots demanded inordinate increases in power. The implications were nothing less than enormous for ships that would eventually be capable of over twenty-five knots. For example, the HMS *Princess Royal* would need 27,000 more horsepower than the HMS *Indefatigable* to travel one knot faster.[36] As might be expected, the required machinery was very heavy. Indeed, few things gobbled up displacement and waterline more effectively than high speed. So fully 2,000 tons and a third of the HMS *Dreadnought*'s length was occupied by engines and boilers—in the first capital ship to feature the space-saving steam turbine.[37] Meanwhile, the elongation of the hull dictated by efficiency produced vast areas of exposed surface demanding armor. But nothing aboard ship was inherently heavier than armor.

The offensive arm of the battleship was likewise prone to gigantism. In the course of a bit more than a century, the 2.5-ton 32-pounder would grow into a 150-ton monster that spit shells 18 inches in diameter.[38] As noted earlier, there were logical reasons why guns should have grown. But beyond a certain caliber, gains in offensive power came only at the cost of enormous accretions in the weight of the pieces themselves. The spiral did not stop there. The ever-more-gigantic guns required ever-more-massive mountings, loading mechanisms, and training devices that were not only heavy but also consumed space that had to be sheathed with still more armor.

Yet the case for large guns seemed unimpeachable. Not only was their effective armor-piercing range much longer, but every increase in caliber produced a far greater increase in the capacity of the shell to carry explosives. "Not quite a geometric progression . . . but it was in that order of ideas,"[39] noted Winston Churchill. So it seemed that simple logic and arithmetic demanded huge warships with a few very large guns.

Once begun, growth took on a momentum of its own. The arguments for further enlargement of any and all parts of the battleship gained force as each component grew bigger. "So I was forced, step by step, as so many others have been before," wrote Bradley Fiske, "to the conclusion that the only solution was to build a ship so large that it could have sufficient speed, sufficient armament, and sufficient armor to whip any ship."[40] Under the circumstances, it was hardly remarkable that naval architects and officers began to attribute a certain inevitability to the process. "You cannot keep ships small," conceded Rear Admiral C. F. Goodrich, "they grow while you sleep."[41]

But during waking hours the forces of military tradition and the human psyche were also at work, subtly encouraging the enlargement of the battleship. Because the modern capital ship was necessarily a combination of several interrelated systems, its design was basically a process of deciding what percent of the total weight each would represent.[42] Since there had been few naval battles in the nineteenth century, the balance that was struck was generally more a product of theory than experience.[43] Given the general state of uncertainty, many a painful compromise was avoided in the name of prudence by simply raising the tonnage of the projected vessel. Although a few, most notably, Admiral Mahan, complained that this expedient was "analogous to meeting household difficulties, not by management but by increasing expenditures,"[44] it proved irresistible to a profession whose whole history had taught its members to equate size with power. As Rear Admiral Joseph Strauss pointed out: "In everything we do the tendency is to make things bigger. We have tied up the idea of size with progress."[45]

Moreover, naval officers were emotionally predisposed to look with favor upon the expansion of their progeny. Admiral Dewey noted with obvious approval, "The increase in the tonnage of ships from 300 to 27,000 tons is a convenient index of . . . a development in naval shipbuilding unrivaled in any equal period of the world's history."[46]

In part the spasmodic nature of technological development was responsible for the gigantic turn of events in naval architecture. By the first years of the twentieth century, the frenzy of innovation that had begun with steam had about run its course for the surface-artillery ship. Armor was about as hard as it would ever be,[47] the possibilities of macroballistics had been pretty thoroughly explored, and the nature of wave resistance severely inhibited any dramatic advances in top speed. A new equilibrium had been established, and it seemed that subsequent increases in battleship power must again be mostly a function of size.

A curious phenomenon had taken place: The fundamentally disruptive force of technology had apparently operated in a manner that removed variables from war upon the sea. Steam propulsion had injected an element of regularity and reliability that greatly facilitated the close coordination and control of fleet tactics.[48] While the evolution of armor and ordnance had served to make the destruction of small ships by large ones more certain than before, it also indicated that future battleships would all be basically alike, differing only in the relative quantities of the various components each carried. Those differences were, in turn, readily reduced to easily comprehended units of measurement that further aided comparison, evaluation, and prediction between ships and fleets. The orderly hierarchical nature of naval warfare could be interpreted as having weathered the storm of mechanization. Meanwhile, it was almost inevitable that Annapolites and their brothers around the naval world would react favorably to the technologies that were inflating the battleship, while at the same time ignoring the development of weapons whose small size in no way detracted from their lethal potential. It would require some explanation, but once officers got over an initial period of confusion and consternation, they awoke to find themselves in the enviable position of having their own predisposition for eternal tactical verities reaffirmed by the revolutionary course of events. Or so it seemed.

II

Steam was taken up with the greatest of reluctance by the United States Navy.[49] The Annapolite's attitude toward the spread of those sooty contrivances was probably typified by Stephen Decatur's statement: "It is the end of our business; hereafter any man who can boil a tea-kettle will be as good as the best of us."[50]

Although a kernel of truth in that gloomy prophecy haunted the thoughts of line officers well into the twentieth century, its political overtones imparted a messianic tinge to the Annapolite's resistance to mechanization. For the introduction of steam propulsion heralded the arrival of a pretender to the naval throne: that wizard of tea-kettle technology, the naval engineer.[51]

Organized in 1842 to provide operatives for the complicated and unreliable engines that line officers found so distasteful, the U.S. Navy's Engineer Corps was a natural center of antagonism for the "naval aristocracy" during the transition from sail to steam.[52] The engineer's presence aboard ship symbolized the growing irrelevance of the Annapolite's special sailing skill and his ignorance of newer forms of propulsion. He was "a mere passenger on board a steamer," according to the ever-combative Engineer-in-Chief Benjamin Franklin Isherwood.[53] By the same token, the "specially educated" engineers felt they were vital to the "navy of the future. . . . Steam was the force of progress, the engineers its masters."[54]

Annapolites perceived the situation far differently. It was, after all, the line officers "who had some familiarity with sea life" who navigated and fought the ship while the engineers were "snoring away below."[55] Accordingly, engineers were refused many of the normal privileges of officers aboard ship, such as access to the wardroom and special berthing facilities.[56] More important, they were denied the rank that might have allowed them to encroach upon the vital command prerogatives of the "naval aristocracy."[57] Along with their fellow staff officers (naval constructors, surgeons, paymasters), the naval engineer was identified by his functional title alone (e.g., Passed Assistant Engineer X or Chief Engineer Y). But the surest way to avoid the encroachment of naval engineers was to limit their numbers by impeding the proliferation of steam.

Yet the Civil War forced the hand of progress. Because of the specialization of the southern economy and its reliance upon importation for virtually all manufactured goods, the Confederacy was particularly vulnerable to economic warfare. It followed that the obvious role for the Union Navy was to blockade the southern coast. Making a reality out of a blockade stretching from Alexandria, Virginia, to Brownsville, Texas, demanded that all but the swiftest blockade runners be caught regardless of wind conditions—a requirement that, in turn, necessitated the wholesale adoption of auxiliary steam power.[58] With admirable energy, Engineer-in-Chief Isherwood did just that, transforming, through new construction and the addition of auxiliary engines, a motley collection of vessels into an efficient steam-based fleet. So by the summer of 1861 the North was able to begin interdicting southern ports.[59]

The Confederacy replied with the classic response of the weaker naval power, *guerre de course*. Although it did supply the South with virtually its only naval successes of the war, commerce raiding, as traditionalists might have predicted, failed in its ultimate objective of forcing the abandonment of the blockade.[60] Meanwhile the "Anaconda" strategy was strangling the South economically. If it was to survive, the garrote of northern ships had to be broken.

In what must have been a mood close to desperation, the Confederate Naval Secretary Stephen Mallory turned to the revolution in naval architecture for salvation. "One armored battleship," he wrote in 1861, "could traverse the entire coast of the United States, prevent all blockades, and encounter with a fair prospect of success their entire Navy."[61] So lured by the ever-sweet siren song of military-technical invincibility, the Confederacy committed the labor of 1,500 men and a considerable portion of its tiny iron-working capacity to the conversion of the captured steam frigate *Merrimac* into the armored central-battery gunship CSS *Virginia*.[62]

Meanwhile, as the *Virginia* was being prepared, the U.S. Navy was searching for an antidote to that theoretically ultimate weapon. The committee of officers appointed to formulate an ironclad policy was hardly sanguine about the possibilities of technology at sea. Shell guns were dismissed as being "of nothing superior to the large and heavy spherical shot," and the committee was equally "skeptical" about the "advantages and ultimate adoption" of armor on cruising vessels. "But," the reluctant Annapolites added, "while other nations are endeavoring to perfect them, we must not remain idle."[63] For that reason, the committee recommended the construction of three ironclads, one of which was a small, ungainly, single-turreted craft, practically without freeboard, and destined to achieve fame as the USS *Monitor*. That radical creature of John

USS Cumberland *versus the ironclad CSS* Virginia. *(Courtesy of the U.S. National Archives)*

Ericsson's fertile imagination was rushed to completion, and on 6 March 1862—not a moment too soon—began its fateful journey to Hampton Roads.

The dramatic events of the next few days captured the popular imagination as few naval engagements have before or since. Yet, more important, they demonstrated with special clarity both the potential and the limitations of military technology.[64]

The South drew first blood. On 8 March the ponderous *Virginia* left Norfolk and attacked what, by previous standards, was a formidable blockading force of wooden vessels—the fifty-gun steam frigates *Minnesota*, *Roanoke*, and *Congress* (sister ships of the original *Merrimac*), the sailing frigate *St. Lawrence*, with fifty-two guns, and the twenty-four-gun sloop *Cumberland*.[65] What followed was little more than slaughter, with the clumsy *Virginia* methodically wreaking havoc on her former sisters, while receiving only superficial damage in return. When nightfall cut short the carnage, the *Virginia* had destroyed two vessels, badly damaged a third, and scattered the rest.[66] It was this depressing scene that greeted the *Monitor's* belated arrival at nine o'clock that evening. But now the stage was set for the next day's climactic encounter between these two primitive ancestors of the mighty dreadnought.

"The day ended in utter frustration." USS Monitor *versus* CSS Virginia. *(Courtesy of the U.S. National Archives)*

On the morning of 9 March the fog lifted over Hampton Roads to reveal the *Virginia* moving away from her anchorage at Sewell's Point, intent upon further destruction. In order to protect the damaged steam frigate *Minnesota*, the *Monitor* steamed out to confront her Confederate adversary. There ensued what historian of ironclads James Baxter called "one of the strangest encounters on record."[67] After a few preliminary shots, the two ships closed to point-blank range and discovered (presumably to their mutual horror), that neither could pierce the other's armor. For the next four hours both sides endeavored without success to pound this revelation to oblivion. With fierce resolution the ships fired round upon ineffective round, all without landing a telling blow. Not unexpectedly, both tried to end the stalemate by ramming, but that too failed, and the day ended in utter frustration.[68]

The inconclusive confrontation provided a glimpse beyond the fiery immediacy of battle to the real nature of the warlike partnership of humans and technology. What had been presumed to be utterly subservient revealed the knack of twisting its master's plans into caricatures. Armor thickness and muzzle velocities were fate's true handicappers there, so that no amount of tactical skill, inspired leadership, or personal courage could keep those cannon balls from merely bouncing off the sides of the two ships. On that day and many others,

technology would prove as capricious as it was willful, first slaughtering promis-
cuously, then sparing all but a few. Hampton Roads would prove an archetype of
future naval events—twisted spectacles in which the death machinery that men
labored upon so lovingly grabbed center stage and turned the ancient and stately
rituals of battle into *Götterdämmerung* burlesques. Meanwhile, human participants would be relegated to the roles of stage props and fall guys. Yet the lesson
was not easily assimilated by creatures so proud and headstrong as ourselves.

The southern plan had failed. The invincible ironclad of the Confederacy
had, like all "ultimate weapons," simply provoked a slightly improved version of
itself. The blockade continued, and the Confederacy would strangle. The North's
Monitor, simply by being there, had won an important strategic victory in odd
contrast to its tactical failure. Much the same could be said of the English Grand
Fleet at a much more elaborate comedy of errors fifty-four years later—Jutland.

Still technology's children, the naval engineers emerged from the Civil War
in flourishing condition. Their numbers had increased from just a few to 2,277
in 1865, and the budget of the Bureau of Steam Engineering had been inflated
to the point that it ranked first in the order of naval requisitions.[69] Moreover,
their leader, the redoubtable Engineer-in-Chief Benjamin Franklin Isherwood,
was determined to win for them a position in the Navy commensurate with their
newly acquired power and numbers. "The War and the progress of the age," he
declared hopefully, "have swept away many of the mouldy prejudices of an effete
regime."[70] Accordingly he proposed a reorganization of the engineers and an
improvement in their rank in relation to Annapolites.[71] Isherwood was equally
optimistic about the future of steam. "The Navy is now, and must ever continue
to be, exclusively a steam navy."[72] Therefore, he enthusiastically supported the
construction of faster but larger and more-expensive warships such as the USS
Wampanoag, which reached an amazing 17.74 knots on her trials, but weighed
over 4,000 tons and cost more than $1.5 million to build.[73]

Isherwood's progressive course was, however, completely out of touch with
the times. At war's end, the United States found itself with one of the largest and
most modern fleets in the world, totaling nearly 700 ships.[74] Yet the country
completely lacked the kind of proximate foes that might have made the maintenance of such a bloated armada advisable.

Under the circumstances, retrenchment seemed eminently logical, and by
1870 only 52 fully commissioned ships remained.[75] Economy became the byword
of the fleet, and with it came technological reaction. Steam engines, because of
their appetite for large quantities of expensive coal, were hardly in vogue. "To

burn coal was so grievous an offense in the eyes of the authorities that for years the captain was obliged to enter in the logbook in red ink his reason for getting up steam and starting engines."[76] For a time there was even talk of making commanders pay for coal if their reasons for using it seemed insufficient.[77] Since the fortunes of the naval engineers were symbolically related to the progress of steam, their importance to the Navy diminished proportionately. Thus, in the four years that followed 1865, the corps was reduced to a mere 319 regular engineering officers.[78]

Meanwhile, the government's policy of naval contraction was in perfect congruence with the reactionary schemes of the line officers. Like any group that thought it saw a possibility of its own extinction, Annapolites were determined to remove the sources of danger when the opportunity presented itself. In March 1869 a board headed by Rear Admiral Louis M. Goldsborough was convened with the purpose of examining all "steam machinery afloat."[79] Its report not only condemned the USS *Wampanoag* and recommended the redesign of all naval steamers to improve their characteristics under sail but also revealed quite clearly the prejudices of the line officers, who dominated the committee. "Lounging through the watches of a steamer, or acting as firemen and coal heavers, will not produce in a seaman that combination of boldness, strength, and skill which characterized the American Sailor of an older day; and the habitual exercise by an officer of [such] a command . . . is a poor substitute for the school of observation, promptness, and command found only on the deck of a sailing vessel."[80]

At a later date naval reactionaries learned to mask their prejudices in appropriately technical-sounding rebuttals. But at the dawn of the Age of Steam, as Elting Morison observed, "They were moved to say . . . they just didn't like her [*Wampanoag*]. And they were simple enough to explain in an official report why."[81]

The line was equally desirous of eliminating the influence of the engineers. Vice Admiral David Porter, who led the "naval aristocracy's" crusade against the usurpers, wrote, "Isherwood had put in a claim to be made rear admiral . . . and to punish him for his folly, we intend not only to strip him and the engineers of all honors, but to make them the most inferior corps in the Navy."[82] Although vulnerable because of their shrinking numbers and utility, the engineers still had one potent weapon with which to defend themselves, bureaucratic camouflage.

Until 1842 a Board of Navy Commissioners made up of the three highest-ranking officers in the service had been responsible for the Navy's administration. In that year Congress, apparently concerned by the board's growing influence, abolished the body and reorganized the Navy Department into several separate bureaus "without collective function or responsibility."[83] The autonomy of the bureaus was enforced by their direct access to and direct appropriations from Congress.[84] In fact, the only means of coordination that the system provided was the guiding hand of the usually inexperienced secretary of the Navy. The decentralized nature of the Navy's administrative apparatus rendered it largely independent of the traditional hierarchical line-officer chain of command, which theoretically governed all aspects of the service. For that reason, the bureaus were natural havens of naval engineers and other staff officers devoid of command prerogatives. And the security of these bureaucratic sanctuaries was matched by their central location. Whereas line officers were frequently aboard ships far from the centers of power, the bureaus and the senior staff officers who ran most of them were clustered in Washington, where the Navy's money was appropriated and spent. The advantage of position translated into political dividends for ambitious naval administrators whose power over the allocation of funds allowed them to establish "a definite community of interests" with the congressional representatives of seaboard states.[85]

Therefore, it was not surprising that the line officer's vendetta against the engineers took the form of an attack upon the bureau system. In 1865 and again in 1869 legislators sympathetic to the line's cause proposed congressional reorganization of the Navy.[86] Each plan featured a commission of high-ranking line officers, known alternately as the Board of Admiralty or Board of Survey, intended to oversee naval administration. "The presumptuous aspirations of the Staff will never be checked till we have a Board of Survey consisting of admirals alone, who . . . could guide the Secretary of the Navy and put an end to 'Wampanoags,' mismanagement, and extravagance."[87]

Although the assaults on the bureau system did not meet with legislative approval, they marked a significant trend in the political objectives of the line. Annapolites would try time and again to superimpose a "council of elders" upon the decentralized administrative structure and technical policy of the Navy. Whether it was called a General Staff or a General Board or a Naval Aide System, its motive was always the same: to bring what appeared to be a chaotic system under the control of the military branch of the service by subjecting it to the strict principles of rank and hierarchy.

The bureau system survived the assault almost uninjured, but the engineers were not so fortunate. Admiral Porter proved a more skilled politician than his blunt antagonist, the engineer in chief. Porter studiously courted the favor of key Republicans and, with the election of U. S. Grant to the presidency, assumed control of the Navy.[88] Isherwood was quickly replaced, and the influence of his corps fell precipitously.[89] An act of 5 August 1882 set a goal of eventually limiting the number of engineers to 100, and by 1896 their ranks had dwindled to a scant 173.[90]

Nonetheless, their memory hung like a dark cloud over the Navy, for their demise symbolized the Annapolites' apparent inability to reconcile mechanization with their own cultural presumptions. Control of the service had been maintained, but only at the cost of pursuing a policy of deliberate technological retrogression, which would shortly make a mockery of the Navy's pretenses to battle efficiency.

The condition of the U.S. fleet until the late 1880s was epitomized by the reply of Oscar Wilde's Canterville Ghost to the complaint of a young American that her country had no ruins and curiosities: "No ruins! No curiosities! You have your Navy and your manners!"[91] Material stagnation was everywhere. For more than twenty years after the Civil War, no seagoing armored vessels were built in the United States, and for armament the Navy continued to rely on antique smooth-bore muzzle-loaders.[92] By 1881 Secretary of the Navy William H. Hunt could report that all but thirty-one American military vessels were unserviceable.[93] Representative John D. Long, who would one day preside over the service as its secretary, termed the fleet "an alphabet of floating wash tubs," regarded by the public as a "marine Falstaffian burlesque."[94]

The fruits of the line's victory were proving bitter indeed. The degeneration of the Navy was a profoundly humiliating experience for Annapolites, who derived so large a measure of their self-image from professional associations with counterparts from other quarters of the naval world. Commander Frank V. McNair's report on fleet maneuvers off Florida in 1874 made no secret of his own dissatisfaction: "The vessels before us were in no respect [those] of a great nation like our own, for what could be more lamentable . . . what more painful . . . than to see a fleet armed with smoothbore guns . . . moving at a rate of 4.7 knots? What inferior force could it overtake, or what superior force escape from, of any of the great naval powers of the earth?"[95] Alfred Mahan echoed those sentiments when he wrote a friend, "If we are made to go from port to port in ships which are a laughing stock . . . you cannot expect that our pride and self respect will escape uninjured."[96]

It was not just the Annapolites' vanity that was being squashed beneath the rotting timbers of the fleet. The Navy's contraction had resulted in a corresponding glut of career officers, especially in the upper grades. Since promotion was strictly by seniority, that meant that advancement all but ceased in the 1870s and 1880s.[97] In a profession where rank meant everything, to be left dangling in midcareer was a punishment of exquisite cruelty.

The frustration suffered by the generation of officers who graduated from Annapolis during the Navy's nadir years 1874–1882 seems to have been particularly severe. Years later Rear Admiral Bradley Fiske, Class of '74, recalled the "crushing hopelessness" of officers his age felt during the "doldrum years."[98] Vigorous, youthful Annapolites like William S. Sims, Albert P. Niblack, Homer Poundstone, and A. L. Key realized that the Navy's survival depended upon reaching some sort of modus vivendi with technology, and they would soon help to build a "new Navy."[99] But the gloomy voyage through the American Gilded Age and the nightmarish possibilities of its repetition were specters not soon forgotten by the service at large.

Yet to truly grasp the mortification of Annapolites we must also take account of events in the rest of the naval world during roughly the years the U.S. Navy was sinking into decay. For if the American line officer's technological counter-revolution had been successfully waged in a power vacuum devoid of nearby naval rivals, that was decidedly not the case in Europe. There, in the closely packed waters surrounding the continent, traditional rivalries persisted, forcing the hand of change and ensuring the rapid and permanent transition from sail to steam, smooth-bore to rifled cannon, oak to armor plate.

At the heart of the matter was the ancient antipathy between France and Britain, fueled anew by a rush to extend their respective overseas empires. As clearly the weaker of the two, France repeatedly raised the technological ante in hopes of tipping the naval power balance in its favor. Consequently, the French were quick to incorporate steam engines into their warships and during the 1850s made a tremendous effort to construct new battleships and convert every seaworthy ship-of-the-line to the new form of propulsion.[100] Despite grave reservations and much soul-searching, the British Admiralty quickly followed suit, matching the French ship for ship.

Thwarted, the French turned to the Paixhans shell gun, and in 1857 the Conseil de Travaux took the next logical step, ordering the construction of the revolutionary wooden-hulled ironclad, *La Gloire*.[101] The year after the French vessel put to sea, the British responded with a still better warship, the *Warrior*, which John Keegan regarded as "the first battleship of the modern age—steam propelled, shell-firing, iron in construction from keel to bulwarks, and heavily armored as well."[102] Keeping the pressure on, the British raced ahead during the 1860s, adding *Black Prince, Resistance, Defense, Bellerophon*, and *Achilles*— the last being capable of fourteen knots, mounting 9-inch-shell guns, and at nearly 10,000 tons in displacement constituting the largest warship in the world.[103]

The French did their best to keep up, spending 3 billion francs on the Navy between 1851 and 1869.[104] But the decisively superior size and quality of the British metallurgical and shipbuilding industries, combined with the traditional British commitment to seapower, kept the Royal Navy comfortably in the lead. Britain's shipyards continued to launch more and better battleships during the 1870s and 1880s, so that by the third year of the latter decade the Royal Navy possessed forty-one of the great vessels—eight more than the combined totals of the next three naval powers, France, Russia, and Germany.[105]

Certainly not all of the new ironclads were great fighting machines—the *Captain*, an early attempt to blend sail and steam with big guns, was so absurdly top-heavy that in 1870 it capsized in a storm and sank with nearly all hands.[106] Nor did the general absence of major naval battles allow a clear idea of exactly how the new ships would fight. Nonetheless, by the mid-1880s the Royal Navy and several of its chief European counterparts had ample opportunity at least to learn how to maneuver a steam-based battle fleet and move it over relatively long distances. Operationally, the steam battleship gave every appearance of having come of age. Moreover, it was destined to reproduce more and more quickly. For almost as the French backed away from battleship building, newly unified Imperial Germany floated forth to dispute the crown of sea power with the Royal Navy, provoking a capital ship–centered arms competition that would be remembered as an archetype of such endeavors and a significant contributor to the eruption in 1914.

Those ultimate consequences remained hidden. What Annapolites saw when they looked toward Europe was unprecedented technological progress, growing naval competence, and the prospect of more and better steam battleships. When they turned to their own navy they found only rot.

III

Phoenix-like, the new American Navy of armor-plated steam battleships arose out of the flotsam of the old.[107] Its origins can be found in the early 1880s when the line's policy of technological retrogression had become too obvious and self-defeating to be ignored any longer. For its part the Navy was gradually forced to the painful conclusion that the maintenance of its credibility as a fighting force required weapons comparable in mechanical development to those of possible adversaries. The course of the service's agonizing reconciliation with contemporary naval architecture can be traced through the recommendations of a succession of committees appointed to study the subject.

In the early summer of 1881 Secretary of the Navy William H. Hunt appointed a Naval Advisory Board, made up of fifteen officers and presided over by Rear Admiral John Rodgers, to study and recommend "the immediate construction of such vessels . . . as Congress would be most likely to approve."[108] The advisory board didn't advocate the construction of armored vessels because it was felt that their expense would cause severe reductions in appropriations for the desperately needed unarmored fleet. Nevertheless, the board did not rule out the possibility of eventually building battleships and recommended that in the future all vessels, armored or unarmored, be constructed of high-quality steel.[109]

Modern ordnance was systematically examined in 1883 by the Gun Foundry Board, a panel composed of officers from both the Army and the Navy. The body grappled with both the technical and economic difficulties involved in the production of large-shell-firing rifles. It concluded that it was advisable to rely on private contractors to supply the forged and tempered billets and then to establish a government-owned naval gun factory in the Washington Naval Yard to complete the manufacturing process.[110]

Finally, in 1885 a joint Army-Navy Board on Fortifications and Other Defenses was named primarily to consider coastal defenses. Nevertheless, it took time to inquire into the capacity of the country to furnish armor plate and the steps necessary for increasing production. Hoping to encourage American arms makers, the board recommended that in the future only domestically manufactured components be employed in U.S. warships.[111] Shortly thereafter, in 1886, naval construction and the heavy industries it required received a tremendous boost when Congress inserted just such a stipulation in an appropriations bill.[112]

Legislative fiat and a true ability to manufacture the specialized steel components necessary for a modern fleet proved to be two different things, however. In fact, the process by which the U.S. steel industry acquired the skills and facilities necessary to forge modern gun mountings and tubes and to roll and treat super-hard armor plate proved to be fairly difficult and expensive. Steel barons, although they would eventually make very considerable profits, were constantly complaining about the technical complexity and high initial investment involved. Nonetheless, by the early 1890s, the foundations of the modern American military-industrial complex were in place, and it was capable of producing domestic armor and ordnance equal to any in the world. Moreover, during that depression-wracked decade, fleet building would come to be viewed as a vast public works project with a considerable capacity to generate jobs and help vital industries through difficult times—perceptions of weapons production that have persisted to the present.[113]

In contrast, however, the initial tangible steps taken by the U.S. Navy to pull itself out of the muck of stagnation were so halting and uncertain that they provided a clear indication that the Navy lacked any central guiding vision. The climate of poverty and tactical uncertainty continued to prevail in the Navy in the 1880s, and what progress there was proved mostly of an experimental nature and confined to the construction of a few unarmored steel cruisers. In short, the Navy's efforts lacked force and coherence.[114] Officers whose entire professional experience had emphasized reverence for tradition and obedience were now required to map the uncharted seas of the future and think creatively about the strategic and tactical capabilities of weapons they didn't particularly like or understand. The Annapolite's unfitness for such tasks and the inadequacy of their confused pronouncements upon the subject were reflected in the low level of naval appropriations that persisted throughout the 1880s.[115] Personal shortcomings notwithstanding, what was required was an institutional rationale for a large, modern steam Navy; without it the problems and possibilities of nautical mechanization would remain largely academic.

At that juncture, amid the chaos, poverty, and gloom, there appeared in the ranks of Annapolites a prophet. As is typical of such beings, his guise was not what his brethren might have ordinarily expected or hoped. No valiant warrior or clever service politician was Alfred Thayer Mahan: He was instead a naval historian, the least likely of messiahs.

"Foundations of the modern American military-industrial complex." A *naval gun factory. (Courtesy of the U.S. National Archives)*

Mahan had a temperament strangely well suited to his task. The son of an austere, scholarly, and somewhat tyrannical West Point professor, Alfred had a lonely childhood that terminated abruptly at the age of twelve when his father began shuffling him from one boarding school to another.[116] When he reached sixteen, the studious youth asserted his independence by applying for admission to Annapolis, a move strongly opposed by his father, who argued that the boy was temperamentally unsuited for military life.[117]

Nevertheless, Alfred persisted in his determination to become a midshipman and enrolled in 1856. For this isolated and introspective youth, nautical indoctrination was particularly effective. In the controlled environment of Annapolis, service loyalty filled the void recently vacated by parental domination. Alfred took to heart the values of the institution and became in outlook an archetypical Annapolite. Although his intellectual brilliance allowed him to graduate second in his class, he shared his messmates' indifference to the technical aspects of his profession, as Robert Seeger points out.[118]

The naval prophet, Alfred Thayer Mahan. (Courtesy of the U.S. National Archives)

There was, however, always something impersonal about Mahan's devotion to the Navy, and it was this quality that led to his ostracism by his fellow midshipmen. In an effort to improve discipline, Mahan broke precedent and reported an upperclassman for talking in the ranks. For this breach of the unwritten code by which all naval cadets lived, Alfred was "put in Coventry" for his final year, being spoken to by a majority of his classmates only when duty required.[119] The incident was symptomatic of Mahan's whole career. He loved the Navy with all his heart but was never really liked by its members.[120] Yet Mahan's unpopularity was in no way detrimental to his usefulness to the service. Aloofness provided him with the objectivity to see beyond the myriad of routine duties and personal associations that dominated the consciousness of most officers and to grasp the real nature of the Navy's problems. Nonetheless, it is equally true that his approach and solutions were seldom anything other than those of a bright but very typical line officer.[121]

Alfred's early career was ordinary in almost every respect. Most of his active service during the Civil War was spent on blockade, watching the South strangle. The duty was boring to Lieutenant Mahan, as it was to the rest of the naval aristocracy.[122] Nor was Mahan any happier than his messmates about the technological turn war at sea had taken or the engineers it had brought to the Navy. With obvious disdain, he wrote: "As if the subtlest and most comprehensive mind that was ever wrought on this planet could devise a machine to meet the innumerable incidents of the sea and naval war. The blind forces buried deep in the bowels of the ship . . . do everything? . . . The stud is all; the rider naught?"[123]

Mahan, nevertheless, shared the horror of other Annapolites at the degeneration of the post–Civil War Navy and remembered with particular bitterness the condescension of a visiting French admiral, who referred to the guns of the future naval prophet's ship as *"l'ancien system."*[124] Clearly, something had to be done, and Mahan was seized with the desire "to raise the profession in the eyes of its members."[125]

His chance came in September 1884 when his former commander, Admiral Stephen B. Luce, invited Mahan to leave the steam sloop *Wachusett*—the most significant feature of which was a permanent list to starboard—to prepare a series of lectures on naval history and tactics to be eventually delivered at the newly established Naval War College, the world's first such institution.[126]

The War College had been the product of both Luce's persistence and a growing realization among officers that if the Navy was ever to be aroused from the doldrums, some form of intellectual foundation had to be created upon which to base modern naval policy. Characteristically, Annapolites looked to the past for guidance. In an 1885 article entitled "The United States Naval War College," Luce wrote that the study of naval history would enable students to "raise naval warfare under steam from the empirical stage to the dignity of a science."[127] Meanwhile, Mahan was trying his best to make naval warfare at least coherent.

For two years the incipient naval prophet worked on his lectures, which in 1890 would appear in print as *The Influence of Sea Power upon History: 1660–1783*, one of the most influential books ever published in the United States. With considerable insight, Mahan cut to the root of the Navy's needs and found them to be basically twofold: First, the unpredictable forces of technology had to be accommodated within a context relevant to naval officers; second, the nation at large had to be convinced of the necessity for a large modern fleet.[128] Mahan's solutions were at all times conditioned by his identity as a member of the naval aristocracy.

Like Luce, he met the dynamic thrust of mechanization with a strategic retreat into the past: "It is doubly necessary thus to study critically the history and experience of naval warfare in the days of sailing ships, because while these will be found to afford lessons of present application and value, steam navies have as yet made no history which can be decisive in its teaching."[129]

What Mahan discovered amid the comfortable relics of times past was calculated to reassure the most apprehensive of Annapolites. Nothing had really changed. The prophet fearlessly maintained that the galaxy of technical improvements that seemed to be turning the naval world upside down was doing so only on a superficial tactical level and consequently did not invalidate the central premises of traditional naval strategy.

Those postulates, as Mahan and every other Annapolite knew, had almost all been laid down and confirmed by the invincible Royal Navy and its ponderous line of battleships in the endless wars of trade of the seventeenth and eighteenth centuries.[130] History had shown time and again the overwhelming importance of fleet concentration and the validity of blockade. Only fights between massed battleships and never raids on commerce had proved decisive upon the seas.[131] For this reason, it was unthinkable to Mahan that seapower (a term he coined[132]) would ever be based on anything other than the possession of a fleet of numerous and largely homogeneous battleships—a modern equivalent of the great Britannic armada of 74s that was once the terror of the high seas.[133] The difficulty with Mahan's assessment of the situation was that it was based more upon historical analogy than technological reality.[134] Unfortunately for the naval prophet and those who took him seriously, he had confused past technical stagnation with the immutability of naval warfare itself. However, Mahan should not be censured too heavily. It would have been hard for any person not intimately involved with the mechanical revolution to foresee that much of what was happening was absolutely unprecedented. For an Annapolite of the classic mold, it was practically impossible.

Whatever its merits, Mahan's capital-ship theory had very definite implications for national policy:

> In the present condition of the Navy . . . the attempt to blockade Boston, New York, the Delaware, the Chesapeake, and the Mississippi, in other words the large centers of export and import, would not entail upon one of the large maritime powers efforts greater than have been attempted before. . . . To avoid such blockades there must be a military force afloat that will so endanger a blockading fleet that it can by no means keep its place.[135]

If that possibility might seem farfetched to Americans separated by an ocean from a European naval world whose battleships were becoming steadily more dependent on friendly bases for fuel and mechanical repair,[136] Mahan made it clear that the uses of a battle fleet were not limited to defeating a blockade. The battle fleet was a basic instrument of coercion and prestige—a necessary and integral part of the aggressive foreign policy that Mahan felt must inevitably be pursued by an industrialized United States. "Whether they will or no, Americans must now begin to look outward; the growing production of the country demands it."[137] Since the only available and profitable outlets for the burgeoning industrial surpluses were the markets of less-developed nations, Mahan prophesied a vast increase in U.S. overseas commerce and resurgence of the once-prosperous merchant marine to carry it.[138] That, however, was bound to lead to friction with other powers struggling to peddle their own manufactured leftovers. "Thus . . . the necessity for a navy . . . springs . . . from the existence of a peaceful shipping, and disappears with it."[139]

Mahan made it clear, however, that the usefulness of the projected American steam armada remained contingent upon certain strategic prerequisites, the fulfillment of which were part and parcel of his master plan. First in his order of priorities was the construction of an Isthmian canal.[140] Such a waterway not only would forge a strong defensive link between the East and West coasts of the United States by cutting in half the 13,000-mile journey around Cape Horn but would also provide a convenient means of transit between the two areas of preferred commercial expansion, South America and Asia.[141] "Along this path a great commerce will travel, bringing the interest of the great nations, the European nations, close along our shores, as they have never been before."[142] Consequently, strategic integrity demanded that the Caribbean be dominated, now more than ever, by the United States and that bases be constructed to guard the approaches to the canal.[143]

Such bases were themselves an important element of seapower in the Age of Steam, without which the ships of the United States "will be like land birds unable to fly from their own shores."[144] The naval prophet maintained that "control of a maritime region is insured primarily by a navy, secondarily, by positions, suitably chosen and spaced one from the other, upon which as bases the Navy rests, and from which it can exert its strength."[145] For that reason, he advocated the establishment of naval outposts along the paths of commercial penetration and consistently favored U.S. acquisition of strategically placed islands such as St. Thomas, Puerto Rico, Samoa, Hawaii, and Luzon, in the Philippines.[146] The defense of those isolated naval bastions would, in turn, be entrusted to the mighty American battleship armada that Mahan dreamed might one day roam the globe.[147]

The fleet was the keystone of his entire system, a doughty shield capable of both ensuring the sanctity of American trade abroad and fending off hostile blows at the Caribbean, the projected canal, or the continental United States itself. This naval prophet had created a comprehensive and interdependent program for national self-assertion, but, as Walter Millis noted, "it is difficult to resist the impression that Mahan's major impulse was simply to produce an argument for more naval building."[148] It would seem that his later widespread fame and influence has tended to obscure the fact that Mahan was first and last an officer in the United States Navy. His work and motivation should be judged accordingly.

National greatness was conceptualized in a characteristically nautical fashion. The model from which he derived his strategic vision was the queen of the naval world, the imperial power par excellence, Great Britain.[149] It was Britain's trade, its merchant marine, its net of overseas bases, its Suez Canal, and, above all, its mammoth fleet that inspired Mahan the Annapolite as he wrote *The Influence of Sea Power*. Yet, the prophet's feat was not merely that of description. This withdrawn, rather sedentary officer had performed a service for the Navy, the likes of which no war hero could equal. He had single-handedly dragged the Navy and the battleship out of the swamp of technologically induced uncertainty and hitched their respective futures to the rising star of American imperialism.

He was not to be a prophet without honor. The work of Mahan was received by Annapolites with approbation bordering on veneration. Filled with inspiration, Lieutenant Commander Richard Rush wrote, "Your books have brought honor not only to yourself, but to the Navy and to the country."[150] Rear Admiral C. F. Goodrich added: "I must tell you how delighted I am by the admirable way you handled so important a topic and how proud I am of your achievements. Let this then convey to you . . . my sincere thanks."[151] The normally reserved W. L. Rodgers gushed: "You cannot imagine what pleasure it has given me to read of your triumphs in England! I congratulate you from the bottom of my heart, and I believe the U.S. Navy can never repay you for the honor and credit you have reflected upon it."[152]

Such effusive displays of gratitude were well warranted. Besides justifying the construction of a large fleet of battleships, Mahan had given Annapolites what they most lacked—faith in the future. He had removed the odium of uncertainty and provided them with an acceptably traditional but apparently unassailable strategic framework upon which to base their efforts.[153] Comprehensive and dogmatic, it removed the necessity for further tormenting thoughts on the basic nature of naval warfare. Officers were now free to concentrate on the tangibles of tactics, training, and ship design so much better suited to their natures and institutions.[154] For those reasons, Mahan's thought was raised to the level of "commandments," the basis for all U.S. naval planning for the next fifty years.[155] Like sermons from a sacred text, his original lectures on seapower were, from 1887 to 1911, faithfully repeated to the congregation of naval thinkers gathered annually to formulate and perfect fleet tactics. The recitations "enforced the lesson[s] that war is an art not a science" and that "the principles of naval strategy are unchanging, no matter to what extent tactics may be modified by modern invention."[156] In such an atmosphere the conceptual unorthodoxy suggested by technological change was all too frequently interpreted as heresy.

The cult of Mahan was not confined just to the U.S. chapter of the worldwide naval fellowship. Because the officers of most fleets shared the same basic corporate memory and were still struggling to contain the same mechanically induced complexities that plagued Annapolites, it was natural that the American prophet should become the subject of the same sort of idolatry on an international scale.[157] The youthful and ambitious fleets of Germany and Japan, impressed as they were by the Royal Navy and its battleships, found Mahan particularly fascinating. He became required reading for officers of the Imperial Japanese Navy, and more of his books were translated into Japanese than those of any other foreign author.[158] Kaiser Wilhelm II, for his part, "devoured" *The Influence of Sea Power*, "trying to learn it by heart." He was so impressed that he ordered that the book become standard equipment aboard all of his ships, where it served as both a monument to the past and an inspiration for Germany's ill-fated High Seas Fleet.[159]

But nowhere did the words of the prophet meet with greater receptivity than in Great Britain.[160] Royal Navy officers had been long waiting for the appearance of a coherent explanation of their success, and when Mahan arrived on the scene, he became, in the words of the distinguished naval historian Arthur J. Marder, "practically the naval Mohammed of England."[161] It could hardly have been otherwise. *The Influence of Sea Power* was at base a eulogy to the Royal Navy and its policy of maintaining the largest battle fleet anywhere. The praise that he received from the most influential body of officers was in itself a significant factor in Mahan's acceptability to the rest of the naval profession. Meanwhile, the glorification of Mahan only led to still further deference being paid to the Royal Navy. So with Mahan in their heads and the overpowering example of Britain's armada close to their hearts, the major naval contenders sailed toward the twentieth century in unison, building battleships.

The intoxicating effect of *The Influence of Sea Power* was not, however, limited to naval officers. Although the key ingredients of Mahan's potent geopolitical brew were primarily nautical, he had also added a generous measure of the contemporary political, economic, and sociological preconceptions shaping his country's domestic and foreign policies.[162] Mahan's timing had been superb: His book appeared precisely when Darwinian nationalism, a growing sense of racial superiority, and dreams of expanding overseas markets were diverting Americans from their previous preoccupation with domestic affairs.[163] As they looked outward, they found that an increasing cordiality and identity of interests between the United States and Great Britain made Mahan's program all the more plausible and attractive.[164]

One of the naval prophet's first civilian converts was the reviewer from the *Atlantic Monthly*, who read all 541 pages of *The Influence of Sea Power* in one sitting and then took the time to write Mahan and congratulate him. "It is a very good book—admirable; and I am greatly in error if it does not become a naval classic. It shows the faculty of grasping the meaning of events and their relations to one another and of taking in the whole situation."[165]

This letter was of some significance, since its author was Theodore Roosevelt, future president and key member of a small circle of political reformers, publicists, and intellectuals who collectively were about to become a dynamic force behind American self-assertion. Anglo-Saxons of upper-class origins and anticommercial leanings, the most important other members of the clique were John Hay, Henry Cabot Lodge, Albert J. Beveridge, Brooks Adams, and editors Whitelaw Reid and Albert Shaw.[166] In one way or another, each had been led to embrace foreign policy as an outlet for excess energy. One and all they dreamed of the day when the United States would play a role on the world stage commensurate with its size and prosperity. As a consequence, they gloried in military power and the prestige it represented.[167] Mahan crystallized their half-formed martial ambitions with a logical and specific plan for national greatness and in the process won both their friendship and attention.[168] Later in the decade of the 1890s, when several of this group had become vastly influential, it was Mahan's program that provided an outline for action.

Meanwhile the naval prophet was gaining civilian converts in still other quarters. Since the secretary of the Navy was responsible for advising both the president and the Congress on naval policy, no plan to build battleships could succeed without his active support.[169] Yet secretaries were generally devoid of technical knowledge and possessed only the rudiments of naval strategy.[170] To such figures, the final-sounding pronouncements of Mahan must have seemed logical indeed.

The first annual report of Secretary Benjamin F. Tracy bore the stamp of the naval prophet throughout.[171] This epochal document ridiculed past U.S. reliance on commerce raiders and called for the construction of "two fleets of battleships"—twelve for the Atlantic and eight for the Pacific. Such a force might not only "raise blockades" and "beat off the enemy's fleet on its approach" toward the United States but could also divert aggression by directly threatening the coasts of distant adversaries. "For a war, though defensive in principle, may be conducted most effectively by being offensive in it operations."[172]

Tracy's successor, Hilary A. Herbert, experienced an even more remarkable conversion. As a congressman from Alabama, he had discounted the usefulness of both steam battleships and the Naval War College. Nevertheless, after reading *The Influence of Sea Power* in 1893, his thought underwent a decided transformation. Not only did he move to ensure the survival of the War College, he also wrote the prophet that he was "particularly struck with your citations from history, of the comparatively little effect of commerce destroyers in bringing war[s] to a successful conclusion, and expect to use in my forthcoming report the information you have set forth in my arguments for building battleships."[173]

Soon the words of the naval prophet could be heard echoing through the halls of Congress. With increasing frequency, on subjects ranging from the size of battleships to the annexation of Hawaii, Mahan was cited by legislators anxious to demonstrate a fluency in naval strategy.[174]

Nautical erudition notwithstanding, Congress showed considerable caution in committing itself to a battleship fleet capable of involving the United States in altercations halfway around the globe. In an effort to circumscribe the fleet's potential field of action, the watershed naval bill of 1890 called for the construction of three "sea-going, coast-line battleships" with deliberately limited coal capacities and ranges.[175] Although such a gesture seems indicative of the legislators' defensive intent, they had, by appropriating money for a squadron of battleships of any sort, unwittingly set the massive Mahanite mechanism in motion. Only a few like Senator Redfield Proctor of Vermont were heard to complain: "A navy is necessary for colonies and colonies are necessary for a navy. . . . That being the case . . . I certainly think we ought to go slowly in the matter of this increase of battleships."[176] Yet, even before the evolution of the steam battleship reached its final, or dreadnought, stage, the United States was destined to spend $96,606,000 preinflation on mixed-caliber ships and to gain several island paradises in the bargain[177] (see Appendix, Table A.1).

There is more than a little irony involved in the portrayal of introverted Alfred T. Mahan as the intellectual Svengali of American imperialism. Yet, the battle fleet that he tied like an albatross around the neck of U.S. policy had vast implications for the future. Whatever its ultimate motivation, the tangible manifestations of American policy during the era of overseas expansion tended to be gestures beneficial to the strategic well-being of the fleet. Far-flung islands were annexed; the Panama Canal was dug—just as the prophet had predicted. Although it is clear that these things were not done solely with the welfare of the fleet in mind, the Navy was a prime beneficiary. And the repercussions of the Navy's agonizing accommodation with technology would continue to be felt by the nation both domestically and abroad. For without Mahan and his "commandments," it is unlikely that a line of battleships would have been anchored in Pearl Harbor on the morning of 7 December 1941.

4

Crusaders in Blue
and the Grail of Seapower

I

In Newport, Rhode Island, amid the summer palaces of the moneyed elite, stood the Naval War College. A haven for intellectuals, the college was merely tolerated by the majority of officers.[1] Nevertheless, it was there that Mahan's theories were reduced to specifics and that a detailed vision of naval policy emerged to guide Annapolites through the troubled waters of technological change. As Lieutenant A. P. Niblack noted, "The Naval War College, like the proverbial prophet without honor in his own country, is really about our only hope of inspiration in case of . . . national troubles."[2]

Yet the precise manner in which the tactical and strategic capabilities of the steam battleship were deduced is cause for some wonder. The nautical future was conjured up by the repeated playing of a series of naval games invented by a retired lieutenant named William McCartney Little and introduced into the War College curriculum by Mahan in 1893.[3]

The games were three in number and embraced all aspects of surface warfare. The first, or "strategic," game was played on actual charts and devised in order to test the practicality of general war plans. When the two hostile fleets came within battle range, the game was either terminated or continued as a "tactical" contest. That was the second variety of naval gaming, intended to measure the combat potential of two opposing lines of battleships. The miniature fleets, composed of model sailing ships painted either red or blue, were maneuvered on a surface resembling a chess board (actually a white-and-black-tiled floor) until one or the other side gained a decisive advantage. Finally, the third

73

game was the "duel," simulating a head-to-head confrontation between two battleships. It was intended to provide the player with experience in handling an individual warship, as well as to test the effect of variations in specific ship characteristics such as turning radius or armor thickness.[4]

Taken as a whole, the games were considered to be a serious analytical tool, an adequate substitute for the battle experience that had become so scarce in the latter portion of the nineteenth century.[5] "When the game-board is not used," Bradley Fiske noted, "people conferring on naval problems can do so only by forming pictures in their own minds . . . while at the same time trying to see the pictures that are in the minds of others—and then comparing all the pictures."[6] As one president of the Naval War College, Captain Caspar F. Goodrich, pointed out in his closing address to the class of 1897:

> Certain truths . . . stand out so clearly that we are led to believe, though their importance may be exaggerated by the game, that they exist in the real game of war. . . . The strategic game shows most conclusively the necessity of concentrating the fighting forces of the fleet. Strong scouting detachments may, and often must, be sent out from the main body, but he who scatters the fighting force (the battleships of the fleet) is vanquished at the outset. The fighting forces should be like a spider at the center of its web. . . . Concentration means strategic life, dispersion strategic death.[7]

Concentration was the keynote, the sine qua non of all prudent tactics and strategy. In terms of fleet composition, concentration was merely another way of saying the admiral with the most ships must win. With the aid of a chart of statistical probabilities, Bradley Fiske was able to give a graphic demonstration of the theoretical consequences of numerical inferiority. If two forces of similar battleships, numbering 10 and 8 respectively, met in combat, the smaller would be reduced to zero before the larger had lost even half of its ships. However, the future appeared even more dismal for a commander foolish enough to allow his fleets to become separated. If a force of 10 was fortunate enough to engage two bodies of 5 each, the outcome would leave the unified party with 5.69 ships whereas his bisected adversary would be reduced to zero.[8]

Numbers, however, were not the only measure of concentration, since, as Lieutenant Commander A. P. Niblack observed, "the key to modern fleet actions is concentration of gun fire."[9] Thus a very few large ships mounting many big guns were necessarily a greater consolidation of power than a more numerous fleet of smaller, less well armed units.[10] It goes without saying that no serious adversary could be expected to construct an armada of naval shrimps doomed by all logic to destruction at the hands of a few juggernauts. Instead, prudence and the general drift of naval architecture dictated an almost automatic escalation to the level of the largest ship possessed by any one naval power.[11] Hence the surest and safest means of reconciling the contradictory ends of numerical and individual concentration was the possession of the largest possible number of the biggest ships available.

Logic and frequent practice on the game boards further clarified the implications of concentration of fleet deployment. Since battleships possessed the "maximum of concentrated destructive power," they were the natural offensive arm of any tactical formation. Operating together as a compact unit, they remained the focal point of the fleet.[12] Radiating around them were auxiliaries sent to probe and scout the enemy.[13] In the no-man's water between battle lines, the successively larger destroyers, light cruisers, and armored cruisers might meet their hostile counterparts in sporadic actions. But because none of these ships carried either heavy armor or very large guns, they were believed incapable of mounting a serious assault against the capital ships. "Battleships are necessary to oppose battleships," wrote Rear Admiral Stephen B. Luce.[14] Therefore, the inevitable result of any contest for control of the sea was presumed to be a test of strength between battle lines. "The first object of the attacking fleet will be to seek the enemy battleships and endeavor to crush them. . . . Should the fleets be of equal force, there will be but little difficulty under ordinary circumstances in bringing about an engagement."[15] The intrinsic importance of such a meeting demanded that the command functions of the fleet also be centered in the battle line, "linked together by the effectual energy of a single will."[16] There, just as on the game boards littered with toy ships, one officer, the commander in chief, was responsible for directing the final intricate maneuvers that would decide the issue.[17]

The tactical formations that he might employ were concocted with the idea of bringing the maximum number of guns to bear on an adversary at the closest possible range. A. P. Niblack explained that "at the Naval War College, in the tactical games, the unit of gun fire is the broadside fire of a ship, for a certain period of time, at 2000 yards range. . . . At 4000 yards the values are one fourth and above; at 3000 yards, one half; and at 1000 yards and less, double."[18]

It was natural, therefore, that the traditional line-ahead arrangement was preferred by tactical theorists. "With two well-handled fleets, the combat may be expected to be carried on with the ships in column and steering in nearly parallel directions, the interval gradually closing, until one threatening to charge and the other heading to meet it, the fleets come together."[19] The goal of this evolution was to flank the enemy's line and cross his T, effectively blanking a large portion of his turret guns while at the same time leaving him exposed to the greatest possible concentration of fire. This, of course, required superior speed. Yet the games at the War College showed that at the relatively short range of from two to four thousand yards where combat was expected, shell damage would probably slow both lines dramatically before that objective could be accomplished.[20] As a consequence, the value of initial fleet speed was minimized in American naval calculations, whereas the importance of big guns and thick armor was maximized.[21] (Quite the opposite view was held by the Royal Navy, whose own war games led them to lay heavy emphasis upon fleet speed, while depreciating the value of armor.[22])

Nonetheless, it was a convincing picture of the future that was painted upon the game boards of the U.S. Naval War College. Regardless of differences over details, technology was not proving to be as revolutionary a force as once feared. The cycle that gave birth to the steam battleship seemed to be stabilizing. Lieutenant Commander Richard Wainwright predicted that "at the present day it looks as if the great strides in the progress of both vessels and weapons had ceased for a time. . . . If this is true, the tactics that are correct for the present time will remain so for a number of years."[23] Continuity was preserved between past and future. The general direction of mechanization had upset none of the traditional features of war at sea. On the contrary, it had apparently reinforced them along several dimensions.

The hierarchy of ship types, which had been so much a part of the Age of Sail, seemed even more firmly founded than before. Whereas all classes had once carried guns of basically the same size and type, now larger ships mounted progressively bigger and more-powerful ordnance. Not only could a warship thus armed overwhelm a weaker adversary by sheer power, it could do so at ranges from which it was impossible for the smaller-gunned foe to reply.[24] To reinforce the point further, heavy warships were now sheathed with armor rendering small guns all the more useless against them. For those reasons, the War College's emphasis upon battleships and its relative neglect of auxiliary's tactics seemed eminently sensible.

The prevalent conception of command held by the theorists at Newport seemed equally in sync with the direction of technological change. It was almost universally agreed that the regularity of steam propulsion and the rapidly advancing methods of communications between ships were making the centralization of command even more advisable than in the days of sail. Bradley Fiske noted that now "one man can make the fleet go faster or slower or stop; he can increase its power of motion or decrease it at his will. . . . He can turn it to the right or left as much as he wishes."[25] Given such complete control, the advantages of a unified command were hard to deny. By minimizing the steps between order and execution and establishing clear lines of authority, such a system seemed bound to dispel at least a portion of the deadly cloud of confusion that inevitably enveloped every battle.

As plausible as all this may have seemed, a closer examination of the War College's preview of naval history reveals its basis to be the assumed validity of a number of key items of belief. The first and most important of these was the primacy of the gun as a weapon of naval warfare. Although the mine and the torpedo had constituted possible alternatives to naval ordnance since the Civil War, they were simply not taken seriously by naval planners. Richard Wainwright thought it necessary "to open the vexing question of the relative importance of modern weapons" but quickly added, "I am a firm believer in the gun as the first and foremost weapon. And it seems to me that it is the only position to be maintained logically."[26] A. P. Niblack concurred in this judgment when he wrote, "In fleet actions, the tactics of the torpedo and ram are incidental to the tactics of the gun, which is of prime importance. This assertion is too fundamental to admit of discussion."[27] The careful gradation of the size and number of guns carried by each class was coming to be a key prop to the entire hierarchy of ships. If guns were replaced by weapons less deferential in their destructiveness, the whole naval structure might be in imminent danger of collapse. The circumvention of the tightly wrought relationship between guns and armor spelled nautical anarchy, a prospect not pleasant to contemplate.

A second important presumption perpetuated by the investigations conducted at the Naval War College was the basically two-dimensional nature of war at sea. Since the dawn of naval history, ships had fought only upon the surface of the sea. That would seem to be almost too basic to mention, except for the fact that things were changing. At the very time the naval theorists were investigating the possibilities of the battleship, human ingenuity was making it possible for people to plunge beneath the waves and to dream of flying above them. Yet, the game board was a tool ill adapted to analyzing the potential of weapons capable of operating on more than one plane. Toy submarines could not dive below its hard surface, nor could model planes be conveniently flown above it. Such weapons might be represented in the games, but their peculiar spatial advantages would not be apparent to officers whose entire heritage and outlook was both literally and figuratively flat. Yet the addition of this third dimension brought complexities to naval strategy and tactics vastly exceeding the scope of the neat, orderly battleship scenario. But the planners strove for certainty. Consequently, they were not eager to embrace methods of warfare fraught with imponderables. Who, after all, would knowingly complicate his life if that could be reasonably avoided?

The liquid properties of the sea were ignored in still another way by the theorists' emphasis on concentration. In a way unknown to land fortifications, capital ships—particularly heavy-metal capital ships—were subject to sudden destruction. Unlike a terrestrial citadel, whose guns had to be reduced piecemeal, a warship was a unitary mechanism, whose offensive power was directly dependent upon the integrity of its other components. A battleship had merely to fill up with water for her entire tactical potential to be eliminated. Even damage sufficient only to reduce her speed by several knots might prove fatal to a capital ship by separating her from the concentrated haven of the battle line, which could not afford to slow down lest its T be crossed. Whatever the case, the larger the ships that were used, the greater the loss to the fleet should one sink. In one sense, then, prudence dictated against the construction of very large vessels.

But battleships grew by a logic of their own, and it was to this resounding beat that naval planners marched. Ironically, Mahan himself, impervious to mechanical imperatives, eventually protested against the lengths to which his disciples had carried the doctrine of concentration. "Unless the country—and Congress—are prepared for practically unlimited expenditures, bigger ships mean fewer ships. Now there are strong military reasons why numbers of ships are wanted; and in view of the steady increase in size, due to increasing demands of each technical factor on the battleship, the time has arrived when the military experts should be directed to consider what the limits of size should be."[28] Yet the patter of moderation was difficult to hear above the roar of progress.

Regardless of the prophet's admonitions, the rites performed atop the gaming tables of the Naval War College had completed Mahan's resuscitation of the battleship. But there was a noticeably contrived and artificial aura to the whole process. Whatever the perceived intentions of the participants, the purposes of the operation had been largely cosmetic—the grafting of an analytical and technological facade upon the presumably unchanged and unchangeable structure of war at sea. The trappings of empiricism were a sham. The logic of the game board was deductive rather than inductive, and the central premise was the indispensability of the sacred vessel, the battleship.

Because the Navy at large was even more susceptible to this kind of reasoning than the intellectuals at Newport, the War College's pronouncements on strategy and tactics were embraced almost without exception. Before long, practical-minded officers such as George Dewey were writing of the "principle of concentration [as] now deemed a necessity for maintaining the vitally important command of the sea."[29] Orders went out to the fleet "that battle formations, as worked out by the War College and forwarded therefrom, be fully understood and be formed without hesitation or confusion under varied circumstances."[30] Soon, like trained circus elephants, the capital ships could be seen performing complicated evolutions (manuevers on a drill field from one formation to another) such as parallels, obliques, diamond fours, and block fours. Countless hours were spent crossing and recrossing the Ts of hypothetical battle lines. Yet no matter how precisely the maneuvers were executed, the signals from the flagship never seemed to cease.[31]

More important than tactics, however, were the general war plans supplied by the War College to the Navy Department, beginning with the Venezuelan crisis of 1895.[32] Prompted by Mahan's strategic ideas and refined on the game boards, these early ancestors of the famous War Plan BLACK presumed the Caribbean to be the focal point of American naval strategy and the objective of all future European threats to the integrity of the Western Hemisphere.[33] According to the scheme, as soon as war was declared, the battleships were to concentrate in the Chesapeake Bay and move en masse to the Gulf of Mexico, there to await the inevitable approach of the aggressor fleet. Its arrival signaled the beginning of a short decisive battle that determined, once and for all, who commanded the seas surrounding North America.[34]

The plan, like almost everything else associated with the steam battleship, took a number of things for granted—not the least of which was the certainty of a European advance into the Caribbean. Implicitly, the scheme conceived of the battleship fleet more as a device to fight other armadas than as an instrument of national security.[35] Nonetheless, it had proved itself on the game boards, and when war came in 1898 the government adopted it as the general basis for its efforts. After spectacular success in this campaign, the basic war plan would continue, at times in utter disregard of objective reality, until the fateful summer of 1917.[36]

At the base of the Navy's enthusiasm for the plan and the theories of Mahan and his disciples was a universal appreciation of the prime instrument of their execution, the battleship. It was at the core of naval existence, a weapon that symbolized practically everything that line officers held to be true about life and war.[37] The commitment of the average Annapolite to this weapon was total on both a rational and an emotional level. Vincent Davis was not exaggerating when he wrote, "They were already in love with battleships and they were faithful lovers."[38] William Sims's enthusiasm for the mammoth vessels was obvious when he wrote a friend, "To command a successful battleship was the best job in the world."[39] Rear Admiral Henry A. Wiley echoed those sentiments when he reminisced: "Nothing I know compares . . . to the command of a great battleship. The responsibility is small compared to the flag command or the command of an army. And yet it is more intimate—greater in the human touch. Take the *Wyoming*, for example. . . . I felt that she was 'my ship.' I knew that, if well handled, she would always respond handsomely. She was almost human."[40] Admiral Yates Stirling was even more graphic in noting, "When I stood on the bridge of *New Mexico* for the first time . . . and gazed down at the two great turrets and then aft along four hundred and fifty feet of massive steel, little shivers went up and down my spine . . . when I stepped down off the bridge, I was as near tears as I have ever been in my life over something inanimate."[41]

Such exaggerated manifestations of loyalty and affection become much more understandable when the morphology of the steam battleship is analyzed further. Like virtually everything in the Annapolite cosmology, the battleship was conceptualized in hierarchical terms. Rear Admiral Harris Laning wrote, "The submarine is the natural prey of the destroyer, the destroyer of the cruiser, the cruiser of the battleship. The battleship stands at the top of the pyramid, invincible to the fire offered by lesser craft."[42] In 1932 the Navy's General Board reported to the secretary of the Navy that "the consensus of naval opinion in our country is that the battleship is the supreme naval type, and that all others are adjuncts or auxiliaries. The fleet is built around battleships, the basic force."[43]

Even the terminology that surrounded the giant vessels betrayed a vertical outlook. The persistent use of the phrase "capital ship" to describe battleships had autocratic overtones hard to ignore. Whereas submarines in the U.S. Navy were named for fish, destroyers for worthy individuals, cruisers for cities, only battleships were named for states. (Nor was this an isolated phenomenon; similarly hierarchical nomenclature schemes were followed by most other navies.)

The appeal of the nautical hierarchy of ships was further enhanced by the smooth manner with which it meshed with the all-important naval rank hierarchy:

> On looking back over the vessels I had commanded, I saw they had the appearance of a stepladder. Of course, I had commanded the little *Paragua* as a lieutenant . . . between being navigator and executive officer, I was given the command of a destroyer, the *Paulding*, of 750 tons. After reaching what is called command rank, that of commander, I had commanded the *Salem*, a cruiser of about 5000 tons, two monitors of 3000 tons, the *Columbia*, of 8000 tons, then two big transports of 20,000 and 25,000 tons. After the war I had the battleship *Connecticut* of 15,000 tons and now the *New Mexico* of 34,000 tons.[44]

Whereas junior officers were obliged to undergo the hardships and cramped quarters associated with smaller ships, the roomy battleship provided staterooms befitting the exalted status of their occupants. There, in an atmosphere of as much Victorian elegance as space would allow, an admiral might contemplate naval affairs confident that his surroundings reflected his own importance.[45] "It seemed only natural and proper," to Rear Admiral Charles Badger, "that when a man had successfully commanded a big ship that he should get a bigger one the next time."[46] Violation of the proper correspondence between rank and command was cause for alarm. When Theodore Roosevelt personally granted William S. Sims stewardship of the battleship *Minnesota* before Sims had reached the grade of captain, W. S. Benson, future chief of naval operations, wrote that "personally I would much rather have seen you promoted to the next higher grade and then given a battleship, than to have established the dangerous precedent of giving battleships to commanders."[47]

The battleship was, in the minds of line officers, a symbol of order and naval propriety, the bulwark against the confusion of battle and the unknown. It was, as its Annapolite defenders would repeat over and over in the 1920s and 1930s, the "backbone of the fleet"—a vital organizing force about which other entities should be arranged. Its absence implied formlessness and chaos—spinelessness.

The uniformity and regularity that their education and careers had taught Annapolites to revere was reflected in the precision of the well-trained battle line. Admiral Wiley wrote:

> I think one of the finest movements of ships made on the round-the-world cruise was coming to anchor off Coronado. . . . The sixteen battleships were steaming at full speed, in line ahead four hundred yards apart. . . . In obedience to signal, the leader of divisions, four flag ships, suddenly turned eight points to starboard,

followed in succession by each ship of the division. They were scarcely straightened out before the signal went up "Anchor," and when the signal left the yardarm, sixteen anchors went down, sixteen sets of colors left the gaffs, sixteen others were run up at the flag staffs . . . thirty-two boats went into the water, thirty-two gangways were lowered, and thirty-two swinging booms swung out. Four lines of ships brought up in perfect line, four columns in perfect column. They had brought up as sixteen well-drilled soldiers.[48]

With such a disciplined force, what surprises could outrageous fortune and the fog of battle really hold?

Such a view was not unreasonable. A great deal about the battleship and the outlook that perpetuated it made sense—sense at least in the way two million or so years of experience had instructed men on the expected outcome of violent encounters. Nature, as well as the history of our species as predators and combatants, had taught us that the big almost always vanquished the small. As Norman Mailer wrote: "Light-weights, welter-weights, middleweights can all be exceptionally good, fantastically talented—but they are still very much in their place. The best light-weight in the world knows that an unranked middleweight can defeat him on most nights, and the best middleweight in the world will kill him every night. . . . [It is] the law of the ring: a good big man beats a good little man."[49]

For Annapolites, this tradition had been borne out by the whole history of naval warfare, and they were not inclined to believe that the new interloper, technology, would change things fundamentally. "A big prize fighter, trained to the ultimate," wrote Commander Homer G. Poundstone, "is invulnerable to smaller-sized fighters. . . . So with the supreme type of battleship in their encounters with smaller units."[50] To Captain Albert L. Key, "the matter [was] too plain to admit of any doubt. In a gun fight between two men, the one that has the longer reach, that can hit harder, and can stand more punishment is bound to win."[51] To Captain E. J. King, "the sole disadvantage . . . resulting from increases of size of a battleship . . . is that it costs more; on the other hand, the larger ship is more powerful, has greater resisting qualities, is faster under all circumstances, and has a greater steaming radius and cruising life. As the greater cost results in better naval return for the money invested . . . this seeming disadvantage is not one in reality."[52] Size was a virtue in and of itself—it connoted strength in a way nothing else could. The Annapolite's every instinct told him that the perfect warship was the perfectly enormous warship.

Yet, it was not mere bulk that caused the battleship to appear so formidable. Never before had a weapon produced such sound and fury. The firing of the great guns, be they those of dreadnoughts or pre-dreadnoughts, was a spectacle to behold. To Seaman Theodore Mason:

> All the machinery and equipment the men operated, all the braid and chevrons and regimentation, were dedicated to one task: loading, elevating, and training the twelve gargantuan rifle barrels, so that they would speak with tongues of orange flame and shattering sound, hurling 1500 pound projectiles across the horizon in lofty decaying curves to descend upon, penetrate, and destroy the ships of the enemy. To speak death was the purpose of the *California* and her sisters of the battleline.[53]

"Inside the turret it was hot," wrote Lieutenant Commander Gary.

> The men about the breach perspire as the massive chamber revolves. "Stand by" sight setters check corrections. Load. . . . A rumble from below. . . . Shell and powder are rammed home. . . . The flagman shouts "Ready" . . . then silent tension until the moment when 200 or 300 tons of guns leap back in recoil as they are fired from the control station. . . . The roar within the turret is tremendous; but it is duller and more distant than the hot blast outside, a blast which will tear off a man's clothes, singe his hair and knock him head over heels if he has been so innocent as to stand on deck nearby.[54]

A British observer noted that battleships "when firing were momentarily blotted out by globes of orange flame followed by the tremendous concussion of the guns whose blast caused ripples and a flurry of spray on the water."[55] Enlisted man Thomas Beyer observed: "The ship trembled as though she had run into a bank of dough and forced herself through. The shell seemed to cut a hole through the air as it was speeding toward the target and when it struck, there was an outburst of applause from all the spectators."[56] Mixing his metaphors nicely, Annapolite Paul Schubert wrote: "There's no sport in the world like gunnery. . . . Men who fire for the first time are frightened white; later it exhilarates them. . . . The complete heat and volume of these full salvoes is an ecstasy of violence. Springing out of her bowels, they seemed to purge her of all trouble and shame."[57] To doubt the absolute relationship between a powerful bark and an equally potent bite under such dramatic circumstances required an iconoclasm not easily found in the orderly ranks of line officers.

A symbol of power for the age: "If battleships ran on land . . . [they] could whip an army of a million men, knock down all the buildings in New York, smash all the cars, break all the bridges." Popular magazine cover, 1917.

"Squat and immovable as castles." USS Minnesota. *(Courtesy of the U.S. Naval Institute)*

Instead, the battleship became a consummate symbol of potency and machismo. In a 1915 fantasy of destruction entitled "If Battleships Ran on Land," Bradley Fiske, who later turned against the mammoth vessels, was to write: "It is a greater example of power than anything else existing. . . . It could whip an army of a million men, knock down all the buildings in New York, smash all the cars, break all the bridges, and sink all the shipping."[58] Reflecting the same mood, Lieutenant Paul Schubert called the dreadnought *Texas* "a hard, tough, shootin', steamin' fool, a trophy grabber, a fighter and a he-man battle wagon."[59]

Visually, the great ships were paradoxes of power and beauty. Great floating fortresses, guns bristling from slab-sided turrets, crowned with massive steel superstructures, they literally oozed defiance. When viewed from either end, they were as squat and immovable as castles. Yet they appeared almost delicate and graceful when seen lengthwise. So to Seaman Mason, "the *California*, with her raked clipper bow, appeared a thing of strange masculine beauty. The piled-up superstructure of command was almost perfectly balanced by the two tall cage masts . . . and by the long-barreled fourteen-inch guns in their superimposed fore-and-aft turrets. Indeed it was the guns that put it all in perspective."[60] If a sailor felt this way, an admiral in command of a herd of these leviathans must have felt powerful indeed. Surely, such a flotilla need not flinch in the face of any other inhabitants of the sea.

The modern ship-of-the-line gave vent to the warrior's romantic impulses, which were soon to be callously disregarded by the course of events and the calculations of a legion of innovative engineers. Aboard his flagship, an admiral could dream of lines struggling for position, thrashing the sea to foam in high hopes of crossing an enemy's line of bearing and unleashing a devastating burst of steel. Because combat between respective ships-of-the-line was individualized, analogies to the duel were inevitable. With caution thrown to the winds, each set of adversaries was envisioned as bravely steaming across the briny field of honor, "where death hurtles fifteen miles through the upper atmosphere instead of flashing at the end of a cutlass."[61] This was warfare as it has been idealized by men ever since Gilgamesh and Homer, a heroic struggle between giants. The battleship epitomized its spirit.

Nevertheless, the steam battleship was a classic example of the dangers of what Lowell Tozer called "the apparent necessity for people to be able to relate anything new to something already familiar"[62]—the tendency to pour new wine into old bottles. Because the battleship was a weapon designed according to the premises of the past, it was ill equipped to deal with the unprecedented. Consequently, it was fatally prone to attack from above and below. Yet in the face of this truth, line officers, like beleaguered sloths, clung all the more tightly to the ship-of-the-line. At first they simply disregarded the threat. Then, when it became too obvious to ignore any longer, Annapolites, along with the mainstream of the naval world, furiously denounced the new weapons and attempt to suppress them. Finally, when the potency of multidimensional warfare could no longer be questioned, the American service and those abroad sought to integrate the new systems into the familiar hierarchy of ships.[63] Until the humiliating morning of 7 December 1941, the de-emphasis, much less the demise, of the battleship remained absolutely unacceptable to the overwhelming majority of line officers. It was their "backbone," their lifeblood—its disappearance implied the end of their world.

II

As the USS *Maine* steamed slowly past Morro Castle at the entrance to Havana Harbor and prepared to anchor on the sunny afternoon of 25 January 1898, none of the ship's company had any premonition that their vessel, the prototype of the growing U.S. battle fleet, was about to be martyred for the cause of Mahan and the fulfillment of dreams of American naval power. As we shall see, the miraculous consummation of the naval prophet's words would begin in the grand Old Testament manner—with fire and brimstone.

The *Maine* was quiet on the evening of 15 February, and most of her crew were already asleep. Although the battleship's visit had been prompted by the growing instability of the lingering Cuban crisis, she had been cordially received by Spanish officials and her stay had been without incident.[64] Below decks in the admiral's stateroom, the *Maine's* captain, Charles D. Sigsbee, had just finished a letter to Theodore Roosevelt, then assistant secretary of the Navy, on the subject of torpedoes, when he was thrown to the floor by a terrific concussion. "After the first great shock—I knew my ship was gone."[65] It was. By the time Sigsbee made his way through the vessel's darkened passages to the poop, the entire forward portion of the *Maine*—little more than a charred twisted mass of steel—was under water. Regretfully, the captain gave the order to abandon ship and, true to tradition, was the last man to leave his battered command.[66] Upon being rowed to the nearby *City of Washington*, Sigsbeen, "looking ten years older," wrote a cable informing Naval Secretary John D. Long of the loss of the *Maine* and many of her crew.[67] Despite his harrowing experience, the captain maintained a rational tone throughout the message, indicating the sympathy of Spanish officers and suggesting that "public opinion should be suspended until further report."[68] His advice would go unheeded.

Serious friction between the United States and Spain over Cuba had begun in early 1895 when the harsh conditions of Spanish rule and the economic decline precipitated by the Wilson tariff's restoration of duties on Cuban sugar led José Martí and his Cuban Revolutionary party to go into open rebellion against the island's colonial administration. For the next three and a half years, Spanish officials tried unsuccessfully to put down the revolt, while the "new" journalism of Hearst and Pulitzer translated their brutality and ineptitude into spiraling newspaper sales.[69] On the pages of the New York *World* or *Journal*, Spain was a crumbling, priest-ridden monarchy, senselessly perpetuating its tyranny over a freedom-loving people, crushing the spark of democracy that pulsed in the breasts of the oppressed. Fed steadily on such a journalistic diet, the American people became increasingly sympathetic to the cause of the Cuban revolution and correspondingly more hostile toward Spain.

But below this penumbra of emotions lay the harder stuff of national interest. Besides Britain, Spain was the only colonial power of any consequence left in the Western Hemisphere. Its remaining possessions there, Cuba and Puerto Rico, if transferred to a more energetic power such as Germany, might seriously compromise the strategic integrity of the United States by providing bases for an aggressor fleet.[70] Moreover, the favorable response to what American intellectual historian Richard Hofstadter termed "disproportionately aggressive" American diplomacy during the Chilean and Venezuelan crises of 1891 and 1895 was a strong indication that the country was in a fighting mood.

It was in that context that the news of the *Maine's* transmogrification was received by the American people. "It was manifest," wrote Secretary Long in retrospect, "that the loss of the *Maine* would inevitably lead to war, even if it were shown that Spain was innocent of her destruction."[71] Beset with the paralysis of a goat confronted by a hungry lion, the Spanish government watched helplessly as the crisis relentlessly escalated to its preordained conclusion. On 25 April, after recognizing the independence of Cuba, the U.S. Congress formally declared war.

Spain had to fight. To do otherwise, to submit peacefully to humiliation, acceding to all U.S. demands, could have produced repercussions that could have spelled the end of the tottering Bourbon monarchy. Spain was a country in the midst of its own epic of decline, a nation whose martial spirit was symbolized by an aged warrior locked in mortal combat with a windmill. Spain would play its part, in the tradition of the armada, with all the fatalism it deserved.

The Spanish Navy, which would bear the brunt of the fighting, was in atrocious condition.[72] Although Spain's officers proved themselves to be brave and self-sacrificing, they were utterly lacking in the technological expertise that had become necessary for survival in naval warfare. Large-scale maneuvers had never been attempted, and drills of all sorts were chronically neglected. General target practice had been held only once in the year before the war, a fact that would become painfully obvious in battle.[73] When in 1897 Admiral Pascual Cervera was informed that he would probably be given command of Spain's fleet in the event of war, his reply was anything but quixotic: "I shall accept, knowing, however, that I am going to a Trafalgar. . . . Allow me to expend beforehand

"Remember the Maine!*" (Courtesy of the U.S. National Archives)*

50,000 tons of coal in evolutions, and ten thousand projectiles in target practice. Otherwise, we shall go to a Trafalgar. Remember what I say."[74]

By contrast, the United States Navy Department faced the first real test of the new battle fleet, forged during the previous years of the decade, with confidence and determination. Since 1896 the Caribbean Plan had been available, along with a subordinate scheme to deal with Far Eastern contingencies. True to Mahan and the strategic studies of the War College, this program called for "blockades, harassments, naval descents on exposed colonies, naval actions whenever they can be brought under fair conditions."[75]

The Caribbean Plan and its addenda were bound to appeal to Assistant Secretary Theodore Roosevelt, who in September 1897 recommended it to his chief.[76] Since the sinking of the *Maine,* which he termed "an act of dirty treachery on the part of the Spaniards,"[77] Roosevelt had been anxious to begin translating the plan into action. But the cautious Long had been satisfied with maintaining the Navy merely on a semiwar footing.[78] That unsatisfactory situation persisted for ten days until 25 February, when the aging naval secretary, wearied by the crisis, decided to take the rest of the day off. Consequently, when Senator Lodge visited Roosevelt that afternoon at the Navy Department, he found his friend in the role of acting secretary of the Navy.[79] Opportunity beckoned.

Secretary Long arrived at the office the next morning to find that "Roosevelt, in his precipitate way has come very near causing more of an explosion than happened to the *Maine*. . . . Having authority for the first time as Acting Secretary, he immediately began to launch pre-emptory orders distributing ships, ordering ammunition. . . . He has gone at things like a bull in a china shop."[80]

Despite his anger, Long did very little in the way of countermanding Roosevelt's instructions, and from that point, the full mobilization of the Navy proceeded smoothly. In March all ships were concentrated into squadrons. This included the Bremerton-based battleship *Oregon*, which promptly began its epic journey around Cape Horn to join the battle fleet in the Atlantic.[81] The Spaniards were rumored to employ torpedo tactics. So, in the same month, almost as an afterthought, the Navy Department bought a number of tugs and yachts to take the place of the torpedo-boat destroyers it had neglected to build.[82] Finally, the War Board, made up of high-ranking line officers and presided over by Roosevelt, was organized to supervise strategy and provide the secretary with professional advice.[83] Though already influential, the board's prestige was considerably enhanced when Mahan himself was called out of retirement to fill the vacancy created when Roosevelt left the Navy Department to join the Rough Riders.[84]

Among the many products of Roosevelt's rampage of 25 February was a telegram addressed to the commodore of the United States Asiatic Squadron, George Dewey: "Order the squadron, except the *Monocracy*, to Hong Kong. Keep full of coal. In the event of war with Spain, your duty will be to see that the Spanish squadron does not leave the Asiatic coast, and then offensive operations in the Philippines.[85]

Roosevelt had handpicked Dewey for that command with just such a contingency in mind. "I knew that in the event of war Dewey could be slipped like a wolf-hound from a leash . . . given half a chance he would strike instantly."[86] He had chosen the right man. To the casual observer, George Dewey might have appeared more suited to a Gilbert and Sullivan operetta than a naval battle. Yet, his jovial manner, flashy clothes, and sybaritic love for good food and drink concealed a man of immense shrewdness and ambition.[87]

Upon receipt of Roosevelt's cable, the enterprising Dewey made haste to prepare his squadron for action. Extra ammunition was ordered and sent. The commodore purchased two steamers full of coal and supplies.[88] Each of his ships became a beehive of activity, their crews kept continuously busy removing flammable woodwork, covering peacetime white hulls and superstructures with slate-gray war paint, and drilling for the last time with the great guns.[89]

Yet as the flagship *Olympia* led its brood out of Mirs Bay, a host of potential dangers must have run through Dewey's mind. There was not a single armor-clad among the six ships that made up his small fleet.[90] Informed opinion among foreign naval officers considered the expedition extremely ill advised.[91] Seven thousand miles separated the force from the nearest U.S. base. Unless Dewey's victory was complete and Manila captured, there would be no shelter for his wounded ships.[92]

There was, however, no real cause for concern. Six hundred miles to the southeast, the Spaniards faced the coming crisis with the enthusiasm of condemned men. As Commander-in-Chief Patricio Montojo later wrote: "The inefficiency of the vessels which composed my little squadron, the lack of all classes of personnel, especially master gunners and seamen gunners, the ineptitude of some of the provisional machinists, the scarcity of rapid-fire cannon, and the strong crews of the enemy all contributed to make more decided the conviction . . . we were going to certain death and could expect a loss of all of our ships."[93] Yet even if morale had been high and the crews skillful, the Spanish vessels were still older and smaller than those of the Americans (see Appendix, Table A.2).

Montojo's only hope was to fend Dewey off with an effective mine field at the entrance to Manila Bay and enough shore-based, high-powered artillery to prevent the field from being swept. Inauspiciously, the Spanish guns were mostly ancient muzzle-loaders, and their mines lacked fuses.[94] Therefore, Dewey's instinctive naval officer's scorn for submarine weaponry was to be rewarded when his force passed Corregidor on the night of 20 April unharmed and practically unchallenged.

Dawn unveiled the Spanish ships clustered together at anchor in front of Cavite.[95] Montojo had chosen to remain a stationary target rather than attempt to maneuver his inexperienced fleet.[96] A few minutes past 5:00 Dewey signaled a close line-ahead formation and led his squadron toward the enemy who, with futile courage, opened fire at the impossible range of 9,000 yards. When the Americans were within 5,000 yards of the Spaniards, Dewey turned to the

Olympia's captain and calmly told him, "You may fire when you are ready, Gridley."[97] Soon the American line was enveloped by smoke and the roar of heavy artillery as it slowly paraded back and forth in front of its hapless opponents.[98] As contempt for Spanish gunnery grew, the range shrank to 2,000 yards.[99]

Shortly after engaging, the Americans were momentarily distracted from their leisurely butchery by the appearance of a small steam launch trailing "a big Spanish ensign" and behaving suspiciously like a torpedo boat. Although American secondary batteries promptly opened fire, they were unable to damage the craft before it approached close enough to be distinguished as a harmless market boat. "But the moral of this incident," wrote Lieutenant Calkins, "is all on the side of genuine torpedo boats."[100]

Nonetheless, the day belonged to the gun and by 7:35, as Dewey drew off to count his ammunition and treat his men to breakfast, the Spanish vessels could be seen to have suffered heavily.[101] Montojo had been forced to abandon his riddled, blood-smeared flagship, *Reina Christina*; the squadron's only wooden ship, *Castilia*, was a mass of flames; the *Ulloa* had been sunk by a shell; and several other vessels exhibited obvious signs of distress.[102] When the Americans resumed firing around 11:00, the Spanish quickly struck their colors. Three hundred and eighty-one had died. This installment on Spain's honor had been paid in full.

Dewey's squadron, in contrast, emerged virtually unscathed. As the commodore and his captains compared notes, they realized to their utter amazement that not a single American life had been lost.[103] Besides being one of the most decisive naval battles on record, Manila Bay had been the first major engagement between Western fleets since Lissa in 1866. Its results would not go unnoticed. Although neither fleet had been composed of the most powerful or modern ships available, it was hard to interpret the battle as anything but a resounding affirmation of conventional naval thought and construction. Steam power had proved reliable under combat conditions; line-ahead tactics were still effective; the destructive power of modern ordnance had been amply demonstrated; and the danger of subsurface weapons had proved a chimera. No one was more impressed with these developments than the architect of victory himself, George Dewey. That was important, since, at age sixty-one, his future had just begun.

When news of Dewey's astonishing victory reached Washington on 6 May, it marked a welcome change from what had been a steady regimen of frustration and confusion.[104] Trouble had begun on 29 April with a report that the Spanish

Lithograph of the Battle of Manila Bay. (Courtesy of the U.S. National Archives)

Admiral Cervera with four cruisers and three torpedo boats had left his base in St. Vincent and was sailing westward.[105] The move did not overly concern the Navy's planners, whose experience with strategical games and the plan left them nearly certain that the Caribbean must be the focal point of the coming campaign. Presuming the Spaniards' destination, after a voyage of 2,700 miles, would be the nearest friendly facilities, they sent Admiral William T. Sampson and the North Atlantic Squadron to intercept him at San Juan, Puerto Rico.

Residents of the Eastern Seaboard drew a different and altogether more frightening conclusion. They feared the missing fleet might suddenly appear at any point along the undefended coast and begin shelling their homes and families. And this nautical nightmare soon manifested itself in political pressure. With more than a touch of bitterness, Theodore Roosevelt described the scene at the Navy Department:

> Members of Congress who had actively opposed building any navy came . . . around to ask each for a ship for some special purpose of protection connected with his district. . . . Not only these Congressmen, but the Chambers of Commerce and Boards of Trade of different coast cities all lost their heads . . .

and brought every species of pressure to bear on the administration to get it to adopt the one most fatal course—that is to distribute the Navy.[106]

But the rising tide of fear soon inundated the foundations of naval theory, and the department was compelled to abandon, or at least modify, the rule of concentration.[107] Consequently, when Admiral Sampson left for Puerto Rico on 4 May, it was without two of his battleships—the *Massachusetts* and the *Texas*—which had been transferred to Commodore Winfield Scott Schley's "Flying Squadron," stationed at Hampton Roads to help guard the imperiled coast.

Worse yet, when the U.S. Atlantic Squadron arrived off San Juan on 12 May, Cervera was nowhere to be found. His elusiveness, like most things Spanish in this war, was more the product of ineptitude and inferior equipment than sagacity. "So while Washington was carrying the Spanish fleet rapidly over the ocean at ten to twelve knots an hour toward a well-defined objective point," wrote Henry Cabot Lodge, "in reality they were creeping along at seven knots an hour and making vaguely for some point in the West Indies, to do they knew not what."[108]

Had the American public been aware of the true condition of this latter-day Spanish Armada, the panic likely never would have occurred. Like its forerunner, this fleet had serious gun problems. Of Cervera's four armored cruisers—*Infanta Maria Teresa*, *Almirante Oquendo*, *Vizcaya*, and *Cristobal Colon*—three had defective breech mechanisms and no reliable shells for their 5.5-inch guns.[109] The newest and fastest of the ships, the *Colon*, did not even have her 10-inch main battery mounted, and the *Vizcaya* was in such disreputable condition that the admiral referred to it as "a boil on the body of the fleet."[110] Cervera's only other hope, the squadron's six torpedo boats, had been so neglected that only two proved fit enough to follow him into battle.

It was this dilapidated force that was ordered on 22 April to leave its safe haven in the Cape Verde Islands and proceed directly to West Indian waters.[111] Cervera's reaction was characteristic: "Nothing can be expected of this expedition except the total destruction of the fleet or its hasty and demoralized return."[112] A melancholia of impending doom must have hung over the Spanish force as it slowly crossed the Atlantic, stopping long enough in Martinique to be spotted by Americans and finally taking refuge in the nearest fortified port, Santiago de Cuba, on 19 May. There Cervera quietly awaited the inevitable approach of the avenging Americans. The respite, however, proved longer than anticipated, for the U.S. Navy was destined to conduct a search, the futility of which brings to mind the later cinematic exploits of the Keystone Cops.

Because Cervera was conceded no longer to constitute a threat to the Atlantic Seaboard, the U.S. Navy was free to concentrate all its forces in the Caribbean. On 18 May Schley's "Flying Squadron" joined Sampson's main body at Key West and plans of the hunt were formulated.[113] Stephen Crane, observing from the New York *World's* press tugboat, captured some of the drama as the ships prepared to leave. "Now in progress is a huge game, with wide and lonely stretches of ocean as the board, and with the great steel ships as counters. . . . The Spaniard made the first move. He played his fleet plump in the middle of the board, and he watches eagerly to see if our next move is a blunder."[114] It was. For the next ten days, the impulsive Schley wandered aimlessly around the coast of Cuba, ignoring orders and looking everywhere but the most obvious spot, Santiago de Cuba, for the stationary Spaniard. By the time he located Cervera (on the morning of the 29th), the commodore had managed to anger both the Navy Department and his immediate superior, the dour Admiral Sampson.

When the latter arrived off Santiago on 1 June, he immediately took personal command of the operation and began relentlessly tightening the blockade. During the day Sampson arrayed his ships, which now included the much-traveled battleship *Oregon*, in a semicircle six miles from the harbor.[115] After dark they ventured much closer and beamed their searchlights upon the entrance in hopes of foiling any nocturnal escape attempts. "The idea of deliberately placing a battleship within a mile or two of the fastest torpedo boats in the world, and then turning on a searchlight to mark her position," wrote Captain Robley D. Evans somewhat dubiously, "was novel at least."[116]

The inventive Sampson even devised a plan to cork the harbor by sinking the collier *Merrimac* at its entrance. That scheme, however, succeeded in little more than creating an instant war hero out of naval constructor Richmond P. Hobson, who somehow managed to survive the ill-fated mission.[117]

Nonetheless, the American commander in chief remained willing to try anything short of actually steaming into Santiago after Cervera. Yet this was exactly what was desired by the U.S. Army's General Schafter, who by 1 July had suffered over 1,000 casualties investing (laying siege to) the city by land.[118] Sampson's reaction to that suggestion was unequivocally negative. "To throw my ships to certain destruction upon mine-fields would be suicidal folly." He did, however, agree to meet the general on the morning of 3 July to continue discussing the problem—an appointment he would live to regret.

In fact, no amount of American bickering or bungling could have salvaged the Spanish position. Facing Cervera's ramshackle squadron was a concentration

of five American battleships (*Texas, Massachusetts, Iowa, Oregon,* and *Indiana*),
two armored cruisers (*Brooklyn* and *New York*), two scout cruisers (*New Orleans*
and *Newark*), and two large armed yachts (*Vixen* and *Gloucester*), all in excellent
condition. The Spaniards' one theoretical advantage, a relatively high fleet speed
of twenty knots, had vanished amid the weeds and barnacles that fouled the
bottoms of their ships.[119] Worse than that, Cervera's vessels were decked and
ornamented with flammable wood, all of which should have been ripped out
long before.[120] His crews were hungry and tired from manning the land defenses
of the city. Any attempt at escape was hopeless. "A sortie," he wrote, "will entail
the certain loss of the squadron and the majority of its crew."[121] Nevertheless,
Governor-General Blanco was convinced the city was about to be captured and
the fleet with it. To avoid that, he ordered Cervera to leave port at any cost.[122]
Hoping to surprise the Americans while at religious services, Cervera chose the
morning of Sunday 3 July for his charge.[123]

That morning found the American blockade somewhat depleted. Not only
were the *New Orleans*, the *Newark*, and the battleship *Massachusetts* coaling
forty miles away in Guantanamo, but at 8:45 Admiral Sampson left the line in
the *New York* and sailed eastward to keep his appointment with General Schafter.[124] At about 9:30 Lieutenant Commander Hodgson, the navigator of Schley's
flagship, *Brooklyn*, realized that the suspicious plume of smoke rising from
behind the hills of Santiago was moving.

Fortune had given the discredited Schley another chance: In Sampson's
absence, command fell to him. "We'll give it to them now! We'll give it to them
now!" he was heard to say.[125] "The Spanish ships came out as gaily as brides to
the altar," wrote Captain John W. Philip of the *Texas*. "Handsome vessels they
certainly were, with flags enough for a celebration parade." As the antagonists
drew closer, the Spanish crews—their fatigue and hunger blunted by liberal doses
of cognac—waited anxiously for the order to fire.[126] "It was a solemn moment,"
wrote the *Maria Teresa*'s Captain Concas. "The bugles [that] gave the signal for
the commencement of battle. . . . [were] the last echo of those which history tells
us were sounded at the capture of Granada. It was the signal that four centuries
of grandeur was at an end and that Spain was becoming a nation of the fourth
class."[127]

After a brief melee, the Spanish column turned west and ran along the coast,
desperately trying to escape. But the ships were too slow. As the Americans drew
to within 2,000 yards, the action developed into a classic parallel line-ahead
chase.[128] One by one the flammable Spanish vessels were overtaken and de-

stroyed. Aboard the *Maria Teresa* Lieutenant Gomez Inas watched awestruck as his ship was blown apart: "First a shell exploded in the Admiral's cabin, setting fire to the woodwork there. . . . Another shell struck the main steam pipe . . . [and] killed or wounded eighty of our men. The fire in the after part of the ship had driven the crews away . . . and the rapid fire guns of the American ships were playing havoc with our men and riddling the upper works of the ship." "It will be useless to fight any longer," muttered Admiral Cervera, and the ship was run on the beach.[129]

Next the *Oregon* closed to 900 yards of *Oquendo* and began raking the unfortunate vessel.[130] Soon the officers of the bridge had been all but annihilated, the forward 11-inch turret exploded, and the dismembered corpses of 130 dead crewmen littered the decks and superstructure. Her wounded Captain Lazaga had no choice but to beach the ship.

The *Vizcaya* was the next victim. She, too, was quickly reduced to ruins and sent, burning furiously, toward the rocks. As the *Iowa* passed the wreck, Robley D. Evans described a scene of almost gothic horror: "The Cuban insurgents had opened fire on the survivors from the shore . . . and I could plainly see the bullets snipping up the water among them. The sharks, made ravenous by the blood of the wounded, were attacking them from the outside."[131] The last Spanish cruiser, *Cristobal Colon*, almost broke free but ran out of high-quality coal and was caught and beached.[132] The Spanish torpedo boats had fared no better. Both the *Pluton* and the *Furor* were sunk by the combined fire of the *Iowa*, *Indiana*, and *Gloucester*. The U.S. Navy's "Fourth of July present to the nation" entailed 323 dead Spaniards.[133]

In contrast to the carnage aboard the Spanish ships, the American line had remained curiously immune to enemy fire. The only battle fatality of the day had occurred when a shell decapitated Schley's yeoman, George Ellis. As if to remind Schley of the realities of battle, the impact had splattered warm blood and brains over the victorious commodore's white uniform.[134] Otherwise, it had been a delightful morning for him. Unexpectedly, fate had granted Schley the one prize more coveted than rank by Annapolites, the opportunity to lead a fleet in a victorious engagement. Admiral Sampson, in contrast, had spent the morning in futile pursuit of the action. By the time he caught Schley, the battle was over and his frustration hardened into open hostility.[135] Both men occupied opposite poles of the naval personality, much like Beatty and Jellicoe in World War I: Schley was a throwback to the sea dogs of the past, genial, impetuous, and utterly uninterested in machinery; whereas Sampson was an archetype of the naval officer of the future, an engineer at heart, careful, and scientifically oriented.[136] Between these two antipodes would flash a controversy over the laurels of victory destined to scar the reputations of both irrevocably.[137]

Personal quarrels notwithstanding, Annapolites had good reason to be thankful for the results of Santiago and the naval war in general. The words of the prophet had come to pass. Tradition had reasserted itself. All the major preconceptions held by the naval establishment had apparently been verified by the course of events. Whereas Manila had been basically an engagement of minor units, Santiago provided an apparently unqualified demonstration of the power of the modern battleship, the continuing validity of blockade, and the soundness of the hierarchy of ships. "Everything goes to prove the value of the battleship," wrote Lieutenant Robert Brinkerhoff, who had observed the action from the *Iowa.* "I value too the moral effect on the men of large ships."[138] The only other pretender to the naval throne, the torpedo boat, had also been slapped unceremoniously back in place by its betters. "The torpedo boats . . . were things of the past," noted Robley D. Evans hopefully. "They had given us many sleepless nights, but when it came to the test of battle, they had done just what many of us thought they would do. They had been disabled and destroyed in the shortest possible time."[139] Lieutenant W. I. Chambers concluded, "It is safe to say that we have shown that if a man of war is ready at all times to open up instantly an efficient, rapid fire, that ship has little or nothing to fear from torpedo boats."[140] The superiority of the monster gunship had never been clearer.

Nonetheless, a closer examination of the firing record of both sides reveals some startling inconsistencies in the generally held picture "that God and the gunners had had their day."[141] Even the excitement of battle and the dense clouds of smoke could not account for the miserable shooting. The Spaniards, who rarely practiced gunnery, had managed to score only 16 hits at Manila and 23 at Santiago.[142] The Americans, who drilled regularly, had not done much better. Firing at a stationary target, Dewey's squadron had hit its adversaries only 170 times, whereas at Santiago 122 of 9,433 shots had found their mark.[143] These figures looked even worse when it was considered that each action had taken place at considerably shorter range than had been expected.[144] Either both sides were inept or long-range naval gunnery was proving to be a much more difficult proposition than had been first imagined. Yet, these embarrassing details were easy for Americans to ignore in the general climate of success.

The Navy's strategic planning had been thoroughly vindicated by the course of events. Amid the civilian stampede for coastal protection, the Navy had steadfastly insisted that Cervera would sail directly for the Caribbean just as the plan said he must. It had all come to pass and the Gulf of Mexico was established more clearly than ever in the minds of Annapolites as the key to U.S. naval integrity. Mahan's War Board had proven "eminently fitted to coordinate the work of the department and the fleet," and its advice on strategy appears to have been accepted without question by the civilian secretary.[145] That was important because the board represented a significant step toward the "council of elders" for so long desired by hierarchically oriented line officers. Soon, at the urging of Mahan and his friend Rear Admiral H. C. Taylor, the War Board would be resurrected and expanded into the General Board of the Navy—a sort of American naval equivalent of the College of Cardinals and a body destined to exert an enormous influence over the formulation of U.S. naval policy and its reliance upon the sacred vessel, the battleship.[146]

Yet the triumph of the prophet had not been limited to professional matters. The geopolitical component of the Mahanite master plan was well on the way toward fulfillment. The war had provided ample confirmation of the fleet's dependency upon bases, and the peace settlement was, in large measure, intended to assure American naval forces ample shore facilities in the future.[147] The United States emerged from the conflict with a net of base sites that not only guarded the approaches to the proposed Isthmian canal but also stretched across the western ocean to the doorstep of Asia. In the Caribbean a coaling station would be built at San Juan, and the base at Guantanamo, leased in perpetuity from Cuba in 1903, would grow into the largest U.S. outpost in the West Indies.[148] Besides Pago Pago in the South Seas, the United States now possessed three of the best anchorages in the Pacific: Pearl Harbor, in the newly annexed Hawaiian group; Apia, in Guam, 3,300 miles west of Honolulu; and Manila Bay, in the Philippines, a bastion that would command the north-south shipping lanes from Japan to the East Indies. Neverthless, far-flung possibilities were not without liabilities. The defense and development of the Pacific bases was a problem fated to frustrate American planners until World War II.[149] Finally, Mahan's first priority, the construction of an interoceanic canal, had received a huge boost from the much publicized voyage of the battleship *Oregon*. With responsibilities in both oceans, the necessity for rapid transport of the battle fleet was now obvious, and construction of the waterway would soon begin.[150] Annapolites could rejoice in their good fortune; their prophet had proved to be a naval messiah.

But Mahan's was not the only reputation enhanced by the Spanish-American War. Fate had also smiled on George Dewey and Theodore Roosevelt, two figures whose future careers had great impact on the continued development of the battle fleet. While Sampson and Schley were canceling each other out as naval heroes, the praise of a grateful nation was focused upon the hero of Manila Bay. There were Dewey cocktails, Dewey laxatives, Dewey arches, Dewey flags, and "Welcome Dewey" in electric lights on the Brooklyn Bridge—but most important of all, there was a promotion.[151] On 2 March 1899 Congress authorized the president to appoint Dewey "Admiral of the Navy, who shall not be placed on the retired list except by his own application."[152] The title was unique in a service whose highest rank had traditionally been rear admiral and whose system of promotion by seniority ensured that no man would remain on this pinnacle for more than a few years. George Dewey, however, could be neither outranked nor removed—the nautical equivalent of immortality. Yet that would have meant little had not the Admiral of the Navy also possessed a keen eye for power and an unwavering faith in both the principle of concentration and the ideas of Alfred T. Mahan. Consequently, when Henry C. Taylor offered him the presidency of the General Board, Dewey—realizing the body's potential influence—jumped at the opportunity. For the next sixteen years he would cling tenaciously to the post, methodically gathering influence and dedicating himself to the construction of a "navy second to none."[153]

Even the good fortune of Mahan and Dewey could not match the meteoric rise of Theodore Roosevelt. Returning home with the Rough Riders in mid-August 1898, he would arrive just in time to begin his successful campaign for governor of New York. Within two years he had been elected vice president. Then on 6 September 1901 President McKinley was mortally wounded at the Buffalo Exposition. Eight days later Mahan's foremost civilian disciple took the oath of office and became the youngest chief executive in the nation's history. The future looked bright for the Navy.

5

Sacred Vessel:
The Dreadnought

I

In November 1900 the enterprising Lieutenant William S. Sims arrived aboard the USS *Kentucky*, which, along with her sister *Kearsarge*, was the latest and presumably the most awesome addition to the growing herd of U.S. capital ships.[1] Fresh from a three-year tour of duty as an intelligence officer assigned to evaluate the latest developments in European naval technology, Sims was naturally interested in the details of *Kentucky*'s armament and construction. What he discovered was not reassuring. Although Sims had been taught "from the day that I entered the Naval Academy . . . that each ship that we launched was 'the latest expression of naval science,'" he found the *Kentucky* to be a treasure trove of naval blunders and antiquities.[2] He reacted to the ship's manifold failings with something akin to moral outrage. "*Kentucky* is not a battleship at all. She is the worst crime in naval construction ever perpetrated by the white race."[3] So great was Sims's consternation that in February 1901 he presented the unfortunate vessel's commanding officer with a detailed bill of indictment to be forwarded to the Navy Department in Washington.[4] "I shall never forget the scene at the wardroom mess table when the criticisms were first discussed. The executive and other officers became pale with rage in denouncing them—and me. However, after much discussion, they were obliged sadly to acknowledge their justice."[5] Not surprisingly, in March Sims received word that he was to be transferred from the *Kentucky* to the monitor *Monterey*, stationed at Canton.

The next chapter in Sims's rather disillusioning reevaluation of U.S. naval efficiency began when, on the way to his new assignment, he broke passage at

Hong Kong, the home of the Royal Navy's Asiatic Squadron. There he met for the first time Captain Sir Percy Scott, the vitriolic wizard of British naval gunnery.[6] A tough, bearded little man, Scott had a colorful personal life and a violent manner; both marked him as an eccentric in a service steeped in Victorian propriety. He was also one of the few officers in the Royal Navy with a mind inventive enough to follow the tortuous path that technology was tracing across the landscape of naval strategy. His friend and fellow iconoclast Admiral Sir John Arbuthnot Fisher would later defend him solely on the grounds of naval efficiency: "I don't care if he drinks, gambles, and womanises; he hits targets."[7] Indeed, Scott's crews had been shooting with uncanny accuracy—80 percent hits at a time when 30 percent was considered very respectable.[8] Such figures made a deep impression on Lieutenant Sims, who was sorely aware of the disappointing American marksmanship at Manila Bay and Santiago.[9]

Playing upon the rapprochement between the two navies, the American lieutenant cultivated the Briton and learned that the key to Scott's success lay in the use of a technique known as continuous-aim firing, a scheme by which the gun was aimed at its target throughout the entire period of a ship's roll. To enable gunners to take full advantage of the system, Scott had improved the naval rifle itself by redesigning the training mechanism and introducing powerful telescopic sights mounted so as not to be influenced by recoil. Finally, in order to provide his crew with frequent practice without prodigal waste of ammunition, Scott devised a system of subcaliber fire based on a mechanism called the dotter, which moved a paper target in front of the mouth of the gun.[10]

Excitedly Sims recorded his discoveries in a second mammoth report to the Navy Department, entitled "The Remarkable Record Target Practice of the HMS *Terrible*." The paper explained Scott's system in great detail and included an embarrassing comparison between the strict rules followed at British target practices and the lax procedure tolerated in the American Navy, allowing a ship to pick its own range and rate of fire.[11] The implication was clear: U.S. warships stood little chance of surviving a hostile encounter with adversaries versed in these revolutionary techniques. Nonetheless, the Navy Department reacted to Sims's gunnery report with the same massive silence that had greeted his exposé of the *Kentucky*.[12]

Not willing to be ignored, the persistent lieutenant began writing for the third time, and in May 1901 produced a voluminous comparison between the defective American capital ship *Kentucky* and a contemporary British vessel, the *Canopus*. Whereas he believed (erroneously as it turned out), "every practicable precaution" had been taken to ensure the safety of the guns and their mechanisms on *Canopus*, Sims made it absolutely clear he considered the *Kentucky* a death trap.

> An impartial consideration of the facts . . . will render it apparent that a battleship built on the same general plan as the *Kentucky* . . . would . . . go into action with all chances very heavily against her inflicting serious damage on a modern battleship of her weight before her guns were put out of action, not to mention the slaughter of her men, and the grave danger of her magazines being exploded.[13]

The reaction of most of the line officers in the U.S. Asiatic Squadron to Sims's forthright statement of his position was interesting. Like his messmates in the wardroom of the *Kentucky*, they were hardly overjoyed at having their attention called to what now seemed rather obvious technical deficiencies. Yet, most agreed with the *Monterey's* Captain Stockton, "that we ought to stand in the light and not be afraid of the truth no matter how unsatisfactory."[14] The naval bureaucracy in Washington, however, remained as profoundly indifferent as ever to Sims's jeremiads. Meanwhile Sims grew "madder and madder with each paper"; and eventually he would take the extreme step of writing the president of the United States of his perception of the deplorable state of U.S. battleship design and gunnery.[15]

Perhaps more than any other American, Theodore Roosevelt personified his age and what it expected of its leaders. On the surface he crackled with aggressiveness, brilliance, and a visceral energy that had propelled him to the top of a society dedicated to getting things done. Yet his character was founded on the same contradictions that would soon cause his fellow human beings to begin the greatest bloodletting in history—a slaughter that would within fifty years bring them to a point at which they could contemplate their own extinction.

Roosevelt was born with a puny body that he struggled desperately to overcome, and his personality and career were deeply affected by a lifelong quest for manliness. Locked in what amounted to perpetual adolescence, Roosevelt exhibited an admiration for all things military and naval that became proverbial.[16] In one sense that was merely symptomatic of a larger fascination with power— almost for its own sake. To such a person the implications of what he called "the wonderful new condition of industrial growth" could hardly be anything other than benign.[17] Technological expertise was at the root of both his own country's phenomenal rise to prominence and the general mastery of the so-called Anglo-

Saxon race with which he identified so closely. It was natural, therefore, that Roosevelt should attach special significance to the continued development of the battle fleet that he and Mahan had worked so hard to foster in the 1890s. It was at once an instrument of war, a bevy of splendid machines, and the most concrete manifestation of national power in an ocean ruled ultimately by force.

The newly installed twenty-sixth president lost little time before defining his position on naval affairs. In his first annual message to Congress in 1901, Roosevelt noted, "The American people must either build and maintain an adequate Navy or else make up their minds definitely to accept a secondary position in international affairs, not merely in political but in commercial matters."[18] The relationship between a strong fleet and a successful foreign policy was so vital in Roosevelt's eyes that he assumed personal control over the service, acting de facto as his own naval secretary through his entire administration.[19]

Roosevelt agreed with Mahan and the naval establishment that an "adequate" Navy consisted chiefly of battleships. "I thoroughly believe in developing and building an adequate number of submarines; I believe in building torpedo-boat destroyers; there must be fast scouts. . . . But the strength of the Navy rests primarily upon its battleships."[20] Therefore, when Congress persisted in cutting his naval budgets, Roosevelt inevitably sacrificed auxiliaries in favor of continued battleship construction. Along with his Germanic counterpart, Kaiser Wilhelm II, Roosevelt followed the latest developments in naval architecture with a rapt attention scarcely exceeded by the best-informed professionals.[21] Consequently, when Lieutenant Sims's fateful critique of American battleship design and armament arrived at the White House, it received the president's immediate attention.

At first Roosevelt was inclined to be dubious. "Sims is a good man, but a preposterous alarmist. Prior to the outbreak of the Spanish War he actually believed the Spanish vessels were better than ours."[22]

However, further inquiry and a second letter from the industrious lieutenant convinced Roosevelt of the truth behind many of Sims's charges. On presidential orders Sims's reports were printed and distributed to every officer in the service.[23] By the middle of April 1902 Roosevelt was writing Rear Admiral Henry C. Taylor, the progressive chief of the Bureau of Navigation: "I am really very much impressed with Sims' letters. . . . I would like a careful memorandum of what he says. I also want to go over the matter with you at length."[24] By September, Roosevelt and Taylor were in agreement that Sims should be appointed inspector of target practice.[25]

Sims's nature and schemes were bound to appeal to Roosevelt. The two men were so much alike that the friendship that sprang up between them was practically inevitable. Sims roared through life at the same frenzied pace as Roosevelt, playing tennis, doing push-ups, jogging and hiking all the while. Throughout his career this restless energy would lead him to confront the salient problems of evolving naval strategy well before most of his colleagues even suspected that such difficulties existed. Moreover, Sims was infused with the same spirit of reform that saturated the president, a deep-seated feeling, born of an inbred philosophical optimism, that things could be set right by creative intelligence. Together they believed that mechanization, both civilian and military, had produced undesired results simply because things had been woefully mismanaged. Fittingly enough, their solution to technology-bred problems could be boiled down to one vague but splendidly all-inclusive word: "efficiency." It was not a very revolutionary motto. Basically, it implied that improved technique, rather than dramatic restructuring, was needed. Yet in the habitual use of that term, as in most things, both Roosevelt and Sims epitomized the mood and essence of progressivism. In that sense Sims was an archetype of the modern, politically sophisticated Annapolite. Unlike Mahan, whose partisan activities never extended beyond supplying his influential friends with a specific course of action and the historical analogies to support it, Sims co-opted the style and techniques of a civilian reformer. It would prove a profitable stance.

Characteristically, the new inspector of target practice carried out his job with boundless enthusiasm. "My opinion formed by my experience . . . was that a personal campaign would accomplish more than tons of paper."[26] Consequently, in late 1902 Sims descended like a tornado on the Atlantic Fleet, peacefully gathered at Culebra, determined to teach them scientific marksmanship. Methodically, he visited each vessel, lecturing tirelessly on the virtues of Scott's system. For three and four hours at a time Sims subjected his captive audience to a merciless barrage of facts, figures, and slashing logic that at one point caused a young engineering officer to cry out in despair, "Judas Priest, can't you talk about anything but gunnery?"[27] Nonetheless, his enthusiasm gradually overcame the initial skepticism of most officers. The evangelical inspector's visit caused the fleet to begin serious practice with the dotters and other devices that had been secretly made available to them by Britain.[28] The climactic test proved an astonishing vindication of Sims's methods. The accuracy of all ships improved dramatically, with the *Alabama* shooting an astonishing 60.5 percent with all guns.[29]

Still, the inspector was not satisfied. His trip to Culebra had convinced him that the sights used by the battle fleet were inadequate to the demands of long-range firing, and soon he composed a lengthy condemnation of American aiming devices.[30] The reaction of the chief of the Bureau of Ordnance was very nebulous as to how he proposed to rectify past errors. A year passed with no attempt made to replace the old sights. Sims again presented his case to the president. Roosevelt's reaction was unequivocal: "I shall give the Bureau an alternative: either they must find the money to resight the Navy with the best possible design of instruments or I shall take the matter up with Congress and tell them that the Navy's sighting devices are obsolete and inefficient."[31] Within two years the battle fleet was completely equipped with new sights.[32]

Although accurate telescopic sights were useful in pointing a gun at a target, finding its range was another matter. The best means of estimating an unknown range was to create an imaginary triangle and find its tangent. But the angles created by a target 6,000 yards or more yards away became too acute and sensitive to be dealt with by individual gun crews located near the waterline. The solution lay in lengthening one of the legs of the triangle by mounting a spotter high above the ship and providing him with the most sophisticated optical equipment. After estimating the range, using trigonometry, the spotter could correct his calculations by observing whether the splash of the shell was in front or beyond an adversary.[33] But as long as naval rifles of all calibers continued to be fired individually and haphazardly, no recognizable splash pattern could be produced. To do that, guns would have to be fired simultaneously in salvoes.[34] "Fire control," as this system was called, had been originated by Sims's friend and associate, Bradley Fiske, in the early 1890s, but had never been implemented.[35] Now, however, the crusading inspector of target practice campaigned for the scheme and was the moving spirit behind the Board on Fire Control, whose recommendations were largely responsible for its eventual adoption by the Navy.[36]

The use of fire control had particularly important implications for naval architecture. Until this time, capital ships had mounted multicaliber main batteries; generally including guns of approximately five, nine, and twelve inches in diameter. Yet, such an assortment tended to confuse spotters, who in the heat of battle were bound to have difficulty differentiating one type of splash from another.[37] Moreover, at the extreme ranges that torpedoes were beginning to necessitate, the steady flight characteristics of the heaviest shells made them considerably more accurate than smaller projectiles.[38] Gradually, it occurred to ordnance experts around the naval world that the resolution of these complications lay in the construction of a battleship with a single-caliber main battery composed of the largest naval rifles available. Such a vessel would not only be inherently more formidable than its eclectic predecessors, but its uniformity of armament would also doubtless simplify the problems of ammunition storage and supply.[39]

Among the first to reach this conclusion was Sims's friend Homer G. Poundstone. Invalided by severe rheumatoid arthritis, the redoubtable "Lbspierre" spent most of early 1902 aboard the USS *New York*, taking morphine and working on a scheme for a "bigger and better battleship."[40] Poundstone produced a memorandum advocating the construction of an all-big-gun ship, which he labeled the *Possible*. Not surprisingly, the document found its way into the president's hands. "Let me congratulate you on your paper on battleships," Roosevelt wrote the aspiring designer in December. "It is excellent, though I am not sure that I can get Congress to take the view I should like it to on the subject."[41] Greatly encouraged, Poundstone began working on blueprints of the proposed ship, which by August 1903 he had completed and circulated to a few of his "most trusted friends."[42]

Among the recipients was Lieutenant Commander W. I. Chambers, who immediately submitted them, under his own name, to the 1903 Naval War College Summer Conference.[43] When the plans were favorably received there, Chambers presented a memorandum on the subject to the General Board in October. His proposal called for a capital ship with a top speed of eighteen knots, a main battery of eleven or twelve 12-inch, 50-caliber guns, and no other ordnance except numerous 3-inch antitorpedo guns.[44]

Admiral Dewey, not fully understanding the principles behind uniform armament, but characteristically impressed by arguments for bigger naval artillery, requested, first in October, then in late January 1904, that the Bureau of Construction and Repair "prepare a tentative design for a battleship with a battery of 12 heavy turret guns, none of which shall be less than 10″, and at least four shall be 12″."[45] The bureau, however, chose to ignore the request, and by midsummer 1904 no plans had been produced.

Nevertheless, the proponents of the all-big-gun ship were undeterred. On 15 July Sims wrote Poundstone, informing him that the "subject is booming" and urging him to send his proposal to the General Board at once "so the executive committee has a chance to mull it over before it comes to them officially."[46] Arthritis retarded Poundstone's progress, however, and on 24 July Sims again pressed his friend for plans of the *Possible*. "Captain Whiskers [Dewey] is liable to forget all about it while mulling over the proper disposition of our fleet when we have 60 battleships."[47]

The chances of that happening increased on 7 September when the Bureau of Construction and Repair unveiled its plans for the next generation of U.S. capital ships. It was not the all-big-gun vessel that the General Board had requested, but a 16,000-ton battleship of mixed armament. Significantly, the bureau was concerned about "not making departures from recently authorized types,"[48] so concerned, in fact, that on 4 October the bureau flatly refused the General Board's next request for blueprints of a uniformly armed vessel.[49] At that point Sims went to see the president, who personally intervened. But the constructors (naval architects) remained adamantly opposed to the proposition. On 17 October they replied to Roosevelt's letter, noting that "nothing has transpired during the past year that would justify extensive changes in the main battery of vessels building or recently designed."[50] The constructors were not so dubious about the technological feasibility of the vessel as they were upset by the all-big-gun ship's implications for the rest of the fleet. There seemed little doubt that the entire mixed-caliber squadron, so painfully acquired, would be rendered irretrievably obsolete by the existence of such a battleship.

On 28 October the General Board hastened to assure the department that this was not the case:

> Having fixed upon the 16,000 ton *Connecticut* as the standard as to displacement and dimensions, there should be no departure from that vessel in the concomitant tactical features of speed and steaming radius without grave reasons, which do not appear to exist. . . . The only features in which a departure should be made from the *Connecticut* are the armor and armament. It is not essential that the guns powers of different ships of a squadron should be identical.[51]

That explanation seemed reasonable to Congress, and on 3 March 1905 it authorized the construction of "two first class battleships carrying the heaviest armor and most powerful armament for vessels of their class upon a maximum trial displacement of 16,000 tons."[52] Still, the designers remained hesitant and on 26 June the chief constructor informed the General Board that a definite design for an all-big-gun ship was still pending.[53]

Almost simultaneously with this announcement came news from abroad that would make the matter appear very much more urgent. Russia's war with Japan, which had not been going well in the first place, had taken a disastrous turn for the worse. After losing its Pacific Fleet at Port Arthur, the czar's naval ministry had risked everything by continuing to send the remaining Baltic Squadron under Admiral Rozhdestvensky halfway around the world to meet the well-trained and well-equipped Japanese. To make matters worse, the rigors of the 18,000-mile voyage and the usual neglect of imperial Russian ships combined to leave the fleet in thoroughly dilapidated condition.[54] As the Baltic Squadron approached the Sea of Japan, exasperated engineers worked next to Orthodox priests, who sprinkled holy water over stripped gears and bent rods.[55] On 27 May Admiral Heihachiro Togo intercepted the Russians off the Straits of Tsushima. Using his four-knot advantage in speed to repeatedly cross Rozhdestvensky's T, the Japanese commander systematically all but annihilated his Russian adversary with merciless gunfire.

In the United States, advocates of "scientific gunnery" and its offspring, the all-big-gun ship, were quick to seize upon the battle as a resounding affirmation of their ideas.[56] Lieutenant Robert McNeely wrote Sims on 30 May that "the authenticated reports of Togo's victory have just arrived; to me it looks like a well-conducted target practice."[57] In June Admiral Dewey noted that the "big guns on battleships," and not torpedo boats, had "decided the battle."[58] To Homer Poundstone, "the torpedoes' success in the Battle of the Sea of Japan and previously were not practicable until the big guns of the battleships had prepared an opening for these hornets of the sea by smashing the mobile torpedo defenses of the enemy."[59]

Although that view was generally held throughout the naval world, it was certainly open to question. It seems, in retrospect, that the role of subsurface weaponry in determining the course of the Russo-Japanese War was universally underestimated at the time. Mines alone were responsible for the destruction of eighteen warships, as many as had been sunk by all other means combined.[60] In addition, Rozhdestvensky seems to have lived in constant terror of being subjected to Japanese torpedo attack. That fear first manifested itself off Dogger Bank—literally thousands of miles away from the nearest Japanese naval combatant—when the trigger-happy Russians opened fire on the British fishing fleet. But that embarrassing interlude proved much less dangerous than Rozhdestvensky's decision to pass the narrow Straits of Tsushima by day in order to avoid nocturnal torpedo attack, thereby losing his fleet's best chance to avoid Admiral Togo.[61]

Even more influential than the results of Tsushima, however they might be interpreted, was the news filtering into the Navy Department that summer from

Great Britain. In 1903 a romantic Italian naval engineer, Vitorio Cuniberti, had published an article in the current edition of *Jane's Fighting Ships* projecting a vessel armed with twelve 12-inch rifles and "a very high speed—superior to that of any existing battleship afloat." Furthermore, it plausibly and melodramatically argued the case for the ship's virtual invulnerability. Cuniberti's *Invincible* not only carried enough heavy armament to quickly reduce any possible opponent to a smoldering hulk but also possessed the speed to escape any trap or combination of numbers against her.[62]

The scheme apparently took seed in the fertile imagination of the flamboyant Admiral John Arbuthnot Fisher who, while stationed at Portsmouth in early 1904, designed just such a capital ship.[63] On becoming First Sea Lord in October, Fisher—who subscribed to the belief that "to beget Surprise you must arrange for Inspiration to go to bed with Audacity"—immediately began a resolute campaign to have his "ideal battleship" constructed.[64]

By the middle of August 1905, Homer Poundstone had learned from friendly British sources that the Royal Navy was definitely "about to lay down the *Dreadnought* [which] . . . will be 20,000 tons full load, 21-knots speed and . . . mount a battery of at least ten 12-inch guns."[65] This vessel would not only weigh 4,000 tons more than the projected all-big-gun *Michigan* and *South Carolina*, but also its revolutionary propulsion system based on the steam turbine would allow it to steam 5 knots faster than the 16-knot fleet speed of the American battle line.[66]

The implications of the HMS *Dreadnought* were not lost on Sims and Poundstone, who immediately recommended that the General Board increase the displacement of its all-big-gun ships.[67] In late September Admiral Dewey asked for authority to expand the *Michigan* and *South Carolina* from 16,000 to 18,000 tons.[68] But the Board on Construction, determined to maintain some semblance of homogeneity in the U.S. battle line, was able to block this proposal.[69] Consequently, the two ships were built according to the original weight limitations.

Yet the constructors' attempts to stem the tide of technology and the chronic swelling of the battleships were soon to prove utterly futile. By early February 1906 the HMS *Dreadnought* was launched with great fanfare, and it quickly became apparent that she would match or exceed all previous speculations as to her character.[70] To make matters worse, it was learned that shortly before the *Dreadnought's* christening, work had begun on three British supercruisers,

USS Michigan, *which along with sister ship* South Carolina *made up the first class of American all-big-gun battleships. (Courtesy of the U.S. National Archives)*

Invincible, Inflexible, and *Indomitable*—all displacing over 17,000 tons, armed with all-big-guns, and eventually capable of an amazing twenty-eight knots.[71]

News from other strongholds of the naval world was equally riveting. Dreadnought fever had taken hold. It was clear that Germany's *Nassau* and Japan's *Satsuma* were being built to match the speed, armament, and bulk of the *Dreadnought*.[72] It was also apparent that other naval powers would soon follow. The day of the first American battle fleet had passed. A new one would have to be built.

II

In the spring of 1906 Congress began to debate the matter. Members were plainly not happy about the gigantic turn in naval architecture. A minority, led by the powerful Senator Eugene M. Hale, who had been one of the congressional architects of Mahan's mixed-caliber fleet, was vehemently opposed to a ship matching the dimensions of the HMS *Dreadnought*.[73] The most intriguing suggestion from this group came from Representative John S. Williams of Mississippi:

> Whereas the British Sea Monster which we are imitating has been named *Dreadnought*—an archaic name—this man-of-war is hereby named *Skeered O'Nuthin* as an expression of our true American spirit; Provided further, that it is hereby made the duty of the first Captain who shall command her to challenge in the nation's name, the so-called *Dreadnought* to a duel à outrance, to take place . . . in sight of Long Island and that on the occasion of the combat the President and his cabinet . . . being fond of the strenuous life, shall be entertained on the quarter-deck as guests of the ship and the nation.[74]

He was ruled out of order.

In spite of the clamor, in early June the USS *Delaware* was authorized by Congress. It was the first vessel in modern U.S. naval history whose tonnage was not stipulated by law.[75] Equipped with steam turbines and designed for twenty-one knots, the *Delaware* would carry a battery of ten 12-inch guns and weigh in at a hefty 20,000 tons.[76] She would be the first member of the second American battle fleet.

News of the *Delaware* found naval journalists as skeptical of the giant ship as were its legislative opponents. The widely respected William Hovgaard "warned against a too rapid increase in displacement of battleships" and pointed out "the drawbacks connected with excessive size."[77] The well-known writer on naval affairs Park Benjamin phrased his objections to what he called "The Shout for Big Ships" in somewhat more poetic terms:

> Let's build another Big Ship!
> We can just as easily settle plans for two as one.
> Let's build another Big Ship every year,
> and meanwhile let's talk about four more.
> Let's get rid of all the battleships we have, quick
> by applying them to a law which sends them to the dump
> if they need repairs.[78]

Yet none of the condemnations of the dreadnought principle was nearly as influential as Alfred T. Mahan's "Reflections, Historic and Other, Suggested by the Battle of the Sea of Japan," which appeared in June 1906. Always the historian, the aging naval prophet, who had retired from active service in order to leave the "monstrous modern" battleship to younger officers, chose to interpret the appearance of the all-big-gun ship, not as a resounding nautical innovation, but as a dangerous lapse in moderation.[79]

Although Mahan's arguments were flawed by a misinterpretation of the Battle of Tsushima and a characteristic ignorance of contemporary technical developments, his observations were undeniably cogent. Mahan concluded that Togo's scouting and choice of position, rather than his tactical advantage of speed, had sealed the Russians' doom. Moreover, "in a fleet today [a dreadnought's] speed will be that of her slower sisters; more *Dreadnoughts* must be built to keep up with her; and upon them in turn, according to the prevalent laws of progress she will be a drag, for her successors will excel her."[80] Suffering the trials of a prophet whose revelations had been seized by zealots, Mahan complained: "We are at the beginning of a series to which there is no logical end, except the power of naval architects to increase size. . . . It is introducing the Navy into a simple trust in bigness and what is worse, an absence of trust in anything but bigness. This willful premature antiquating of good vessels is a growing and wanton evil."[81]

Finally and perhaps most significantly, Mahan worried about the growing distance between naval antagonists. "The fleet which has thus placed its dependence on long-range fire has with it assumed the naval tone and temperament associated with the indisposition to close. . . . I think appeal can be made confidently to history that the navy, which, for any reason, habitually seeks to keep the enemy at a distance, in order to secure a preliminary advantage, usually fails to achieve a decisive success."[82]

The article constituted a potent critique, and even the president's faith in the dreadnought type was shaken by the prophet's logic. So on 30 August Roosevelt had his personal secretary write Sims a letter asking him to reply to Mahan's essay.[83] Sims's rebuttal, which was eventually published in the December 1906 *United States Naval Institute Proceedings*, was technically devastating.[84] Although exposing numerous errors and anachronisms in Mahan's preference for multicaliber rifles over all-big-gun armament, Sims nonetheless proved himself woefully incapable of addressing the larger issues raised by the naval prophet: "I can understand an individual being willful and wanton, but I cannot believe that the navies of the world would without good cause be suddenly and uniformly inspired in this manner. On the contrary, it seems to me that the mere fact of there being a common demand for such large vessels is conclusive evidence that there must be a common cause that is believed to justify the demand."[85] This might be interpreted as begging the question, but it was persuasive enough for Roosevelt. Consequently, in late September he wrote Commander Sims that he "regarded his article as convincing and had modeled the recommendations in my message accordingly."[86]

Sims's fellow Annapolites were, if anything, even more enthusiastic about the article than the president.[87] To all involved it seemed that Mahan had been proved as obsolete as his mixed-caliber fleet. Gently but firmly, he would be removed from the naval pulpit and carted off to an honorable place in the naval sepulcher. From that point, it was primarily to Sims and his friends that Roosevelt looked for advice on matters of naval construction. Indeed, in October 1907 the president wrote his new naval protégé, "Is there any point you would especially like me to bring out in my annual message, or any other action you would recommend my taking?"[88]

Still Congress maintained its reservations and refused to authorize more than one duplicate *Delaware* in 1907.[89] Meanwhile Roosevelt bided his time. He was perfectly aware that a building program on the order of the one he was contemplating required a spectacular demonstration of the Navy's usefulness. That would not prove to be a great obstacle, however: No one had ever accused the rough-riding president of lacking showmanship.

By the middle of June 1907, Roosevelt had decided to send the entire American battle line on an epochal journey, first to the Pacific and then around the world.[90] The motives usually assigned to this ostentatious odyssey are numerous. Certainly, the arrival in Pacific waters of an American fleet roughly twice the size of the Japanese would have a chastening effect upon the newly victorious Asiatic power. In addition, Roosevelt emphasized the Navy's need for practice in navigation, fleet maneuver, and repairing machinery while at sea.[91] After the example of the unfortunate Russians in 1905, there was some question as to whether a large steam-powered fleet could undertake such a lengthy voyage and expect to remain in battle-worthy condition. But none of those explanations account for the theatrical nature of the voyage. The entire enterprise was conceived with an eye toward publicity. It was to be the final mission of the trusty troupers of the mixed-caliber fleet: to drum up enough public support for the construction of their successors.[92] So on 16 December 1907, amid as much fanfare as he could muster, Roosevelt bade farewell to the sixteen freshly painted battleships. Slowly, lined up like mechanical pachyderms, the white elephant fleet headed out to sea to begin its circus tour.

On 14 April 1908 in a special message to Congress, the president made explicit what had only been implicit in the voyage of the "Great White Fleet." He explained that there had occurred

> a radical change in the building of battleships among the great military nations— a change . . . which doubles or more probably trebles their effectiveness. Every other great nation has or is building a number of ships of this kind; we have provided for but two. . . . Under these conditions, to provide for but one or two battleships a year is to provide that this Nation, instead of advancing, shall go backward in naval rank and relative power. . . . There is imposed on me a solemn responsibility. . . . I earnestly advise that the Congress now provide four battleships of the most advanced type.[93]

Congress angrily cut his four capital ships to two, but in the end Roosevelt had his way. The fleet would be rebuilt—this time with dreadnoughts.

In Europe the introduction of the dreadnought type compounded the tensions that surrounded the ugly naval race that had been brewing between Great Britain and Germany since the late 1890s. In Britain Admiral Sir Frederick Richards wrote: "The Russian fleet had practically ceased to exist, the French in low water, Germany and the United States doing nothing sensational. That was the moment selected by the British Admiralty to start an international competition the end of which no man can foresee."[94]

Even Fisher spoke of the "unanimous naval feeling against the *Dreadnought* when it first appeared."[95] The influential Admiral Sir Reginald Custance questioned the validity of the ordnance data that was largely responsible for the ship's construction. "Opinion is misled by the results obtained in 'battle-practice' . . . [where] ships fire singly in smooth water, whereas the normal conditions in action will be that several will fire together, and possibly in rough sea."[96] Moreover, Custance noted that the "misty and foggy atmospheric conditions of the North Sea" would generally "force fleets to engage at short ranges of less than 6000 yards."[97] Sir William White, the former director of Naval Construction, labeled the all-big-gun concept as the "policy of Goliath." He wondered whether "it is the best policy to concentrate in a single ship enormous gun-power. . . . Underwater attacks—by submarines, mines, and torpedoes—cannot be regarded as relatively unimportant considering what happened in the Russo-Japanese war. . . . It cannot be disputed that an extreme concentration of fighting power in single ships of enormous size may be accompanied by large relative losses."[98]

Nonetheless, Fisher's audacious and determined effort to have an all-big-gun ship actually built produced a momentum that even the most reasoned criticism proved powerless to slow. Besides, the Royal Navy's upstart rival across the North Sea was known to be laying down Teutonic equivalents of the *Dreadnought.* Consequently, Britain began building ships with an increasing frenzy that would climax in 1909 with Parliament's authorization of eight of the mammoth warships. Winston Churchill, astonished by the progenitive powers of military technology, later commented: "The Admiralty had demanded six ships; the economists offered four; and we finally compromised on eight."[99]

The Germans, for their part, were probably even more inconvenienced by the appearance of the all-big-gun ship than the other major naval powers. The Germans' most important strategic waterway, the Kiel Canal—a sixty-one-mile shortcut between the Baltic and the North Sea—had been built in 1886 and, consequently, had locks that could accommodate no ship larger than 13,000 tons.[100] Germanic dreadnoughts would automatically necessitate alterations to the canal, costing 12.5 million pounds sterling.[101] Yet the chances that Germany would abstain from the naval challenge were minimal.

Its strident emperor, Kaiser Wilhelm II, matched even Theodore Roosevelt's enthusiasm for battleships, having the habit of drawing hypothetical examples on the backs of envelopes.[102] Born with a withered arm, Wilhelm appeared to look upon his fleet as an extension of his own personality. "All the years of my reign," he once told the king of Italy, "my colleagues, the Monarchs of Europe, have paid no attention to what I have to say. Soon, with my great Navy to endorse my words, they will be more respectful."[103] As a result of untiring study, he became an expert in naval affairs and followed, with "fanatical interest," every detail concerning the budding High Seas Fleet, developing in the process what amounted to a near obsession with what he called a "fast capital ship," a vessel combining the strength and firepower of a battleship with the speed of a cruiser.[104] But most of all, the "Kaiser want[ed] a fleet like that of England."[105] From his earliest childhood, Wilhelm had been fascinated by British ships.[106] He took his commission as an admiral of the British Navy seriously "and never concealed the pride with which he donned the British uniform, with its deep gold cuffs and cocked hat."[107] Consequently, when the *Dreadnought* appeared, Wilhelm's instinctive reaction was to duplicate it.

Even if the Kaiser had been utterly uninterested in weaponry, the logic that had given birth to the High Seas Fleet demanded that Germany follow Britain's lead in constructing dreadnoughts. "Risk fleet" was the term Admiral Alfred

Peter von Tirpitz used to describe his subtle attempt to paralyze the Royal Navy. It was premised on the construction of a fleet just large enough to prevent the strongest existing navy from challenging it without fatally weakening itself.[108] For the Teutonic deterrent force to remain credible, its size and power had to be kept in some meaningful relationship to that of the Royal Navy.[109] Roughly, that would translate into the construction of seventeen all-big-gun battleships and five dreadnought battle cruisers before the fateful August 1914.[110]

By underwriting the step-by-step perfection of the surface artillery ship, the mainstream of the naval world had led itself out upon a technological limb. If the processes of mechanization are analogous to those of evolution, then the dreadnought can be compared to the dinosaur—Mother Nature's own Mesozoic experiment with centralization. The weapons revolution had subtly, but nonetheless decisively, altered the character of the ship-of-the-line. The capital ship was no longer a brawler built to slug it out at point-blank range but a weapon of precision, whose entire destructive potential depended upon the pinpoint accuracy of a relatively few guns firing at ranges exceeding eight miles.

It was largely a fantasy: The developments in scientific marksmanship that were claimed to make this possible had in fact been largely overrated. Undeniably, great relative improvements in accuracy had been achieved through the methods of Scott and Sims. But those gains were more a function of the inefficient practices of the past than the efficiency of the new system. Hypothetically, if a weapon was able to hit a target once in a hundred times, whereas before it had missed every time, this was an advance of 100 percent. Nevertheless, in the larger context the weapon would still have to be considered a very imprecise instrument. That was largely the case with naval gunnery.

As Sims himself would later admit, "Roughly speaking there are about two dozen causes for the inaccuracy of a gun."[111] Besides the rolling of the sea, among the factors that could interfere with the precision of a discharging naval rifle were the weight of the powder charge, the temperature at which it burned, the number of rounds that had been fired through the barrel previously, the velocity of wind, the air density, the firing platform's momentum, and the error caused by the rotation of the shell.[112]

To compound matters, the optical devices that had been developed to aim the great guns were subject to their own set of problems. Light, upon which all high-powered telescopic sights depended, grew progressively more dim as distances increased.[113] Consequently, range finders became erratic at maximum ranges in cloudy weather or less-than-ideal lighting conditions.[114] But even if the

"The interference caused by the volume of funnel smoke . . . might easily result in the defeat of the superior fleet." USS North Dakota. (Courtesy of the U.S. Naval Institute)

skies were clear and the day bright, the volumes of smoke and heat produced by two battle lines were bound to obscure and distort the vision of both sides.[115] As Sims was aware in 1910, "the interference caused by the volume of funnel smoke, and from the guns while steaming at high speed might easily result in the defeat of the superior fleet."[116]

The dreadnought concept was a classic example of technology overreaching itself. The complexities involved in truly accurate firing at the contemplated ranges simply overwhelmed the means available. Recently, both John Sumida and Stephen Roskill argued that if the British Admiralty had only adopted the so-called Argo Clock fire-control system developed by Arthur Pollen around 1905 rather than the cheaper, simpler, and quite probably less accurate Dreyer table, then the dreadnought might well have lived up to expectations.[117] Yet those authors missed a larger point, in effect falling prey to the same chain of fallacies that fooled the dreadnought's inventors. There were simply upper limits on the accuracy of any system based on optics and mechanical computation. And as long as they were relied upon, the dreadnought was destined to be a tactical underachiever, whose few successes were based largely on the vulnerability of its own ammunition stores, particularly in the case of the battle cruiser. Had radar-based range finders and electronic computers been in existence, dreadnoughts could have been effective weapons; but with extant fire control, the great ships were preordained to relative impotence.

Meanwhile, the naval world's ordnance experts remained blind to the short-comings of long-range gunnery. "I had never heard an intimation from anybody," wrote a somewhat rueful Bradley Fiske at the end of World War I, "that anyone realized how easy it would be to prevent range finding."[118] Nonetheless, their shortsightedness was understandable. They were men whose every professional impulse told them that the dreadnought was the natural culmination of a type that had been evolving for hundreds of years, rather than a cul de sac. Until war came to show them, they could know no different. In the interim, dreadnoughts multiplied, ranges grew longer, guns waxed larger—while submarines were ignored and torpedoes neglected.

III

In terms of the institutional future of the United States Navy, the introduction of the dreadnought was a profoundly significant act. For the first time the impetus for technological reform had come from line officers rather than from the technical branches of the service. That was no accident. Whereas the Navy of Mahan had carefully and suspiciously dealt with mechanization, Sims and his colleagues were truly enthusiastic about the possibilities of machinery. Unlike their predecessors, the new breed of Annapolites was ready to follow the dictates of technology with something approaching an open mind.

To a significant degree, the stagnation of the United States Navy in the 1880s had conditioned the membership, goals, and outlook of the officers who would eventually sire the American version of the all-big-gun ship. For one thing, the plight of the service had a direct relationship on the career aspirations of those Annapolites who graduated between 1874 and 1884.[119] As the Navy shriveled, its need for junior officers diminished proportionately. The trend was ratified by Congress in the act of 5 August 1882, which had the effect of limiting the number of commissions granted to the top 25 percent of each class.[120] Although that law probably did very little for morale at the Naval Academy, it did ensure that none but the brightest Annapolites were permitted to join the "naval aristocracy" during this period.

Intellectual ability was not the only trait held in common by those young Annapolites. Their own frustrating circumstances tended to produce a self-conscious group; its members looked to each other for friendship and support and held views sharply differentiated from those of their seniors. The center of this clique, as is usual in military organizations, was dominated by a few outstanding individuals. There was, of course, Sims himself. Graduate of the class of 1880, this irrepressible officer came to personify the whole movement. Besides Sims, there was Bradley Fiske—described by the former as "one of the few thinkers in the Navy"—he was highly ambitious and a remarkably talented inventor holding patents on key devices such as the battle-order telegraph, the electric turret-turning mechanism, and a telescopic sight.[121] Fiske's passion for machinery was shared by the third member of the triumvirate, William F. Fullam, a gifted officer who consistently demonstrated an iconoclasm rare among Annapolites, eventually being one of the first to realize that naval warfare in the twentieth century would no longer be concerned with just the surface of the sea but was bound to become three dimensional.[122]

Surrounding this inner circle were several equally enthusiastic, but somewhat less visible, officers. They included Ridley McLean, Albert Lenoir Key, A. P. Niblack, Washington Irving Chambers, Richard Wainwright, and the first American all-big-gun advocate, Homer Poundstone.

Ironically, the course of naval reform as conceived and managed by that group really began with an enforced period on land. After the 1883 discontinuance of repair funds for wooden vessels and the subsequent decommissioning of most of those rotting veterans, many junior officers were forced ashore for periods of up to five years.[123] There, explained an older officer, they "naturally became interested in the absorbing question of rebuilding the Navy."[124] Yet, unlike previous naval reformers, the techniques and attitudes of this group tended to reflect the tides of change that were beginning to stir the surrounding civilian society. In nature and method Sims and his friends became service equivalents of those adhering to the political movement known as progressivism. The zeal and activism of civilian insurgency was echoed in their statements. "Our profession demands that we should . . . heartily encourage every officer who is trying to do something," wrote Fullam to Fiske. "We need do-ers in the Navy."[125]

If these young Annapolites were insurgents in outlook, they were muckrakers in method.[126] Whereas the "average naval officer . . . was brought up to . . . 'think of' the word publicity as an anathema,"[127] the nautical progressives became experts in the technique of public information. "The new navy was," in the words of Bradley Fiske, "the child of a public opinion created by naval officers."[128] Their abiding belief in the purgative value of fact led them to concentrate on exposure as a means of self-expression. Consequently, it comes as no surprise that Sims and his colleagues cultivated close ties with the leading reform journal of the day, *McClure's* magazine.[129]

Yet the insurgent Annapolites' excuse for publicizing naval malpractice seldom varied. They were interested solely in promoting "efficiency." Characteristically, the naval reformers transformed the previously haphazard act of loading and firing a naval gun into a ritual of such precision that Frederick Winslow Taylor, the father of all "efficiency experts," called it "the finest example of scientific management that I know of."[130]

The naval insurgents' concern for "efficiency" was also indicative of a much greater familiarity with machinery than their seniors possessed. Their extended assignments ashore had been spent in shipyards observing and supervising the construction of the latest in naval weaponry.[131] Memories of sail were fading. This generation had begun their careers when the Navy was in shambles and possibly doomed. It was natural that they should associate the Navy's resurrection with its mechanization. It would be difficult for such men to believe technology to be the dangerous force early Annapolites had imagined.

Nevertheless, a commitment to mechanical sophistication inevitably revived serious institutional complications for the Navy. It became increasingly clear to men like Sims that the lack of interest in technology affected by most line officers was endangering their control of the service.[132] With the reconstruction of the fleet had come the necessity of opening the service to numerous naval architects (or "constructors" as they were officially designated), engineers, technicians, and other staff types needed to design and operate the complicated new warships. After the war with Spain, civilian-oriented occupations actually began to predominate in the Navy.[133] "There seems to be a member of the staff under every rock you overturn these days," muttered William F. Fullam.[134]

To make matters worse, that unruly, unmilitary horde, by virtue of technological expertise, had steadily gained control over the design and construction of the Navy's warships. "Soon after we commenced to build a real fleet," wrote Richard Wainwright, "the Department constituted a new Board . . . which recommended to the Department the military characteristics of all new vessels."[135] Of the six bureau chiefs who made up this Board on Construction, only the chief intelligence officer and the head of the Bureau of Ordnance represented departments ordinarily dominated by line officers.[136]

The insurgents believed that their fellow Annapolites were largely to blame for their own predicament. Sims felt "it was the line's neglect of its own military job that permitted the material bureaus to entrench themselves so completely. . . . The line did not give bright cadets a special course in military principles that should govern the construction of ships . . . [and] has never until lately given the subject much thought."[137] "Battleships are now great machines," he later wrote Roosevelt. "A turret and its guns with their elevating and training gear, ammunition hoists, etc. is a mass of machinery. To handle them efficiently line officers must be competent engineers."[138]

As far back as the late 1880s activists like Richard Wainwright had attempted to rectify the situation by helping Annapolis Superintendent William Sampson introduce "practical and progressive" courses in electricity, naval architecture, steam engineering, and modern gunnery.[139] When Sampson appeared before a congressional committee in 1888 to argue for the replacement of the academy's ancient wooden sailing vessels with a modern steam training ship, his request brought a "veritable broadside" of criticism from senior Annapolites. So great was the furor that the replacement of the wind-borne veteran was postponed until 1901.[140] Yet time, expediency, and the momentum of technology were on the side of the insurgents. Gradually, as reactionary seniors retired, progressives were able to bring the training of line officers into a more realistic relationship with contemporary naval practice.

If line officers were to gain a meaningful dominion over their own machinery, they would have to eliminate their competition at the controls. By the late 1890s the despised naval engineers were enjoying a mild resurgence, after Porter's purge and the lean years of the Gilded Age had decimated their ranks. The insurgent Annapolites, however, were determined to remove the engineers' influence once and for all. "Marines and Engineers. They are both fighting a losing game and they know it," Captain C. H. Davis confided to Fullam.[141] The end came in May 1899 when Congress ordered the Corps of Engineers abolished and its members amalgamated into the line.[142]

Leaving half-trained Annapolites in charge of complicated machinery, once tended by experienced engineers, would prove to be not without its hazards. In 1905 the gunboat *Bennington* exploded, with the loss of sixty-six crew members. An investigation showed that its engine room had been commanded by an ensign who before being stationed there had never seen a boiler.[143] Nevertheless, a larger and more symbolic purpose had been served by the amalgamation. For the first time in half a century, the line could truly claim to control its own ships.

With executive backing assured, the progressive line officers began to grow more strident. It is in that context that Sims's criticisms of the construction of the U.S. battleships must be interpreted. Although the crusading lieutenant probably saw little dichotomy between his political motives and his moral outrage at the supposed inefficiency of American warships, his attacks inevitably reflected on the competence of the staff-dominated bureaucracy that had designed the vessels.[144] Progressive Annapolites were in complete accord with Admiral Mahan's advice to President Roosevelt:

Size and other qualities [of warships] are now determined by administrative officers. The sea officer is not represented. . . . What is needed supremely is an organ, wholly detached from administration, to evolve conclusions which shall stand for the professional opinion of the instructed sea officer; of the man who cares nothing about the administrative processes, but simply for the fighting efficiency of the ship.[145]

It seemed to William L. Rodgers that Admiral Dewey's "General Board [was] a beginning of such a military organization."[146] Although established primarily to coordinate war plans, the General Board had, from the beginning of its existence, taken it upon itself to recommend to the secretary the type and number of ships it felt should be built each year.[147] In the eyes of the insurgents, the General Board's competence in that sphere increased in direct proportion to the resistance of the Bureau of Construction and Repair and the Board on Construction to the all-big-gun ship. What must have seemed to the naval architects as healthy skepticism and a desire to avoid the unnecessary replacement of an expensive mixed-caliber fleet appeared to Sims and his colleagues as muddle-headed conservatism of the worst sort. Consequently, by the beginning of 1908 the progressives had made up their minds to eliminate staff influence from the designation of ship characteristics.

The first blow fell in January when Henry Reuterdahl published an article in *McClure's* entitled "The Needs of Our Navy," which Sims had helped him write.[148] Briefly, the piece was a catalogue of the submerged armor belts, exposed turret housings, and open ammunition hoists that had plagued U.S. battleships in the past. "How is it possible that blunders of these proportions can be perpetuated?" wondered Reuterdahl.

The answer to this is simply that no human being is responsible for this thing. It is done by the system—an organization so constituted that its very nature compels it to perpetuate mistakes. . . . What is needed is quite clear. . . . There must be in our Navy some general expert board, made up of men with ample experience in sea-going service, in which is centered the responsibility for advising the Secretary on all matters pertaining to the efficiency of the Navy.[149]

The effect of the article was like a bombshell, with newspapers around the country carrying summaries of the story and many printing editorials expressing surprise and concern.[150]

Evidently sensing that their position was threatened, the constructors sought help from Congress. In early 1908 their powerful ally, Eugene M. Hale, chairman of the Senate Committee on Naval Affairs, introduced a measure intended to abolish the General Board.[151] Ultimately, the proposal failed to gain legislative approval, and after a complex dispute over the configuration of the dreadnought *North Dakota*, the influence of the construction corps over the basic features of American battleships declined rapidly. In January 1909 Naval Secretary Truman H. Newberry ordered the membership and influence of the General Board increased as part of a larger reorganization of the Navy Department. Eventually, at Sims's urging, Taft's naval secretary, George von Lengerke Meyer, abolished the Board on Construction and charged the "General Board with the determination of purely military details of all new ships."[152]

The insurgents were not satisfied with line control of the Navy's technological development. The decentralized administrative structure still provided sanctuaries within the autonomous bureaus where staff influence might fester uncontrolled. To nautical progressives like Homer Poundstone the solution lay in the establishment of a "General Staff for the Navy, to have control and direction of all military considerations relating to naval efficiency, including authority to enforce its determinations."[153] Such an arrangement at last would subject the disorderly naval bureaucracy to the principles of hierarchy and command so revered by Annapolites. Yates Stirling hoped that "the General Staff would form the crown piece of our naval structure, and upon its efficiency and infallibility, the destiny of the nation on the seas may well depend."[154]

Spurred by gains over technical policy and the knowledge that Roosevelt's term as president would end in March 1909, Sims wrote the chief executive suggesting the appointment of a commission to investigate institutional reform.[155] Roosevelt, realizing that alterations of the magnitude the insurgents proposed would require legislative authorization, and that Congress regarded with deep misgivings a full-fledged General Staff, did nothing throughout the fall of 1908.

Finally, in January 1909 the chief executive appointed a distinguished committee of retired naval secretaries and line officers to decide "how to best recognize and emphasize the strictly military branch of the Navy."[156] Not surprisingly, the commission recommended a reorganization that, although not creating a General Staff, would have the effect of centralizing all executive authority in two councils, both dominated by line officers.[157] Congressional contempt for the proposal was equally predictable. Submitted to the Senate on 27 February, it was ignored until the end of Roosevelt's term.

The insurgents, while remaining firm in their determination to establish a General Staff, ultimately settled for half a loaf—a system of line officer "naval aides" who would sit on the expanded General Board and execute its advice. The aide for operations not only supervised the movement of the fleet but would prove to be the forerunner of the chief of naval operations. Prior to the emergence of the office of the chief, however, the aide system proved more significant as an indication of the growing power of the General Board than as an administrative agent. Just as Admiral Dewey had maintained, the council of elders would prove "a natural center and head" of the Navy's thought and planning.[158]

On the whole the insurgent Annapolites' efforts at reform had prospered. The American dreadnought was a reality, the naval engineers and the Board on Construction were memories, and a body of line officers kept close watch over the suspect bureau system. But success at generating momentum for change was in large part a function of the degree to which the insurgent program catered to the traditional prejudices of line officers. Dreadnoughts were, after all, the biggest, loudest, most ominous-looking examples of naval architecture yet devised. The insurgents had encouraged the study of machinery among antitechnological Annapolites. That, however, could be seen as largely a defensive measure to thwart the ambitions of the staff. It was even possible to interpret the General Staff concept as a throwback to the Board of Navy Commissioners and the line's ancient crusade to impose a strictly hierarchical chain of command over the service's autonomous administrative structure.

To a remarkable extent the fortunes of Sims and his colleagues paralleled the history of the civilian Progressive movement. As long as the progressives remained within the naval mainstream, they thrived. Yet as soon as they found themselves moving against the grain, they encountered frustration from all sides.

Like most members of the Progressive movement, the insurgent Annapolites had an enormous faith in internal reform and the salutary effect of competition. Consequently, the Navy's policy of promotion by seniority was a natural source of irritation. Yates Stirling was typical in complaining that "promotion by seniority, waiting for a dead man's shoes, is a sad blow to efficiency."[159] "In all walks of life, except the American Navy, men compete for their position and their reputation," noted Sims.[160] Yet the insurgent opposition to this arrangement was not based solely on principle. Insurgents had seen their own careers blocked by the Navy's chronic oversupply of officers and inability to eliminate incompetents. So congested was the system that in 1896 there were still lieutenants in the service who had joined it during the Civil War.[161] Because the scheme retarded the advancement of the most-talented and aggressive officers, the American naval high command had the oldest and least-experienced officers in the world.

Despite all this, the progressive line officers' belief that the system could be easily replaced proved to be naïve. A reverence for ascribed status and the regularity of career progression were very fundamental elements in the orderly, hierarchical world of the naval officer. The introduction of a scheme of advancement based on purely competitive values was, to many Annapolites, almost anarchistic.

As Sims wrote dejectedly in 1906, "If the members of any military organization . . . were asked to decide this question by vote, 'Selection' would be snowed under every time."[162] Not until 1916, at the insistence of egalitarian Secretary of the Navy Josephus Daniels, was the system modified in the direction of promotion by selection.[163] Nevertheless, the nine rear admirals who served on the board established to make all promotions proved so conservative in their judgments that the salutary effects of the change were all but counteracted. In 1919, after a careful study, Albert Gleaves concluded that "the same officers would have been available for command afloat whether promotion had been by selection or by seniority."[164]

The experience should have been instructive to the insurgents. There were very definite limits to the possibilities of reform in the United States Navy. But that would not become fully apparent to Sims and his associates until they realized the futility of building dreadnoughts and sought to replace them with more effective alternatives.

IV

While Sims and company looked toward the technological future, the fulfillment of Mahan's strategic prophesies remained uppermost in the minds of the naval establishment. For direction the mass of conservative Annapolites sought the guidance of the Navy's council of elders. The General Board would become the Cardinalate of the Church of Naval Theory, and affable George Dewey, the truest of believers.

More than any other figure it was the Admiral of the Navy who was responsible for the construction of the fleet of dreadnoughts that was the U.S. first line of defense until 7 December 1941. Operating behind a mask of grandfatherly charm exceeded only by that of Dwight D. Eisenhower, Dewey proved to be one of the most astute politicians ever to wear the uniform of a U.S. naval officer.[165] He was, for over a decade, the most celebrated military man in the United States, but he never abused the privilege. By 1916 propagandist George Creel could write that "as an officer, he commands the respect of the nation; as a man, he commands the love of the nation."[166] Except for one brief and ill-considered foray into presidential politics, he remained high above partisan issues. His one public position was a single-minded determination to increase the size and reputation of the Navy. He rarely spoke to the press. But when he did, his voice carried considerable impact.

Dewey's service image was as modest and deceptive as his public one. As the one and only Admiral of the Navy he was not only immune from mandatory retirement, but he also outranked every other officer in the service. Yet he carefully avoided flaunting his prerogatives. He chose instead the subtler and ultimately more effective alternative of leading by example. The insurgents, whose activist temperaments precluded an appreciation of the finer arts of manipulation, treated the admiral with the mixture of deference and condescension that young men reserve for the old and successful. To the insurgents he was an accidental figure, "Captain Whiskers," the old gent who happened to be head of the General Board they so strengthened. They greatly underestimated him. Dewey ran the General Board with an iron hand, exerting great influence over the choice of members and maintaining a virtual veto power over its decisions.[167] The board's power was always purely advisory, and until 1916 it lacked even statutory recognition. Yet, as Richard Wainwright later wrote, "It was more the knowledge that Admiral Dewey was President of the Board that gave any weight to its decisions than any public knowledge of the composition and workings of the Board."[168] In all matters pertaining to naval strategy and construction the voice of the General Board was the voice of George Dewey. That was perfectly acceptable to the mass of Annapolites. For no more representative U.S. naval officer could be found than the amiable Old Admiral.

Admiral George Dewey, the rock upon which the church was built.
(Courtesy of the U.S. National Archives)

From the policy statements that emerged from the board, it is clear that Dewey perceived the defensive prerequisites of the United States entirely from within the context of a strategic picture synthesized by Mahan and elaborated by the Naval War College before the turn of the century.[169] Such a view presented certain very basic problems to naval planners. The first and most fundamental difficulty was the geographical configuration of North America, which had as one of its main features two long and exposed coasts separated by a 13,000-mile journey around Cape Horn. Even after the passage of the Spooner Bill in June 1902 had assured the construction of the Panama Canal, the remaining continent-wide distance might prevent the fleet from being concentrated in an emergency. Consequently, questions of ship disposition assumed considerable importance.

Of course, the "commandment on concentration" clearly decreed that the fleet must never be separated. But political reality tore strategists from the straight and narrow path of rectitude. A unified fleet meant that one coast would always be left undefended. Given the growing power and aggressiveness of the German Navy in the Atlantic and the Japanese in the Pacific, that result became increasingly more unpleasant to contemplate. It was equally hard for planners to ignore the nightmarish memories of 1898 and the constant badgering of politicians like California Senator George Perkins, who "demanded that at least one-half of our battleships shall be stationed in the Pacific Ocean."[170]

In the face of such an excruciating choice, strategists chose the course of vacillation. In the summer of 1903 the consensus at the Naval War College was that the fleet should be concentrated in the Atlantic.[171] In early 1905 the board reversed field when it recommended a policy of maintaining battle fleets in both oceans as soon as twenty capital ships had been completed.[172] Still on the fence, in April 1907, the General Board simultaneously endorsed the principle of concentration and the construction of a "Two Ocean Navy."[173] In November 1909 it was announced that the rapidly expanding German High Seas Fleet had overtaken the United States and had become the second-largest navy in the world. "The natural sequel," wrote naval historian William R. Braisted, "was the Board's return a year later to its earlier opinion that battleships should remain in the Atlantic."[174] So it went. No matter how the ships were shuffled, there were never enough.

To make matters worse, naval planners were discovering Mahan's interoceanic network of bases to be something of a mixed blessing. If war came, naval outposts would have to be defended. In the case of the Philippines that meant the transportation of the battle fleet across 8,000 miles of potentially hostile Pacific Ocean to the home waters of the Japanese.[175] Indeed Japan's *Zengen Sakusen* (Operation Attrition) of the 1930s envisioned just such a campaign.[176] The natural answer was a fleet large enough to be able to suffer heavy casualties and still retain a numerical advantage. In the conclusions it drew for naval policy, the Pacific "bad trip" bore a marked similarity to the ship-shuffling routine: Both called for more battleships.

That was the key to everything. If the Navy's war plans and the strategic thinking of the General Board had only a tenuous basis in reality, it was because they sought to fulfill other criteria. The facts that the High Seas Fleet was thoroughly bottled up in the North Sea by geography and the Royal Navy, that it lacked the coal endurance to cross the Atlantic if it somehow escaped, and that Germany had no bases in the Western Hemisphere to shelter such a force if it somehow got there were all basically irrelevant.[177] Japan's inability to lay down (begin to construct) any new battleships between 1905 and 1909, the small size of its industrial base, and its chronic shortage of funds for naval construction were equally unimportant.[178] Even Congress's persistent refusal to endorse the construction of large-scale naval facilities west of Hawaii could be overlooked.[179] Admiral Dewey and the members of the General Board knew what they were doing, just as Mahan had known in his heart that all those inconsistencies and non sequiturs were irrelevant to the real meaning of seapower. Ultimately, only the size and efficiency of one's battle fleet mattered. All else could be improvised.

However, that fact could never be stated overtly. So civilian bewilderment in the face of the Navy's plans grew apace, as illustrated by the remarks of Representative John J. Fitzgerald at a Navy League banquet in 1913:

> Those who originally asserted that the Panama Canal would almost double the strength of our Navy, claim now that the Panama Canal makes a stronger navy necessary. Formerly they claimed that our isolation was our protection against foreign attack and now they claim that our isolation is our weakest point. Formerly Japan's naval standard was held up to Congress as a standard to be held in view, and now it is Germany's. . . . If you would only frankly give us the real reason why an increase in the Navy is required . . . we would soon arrive at a satisfactory conclusion.[180]

In fact the core of the Navy's reasoning had long been on record. During the first years of the General Board's existence, its advice on naval construction was restricted to annual recommendations as to the type and number of ships it felt should be laid down. However, in February 1903 Admiral Dewey broke precedent with a letter to the secretary of the Navy that would prove to be a turning point in the ill-starred career of the American capital ship:

> The General Board is of the opinion that the defense of the coasts, insular possessions, commerce and general maritime interests of the United States requires the maintenance of a fleet based upon an effective strength of 48 first-class battleships . . . [so that] for every four battleships, the fleet should be composed of 2 armored cruisers, 4 scout cruisers, 4 large sea-going torpedo boat destroyers. . . . The General Board recommends the adoption of a continued naval policy to be pursued by Congress in making appropriations, whereby the strength of the fleet shall be increased regularly at the annual rate of four first-class battleships, with vessels of other types in the proportions named, until it reaches the limits stated above.[181]

It was a frank, if otherworldly, document. The manner in which the number forty-eight had been arrived at typified the whole proposal. As ex-secretary of the Navy John D. Long recalled: "Every State, of course, desired to have its name given to a man-of-war. No state was content with anything less than the biggest battleship." There would soon be forty-eight states, so there would have to be forty-eight battleships.[182] If Congress or the presidential administration took to slicing General Board proposals for battleship construction in half and eliminating most auxiliary types, the dreams of the monster fleet survived intact in the mind of its father, patient George Dewey (see Appendix, Table A.3). To him it made perfect sense. The phantom armada with its neat mathematical relationships between capital vessels and auxiliaries was a triumph of symmetry and order, an ideal type fixed in the minds of the naval establishment by literally hundreds of years of experience.[183]

In 1910, after both Congress and the executive had amply demonstrated their unwillingness to endorse the construction of the giant fleet, "the Board reconsidered the entire question and concluded that the recommendations made in 1903 were not excessive, but moderate." Furthermore, it noted that "the great increase in the country's wealth since then" and the "phenomenal and unexpected" naval development of both Germany and Japan "make adherence to the principle on which that program was based more vital today than when that program was set forth." The proposal's lack of success was "mainly due to a failure on the part of Congress to appreciate the facts in the case." Characteristically preoccupied with past naval tribulations, the board wrote:

The Navy has never recovered from the weakened condition into which it was permitted to fall after the Civil War. . . . Before the Spanish War the Navy was on the way to attaining a sufficient strength for the position then occupied by the United States but the end of the Spanish War left the country with such vulnerable and distant possessions that the responsibilities of the Navy were tremendously increased. To meet these responsibilities the General Board framed its recommendations in 1903; and until these recommendations are carried out, the Navy will not have attained a strength which will justify the General Board in recommending any reduction from the number then recommended.[184]

No statement could have portrayed the naval point of view better. The bitter memories of the post–Civil War period clouded the whole surreal seascape. A world was revealed where foreign powers were hostile, greedy, and forever building ships; where the United States always defended its most far-flung possessions with the pride of its navy, and where battleships were the ultimate arbiter of disputes.

On 1 July 1914 the General Board again called attention to its original statement of 1903.

The basis of the fleet recommended was 48 battleships. . . . The advance of progress and the invention of new ideas . . . have changed the proportion and character of some of the lesser units. . . . But the fundamental fact that the power of a fleet is to be measured by the number and efficiency of its heavy fighting units, or battleships, has remained unchanged; and all the recommendations of the General Board have consistently followed a policy looking to the creation of a fleet founded on a battleship strength of 48.[185]

As long as the fragile fabric of peace remained intact, civilian officials could conveniently ignore such grandiose propositions. But in exactly one month Europe would be plunged into general war, and questions related to the defense of the United States would automatically assume a much greater urgency. Both Congress and the executive would weigh the recommendations of the military with a new sense of respect. Patient George Dewey would be waiting, ready to transform his Phantom Fleet into a splendid reality.

If the strategic pronouncements of the General Board were largely overlooked by civilian officials prior to the beginning of World War I, the boards advice on the military characteristics of warships was taken a great deal more seriously.[186] In fact, after the insurgents had broadened the board's jurisdiction over technical matters, its power in that sphere became almost absolute. The implications for naval architecture were noted by Naval Constructor R. D. Gatewood: "In this country the expenditures per unit ship seem not to be so potent a factor in the minds of Congress and the people as is the actual number of battleships appropriated for each year. It seems, therefore, that it is not a question of how best to spend a fixed amount of money but rather, how best to design and build a fixed number of units."[187]

It was an open invitation to approve the largest possible ships, and the members of the General Board did not turn it down. Since 1903, Dewey "had looked with much favor upon the idea of increasing the size of future battleships."[188] U.S. ships had carried larger guns and thicker protection than European vessels since the days of Joshua Humphrey's stout-sided sailing frigates, and Dewey was no man to break with tradition.[189] It was largely on this basis, and not on the minute calculations of insurgent ordnance experts, that Dewey and the naval establishment came to accept the dreadnought.

Arguing for the adoption of a particularly large gun of dubious merit, the Old Admiral would note that "in this matter, besides the material advantage we must not overlook the confidence begotten in a ship's company by the conviction that its ship is equal to the best. . . . The tendency of all navies for centuries have been toward increases in displacement and increases in weight of armament. There is no indication that this steady movement is now approaching an end."[190] Not if George Dewey could help it. In 1905 he wrote Rear Admiral Caspar F. Goodrich that "we have merchant ships of 40,000 tons displacement—Why not battleships of the same size? But I fear Congress is not educated up to that point!"[191] They would be.

The dreadnoughts approved for construction by the General Board prior to the beginning of World War I were steps on a staircase spiraling toward this goal. Beginning with the 20,000-ton *Delaware* and *North Dakota* of 1906 and 1907, the progression led steadily upward to the 21,825-ton *Utah* and *Florida* of 1909, to the 26,000-ton *Arkansas* and *Wyoming* of 1910, to the 27,000-ton *New York* and *Texas* of 1911, to the 27,500-ton *Oklahoma* and *Nevada* of 1912, to the 31,400-ton *Pennsylvania* and *Arizona* of 1913.[192]

The relentless swelling of the U.S. battleship, however, eventually aroused congressional ire. On 16 July 1912, an angry "Pitchfork Ben" Tillman submitted a resolution,

the object being to find out from authentic and reliable sources the maximum size and maximum draft, the maximum thickness of armor to make the very best battleship that the world has ever seen or ever will see. . . . Let us find out just how far we can go with any degree of safety and go there at once. Let us leave some money in the Treasury for other more necessary and useful expenditures such as good roads, controlling floods in the Mississippi, draining swamp land in the South and irrigating the arid land in the West.[193]

The sarcasm of this request was not lost on the Navy Department. On 18 July, after consulting with the General Board, Acting Secretary of the Navy Beekman Winthrop replied curtly: "There is a constant and steady evolution in the construction of battleships and considering the developments made in the past few years . . . it is absolutely impossible to state the size of the . . . best battleship the world will ever see."[194]

The senator, however, was not satisfied. He wrote Winthrop the next day that "it seems to me that you are disposed to fall in with the idea which some people have put abroad that I am joking; but you were never more mistaken in your life. . . . I want an authoritative answer from the Navy Department not later than next Saturday night, July 27."[195] On 23 July the Bureau of Construction supplied the General Board with the necessary figures, which were duly passed on to Tillman. "The limiting dimensions of the Panama Canal locks are understood to be 1000 ft. × 110 ft. × 40 ft. Assuming ships dimensions approaching as nearly to these as safety in operation would appear to justify, a vessel of seventy-four thousand tons could be constructed."[196] The Navy's reluctance became somewhat clearer. There were, after all, some restrictions on the potential size and bulk of the great armor-plated leviathans.

So the Isthmian canal—the dream of the prophet Mahan and a generation of Annapolites—would eventually become the object of naval frustration. Considerable time and effort had gone into making the waterway a reality. Before it was finished Theodore Roosevelt would instigate a comic opera revolution in Panama to obtain construction rights; Colonel William Gorgas would be lionized for wiping out yellow fever, malaria, and bubonic plague from one of the most-disease-ridden areas on earth; the nation would marvel at Colonel George W. Goethals and his Gaillard cut from which 211 million cubic yards of earth would be removed; 43,400 laborers would be employed at one time; $380 million would be spent; and ten years consumed.

But that was not enough. The canal would barely be in full operation before the General Board began complaining that its locks were too small for the warships of the future. By 1919 the largest American battleship was just 4 feet

narrower than the 110-foot width of the locks.[197] Faced with the same predicament as the Germans, whose Kiel Canal had been outgrown by the advent of
the HMS *Dreadnought*, the General Board acted predictably. With complete
disregard for political and economic reality, it recommended that the locks be
widened to 135 feet immediately or that a completely new canal be built to cover
the inevitable increase in the size of ships.[198] The recommendations were, of
course, ignored, and the canal would become a sort of strategic hymen whose
stolid imperviousness to the swelling dreadnought would frustrate Annapolites
until Pearl Harbor.

The General Board's obsession with large battleships was symptomatic of its
outlook toward technology in general. Technology was to be used for Annapolite
purposes and strictly according to a clearly defined set of cultural prerequisites.
Therefore, it was at once very ironic and extremely fitting that the insurgents
should have taken the design prerogative away from the engineers of the staff
and delivered them to the Navy's oldest and most conservatively oriented body
of officers. Of course, they had expected the General Board to become a
progressive bastion, controlled by a new breed of engineer-Annapolite. But they
had overlooked both the general drift of naval administrative tradition and the
subtle but pervasive influence of George Dewey. In retrospect, even insurgent
member Bradley Fiske had to admit that "Admiral Dewey handled the Board
with exceeding skill, keeping himself in the background and never taking part in
any discussions, but nevertheless keeping a tight rein, which all of us felt but
none of us saw."[199] Consequently the board became, among other things, a synod
dedicated to the maintenance of naval orthodoxy and the suppression of heretical
innovation.

Once the basic configuration of the all-big-gun battleship had been established, changes that went beyond increasing the size of its guns or the thickness
of its armor were resisted with considerable tenacity. Although the steam turbine
had been one of the most successful features of the original HMS *Dreadnought*
and had, at insurgent insistence, been installed on every American capital ship
since the *Delaware*, the General Board remained unconvinced of its superiority.
The turbine, which consisted of a rotor attached to a large number of blades and
a nozzle that directed steam under high pressure against those blades, operated
on a principle entirely different than that of the familiar reciprocating steam
engine. Consequently it was suspect. On 14 December 1910 the General Board,
in one of its more reactionary moments, announced that reciprocating engines
would be reintroduced on the projected battleships *Texas* and *New York*.[200] Not

Top: *"Swelling battleship and the strategic hymen."* USS Missouri *transits the Panama Canal in 1915.* Bottom: USS Idaho *passes through the canal approximately a decade later. (Both photos courtesy of the U.S. Naval Institute)*

until 1912 would Admiral Dewey recant and admit "that the reciprocating engine has about reached its upper limit of speed and performance and that the step to turbines must be taken very soon if higher speed is demanded."[201]

Speed, however, was an expendable commodity in the eyes of George Dewey and his colleagues. Atavistic memories of the ancient ship-of-the-line arose to remind them that it was big guns and stout hulls rather than fleetness that decided naval battles. In fact that was a canny assessment, and the General Board's pronouncements on naval construction retained a healthy skepticism in regard to the speedy new dreadnought battle cruisers that were all the rage in the rest of the world's navies.[202] By contrast, insurgents like Sims were captivated by a romantic illusion of a supercruiser fast enough to bring any scout to bay, cross any T, and big enough to trade punches with the mightiest dreadnoughts.[203] The battle cruiser was a sort of nautical equivalent to the sports car, expensive, trim, fast, and powerful—yet lightly built and vulnerable. Though their inventor, Admiral Sir John Fisher, referred to them proudly as "New Testament ships," George Dewey, an Old Testament holdover, sensed heresy. Consequently, the type was avoided until the massive expansion of the American capital ship program allowed their inclusion.

If the battle cruiser seemed blasphemous to the General Board, other, more original, variations on the dreadnought theme were even less welcome. A case in point was Lieutenant Commander Frank H. Schofield's torpedo dreadnought. In January 1907 Schofield (destined to become a key member of a second generation of naval iconoclasts, who would inherit the torch of reform from Sims and the original insurgents) sent a letter to the General Board suggesting it carefully consider a capital ship armed with torpedo tubes alone.[204] Given the torpedo's inherent destructiveness, the young lieutenant commander had reasoned that such a vessel might "deliver an attack . . . equivalent to that likely to result from the gun fire of many vessels of the first class."[205] Since the vessel no longer had artillery to be kept clear of waves, it could be built with an extremely low profile, making it very hard to hit. Moreover, the weight saved by removing the guns could be used to armor thoroughly those few exposed areas.

But if the ship appeared "invulnerable to gun fire," there was nothing in the promising design to protect it from destruction at the hands of the naval establishment. After conducting a half-hearted preliminary test on the tactical-game board, the president of the Naval War College predictably sent the General Board an unfavorable report on the projected vessel.[206] Dewey, in turn, wrote the secretary of the Navy recommending a "long trial on the game board." "At least," he added with characteristic kindliness, "the scheme indicates original thought and careful study on the part of Lieutenant Commander Schofield along important professional lines."[207]

After three and a half years the results of the so-called long trial were published. Not unexpectedly, they were unfavorable. Schofield exploded. He accused the Naval War College of "using inexperienced players on both sides" and, more significant, of adopting "game board conventions that did not represent the truth within what I consider to be reasonable limits. . . . Any type of vessel can be defeated on the game board if suitable conventions are adopted."[208] With a stroke, the angry officer cut through the mock empiricism of the game board ritual and exposed its contrived nature.

Perhaps smelling the opportunity for some revenge, the Bureau of Construction and Repair leaped to Schofield's aid and recommended that a torpedo battleship be included in the 1913 building program. But the General Board was adamant. "The gun is the paramount naval weapon," Dewey wrote the secretary of the Navy. "The General Board cannot recommend at the present time the construction of a large and expensive ship approximating in cost that of a modern battleship for the sole purpose of carrying a weapon which in the present state of development, is inferior to the gun . . . in velocity, range, and accuracy."[209] The line had to be held.

Of course the turbine, the battle cruiser, and even the torpedo dreadnought were relatively minor deviations from the established orthodoxy. They were safe enough to be discussed. Yet there were several really revolutionary developments maturing during the period between the Spanish-American War and the outbreak of World War I—developments destined to shatter the naval establishment's carefully wrought plans and expectations. These were all but ignored, not only by the General Board, but also by the naval establishment both in the United States and abroad. They had to be. To study them seriously would have undermined not just individual ship appropriations but the entire logic of the battleship as well as the naval establishment's accommodation with technology.

6

The Evil Below . . . and Above

I

Heresy lurked beneath the waves. Traditional naval belief was founded on a profound misperception of water, upon which all else rested. Unlike land-based cathedrals, it was the battleship's misfortune to float in a physical medium even less substantial than the body of belief that had brought it into existence. Despite all assertions to the contrary, there was simply no such thing as an unsinkable ship. But the ocean's eternal willingness to swallow leaky ships was strangely contradicted by its remarkable noncompressibility when subjected to sudden stress. This quirk of physics was the fatal flaw in the logical structure that supported the surface vessel. Because of the immense inertial resistance exerted by water, the entire force of a submerged explosion next to a ship will be drawn inward through the hull (which after all is filled with very compressible air), along the line of least resistance. Seen in this light, a battleship was, not the impregnable floating fortress perceived by Mahan's followers, but basically a bubble clad in a thin layer of steel. To compound matters, water was capable of being used as a medium of transport to great depths, making it possible to approach and attack a surface vessel from below.

All this remained irrelevant through most of the long era of sail, since the difficulties involved in underwater warfare remained safely insurmountable. The tightly wrought logic of surface warfare stood unchallenged. But with the dawn of premeditated technological innovation, it became inevitable that this matrix of possibility would be exploited and utilized. The implications for the naval establishment were shattering. The naval world had accepted the steam-armor-gun revolution largely because it fit neatly into its traditional conceptual framework. Submarine warfare, in contrast, was an utter breach of tradition. Therefore it is not surprising that the early research and development of underwater weaponry were conducted almost entirely by civilians and in several instances by real revolutionaries.

The idea of underwater attack stretches back to the late fifteenth century, but only as a concept and a forbidden one at that. Leonardo da Vinci proposed a submarine in his *Notebooks* and then decried the possibility in literally the same sentence.[1] That attitude of basic disapproval persisted between the end of the Wars of Religion and the beginning of the age of democratic revolution, according to Alex Roland, the foremost authority on the origins of underwater warfare.[2]

Yet on the water, just as on land, revolutionary fervor soon overcame the spirit of moderation. In 1775 in North America, Yale student David Bushnell vowed to destroy the British oppressor's key advantage over the rebellious colonies: seapower. But before he made the attempt, time profitably spent in the college library led him to a unique plan as to how it might be done. First, he came to understand the nature of underwater explosions, realizing that a naval mine's effectiveness depended upon its being submerged well below the surface.[3] Next, his reading apparently led him to the earlier designs of Cornelius Dribbel and Denis Papino for submersible craft.[4] Using these concepts, Bushnell set about constructing the *Turtle*, a diving-bell-like vessel, maneuvered by vertical and horizontal screws, with which he hoped to attach zero-buoyancy charges to the bottoms of British warships. Although the *Turtle*'s single mission against the sixty-four-gun HMS *Eagle* failed—largely through bad luck—the very audacity of the scheme was highly suggestive.

Twenty-five years after Bushnell completed the *Turtle*, in 1801, Robert Fulton briefly gained Napoleon's interest by constructing a four-man submarine, *Nautilus*, and a series of towed, zero-buoyancy contact mines he called torpedoes. When the emperor lost interest, Fulton went to Britain, where William Pitt encouraged him to try out the explosive devices against the French squadron at Boulogne. On the night of 2 October 1805 one of Fulton's torpedoes succeeded in destroying a pinnace and its crew of twenty-one.[5] Although the experiment was generally seen as a failure and torpedoes were quickly dropped, at least one Englishman, Earl of St. Vincent and First Lord of the Admiralty Robert Jervis grasped their significance: "Pitt was the greatest fool that ever existed, to encourage a mode of warfare which they who commanded the seas did not want, and which if succeeded, would deprive them of it."[6] Those were prescient remarks indeed.

By 1843 a mine designed by Samuel Colt, employing electric means of ignition, had successfully destroyed a vessel in motion five miles out at sea.[7] But it was not until the American Civil War that the formidable nature of the weapon became apparent. Mines were employed, particularly by the blockaded Confederacy, to protect estuaries and harbors and succeeded in sinking a total of twenty-eight vessels.[8] Although the mine's success was not repeated in the war of 1898, that was due more to the apathy of the Spaniards than to any deficiency in the weapon itself. By the beginning of the twentieth century, the quantity and quality of mines had improved to the point of making close blockade extremely dangerous.[9] Although that danger was destined to bring about major changes in the conduct of war at sea, mines remained strictly coastal weapons, most effective in geographically constricted areas, but almost worthless on the high seas. Moreover, to be useful, a mine field required the unwitting cooperation of the enemy battle fleet in venturing within the danger zone. Essentially passive weapons, mines were warheads without delivery systems. It was that shortcoming that gave rise to the true torpedo.

The year 1864 marked the conception of what battleship historian Richard Hough called "the most destructive weapon at sea until the arrival of nuclear power."[10] At this time one Captain Lupius of the Austrian Navy designed a small, self-propelled torpedo carrying a charge of gunpowder, to be detonated by a pistol in the nose, and powered either by steam or a clockwork. Hearing of Lupius's work, an Englishman named Robert Whitehead, who was at the time managing an engineering plant in Fiume, became intensely interested and took over development of the weapon.[11] The first Whitehead torpedo, constructed in 1866 with the help of Whitehead's twelve-year-old son, was a rather feeble device. Driven by compressed air, it managed a speed of six knots over a short range but was very erratic in its vertical motion—a potentially fatal shortcoming because it was likely to pass harmlessly under its target. However, Whitehead was able to correct the difficulty in 1868, with the introduction of a hydrostatic depth regulator, which added immensely to the practicality of the torpedo.[12]

In 1885 accuracy was further enhanced, with the addition of a gyroscopic rudder control, an American invention.[13] As the mechanical details of the Whitehead torpedo were worked out, its performance steadily improved. By 1900 the torpedo's maximum speed had increased to twenty-nine knots, and its effective range stretched to 800 yards.[14] But it was also clear that, unlike the gun, the torpedo's development was not at all near its technological limits.[15] Moreover, the torpedo promised to be intrinsically a more destructive weapon than the naval gun. Besides capitalizing on the noncompressibility of water, the torpedo was inherently capable of delivering a much larger payload than a comparable shell. Whereas an armor-piercing shell carried a charge amounting to no more than 5 percent of its total weight, more than 20 percent of the much larger torpedo was devoted to explosives.[16] However, because torpedoes would always be somewhat limited in range, conceptually they amounted to the last stage of a delivery system.

By nature, in order to be truly effective, torpedoes required another vehicle to transport them within range of the target. There were two possibilities.

The first was to mount the deadly mechanical fish on a small, fast auxiliary surface craft. The appearance of the so-called torpedo boat in the early 1880s created an uproar that at its height would see the navies of Germany, Austria, and Russia momentarily abandon their battleship programs.[17] But nowhere was its impact greater than in the French Navy, which had suffered for centuries from the guns of British battleships. Admiral Theophile Aube and his fellow theorists of the "Jeune Ecole" hailed the torpedo boat as the warship of the future. They reasoned that industrial Britain's increased dependence on foreign commerce and the introduction of the torpedo had tipped the scale in favor of *guerre de course*, thus rendering Britain's huge battle fleet superfluous.[18]

Aube's logic was penetrating and ultimately supported by the course of events, but in the long drought of peace that stretched over the nineteenth century, hard to prove. Amoeba-like, the ponderous weight of naval tradition reasserted itself. The thesis of Mahan's *The Influence of Sea Power* had buttressed the venerable hierarchy of ships, while the development of quick-firing secondary armament, underwater structural subdivision, and bulky torpedo nets gave at least the illusion of security to battleships. (Richard Hough noted that although such nets proved largely worthless against torpedoes, the unfurling of those defenses provided a viable substitute for sails, and the smartness with which a vessel deployed its nets upon anchoring compared in importance with the style and rapidity with which the main and top gallant had been rigged by an earlier generation of seafarers.[19])

To deal with the pesky craft in a more active manner, the British Navy began developing fighting vessels specifically designed to hunt and destroy them. After experimenting unsuccessfully with a torpedo-gunboat, in 1893 the Royal Navy concluded that a vessel capable of performing this mission must be a torpedo boat itself, only larger, faster, and better armed.[20] The useful type that resulted came to be known as "destroyers," which were universally adopted as the prime means of protecting a battle fleet from harassment. The torpedo boat, however, quickly fell in disfavor. To the mind of the conventional naval strategist, it seemed only proper that the potent torpedo armament of the destroyer should be turned to defensive purposes. Meanwhile, its offensive potential was largely ignored. So, by a neat sleight of hand, the naval establishment domesticated a potentially very dangerous weapon.

The experience of the American flotilla typified that attitude. After the perceived failure of torpedo boats in the war of 1898, they were relegated to oblivion and replaced by destroyers. The role of the destroyer, however, would be decidedly circumscribed. By 1903 destroyer commander J. V. Babcock was complaining: "In search problems we were not allowed to scout. Except when carrying a message to a ship in the rear, we were out of position when we got over 100 yards from the [battleship] *Texas.*"[21] So limited was the destroyer's mission that it occurred to L. H. Candler Keit, commander of the Atlantic flotilla, that its use as a dispatch boat might indeed be its most important duty in the eyes of the high command.[22] In 1910 Sims ruminated on this problem. "I have always assumed that the destroyer was built, i.e., to protect the battleship. . . . If the destroyer is not to be used as part of the torpedo defense, then what have we built them for? . . . I can see but two possible uses—either as a scout or as a torpedo boat."[23] The very fact that he could ask such a question was illustrative of the degree to which the whole subject had been swept under the naval carpet.

II

But, in fact, the destroyer's fate was a happy one when compared with what was in store for the second major means of delivering torpedoes: the submarine. Since at least the time of David Bushnell it should have been clear that by diving beneath the surface of the sea, a warship could potentially become both invisible and virtually invulnerable to conventional weapons.[24] Moreover, it should have been similarly apparent somewhat later that a submerged craft was a particularly good candidate for torpedo armament, since torpedoes, unlike guns, could be fired underwater. But until the late 1870s the absence of a suitable power source and the mistaken belief that a submarine must always descend and rise on an even keel had prevented experiments in that direction from becoming anything other than unworkable prototypes or death traps for their crew members. Then a young Irish Nationalist immigrant to the United States named John P. Holland began serious work on a practical submersible warship.[25]

Motivated at least in part by the dream of a weapon that would humble the British battle fleet, and financed with $60,000 of Sinn Fein money, Holland in 1881 built the *Fenian Ram*.[26] Designed to dive by planing, the vessel could "remain quite a long time submerged [at rest], probably three days; it could shoot a torpedo containing a 100 pound charge . . . probably three hundred yards over water."[27] But the craft's underwater range was severely circumscribed by the high oxygen consumption of its single Brayton petroleum engine, which was its sole means of propulsion on the surface and below.[28] Throughout the 1880s Holland struggled virtually unassisted with that and other problems associated with the perfection of the submarine, hoping all the while to obtain from the U.S. Navy a formal contract to build one.

The Navy, however, remained unimpressed by the many arguments in favor of submersible warships. Twice, in 1888 and in 1889, the department opened competition for experimental submarine designs only to terminate them without issuing a contract.[29] Finally, in March 1893, after Congress had passed an appropriation to cover the reopening of the contest, the Navy called for new designs.[30] Holland's proposal won easily and in early 1895 he was awarded a contract to build a submersible craft, which would come to be known as the *Plunger*. Holland's plan for the vessel incorporated the revolutionary idea of combining battery-powered electric motors for submerged work with a conventional steam engine for surface propulsion.[31] But the excessive heat produced by its boilers and the Navy's insistence upon three engines, triple screws, and even-keel submersion foredoomed the complicated craft to failure.[32] Nevertheless, Congress remained optimistic about the submarine's future and in June 1896 authorized the Navy to purchase two more boats, providing they passed all the performance requirements.[33]

Holland set to work with renewed energy, this time producing a planing vessel according to his own specifications. The operational success of the new boat, the *Holland VI*, was primarily due to its use of the newly developed internal-combustion engine in conjunction with electric power. The new engine was small, economical, and cool enough in operation to make serious submarining at last possible.[34] Despite the fact that the *Holland VI* had run submerged twice the distance originally demanded of the *Plunger*, the department hesitated to accept her. "What will the Navy require next," fumed the long-suffering inventor, "that my boat should climb a tree?"[35] But it was not until April 1900, after three boards of inspection had thoroughly scrutinized the craft, that the Navy consented to purchase *Holland VI.*

Yet, the Annapolites' reluctance to adopt the submarine was tempered by a confidence that it would never be anything more than a coastal defense weapon of severely limited range. In early 1896, Lieutenant Commander Kimball, one of the Navy's few ardent advocates of underwater warfare, had asked the Senate Committee on Naval Affairs to "give me six Holland submarine boats . . . and I will pledge my life to stand off the entire British squadron ten miles off Sandy Hook without any aid from a fleet."[36] But he made no mention of going any further out to sea. Although George Dewey testified before Congress in March 1900 that "with two of those in Galveston, all the navies in the world could not blockade that place,"[37] he remained mute on the subject of the submarine's role with the fleet at sea. "She will never revolutionize modern warfare, but then no vessel will do that," wrote Commander Richard Wainwright of the submarine. "But for coast defense purposes, she is of inestimable value as an addition to our Navy."[38]

The Spanish-American War would prove to be the last time surface warships could operate in relative disregard of subsurface defenses. But to the mind of most Annapolites, the prospect that underwater weaponry had rendered close blockade impracticable was not exactly catastrophic. Blockade duty was boring, arduous, and universally hated. Moreover, it was assumed that stationing a fleet very close to an adversary's coast could be sacrificed without serious consequence to the doctrine of seapower, as long as the fleet remained within striking distance. That was not necessarily the case. The glowering presence of the superior battle fleet had long been the cornerstone of traditional naval strategy. The more distant that presence became, the greater was the likelihood that the smaller fleet might escape without provoking a decisive engagement. And perhaps more to the point, surface blockaders had virtually no way of disputing the passage of vessels that passed beneath them. For submarines, surface blockade, either close or distant, was largely irrelevant. So what had once been a simple system of direct confrontation would become increasingly more cumbersome and ephemeral as time went on.

Blockade was far from the last traditional feature of naval warfare that would be gravely affected by the appearance of the torpedo-firing submarine. Whereas a gun was most accurate when shot at an approaching target (its T crossed), the reverse was true of the torpedo, which was most likely to hit an opponent broadside.[39] The implications for parallel line-ahead tactics were not promising. "When battleships are in line," explained strategist Bernard Brodie, "the space between ships is about 400 to 500 yards and the length of each ship is some 250 yards. That means that any torpedo discharged in the general direction of the enemy line from a distance within its maximum range will have about two chances out of five of making a hit. Some torpedoes run erratic courses but so long as they run at proper depth they would have to be extremely erratic to miss a battle line."[40]

Inexperienced with the ways of technology, the naval world failed to understand that the submarine-torpedo system, unlike the gun–surface ship combination, was at the beginning of its cycle of evolution. Spectacular improvements in performance could be obtained from even modest investments of time and effort. Consequently, once the major powers undertook even limited programs for submarine weapons development, it became a practical certainty that the delicately balanced theories of surface tactics would be pulled increasingly out of phase with reality. As the submarine's destructive potential grew by leaps and bounds, the technologically mature battleship could answer only with steadily more metaphysical demonstrations of its own capabilities.

Like some hidden corrosive agent, the quiet, relentless progress of underwater weaponry would eat away the battleship's very reason for being. The growing range of the torpedo would push battle lines further and further apart in a vain effort to stay beyond the reach of these deadly exploding fish so likely to hit a file of ships.[41] "If a fleet might otherwise close and reduce the range in an action to increase the effect of gun fire," a panel at the Naval War College wrote ominously in 1909, "the torpedo would prevent its closing within effective range."[42]

As much as anything, it was the extended reach of the torpedo that forced the naval world to replace the mixed armament and crude sights of the pre-dreadnought era with a few monster artillery pieces of uniform caliber able to fire a shell to the horizon, pieces trained by optical equipment whose requirements consistently exceeded the equipment's capabilities. There was more than a little irony in the effort to avoid the torpedo just when its submarine bearer was gaining access to the high seas.

Far from being tied to coastal waters, the submarine's sea-keeping ability would soon amaze even its most ardent supporters. By 1910 Lieutenant D. C. Bingham, a young student at the Naval War College, disturbed by the Navy's neglect of the submarine, was claiming that "it no longer belongs in the class of landlocked harbor vessels, in which class so many in our Navy place it, thereby retarding its development, but . . . it is a seagoing craft, able to keep the sea at all times and in all conditions of weather, and able to submerge within three minutes after sighting an enemy and thus absolutely protected and ready to deliver its attack."[43]

Bingham was correct. Previously, submarines using gasoline engines had been prone to sudden explosion and capable of traveling barely 1,000 miles without refueling. But in 1908, as the result of prior experiments, the Royal Navy launched the initial D-class submarine, the first such boat equipped with a diesel engine requiring no ignition apparatus and burning safe oil fuel.[44] Still more important, the new engine more than doubled the submarine's range, to over 4,000 miles.[45] Four years later the German Navy completed the diesel-powered U-19, with a range of 7,600 miles, one of the most effective naval weapons ever launched.[46]

The day of the interoceanic submarine had truly arrived. When war came in 1914, the submarine would wander far and wide, ready to attack any fleet unfortunate enough to venture within range. But the threat that the submarine presented to military targets was destined to prove secondary to the challenge it posed as a commerce destroyer. That potential was not at first obvious. Even the far-sighted Admiral Aube never made the connection between *guerre de course* and the submarine.[47] But when the time came, the submersible warship was ready to revolutionize the menace to ocean-borne trade and threaten to turn the traditional conception of seapower upside down.

Nevertheless, the fear and dislike that the submarine inspired among almost all members of the international naval fraternity cannot be attributed solely to its destructive potential. It was despised as much for what it symbolized as for what it might accomplish. The submarine and its torpedo armament flouted almost every value that had come to be associated with the proper and traditional conduct of war at sea. It was, in short, a snake among weapons.

The fact that underwater weapons had, quite literally, added another dimension to the heretofore flat world of the naval officer was certainly not interpreted as an unvarnished blessing. As Arthur J. Marder noted, "Many old salt horses doubtless disliked a weapon which added further complications to the means and character of naval warfare."[48] The submarine was not a predictable weapon. Unlike the carefully regulated and articulated surface fleet, the submarine by nature traveled alone or in small groups not ordinarily subject to the control of higher authority. It was the nautical counterpart of the guerrilla fighter—invisible, ubiquitous, capricious, and terrifying.

To make matters still worse, both the submarine and the torpedo operated in fundamental oblivion with respect to the naval hierarchy of ships. Because submarines sought invulnerability through stealth rather than size, they tended to be small replaceable craft not likely to impress officers used to the ponderous bulk of the battleship. But because the torpedo was self-propelled and therefore required no complicated launching devices, even the most diminutive of warships now had the ability to carry a weapon capable of sinking the largest. The entire rationale for the ships' hierarchy had been undermined. To the conventionally oriented officer, such a situation must have seemed not only potentially disastrous but also tantamount to tactical insubordination.

Even the quiet discharge of the submarine's lethal torpedoes must have seemed queer to a naval establishment accustomed to the reassuring thunder of great guns. The submarine was simply not a weapon based on confrontation, and therein lay a major reason for its unpopularity both among Annapolites and the rest of the world's naval officers. The whole manner of their attack implied skulking, treachery, and deception, qualities warriors had traditionally disdained. "It may be observed," wrote Bernard Brodie, "that torpedo attack, particularly when carried on with the submarine boat, from the very beginning ran up against the execration of the naval profession, who for the most part vehemently expressed their detestation of its ungallantry, immorality, and total contravention of the accepted laws of war."[49] "Submarines are no good." wrote Lieutenant Bingham unhappily. "This opinion is, in fact, almost universal."[50] British Admiral A. K. Wilson echoed those sentiments when he described the weapon as "underhanded, unfair, and damned un-English."[51] To Annapolite Yates Stirling, "The opinion of the Bureau of the Navy Department [toward the submarine], seemed to be expressed in the saying 'The best way to exterminate vipers is in their nests.' "[52] "To the Navy," wrote Lieutenant Commander Charles Gary, "the submarine is a 'pig-boat,' and 'pig-boats' are pariahs—useful but dangerous craft, their crews unenvied, even by the gentlemen in dungarees who lurch along the uneasy decks of the destroyer, condemned [as submariners were] to go their way in solitude."[53]

The term "pig-boat" was particularly apropos of living conditions on a submersible. In contrast to the commodious battleship, the submarine was an alien and hostile environment where the starch of naval custom quickly wilted and dress whites were soon stained with grease. After studying life aboard a submarine, U.S. Naval Constructor E. S. Land concluded that "the general conditions . . . can best be described by one word 'hoggish.' Ability to sleep better than anticipated. Ventilation better than expected. Smells of fuel oil, lubricating oil, garbage, humans exceedingly obnoxious. . . . Speaking from a physiological point of view, constipation forms a serious problem in going to sea in submarines."[54]

John Holland had complained acidly, "The Navy does not like submarines because there is no deck to strut on."[55] Indeed, the confined quarters of the submarine provided very little room for any activity at all. Even in the largest and best equipped boats, the claustrophobic quarters, the acid fumes from the batteries, the frequent changes in temperature, the extreme humidity, and the high noise level frequently undermined the health of even the most robust submariner.

To compound matters, "the mental and psychological strain of submarine service, even in peace-time, is terrible," noted Lieutenant Commander Gary. "In time of war it involves long cruises, the knowledge that one is constantly hunted like a wild animal, and that at the end, in all probability, awaits the most horrible of deaths."[56] Under the circumstances, it is not difficult to understand why most officers and men assiduously avoided submarine duty. To the world naval establishment, this unfortunate weapon combined all the advantages of a death trap with the charm of rank heresy and was for that reason systematically suppressed in favor of the more noble battleship.

The feeling against submarine weaponry was probably greatest at the hub of the naval world, in Britain. Therefore, it was not until 1904, when the iconoclastic Sir John Fisher was made First Sea Lord, that a serious development program was finally begun.[57] And in spite of the brilliant early work with the introduction of the diesel, Fisher could still claim, "not only Admirals afloat, but even politicians ashore dubbed the submarine as playthings, so the money had to be got by subterfuge."[58] The attitude of the Royal Navy toward the new weapon was epitomized by an incident that took place in the North Sea during maneuvers. A young submariner, after torpedoing the hostile flagship for the third successive time, respectfully suggested by signal that the larger vessel leave the action. "You be damned!" was the answer he received.[59]

Although not so vehement in their condemnation, the Royal Navy's three major rivals pursued a basically similar policy in regard to submarines. In the Orient the Imperial Japanese Navy built submersible prototypes but concentrated on the capital ships that had won it fame at Tsushima.

The German Navy's underwater weapons program was, in terms of technical achievements, a remarkable success, which would culminate in 1912 with the introduction of the revolutionary *U-19*. Yet the secretary of state for naval affairs and architect of German naval policy, Grand Admiral Alfred Peter von Tirpitz, was as loyal to the battleship as his Mahanite Kaiser. "The creation of sea power," he steadfastly maintained, "could only be done by the institution of a battle-fleet."[60] Consequently, from 1895 to 1914, the German Navy spent the equivalent of an uninflated $1.5 billion on a surface armada destined to meet the enemy only fleetingly, while submarines remained distinctly a secondary priority.[61] So when war came there would be just twenty fully battle-worthy U-boats ready for action.[62]

In the United States Navy, the perfection of the submersible warship proceeded haphazardly at best. Yates Stirling noted that "the Department had been inclined to give the submarine arm little consideration."[63] Some progress was made, but the attitude of the average Annapolite was one of negativism and ignorance. "When an officer advocates an extensive submarine program," wrote Ridley McLean, "he either opens himself to an unkind interpretation of his motives, or to the soundness of his views, in desiring to supplant the capital ship with the submarine building program."[64] Lieutenant Bingham, on the basis of questions such as, How far can you see under water? concluded in 1910 that "knowledge of the submarine in the service-at-large today, and I do not refer to knowledge of details, is almost nil."[65] Up to that date no formal strategic study of the submarine's uses in war had been attempted, nor was any contemplated by the U.S. Navy.[66]

The situation would not improve quickly. When the United States finally entered World War I in 1917, after three years of fighting during which the submarine had demonstrated extraordinary combat capabilities, the General Board of the Navy still had not undertaken any serious examination of the submarine's offensive or defensive qualities.[67] A year earlier, in 1916, submersibles had finally been permitted to participate in war games. But Rear Admiral A. W. Grant complained that they were grossly handicapped by rules that allowed a surface vessel to put them out of action merely by firing one blank charge. (A later test devised by Grant showed that only 2 of 1,545 shots would actually hit a conning tower–sized target set up at a reasonable distance from a battleship.)

Because the Navy's aversion to the submarine was largely a function of professional prejudice, by and large it was not reflected in the minds of legislators in Congress. There the new weapon found an interested and sympathetic audience infatuated with its destructiveness and economy. From 1902 through 1909, Congress authorized the building of twenty-seven submarines and was probably responsible for the program's continued existence.[68] Yet no amount of legislative support could counteract the general climate of apathy and hostility that surrounded the U.S. Navy's submarine-development program. Consequently, when the United States entered World War I, it was without a single submarine fully up to the technical standards of the European combatants, particularly the Germans. The attitude that had led to that state of affairs was epitomized by George Dewey's answer to a letter reminding him of his earlier praise of the submarine's potential effectiveness in 1900: "I have to state that I never said that submarines rendered the battleship obsolete. . . . Please consider this reply to your note for your own personal information, as I prefer not to be quoted on this matter in any manner."[69]

III

The naval reaction to the airplane was similar. After Wilbur and Orville Wright's initial success in December 1903, the development of the flying machine proceeded rapidly. In 1910 Glenn Curtiss flew nonstop from New York to Albany and announced that the military significance of the feat was clear. "The battles of the future will be fought in the air! Aeroplanes will decide the destiny of nations."[70] To prove his point, the New York *World* erected a wooden target in an upstate New York lake and had Curtiss bomb it. The target was shaped to resemble a battleship.[71] If that was an omen, however, the General Board did not recognize it. On 14 January 1911, Eugene B. Ely, flying a Curtiss biplane, successfully landed on the rear deck of the USS *Pennsylvania*. Taking off from the same platform, Ely then flew back to shore.[72] The ship's captain, C. F. Pond, was so impressed with the experiment that he wrote the department "desiring to place myself on record as positively assured of the importance of the aeroplane in future naval warfare."[73] He too was ignored.

Rather than look to the sky, the members of the General Board found it easier to bury their collective heads in the sand. Therefore, until almost the eve of the U.S. entry into the Great War, the board simply remained mute on the subject of aviation. Finally, on 24 June 1916 the board issued a statement, but it was not calculated to reassure air enthusiasts. "Aeronautics," the board noted, "does not offer a prospect of becoming the principal means of exercising compelling force against the enemy." Rather, it predicted that the future role of the plane would be limited to scouting and spotting the fire of heavy ships. As for bombing, the board advised the Navy that it might as well "omit heavy weight carrying types . . . since inaccuracy in aiming forbids . . . valuable service against anything but large land targets."[74]

Ignoring the unorthodox and concentrating on the development of familiar weaponry were acceptable—even preferable—as long as the naval world remained free of serious and prolonged warfare. By almost any reasonable standards, noble but ineffective weapons were more desirable than their deadlier, less ethical, counterparts. But in 1914 the world would cease being reasonable, and the major navies would have to face a deluge of violence. And in such an environment, decency, tradition, and the logic that had brought forth the modern battleship would become simply irrelevant.

7

Trial by Fire:
Battle in the North Sea

I

In 1914, for the first time in a century, Europe found itself immersed in general war. As the terrestrial conflict settled into a ghastly stalemate, the war at sea pitted the presumably incomparable British Grand Fleet against the brash challenger from across the North Sea, the German High Seas Fleet. At last the mighty dreadnoughts would prove themselves to be the formidable weapons sailors everywhere knew them to be—or so the naval world fervently believed. In fact, things were destined to be a great deal different. Reality and that silent arbiter of human affairs, technology, had finally caught up with a naval establishment totally committed to floating leviathans calculated more to inspire fear than to deal death. What ensued was unlikely to reassure those who placed much stock in people's ability to plan their futures.

As war sank its talons into August 1914, the officers of the Grand Fleet had every expectation that they soon would, as King George V had written them, "revive and renew the old glories of the Royal Navy and prove once again the sure shield of Britain and her Empire in the hour of trial."[1] In addition to a victorious tradition that stretched almost beyond recollection, the Royal Navy enjoyed a comfortable, if not extravagant, lead over Germany both in auxiliaries and in the all-important category of capital ships. Britain could match Germany's seventeen dreadnoughts and five battle cruisers with twenty-one all-big-gun battleships and nine battle cruisers of its own.[2]

Yet in the eyes of the British Admiralty, that was not enough, and temptation manifested itself in the form of two modern ships-of-the-line nearing completion at Armstrong's shipyard on the River Tyne. The dreadnoughts *Osiman* and *Rashadish* were, however, Turkish, paid for by the contributions of patriotic but impoverished peasants in hopes of boosting the sultan's fleet, which had fallen on evil days.[3] But the facts surrounding the ships' ownership were conveniently blurred by the necessity of the moment. Giving little thought to any consideration beyond those dictated by the certainty that the largest fleet must inevitably prevail, the Admiralty, in the words of Winston Churchill, "found it necessary . . . to requisition the two Turkish battleships."[4] Needless to say, the Turks were mortified. Retribution for this rather naked act of theft would come quickly and in the most appropriate possible manner, however.

Far away in the Mediterranean an apparently unrelated drama was being acted out. Although Germany had no foreign dreadnoughts to commandeer, the strategists of the Royal Navy expected that their adversaries would move quickly to concentrate the High Seas Fleet by recalling the powerful battle cruiser *Goeben* and her consort, the light cruiser *Breslau*, from Pola, in the Adriatic, and directing them to the North Sea.[5] The British, however, were in an excellent position to prevent such a union. As it happened, they had two forces in the Mediterranean capable of overpowering the modest German flotilla. The first, consisting of the fated battle cruisers *Inflexible, Indefatigable,* and the *Indomitable,* was commanded by the mediocre but charming Admiral Sir Berkley Milne (known as "Arky-Barky" to the service).[6] The second British squadron, led by the imposing Admiral Ernest Troubridge, was weaker, but none the less sufficient, being composed of the four armored cruisers *Warrior, Defense, Black Prince,* and *Duke of Edinburgh.*[7]

Presuming that *Goeben* and *Breslau* must inevitably try to break out through the Straits of Gibraltar, Milne positioned his battle cruisers to "prevent the German ships from going westward."[8] Admiral Wilhelm Souchon, the German commander, had no such plans. Instead he had received an abrupt and startling message form the High Seas Fleet's creator, Grand Admiral Tirpitz: "Alliance concluded with Turkey. *Goeben* and *Breslau* proceed immediately to Constantinople."[9] There remained in his path, however, the four British armored cruisers. Although hardly optimal fighting vessels, all were 14,000-ton ships mounting a total of twenty-two 9.2-inch guns, against which the Germans had only the *Goeben*'s ten 11-inch guns.

Nonetheless, as the two forces converged, Fawcett Wray, Troubridge's flag captain, was providing the admiral a primer on gunnery and naval reality from the perspective of an ordnance specialist. In his scheme of things, the British force was doomed. *Goeben*, using its superior speed and gun range, had only to steam around its British adversaries, picking them off one ship at a time. According to the logic that had produced the all-big-gun ship, the *Goeben* did constitute a superior force. So Troubridge, bowing to the dictates of the game board, gave up the chase. Wray told him, "Admiral, that is the bravest thing you have ever done in your life."[10] The Admiralty would not agree, and Troubridge was court-martialed for his efforts—or lack of them.[11]

As for the Germans, they swept by the British force and arrived unscathed three days later in the Dardanelles, and the *Goeben* would remain among the most fortunate and successful of dreadnoughts. Although her guns would seldom fire a shot, no other battle cruiser, however heroic, could claim to match the *Goeben*'s accomplishments. For when Souchon landed at Constantinople, he was informed by German diplomats that his flotilla had been sold to the Turkish government "as replacements for the two the British stole."[12] The *Goeben* would be renamed *Yavuz Sultan Selim*, her German officers would take to wearing fezzes, and Admiral Souchon would lead the Turkish Navy. The Turks in their gratitude would enter the war against Britain and its allies.[13] Britain's original one-sided transaction had not turned out at all well. It had gained two dreadnoughts but acquired a nationful of enemies in the process.

There could have been no better warning that this was not to be a conflict that went according to plans. Indeed, the war's convoluted beginning was just a prelude. The occurrences surrounding the *Goeben* affair were highly suggestive of the participants. As befit the venerable juggernaut of the naval world, the Royal Navy's ponderous attempts to crush the fleeing German battle cruiser were in strict accordance with the rules. The Germans, in contrast, had shown considerably more ingenuity and willingness to improvise. But they had also run away.

Both reactions were characteristic of the youngest of Europe's great navies. In odd contrast to the other members of the international naval fraternity, the German Navy could best be described as liberal, bourgeois, and technological in orientation. As the sole truly national institution in the volatile half-finished German Empire (the army remained essentially Prussian), the navy was immensely popular. Indeed, the fleet became, in the words of Jonathan Steinberg, "the spoiled child of the Kaiser and also of the Reichstag and the German bourgeoisie generally."[14] The composition of the German naval officer corps reflected this power base. With relatively few exceptions, the High Seas Fleet's flag officers were of middle-class origin and, judging by Admiral Reinhard

Scheer's refusal of a title after Jutland, proud of it.[15] After visiting a number of the ships of the Teutonic battle fleet, the crusty Admiral Sir Percy Scott "found that only a small percentage of the officers were gentlemen.[16]

Just as the spirit of the middle class pervaded the corporate personality of the German naval command, it found its tangible manifestation in the ships of the High Seas Fleet. They were solid products of a society that placed special emphasis on quality, floating exemplars of German craftsmanship and Kultur.[17] Built with a combination of careful attention to detail and a ready acceptance of new ideas, they would prove themselves rugged and durable. Unlike the mass of his profession, the sagacious Tirpitz had foreseen the destructive potential of subsurface weaponry. Consequently, he had taken special pains to ensure that the hulls of German dreadnoughts were minutely divided into watertight compartments and specially reinforced against explosive shock.[18] The British would find them very difficult to sink.

At the other end of the naval hierarchy, German U-boats in 1914 were years ahead of their time; silent, invisible bearers of the deadly torpedo, whose reliability was truly remarkable when compared to the sputtering craft that generally passed for submarines in the other major navies. Yet material excellence alone would not suffice.

Blessed with the active inventive virtues of the middle class, the officers of the Imperial German Navy were plagued with the most bourgeois of afflictions, an inferiority complex—on an institutional scale.[19] The massive steel architecture of the High Seas Fleet proved incapable of dispelling the uncertainties of this adolescent service. Even the flight of the *Goeben* was probably as much motivated by fear of the British as it was by astuteness.

The Germans never really believed that they could beat the British. Calculations were inevitably couched in negative terms, emphasizing potential losses rather than the gains that might accrue from engaging and injuring the enemy. This state of mind was nowhere more evident than in Reinhard Scheer's description of the psychological climate surrounding the Royal Navy: "The English Fleet had the advantage of looking back on a hundred years of proud tradition which must have given every man a sense of superiority based on the great deeds of the past. This could only be strengthened by the sight of their huge fleet, each unit of which in every class was supposed to represent the last word in the art of marine construction."[20] It must have seemed to the Germans that Woden himself might be required to defeat such an enemy. Such pessimism would cost them the war at sea. For the Germans' insecurity was the ultimate insurance that they would persist in fighting according to the rules dictated by the British.

But as is sometimes the case with idolaters, the Kaiser's naval officers failed to discern that the object of their adoration had feet of clay. In spite of its numerous advantages, the Royal Navy was an institution flawed at many points. Time and combat would beat through the impressive facade to reveal a system so tied to a particular set of assumptions as to be practically incapable of adjusting to reality. Not having fought in a hundred years, it had rusted from within; institutionally, its gears were frozen and its joints seized. Rigidity was the keynote and centralization the order of the day. The widespread use of the wireless had concentrated command functions to a degree undreamed of in the seventeenth and eighteenth centuries. Captain J. H. Godfrey noted that "the ideal of the one superman on the remoteness of the flagship bridge was one to which the service gave unquestioning allegiance, and was drummed in from the day a naval cadet joined his first gun room."[21] Yet in practice such a system was bound to result in what Arthur J. Marder called "an acute form of tactical arthritis."[22] Admiral Sir Percy Scott told the story of a certain captain who signaled his flagship asking permission to hang out his laundry. When the request was granted, a heated discussion ensued as to whether this was Scott's prerogative or if he should have forwarded the message by wireless to his immediate superior only ten miles out at sea.[23] It was not an isolated occurrence. Messages were flashed to the Admiralty "requesting permission to issue an extra ration of lime juice."[24] Technology had made it possible for a few men to decide virtually everything, or so it seemed.

That petrification of thought and action found its material representation in the Royal Navy's overwhelming reliance on the gun as an engine of destruction. To the officers of the British fleet, it was the decisive weapon par excellence, just as it had been for the past 450 years, and just as it would always remain. If the Germans considered mines and torpedoes matters for serious consideration, then that was simply evidence of their inexperience. Symbolic of this contempt was the HMS *Vernon*, a rotting wooden ship-of-the-line docked at Portsmouth, which served as the makeshift home of prewar British mine and torpedo development. Big guns on big ships won battles.

It was taken for granted that British ships were superior: Their guns were larger, and they were faster. Besides, British dreadnoughts were the standard by which all other warships were measured. If time would show them to be carelessly built and prone to sudden destruction, they never lost their mystique. Whatever happened, the Royal Naval officer never lost his confidence in British men and matériel.[25] The officers were supremely, if unjustifiably, sure of themselves. If their ships blew up underneath them and German submarines seemed to lurk everywhere, the British would maintain their composure. Such aplomb, as much as anything else, undid the fierce but neurotic Hun.

It was to have been a short, decisive contest in the North Sea. It was taken for granted by the British that the High Seas Fleet would quickly offer battle and be just as quickly smashed. "Oh, these things are generally over in a few months!" maintained Admiral Sir Reginald Custance.[26] On the German side, as Admiral Scheer explained, "there was only one opinion among us, from the Commander-in-Chief down to the latest recruit, about the attitude of the English Fleet. We were convinced that it would seek out and attack our fleet the minute it showed itself and wherever it was."[27] Both were expecting the other to make the first move. Yet neither side budged.

Very much aware that his capital ships were outnumbered, Kaiser Wilhelm was not anxious to provoke a climactic and potentially disastrous encounter. "The Emperor did not wish for losses of this sort," grumbled the more aggressive Admiral von Tirpitz, "the loss of ships was to be avoided, fleet sallies and any greater undertakings must be approved by his majesty in advance."[28] From the beginning the orders sent to Admiral von Ingenohl, the Kaiser's commander in chief, stressed the importance of preserving the High Seas Fleet.[29] It was better to let the aggressive British blockade them and be decimated by mine fields and torpedo boats in the shallow, restricted waters of Heligoland Bight.[30] Then when the sides were equal, the Germans might risk battle.

Although they had little regard for underwater weaponry, the British were not about to commit suicide. They had not quickly forgotten that in one day Admiral Togo had lost a third of his battleship strength to mines while blockading Port Arthur during the Russo-Japanese War.[31] Mine fields had made the traditional close blockade simply too dangerous.

Consequently, by 1911, the Royal Navy had developed a new policy of "distant blockade." The Germans would be confined to the North Sea by the British fleet poised at some northern anchorage, ready to spring into action the moment word arrived that the High Seas Fleet had sailed.[32] But it was largely forgotten that the North Sea, although small by oceanic standards, still encompassed 120,000 square miles of water in which the Germans might prove very difficult to locate. In truth, "distant blockade" was to naval strategy what the "emperor's new clothes" were to menswear. Both required faith on the part of all the participants.

The upshot was that almost nothing happened in the first few months of the war. The only surface action worth mentioning took place on 24 August in German waters off Heligoland, when Admiral Beatty and three British battle cruisers trapped and sank the light cruisers *Köln*, *Mairoz*, and *Ariadne*.[33] But rather than filling the High Seas Fleet with resolve to protect its auxiliaries in the future, the action only confirmed the German Navy's exaggerated respect for the British.[34] More than ever, the Kaiser was determined not to risk his capital ships. They were ordered not to stray beyond the Heligoland Bight and to engage the enemy only if certain of a definite superiority in numbers.[35] It was becoming abundantly clear that the Germans were not about to fight.

The sanguinary leadership of the Royal Navy oozed with frustration. In a September speech First Lord of the Admiralty Winston Churchill stridently asserted that if the High Seas Fleet did not come out, "it would be dug out like rats from a hole."[36] A month later, however, Captain Herbert Richmond found the First Lord in "low spirits . . . oppressed with the impossibility of doing anything . . . unable to strike at their fleet."[37]

A bitter mixture of frustration and helplessness permeated the service. Commodore Reginald Tyrwhitt was typical in finding some consolation in the thought that "we in the Navy are not doing much, but if the Germans won't come out, what can we do?"[38] Yet in reality the Royal Navy was hardly less cautious than its timid opponent. The battle fleet was, in the words of Winston Churchill, the "crown jewels," a force to be risked only in the most dire of emergencies.

That cautious spirit was personified in the figure of John Rushworth Jellicoe, the commander in chief of the Grand Fleet. A protégé of Fisher's and handpicked by the Admiralty for his stability and administrative ability, Jellicoe was determined "not to leave anything to chance in a Fleet action, because our Fleet was the one and only factor that was vital to the existence of the Empire."[39] The perceptive Lord Fisher later wrote, "Jellicoe had all the Nelsonic attributes except one—he is totally wanting in the great gift of Insubordination."[40] It would prove his undoing. For all Jellicoe's methodical planning, he could never dispel Churchill's fearful admonition: He was "the one man who could have lost the war in an afternoon."[41] When battle came at last, he would act correctly, but strictly according to the rules, and opportunity would slip irrevocably from his grasp.

Excessive caution was never a problem with Jellicoe's understudy, Sir David Beatty, the leader of the battle cruisers. No one could have been better suited to those swift, flamboyant craft. From the rakish angle of his cap to the trim unorthodox lines of his custom-tailored uniform, the dashing, handsome Beatty was the embodiment of naval heroics. Married to the immensely wealthy and unstable daughter of Marshall Field, Beatty was something of a tragic figure personally. Tormented by his wife's infidelities, he nevertheless remained almost as prominent at the hunt and in the posh drawing rooms of London as he was upon the bounding main.[42] But for all his wealth and savoir faire, Beatty was primarily a fighter. Never deeply involved with weapons development,[43] he had risen through the ranks on raw courage. Wounded on numerous occasions, he had been promoted to flag rank in 1910, shortly before his thirty-ninth birthday— the youngest admiral since Nelson. If any officer could bring the elusive Hun to bay, it was "Beatty of the battle cruisers."

Yet he would prove hardly more successful than the rest. After Heligoland very little happened, and by the middle of September 1914 he was beginning to worry that "the rascals will never come out but will only send out minelayers and submarines."[44] Eight more months without a general fleet action transformed his apprehensions into acute self-reproach:

> I heard rumours of terrific casualties [on the Western Front]. . . . I don't think
> . . . you will ever realize the effect these terrible happenings have upon me. It
> seems to turn everything upside down in my mind and leave only the desire to
> do something, to destroy, to inflict punishment upon the German head. And I
> feel we are so impotent, so incapable of doing anything for lack of opportunity,
> almost that we are not doing our share.[45]

Beatty need not have been so hard on himself. The stalemate upon the surface of the North Sea was the fault of no one man or group of men. Self-determination dangled helplessly in the claws of technology. It was the nature of the battleship itself that was preventing a decisive encounter. Like war clubs too heavy to wield, dreadnoughts required victims willing to remain stationary long enough to be destroyed. That was a problem when they fought each other; but to even a greater degree they would be sidestepped and ignored by a foe to whom stealth meant everything and chivalry nothing.

II

Just as mammals had skulked across the Mesozoic landscape to eat the eggs of the earth-shaking dinosaur, the untried submarine slipped practically unnoticed into the waters between England and Germany to dispute the crown of seapower with the ponderous battleships. Yet the assault from beneath the waves did not come without warning. In December 1913, Admiral Sir Percy Scott, the man whose innovations had begun the ordnance revolution that made the all-big-gun ship possible, wrote a remarkable letter to the *London Times*:

> The introduction of vessels that swim under water, had in my opinion, entirely done away with the utility of the ships that swim on top of the water . . . [just] as the motor vehicle has driven the horse from the road, so has the submarine driven the battleship from the sea. . . . The . . . function of a battleship is to attack an enemy's fleet, but there will be no fleet to attack as it will not be safe for a fleet to put to sea. . . . If we go to war with a country that is within striking distance of submarines . . . that country will at once lock up their Dreadnoughts in some safe harbor, and we shall do the same.[46]

Scott's letter was not warmly received by his brother officers. Six distinguished admirals made their disapproval known in print, while countless others dismissed it as obviously the ravings of a fool.[47]

The attitude of profound contempt for the submarine held sway among the British for about a month after the beginning of the war. But things soon began to go wrong. On 8 September 1914, word arrived that the light cruiser *Pathfinder* had been sunk by *U-21*.[48] However, *Pathfinder* was a relatively small ship, and its destruction was considered more of a fluke than a portent.

Then disaster struck. Although close blockade had been abandoned by capital ships, British cruisers were, nevertheless, regularly making their presence known in German coastal waters. On 23 September, shortly before dawn, the *Cressy*, *Hogue*, and *Aboukir* were completing a leisurely sweep of the Broad Fourteens, twenty miles northwest of the Hook of Holland, when they were sighted by the German submarine *U-9*. The three British warships, steaming at barely ten knots, without destroyer protection, remained blissfully unaware of the danger as the U-boat's young captain Otto Weddigen ordered his little craft submerged and moved to head them off.[49]

As he peered through his periscope and the slim shapes loomed larger in the half-light, he realized that they were no small game. Armored cruisers, they were old and lacking underwater subdivision, but nevertheless each displaced 12,000 tons and mounted 9.2-inch guns.[50] Determined not to miss the opportunity of a lifetime, the young submariner closed within a few hundred yards of *Aboukir* and at 6:30 A.M. fired a single torpedo. Within seconds Weddigen saw "a fountain of water, a burst of smoke, a flash of fire, and part of the cruiser rose in the air. . . . She had broken apart and sank in a few moments."[51]

While the *Aboukir* was in her death throes, her captain had signaled her two remaining consorts to come closer to pick up survivors.[52] As they approached, the unseen German executioner pumped two torpedoes into the *Hogue*. Ten minutes later she too would capsize and slip beneath the surface. Seeing this, the *Cressy*, like a terrified beast, began zigzagging wildly and firing her guns at nothing in particular. And to no avail. *U-9* surfaced and, after taking careful aim, launched two more of the deadly fish. "My crew was aiming like sharpshooters," wrote Weddigen, "and both torpedoes went to their bull's eye."[53] *Cressy's* hull split open and her boilers ruptured; it was immediately clear that the cruiser had been mortally wounded. At 7:30 A.M. she joined her sisters at the bottom of the sea. An hour had passed, and 1,459 men had died.[54] In terms of casualties, it was greater than the cost of Trafalgar, the worst wartime disaster the Royal Navy had suffered in almost three hundred years.

But it was more—far more. Deep in the collective imagination of the naval establishment a laughing voodoo priest had just slipped into the spotless chapel of naval orthodoxy. As he danced his obscene dance, he would pollute icon after icon. Naval officers would struggle desperately to beat the image back into the subconscious. But the fact remained; the naval world was staggering on the edge of the void; its proudest member confronted with a weapon for which she had no defense.[55] In some weird approximation of mortal vengeance, or perhaps just coincidence, the HMS *Dreadnought* rammed and sank Weddigen's submarine in March 1915.[56] It was merely bravado. There were not yet any counters for submersibles.

All the Royal Navy had were absurd panaceas. Picketboats armed with blacksmiths' hammers were sent out to smash periscopes in the first patrols off Portland Harbor.[57] When that scheme didn't work, the little craft were armed with large steel nets intended to catch submarines like cod or sea bass.[58] Sea gulls were trained to perch upon periscopes to make them more visible.[59] The Royal Navy even attempted to teach sea lions to search out the unwanted submerged intruders. The sea lions, however, showed little interest.

Serious efforts to deal with the problem were hampered by the fact that the Admiralty's prewar committee on the submarine threat had actually been disbanded at the outbreak of hostilities.[60] It was not until the formation of the Board on Invention and Research in July 1915 that the British Navy made a wholehearted effort to generate effective countermeasures. Progress was slow, however.

Not before June 1917 were hydrophones, the first workable acoustical detection system, and depth charges available in sufficient quantities to allow surface craft to menace submarines regularly.

Meanwhile, as American insurgent William Fullam observed, "the battleship was no longer unafraid!"[61] The days following the calamity in the Broad Fourteens brought further unpleasant discoveries that served to delineate further the true proportions of the danger. U-boats were beginning to be sighted in the upper portions of the North Sea, lying in wait for the Grand Fleet.[62] At first, it was thought that they were operating from a floating base that could be destroyed, but gradually the British came to realize that the endurance of the German submersibles had been vastly underestimated. In fact, the deadly *U-19* had a range of almost 8,000 miles and from the beginning had been capable of striking anywhere in British waters.[63]

Even the main base of the Grand Fleet at Scapa Flow, thought to be too remote to require submarine defenses, now seemed subject to attack.[64] An uneasy Jellicoe wrote Churchill at the end of September 1914: "I long for a submarine defense at Scapa; it would give such a feeling of confidence. I can't sleep half so well inside as when outside, mainly because I feel we are risking such a mass of valuable ships in a place where, if a submarine did get in, she practically has the British Dreadnought Fleet at her mercy up to the number of her torpedoes."[65]

Hoping to prevent such a catastrophe, Jellicoe, earlier in September, had ordered the Grand Fleet to leave Scapa after a "periscope" (now thought to have been a frolicking seal) had been sighted within. The wandering armada found a new home in remote Loch Ewe on the northwest coast of Scotland.[66] But the stay proved short-lived. On 7 October a submarine was reported inside the anchorage, and Jellicoe ordered his massive charges to return to Scapa. But no respite was to be found there. On 16 October, nervous lookouts thought they spotted a periscope and the track of a torpedo among the slumbering capital ships.[67] Again the fleet was hastily transferred, this time to Loch Swilly, on the north coast of Ireland, more than three hundred miles away. Top predators for almost half a millennium, battleship dwellers now felt the terrified helplessness of the preyed upon. "We are hunted about the sea and have nowhere we can rest," wrote a depressed officer on the HMS *Lion*.[68]

The stay in Loch Swilly did little to ease the fears of the Royal Navy. On 27 October, the dreadnought *Audacious*, while preparing for target practice, struck a mine thought to have been laid by a submarine.[69] After a desperate twelve-hour struggle to save the grievously wounded ship, she blew up and sank. Three months before, the indiscriminate mining by the Germans had been considered little more than a nuisance. ("It will be months before the North Sea is safe for yachting," Commodore Reginald Tyrwhitt had written complacently in August.[70]) Now one of the most modern and best protected ships in the fleet had been destroyed with ridiculous ease at absolutely no cost to the enemy.

The incident, coming on top of all his other troubles, seems to have thoroughly unnerved Jellicoe. On 30 October he wrote the Admiralty a letter with momentous implications for the future.

> Experience of German methods makes it possible to consider the manner in which they are likely to be used tactically in a fleet action. They rely to a great extent on submarines, mines, and torpedoes, and they will endeavour to make the fullest use of these. . . . If the enemy turned away from us, I should assume the intention was to lead us over mines and submarines, and decline to be drawn. This might result in failure to bring the enemy to action as soon as is expected and hoped, but with new and untried methods of warfare, new tactics must be devised.[71]

The document brought not a word of protest from the Admiralty, and the cautious commander in chief was left with the decided impression that it articulated the current policy. So, even if the High Seas Fleet could be persuaded to fight, the British no longer dared to close in for the kill.

The officers of the Grand Fleet must have been thoroughly rattled by 9 November, when they returned to their base at Scapa, still far from being secured against submarines. But they had no way of knowing that this part of their ordeal was almost over. German submarines soon desisted from actively stalking Britain's dreadnoughts. The wolves of the sea had found fatter, tamer flocks to plunder.

Eighteen months before the war began, A. Conan Doyle, the opium-smoking creator of Sherlock Holmes, had written *Danger*, a remarkable war fantasy describing a dispute between Britain and Nordland, an imaginary small European state. Lacking an adequate surface navy, the latter's king was about to submit, when he was reminded of his flotilla of eight submarines by an enterprising officer, John Sirius. "Ah, you would attack the English battleships with submarines?" inquired the worried monarch. "Sire, I would never go near an English battleship."[72]

Instead, Sirius proposed to wage a merciless campaign against merchant shipping, thus striking directly at the island kingdom's greatest weakness, an absolute dependence upon seaborne foodstuffs. The plan was put into operation and numerous transports were sunk without warning. "What do I care for the three mile limit or international law?" growled Sirius at one point.[73] England was quickly pushed to the edge of starvation and forced to accept a humiliating peace.

The story was hardly popular among the British. Despite Doyle's repeated attempts to confront leading editors and naval men with the tale, he found himself ignored.[74] It was no wonder. Doyle the civilian had made the connection between *guerre de course* and the submarine, which the naval establishment had studiously avoided.

The Germans, however, were more interested. The book was called to the attention of Admiral Tirpitz and the Naval High Command,[75] who kept it in the back of their minds through the first frustrating months of war. Submarines were used against Allied transports, but only after the crews had been warned and evacuated. International rules were observed.[76]

Then on 7 November 1914, the chief of the Naval Staff, Admiral Hugo von Pohl, proposed a change.

> As England is trying to destroy our trade it is only fair if we retaliate by . . . all possible means. Further as England completely disregards International Law in her actions, there is not the least reason why we should exercise any restraint in our conduct of the war. We can wound England most seriously by injuring her trade. By means of the U-boat we should be able to inflict the greatest injury. We must therefore make use of the weapon, and do so, moreover, in a way most suited to its peculiarities. . . . Consequently, a U-boat cannot spare the crews of steamers but must send them to the bottom with the ships. . . . The declaration of blockade is desirable in order to warn neutrals of the consequences. The gravity of the situation demands that we should free ourselves of all scruples.[77]

It was hardly a stirring manifesto. In fact the Naval Staff seemed very defensive about unleashing this cur among weapons. The tone of the document may have bothered the German chancellor, Theobald von Bethmann-Hollweg, who expressed serious doubts about both unrestricted submarine tactics and the idea of declaring a blockade against Britain. Already worried about neutral sentiments in both Europe and the United States, the chancellor was particularly concerned that such methods might drive Italy and the Balkans into the Allied camp.[78] But the submarine was the only weapon in Germany's naval panoply achieving noteworthy successes, and the pressure to use it indiscriminately grew daily as land casualties mounted. Finally, on 4 February 1915, after meeting with Tirpitz and von Pohl, Bethmann capitulated,[79] and the waters around Great Britain and Ireland were declared a war zone, where all merchant vessels, including neutrals, might be sunk without warning.[80]

The Germans only had twenty-two operational submarines at the time, and the blockade was interpreted at first as a bluff[81]—a sort of cheeky caricature of the classic British strategy. But after a hesitant first few weeks, German submarines began sinking merchant tonnage at a steadily increasing rate. By the end of April, British losses stood at thirty-nine ships displacing 105,000 tons.[82] Still that was less than 0.25 percent of Great Britain's shipping and could be dismissed as nothing more than a nuisance by an Admiralty determined not to flinch.[83]

On 7 May 1915 something happened that could not be ignored. The giant 32,000-ton luxury liner, *Lusitania*—whose continued presence on the New York–to–Liverpool run symbolized British control of the seas—was torpedoed off the coast of Ireland by *U-20*. Heavily laden with munitions, the ship blew up and sank in eighteen minutes, with the loss of 1,198 lives, including 128 Americans.[84] To many, it seemed little more than mass murder. An outraged Woodrow Wilson wrote: "The sinking of passenger ships involves principles of humanity which throw into the background any special circumstances. . . . The Government of the United States is contending for something much greater than mere rights of property or privilege of commerce. It is contending for nothing less high and sacred than the rights of humanity."[85]

But it was not merely the destruction of vessels carrying noncombatants that had offended the U.S. president: It was the manner in which it was done. "No nation, nor group of nations," he wrote to Senator William J. Stone, "has the right, while war is in progress, to alter or disregard the principles which all nations have agreed upon in mitigation of the horrors and sufferings of war."[86]

The British were quick to join the chorus of condemnation. Considering the Royal Navy's neglect of antisubmarine weaponry and persistent opposition to merchant convoys for fear of depleting the Grand Fleet's destroyer screen, there was probably little else that could be done. Nevertheless, it was surprisingly effective. The broadside of propaganda emanating from Britain during the summer of 1915 had the effect of solidifying world opinion against unrestricted submarine warfare at a time when British merchant losses climbed to 135,000 tons per month.[87] Then on 19 August the White Star liner *Arabic* was torpedoed off Ireland by *U-24*, with the loss of forty lives, including three Americans.

Wilson reacted immediately, threatening to suspend diplomatic relations with Germany unless such practices were suspended.[88]

The German response was interesting. Although it was apparent that the United States was not about to go to war, the Germans, nevertheless, conceded on every point.[89] By the end of September the submarine campaign had been virtually abandoned, and with the exception of a short two-month spate of sinkings in the spring of 1916, it would not be taken up again until February 1917. Something remarkable had happened. The Germans had deliberately relinquished a potentially decisive weapon at a critical point in the war. Furthermore, they had been motivated to do so more by moral pressure than by fear of reprisal. This conclusion becomes even more astonishing when the relatively light casualties of the submarine campaign (fewer than 13,000 throughout the course of the war[90]) are compared to the prodigious destruction of lives on the Western Front. The submarine could hardly be called a wanton killer.

Rather it was the nature of the weapon that offended. The newest member of the international naval fraternity had broken a code that transcended casualty figures or even winning or losing, and what the Germans felt must have been akin to guilt. Chief of the Naval Cabinet Admiral George von Muller referred to the submarine as a "desperate measure."[91] Admiral Scheer thought it necessary to ask whether "it really made any difference purely from a moral point of view, whether those thousands of men who drown wear naval uniforms or belong to a merchant ship bringing food and munitions to the enemy."[92] Of 1916, a year that could have been used to expand the German underwater fleet dramatically, Commander Bartenbach wrote, "One has the feeling that instead of building every possible submarine regardless of consequences we are trying to avoid having too many.[93] Even hard-bitten Admiral Tirpitz was forced to admit: "Our appearance of an uneasy conscience encouraged the English case that the campaign was immoral. By this most unwise behavior we made it more difficult and dangerous to resume the campaign. . . . It seems as if even from our own point of view we were sinning against humanity."[94] Meanwhile, the year-and-four-month suspension gave the British time to develop the antisubmarine weapons and defensive procedures that eventually defeated the climactic unrestricted campaign of 1917.[95] Similarly, the Americans, when they finally did go to war, were in much better condition to become a decisive factor along the Western Front than they would have been had they entered in 1915.

So technology had offered the crown of seapower to the officers of the German Imperial Navy. But something had stopped them on the terrifying brink of success. Perhaps it was their own institutional insecurities, or it may have been simply loyalty to the battleship and acceptance of the immorality of submarines—or possibly they had noticed a strange glow in their benefactor's eyes and the sharpness of its teeth.

III

The Germans' chronic irresolution was likewise apparent in the few surface actions that did manage to develop during the first year of the war. On 1 November 1914 Sir Christopher Cradock and his force of three old cruisers and an armed merchant steamer blundered into Vice Admiral Count Maximilian von Spee's much superior five-ship squadron off Coronel, along the coast of Chile.[96] Von Spee hesitated until the sun had set and the British ships were clearly outlined in its afterglow. Under such ideal conditions, the German flotilla, which included the powerful new armored cruisers *Scharnhorst* and *Gneisenau*—both crack gunnery ships—proceeded to blow the British out of the water. By nightfall the armored cruisers *Monmouth* and *Good Hope* were sunk and Cradock and 1,600 of his men were dead.[97]

As soon as the battle was over and the magnitude of his victory became known to him, von Spee began acting like a condemned man. When he pulled into Valparaiso to await further orders, he was greeted as a hero. Yet he remained melancholy. He declined to drink to the "damnation of the British Navy" and at one point even refused a bouquet of roses thrust into his hands by an admirer. "Keep them for my funeral," he observed grimly.[98] But if von Spee's premonitions of doom were real, he did little to avoid his fate. Instead of rounding Cape Horn as quickly as possible and attempting to break through to the High Seas Fleet before the British had a chance to react, the dispirited German dawdled along the west coast of South America until 1 December.

Meanwhile the disaster off Coronel seemed to snap the Admiralty out of its lethargy. The new First Sea Lord—none other than John Arbuthnot Fisher, brought out of retirement at age seventy-four—moved quickly to avenge his friend Cradock. At last Fisher had found a job tailor-made for his most flamboyant creation, the dreadnought battle cruiser, and he drew a noose of the giant ships around von Spee and the Germans. In the Pacific the battle cruiser *Australia* was alerted, and the *Princess Royal* was pulled out of Beatty's battle cruiser squadron and sent to the Caribbean to prevent von Spee's passage through the

Panama Canal.[99] But more important, the battle cruisers *Invincible* and *Inflexible* were hastily made ready for sea and sent to the South Atlantic, the Germans' most likely avenue of escape. Appropriately enough, the "admiralissimo" of this two-ship armada was ex-chief of the Naval Staff, Doveton Sturdee, the man who had presided over the Admiralty's dilatory efforts to reinforce Cradock and whom Fisher had called a "pedantic ass."[100]

Whatever the circumstances, Sturdee was not a man to be rushed. Instead of proceeding immediately to his temporary base in the Falkland Islands, he paused for target practice and waited off the Abrolhos Rocks to be joined by four armored cruisers (*Defense, Canarvon, Kent,* and *Cornwall*) and two light cruisers (*Glasgow* and *Bristol*). It didn't matter. His timing would be perfect. Arriving in Port Stanley at 10 A.M., Monday, 7 December, Sturdee immediately ordered his men to begin replenishing the ship's coal bunkers and cleaning her boilers. As dawn broke crystal-clear on Tuesday morning, they had almost finished.

At nearly the same moment, von Spee was steaming into view of the Falklands, intent upon shelling its wireless station, a target that the majority of his captains had told him was not worth the effort.[101] As the Germans drew near Port Stanley, the lookouts reported that not only were there warships in the harbor but that two of the vessels possessed tripod masts, an unmistakable feature of British dreadnoughts. Like George Dewey at Manila Bay sixteen years before, von Spee had the good fortune of coming upon a stationary enemy. If he had to fight a superior force, he could not have asked for better conditions.[102] But the combined reputation of the dreadnought and the Royal Navy undid the German commander, and he fled in terror to the southeast without firing a single shot.

Sturdee, in contrast, reacted to his adversary's unexpected arrival with characteristic nonchalance. "He [von Spee] came at a very convenient hour, because I had just finished dressing and was able to give orders to raise steam and go down to a good breakfast."[103] The twenty-six-knot *Invincible* and *Inflexible* were ready to leave Port Stanley at 10:00 A.M. and by 12:48 were within range of the last ships in the German line.[104] While the British armored cruisers pursued von Spee's three light cruisers, the two capital ships concentrated on the largest German units, *Scharnhorst* and *Gneisenau*. Using his edge in speed and the superior range of his guns to maximum advantage, Sturdee was able to stay clear of hostile fire while leisurely pounding his hapless opponents into rubble. Just after 4:00 P.M., the flagship *Scharnhorst*, "looking pretty sickly," as Commodore Edward Bingham described it, "rolled quietly over on one side, lay on her beam ends, and then took a headlong dive."[105] Not one of her 750 crew members, including von Spee, escaped the icy plunge. The *Gneisenau* lasted until 6:00 P.M., suffering in the process over fifty direct 12-inch hits and 600 casualties.[106] Her decks littered with dismembered corpses and burning furiously, *Gneisenau*'s Captain Maerker ordered her abandoned shortly before she sank outright.[107] But the battle-weary German sailors stood little chance in the thirty-nine-degree Fahrenheit water. As boats from the *Invincible* and *Inflexible* struggled to their rescue, albatrosses attacked viciously, fighting greedily for the human spoils of battle.

That portentous twilight scene had little effect upon the unrestrained joy of the victors. "It was an interesting fight off the Falkland Islands, a good stand-up fight," Doveton Sturdee later wrote.[108] Indeed, it was a fight tailor-made for the Ancient Mariner mentality that Sturdee epitomized. The dreadnought principle, the hierarchy of ships, and the ponderous mass of traditional belief they rested upon had all been vindicated on 8 December. "And the above accomplished under the sole direction of a Septuagenarian First Sea Lord," wrote Fisher with customary modesty, "who was thought mad for denuding the Grand Fleet of our fastest Battle Cruisers and send[ing] them 14,000 miles on a supposed wild goose chase. . . . And how I was execrated for inventing the Battle Cruiser!"[109]

Seen from another perspective, the action off the Falklands was a testimony to the fragility and artificiality of naval orthodoxy. All the postulates had worked only because the battle was an unusual one, bearing more resemblance to the miniature Armageddons of the game board than to reality at sea in 1914. The most southerly naval engagement in history (until the 1982 Falklands campaign), the battle had transpired on the rim of the Antarctic, thousands of miles from the real action of the war at sea and the submarines that were its dominant feature. It is questionable whether the British battle cruisers would have pursued von Spee's smaller ships so fearlessly had they noticed even a single periscope off Port Stanley. Indeed the Falklands battle was the last action of the war settled by gunfire alone.[110] Conditions had been perfect—unlimited visibility, calm seas, and all the time in the world. If the naval gun was ever to show its true deadliness, it would have been here. Yet ballistic performance had been unimpressive. On several occasions accumulated cordite smoke had obscured the vision of the range finders so badly that firing had to be suspended.[111] Yet even when they could see, the British spotters and gunners using the Dreyer fire-control tables had a great deal of trouble hitting their targets at the 14,000-yard range necessary to remain clear of German secondary fire. In all, 1,174 12-inch shells had been fired by the two battle cruisers, with a mere 5 percent of them finding their mark.[112]

Even more troublesome was the fact that each of the German ships had required at least fifty major caliber hits to be dispatched. They were hardly the clean, almost antiseptic kills that men like Poundstone, Cuniberti, and Fisher had imagined when they first conceived of the dreadnought. Besides, *Scharnhorst* and *Gneisenau* were only armored cruisers, a depressing thought in itself. For as 1915 began, it remained true that no dreadnought had yet been able to engage another of its kind in mortal combat. But that, at least, was destined to change shortly.

In the waning months of 1914 the High Seas Fleet had resorted to hit-and-run raids on the English coast, sending its battle cruisers to bombard Yarmouth in November and Scarborough and Hartlepool in December. Although strategically meaningless, those forays did serve the purpose of providing the German crews with something approaching combat experience, thereby building their confidence. But the incursions were very much more dangerous than the strategists of the High Seas Fleet imagined.

The raids had been a direct slap in the face of the Royal Navy, making it look as if it could not even protect its own coast, and provoking English anger as nothing else would until the sinking of the *Lusitania*. But in the case of the coastal raids, the Admiralty had the technology to match its fury. Unlike the Germans, the British naval establishment had shown an early interest in capitalizing on the newly invented radio in ways beyond simple communication. Consequently, as the war began, the British alone possessed workable radio direction finders and the means to intercept hostile wireless transmissions. The significance of this advantage increased a thousandfold when the Russians recovered a complete copy of the German codebook from the sunken cruiser *Magdeburg* and passed it on to London in late October.[113] For the remainder of the war, the British, by closely monitoring the volume of enemy radio traffic and deciphering selected messages, were able to piece together a very accurate picture of what the Germans planned to do.

It was for this reason that on 23 January 1915 the Admiralty could dispatch Beatty and his five battle cruisers (*Lion, Tiger, Princess Royal, New Zealand,* and *Indomitable*) to Dogger Bank, with the strong belief that awaiting them there would be the normally resolute but unsuspecting Rear Admiral Franz Hipper with but three ships of the same type (*Seydlitz, Moltke, and Derfflinger*) plus the large armored cruiser *Blucher*. Winston Churchill described the atmosphere of tension and romance that pervaded the Admiralty headquarters during the early hours of 24 January: "Only one thought could reign—battle at dawn! Battle for the first time in history between the mighty super-Dreadnought ships!"[114]

As Hipper steamed into view the next morning and recognized the telltale masts of the British battle cruisers, he reacted just as German commanders had since the beginning of the war—he reversed his course and ran for his life. But the snare, it seemed, had tripped perfectly. As Beatty took up the chase, he had every reason to expect a great victory. Besides a numerical advantage of five to four, his ships possessed a three-knot superiority in fleet speed and were armed with heavy guns that averaged two and one-half inches bigger than those of their adversaries.[115] On any game board worth its name, such a combination would inevitably mean the annihilation of the weaker party.

As the flagship *Lion* drew within 17,500 yards of the fleeing *Seydlitz* at the head of the German column, it seemed as if the slaughter was about to begin. A 13.5-inch British round penetrated the barbette of the unfortunate vessel's aftermost turret and ignited the charges about to be loaded. Within moments 159 human beings were roasted alive. Smoke and flames rose a hundred feet high, and the loss of the vessel was only prevented by the prompt action of an executive officer who flooded her magazines.[116]

Meanwhile the last ship in line, the slow, undersized *Blucher* (8.2-inch guns), had been battered successively as each British battle cruiser caught up with the retreating Germans. By 10:00 A.M., *Blucher* could be seen limping badly, her speed down to seventeen knots. On board the charred *Seydlitz*, a thoroughly shaken Franz Hipper felt that any attempt to support the stricken ship would "lead to heavy losses. So I turned again to SE—and left the *Blucher* to her fate."[117] There seemed, for the moment, little hope for the remaining German warships. The weather was clear, the day was young, and the Fatherland was still far away.

At that point, however, events began falling under the sway of Murphy's Law. In short succession Beatty saw first the engines, then the radio, of his flagship *Lion* knocked out by shell fire, then "personally observed the wash of a periscope . . . on our starboard bow" (there were no enemy submarines within sixty miles), and finally sent his squadron a confusing message by flag, which caused them to break off the chase.[118] As their dreams of a decisive victory vanished over the horizon with the fleeing German squadron, the British were left only *Blucher* to gnaw on.

The end of the Blucher. *(Courtesy of the U.S. National Archives)*

They made the most of the occasion, however, closing in for the kill at point-blank range. Overhead in *Zeppelin L5*, Lieutenant Commander Heinrich Mathy watched helplessly as "the four English battle cruisers fired at her together. She replied for as long as she could, until she was completely shrouded in smoke and apparently on fire."[119]

Salvo after salvo poured in and the ship's interior gradually came to resemble a landscape of hell. "All below between decks was pitchy darkness only lighted up by the bursting shells as they penetrated and massacred the crew literally by the hundreds. . . . In the engine-room a shell licked up the oil and sprayed it around in flames of blue and green, scarring its victims and blazing where it fell. Men huddled together in the dark compartments, but the shells sought them out."[120] Mercifully she rolled over and sank at 12:10 P.M. Once again death had not come easily.

But seen from British eyes, the demise of the *Blucher* had been rather more glorious—the heroic end to a great ship killed at last by something approaching its peers and not by some underwater bit of treachery. The official naval historian, Sir Julian Corbett, wrote, "As an example of discipline, courage, and fighting spirit her last hours have seldom been surpassed."[121] To add a final dash of drama, technology obligingly recorded the scene for posterity: A spectacular photograph caught the *Blucher* capsized, the remains of her crew clambering over her hull, looking like the barnacles on a diving whale. Now every British newspaper reader might share at least a portion of the excitement over morning tea.[122] The country glowed with pride. Coming on top of the Falklands campaign, what more spectacular reaffirmation of the Royal Navy could be desired?

But therein lay the problem. The theatrical conclusion of Dogger Bank obscured what had actually taken place. The main body of the enemy had escaped, and the captains of the individual British battle cruisers had shown a notable lack of initiative in not pursuing them more closely. Moreover, British gunnery had again proved ineffective. During the chase the range had seldom dropped below 12,000 yards, smoke remained a problem, and spotters had consistently confused their own salvo splashes with those from other ships.[123] Consequently, with the exception of the damage done to *Blucher* and the single pyrotechnic hit on *Seydlitz*, Beatty's gun layers had scored but five other hits all day, or 0.5 percent of total shells fired (the German figure was 2.1 percent).[124] Yet unpleasant realities were easily forgotten in the euphoria of the British victory.

Dogger Bank, however, had precisely the opposite effect upon the Germans. Undeniably, it had been a humiliating defeat for the High Seas Fleet. Its commander in chief, Admiral Ingenohl, had failed to come to the aid of the battle cruisers and was dismissed on 2 February 1915. To make matters worse, the Kaiser was furious at the loss of the *Blucher* and prohibited further forays into British waters.[125] A year passed before German capital ships would show themselves in the North Sea again. But the enforced idleness gave the officers of the land-locked fleet time to reflect on what went wrong, and one very ironic lesson about the modern battleships emerged. The artillery shells most likely to sink a dreadnought were her own. The insufficient antiflash devices between the *Seydlitz's* turret and barbette had almost allowed the flames ignited by the British shell to reach the ship's magazine and oblivion. It could have happened to any other unit in the High Seas Fleet. The Germans took immediate remedial action: The next time the Kaiser's floating champions went into action they would be relatively fireproof.[126] The British, however, had the benefit of no such warning.

IV

So both sides sank back into nautical purgatory, locked in an apparently interminable stalemate. By spring 1916, the decisive battle seemed no nearer than before and many members of the Royal Navy were on the edge of despair. A young officer aboard the dreadnought *Hercules* was typical in writing: "The deadly monotony of the work of the Grand Fleet will probably never fully be realized by any but those whose fate it was to wait day after day and week after week for the longed-for encounter with the enemy. Only that ever-present hope carried us through that dreary second winter of war."[127]

Yet forces were at work that would shortly put the fortunes of both fleets on a collision course. For one thing, there was a new commander of the High Seas Fleet. Vice Admiral Reinhard Scheer, since the beginning of the war, had been a leader among the younger officers who pressed for the German battle fleet to take the offensive.[128] Now as its chief, this aggressive and skillful officer had his opportunity. For in February 1916 pressure to resume unrestricted submarine warfare had forced Bethmann and the government to unleash the High Seas Fleet as the lesser of two evils. Limited battle fleet sorties were again possible.

Scheer's plan was ingenious, aimed at taking advantage of both the proverbial aggressiveness of the British and the technology of the Germans. Hipper's battle cruisers were to be used as decoys to lure units of the Grand Fleet (specifically Beatty's) over a U-boat trap and then into the waiting grasp of the rest of the High Seas Fleet.[129] Like the earlier German attempts at attrition, Scheer's scheme assumed it would be possible to engage part of the British fleet without drawing in the whole. (A string of zeppelins were to be stationed off the English coast to warn the High Seas Fleet in the event Jellicoe came out in force.) But beneath all its gadgetry, the plan was a naïve one, overlooking the essential fact that nothing prevented the British from trying to do the same thing.

As it happened, that was exactly what the British were planning.[130] By the spring of 1916 John Jellicoe had reluctantly come to the conclusion that the Grand Fleet had better do something valorous soon. Its destroyers were slipping away to fight submarines, and civilian politicians were showing less and less reverence for the supposedly omnipotent but increasingly stationary role of the battle fleet. Therefore, in what must have constituted a flash of daring for such a methodical man, Jellicoe decided at the end of May to draw the coy Teutonic dreadnoughts out by dangling David Beatty before them just off Jutland Banks.[131]

"Thus in the early summer of 1916," wrote Richard Hough, "caution was now going to be thrown to the winds. Inferior forces from both sides were going to be lured into traps."[132] Whatever the motives of the players, the stage was finally set for the long-awaited battle royal. The logic that had given birth to the dreadnought and had supported the naval world for more than a century since Trafalgar would at last be subjected to a test of reality. And in the heat of Armageddon that logic would fail. Moreover, the torpedo and the submarine would cast a fatal shadow over the whole proceedings. The nautical leviathans would have their thunderous showdown, but not without keeping an eye out for the tiny deadly vipers that struck from below.

On 30 May the Admiralty's radio surveillance unit, noting the large volume of German naval transmissions, managed to decipher a message from Scheer ordering the High Seas Fleet to sea on the following morning.[133] The news was instantly relayed to Beatty at Rosyth and Jellicoe at Scapa.[134] By 9:30 P.M., surrounded by legions of destroyers and eight cruisers, the six sleek sisters of the British battle cruiser squadron (*Lion, Tiger, Princess Royal, Queen Mary, New Zealand,* and *Indefatigable*), trailed by the four twenty-five-knot, 15-inch-gun superdreadnoughts of Hugh Evan-Thomas's Fifth Battle Squadron, had slipped past the cheery, glowing cottages that lined the Firth of Forth and headed into the gloom of the North Sea. By 2:00 A.M., they had been sighted by *U-32*, which, after firing two torpedoes unsuccessfully, relayed the information to Scheer.

At the same hour, 175 miles to the north, trawlers swung open the massive gates of the antisubmarine nets and the armor-plated inmates of Scapa Flow began to file out. Three divisions of eight battleships, plus the three battle cruisers of Rear Admiral Horace Hood, twenty-seven dreadnoughts in all, passed slowly in succession seaward. Thanks to the radio intercepts, Britain's armada sailed four and one-half hours before the first German units left Jade.[135] By midnight, 148 British ships and 60,000 men were steaming in neatly ordered ranks toward destiny, essentially under the command of one man—a very cautious man, John Jellicoe. It must have seemed to the members of this overcentralized little universe that every possible contingency had been taken into account.

It was a worried Reinhard Scheer who led the High Seas Fleet from the safety of its anchorage of Wilhelmshaven in the early hours of 31 May. Adverse winds had prevented the zeppelins from flying and only four U-boats were in a position where they could see the Grand Fleet leaving harbor. Only the knowledge that his submarines could not remain on station past 1 June had forced Scheer's hand.[136] As the stocky, bearded figure stood impassively on the bridge of the *Friedrich der Grosse*, the possibility that his own sixteen dreadnoughts and Hipper's five battle cruisers might somehow blunder into the massed Grand Fleet must have danced before his mind's eye like some terrifying vision.[137] Consequently, it was with extreme circumspection that the Germans moved north along the coast of Denmark—Hipper first with the battle cruisers and Scheer following sixty miles behind. By 2:00 P.M., Hipper's force had reached

Jutland Banks. To the west the light cruiser *Elbing* noticed a suspicious merchant steamer, *N.J. Fiord*, and sent two destroyers to board her.

Unbeknownst to the Germans, the British light cruiser *Galatea*, a scout for the battle cruiser squadron, had just sighted the same innocent transport.[138] As the British warship moved to investigate, one of the destroyers "was observed . . . by her stump foremast and tall mainmast to be a Hun."[139] At 2:18 P.M., *Galatea* hoisted the general flag signal: "Enemy in sight."[140] A few moments later she was exchanging shots with the *Elbing*. The battle of Jutland had begun.

David Beatty's reaction to *Galatea's* contact was instantaneous. The ever-aggressive admiral turned his battle cruisers sharply to the east, hoping to cut off the enemy. By doing this, however, he opened a ten-mile gap between himself and the four superdreadnoughts of Admiral Evan-Thomas.[141] That was not the only unfortunate consequence of Beatty's impetuous maneuver: It also put the British battle cruisers on a collision course with Franz Hipper.

At 3:30 P.M. the German admiral spotted his old nemesis and immediately reversed the course of his battle cruisers as if to flee.[142] Beatty took the bait like a hungry game fish, and by 3:45 P.M. both forces were steaming in parallel line ahead to the east-southeast, headed directly toward Scheer. Three minutes later, the range dropped to around 15,000 yards and firing began.[143] To eager German eyes, events seemed to be unfolding magnificently and according to plan. The British, of course, were equally certain that things were developing just as they intended. To an officer aboard the *New Zealand* near the rear of Beatty's line: "It was hard to believe that a battle was actually commencing: it was so like [an] exercise the way in which we and the Germans turned up on to more-or-less parallel, and waited for the range to close before letting fly at each other. It all seemed so very cold-blooded and mechanical, no chance here of seeing red, merely a case of cool scientific calculation and deliberate gunfire."[144] Or so it appeared the instant before the fantasy called dreadnought was overwhelmed by the anarchy of events.

The first surprise came from the five German battle cruisers, which more than held their own with Beatty's six heavier-gunned ships as they beat their way eastward. At about 4:00 P.M., on the bridge of the *Lion*, Lieutenant W. S. Chalmers found himself enveloped in a hail of German shell fire:

All around us huge columns of water higher than the funnels were being thrown up as the enemy shells plunged into the sea. . . . At about this time a blood-stained Sergeant of the Marines appeared on the bridge. He was hatless, his clothes were burnt, and he seemed to be somewhat dazed. I asked him what was the matter; in a tired voice he replied: 'Q turret has gone, sir. All the crew are killed.' . . . I looked over the bridge. The armored roof of Q turret had been folded back like a sardine can, thick yellow smoke was rolling up in clouds from the gaping hole and the guns were cocked up awkwardly in the air.[145]

Yet the damage had nearly been a great deal worse. Just as with *Seydlitz* at Dogger Bank, the explosion had flashed down the barbette and almost reached the magazine. Only the prompt orders to flood the area by the dying turret commander, Major F.J.W. Harvey—both his legs ripped off by fragments—had saved the ship.[146]

But unlike the Germans, the British were not to be granted time to modify their vulnerable loading mechanisms. A few minutes later, in the rear of the British line, three shells from *Von der Tann* simultaneously penetrated *Indefatigable's* upper deck and exploded deep inside the hull. Already sinking by the stern, *Indefatigable* fell out of line when the next salvo hit her near the A turret.[147] The explosion ignited powder bags in the loading chamber, which in turn sent great tongues of flame into the magazine. An officer aboard *New Zealand* reported: "There was an interval of about thirty seconds; at the end the ship blew up, commencing from forward. The explosion started with sheets of flame followed by a dense, dark smoke cloud which obscured the ship from view. All sorts of stuff was blown into the air, a fifty foot steamboat being blown up about 200 feet, apparently intact though upside down."[148] When the smoke cleared, *Indefatigable* was gone. Out of a crew of 1,017, only 2 survived the blast, spotters in the fighting tops, who had watched their ship disintegrate beneath them.

Momentarily shaken by the loss, Beatty steamed to beyond firing range and waited for Evan-Thomas and his four swift battleships to catch up. Then, fortified by a nine-to-five numerical advantage, the dashing admiral reentered the fray.

Yet adversity was not yet finished with the British. Almost immediately the third ship in the line, the new 26,000-ton battle cruiser *Queen Mary*, found herself in a 15,000-yard duel with two Germanic opponents, *Derfflinger* and *Seydlitz*. The *Queen Mary* was the champion gunnery ship of the Royal Navy, and her heavy 13.5-inch guns seemed at first to be prevailing. Around 4:20 P.M., Commander George von Hase, aboard the *Derfflinger*, was amazed to discover he could actually see the salvos "like elongated black spots" zooming toward his ship, "and I had to admit the enemy was shooting superbly."[149] But *Derfflinger* was not long in retaliating. At 4:24 she dropped a trio of 12-inch shells on *Queen*

Mary's Q turret. Two minutes later, two more of her heavy rounds landed near the same place. As an amazed von Hase watched: "First of all a vivid red flame shot up from her forepost. Then came an explosion forward which was followed by a much heavier explosion amidship. Black debris flew into the air and immediately afterwards the whole ship blew up with a terrific explosion: a gigantic cloud of smoke rose, the masts collapsed inward [and] the smoke hid everything."[150]

Twelve miles away in the midst of the holocaust was Petty Officer E. Francis, a resident of the stricken vessel's X turret.

> Everything in the ship went as quiet as a church, the floor of the turret bulged up and the guns were useless, I put my head through the hole in the roof of the turret; the after 4-inch battery was smashed out of all recognition and the ship had an awful list to port. . . . I went out through the top . . . something seemed to be urging me to get away, I must have covered nearly fifty yards when there was a big smash and the air seemed to be full of flying pieces, I heard a rush of water, which looked very much like surf breaking on a beach, and realized it was the suction or back wash from the ship which had just gone.[151]

Twelve hundred forty-eight out of a crew of 1,266 died.[152]

The British were being thrashed. The battle was scarcely an hour old, and they had already lost two capital ships and barely saved a third, while doing practically no damage to a thoroughly outnumbered enemy. It was not the sort of performance that perpetuated myths. Like some aging prizefighter, the Royal Navy had reached the point when a brilliant past could not hide present sluggishness. On the bridge of the *Lion* David Beatty turned to his flag captain and said, "There seems to be something wrong with our bloody ships today."[153]

There were, in fact, a great many things wrong with the British battle cruiser on this and any other day. Products of John Fisher's febrile imagination, they were the purest of dreadnoughts, sacrificing everything for speed and big guns. Who, after all, had needed armor in the prewar game board–land where the victors either outranged or outran their opponents? They had been billed as "invincibles." Now in the heat of combat, the British battle cruisers, with their flimsy turret and deck armor, and their flame-conducting loading mechanisms, were little more than intricately wrought bombs. And the giant British guns, for which so much else had been sacrificed, were not only shooting with their customary inaccuracy, but they were also firing inadequate armor-piercing projectiles with the exasperating habit of exploding before piercing armor, thus largely negating their destructive effect.[154] Machinery, the British were learning, had no respect for reputations.

Hipper's battle cruisers, in contrast, had been built according to less doctrinaire specifications. They were a bit slower, but they had something approaching adequate armor.[155] Their guns were smaller, but they were thoroughly tested and equipped with quick-hitting stereoscopic sights—which, while hardly optimal, were clearly better suited than the British coincidence type to the fleeting moments of combat that were to be the dreadnought's lot. The opening rounds had shown the Germans to be clearly superior on a ship-for-ship basis. Now, as they approached Scheer's battle line, the officers of Hipper's squadron must have sensed a knockout.

If they did, they were overoptimistic. For as Beatty drew near, his scouts spotted something. "We were about 1500 yards ahead of our battle cruisers and 13,000 from the enemy [Hipper]," recalled Lieutenant William Tennant on the bridge of the light cruiser *Nottingham*, "when suddenly out of the mist on the port bow a line of big ships appeared."[156] After a few moments of investigation by the scouts, the signal went out to Beatty and Jellicoe, "Have sighted enemy battlefleet bearing S.E., course N."

The battle cruisers reacted quickly and managed to reverse their course just before they came within range. But as each of Evan-Thomas's four battleships swung around the same pivotal point, it was subjected to the concentrated fire of Scheer's seven-dreadnought Third Battle Squadron.[157] Yet the Germans were unable to score another kill. Moreover, accumulated smoke was beginning to have a detrimental effect on German sight-setters, and from that point in the battle their marksmanship decreased steadily.[158] By 5 P.M. both British squadrons would be clear and leading the combined German force straight into the jaws of Jellicoe, just fifty miles to the northwest.[159] So on the verge of a Teutonic triumph, Fate had rewritten the script and reassigned the parts. In the new version of Armageddon, the High Seas Fleet found itself in a much more accustomed role—that of the victim.

Meanwhile the new protagonist, the unassuming John Jellicoe, was rapidly approaching the climactic few moments of his life, tortured by doubt. He was the absolute master of one of the clumsiest weapons in history. Too massive to cruise in line-ahead formation, the Grand Fleet moved south in six columns of four dreadnoughts apiece. Before it could fight, all twenty-four of these lumbering monsters had to be deployed in a single file, an operation that took twenty minutes under the best conditions. Should it be done prematurely, the Germans would be left with a last opportunity to maneuver and escape. But should Jellicoe hesitate beyond a certain point and be confronted by an already-deployed High Seas Fleet, while still massed in an easy-to-hit rectangle, then the results could be fatal.[160] The split-second timing necessitated by the modern battleship's unwieldiness was thoroughly compromised by another of its characteristics. Guns that fired to the horizon demanded that all last-minute maneuvering be accomplished while the enemy was still out of sight, and this, in turn, left the beleaguered Jellicoe totally dependent upon his scouts for news of Scheer's speed, course, and distance.

Accurate information, however, was destined to remain a scarce commodity on the bridge of the *Iron Duke* that critical afternoon of 31 May 1916. In the heat of combat, Jellicoe's advance units simply neglected to stay in touch, leaving him to stare helplessly into the mist trying to fathom somehow what lay beyond. Between 4:45 and 6:06 P.M., Beatty sent not a single message to his commander. Evan-Thomas, who had been within sight of the German battle fleet until 5:25, remained equally mute.[161] Meanwhile, the two armadas were converging at a combined speed of over forty knots. Moment by moment the tension must have risen to an unbearable pitch. But Jellicoe remained calm, speaking quietly, eyes always on the horizon. Then the rumble of distant heavy artillery became audible over the hum of the ship's machinery, and for a moment his composure slipped. "I wish someone would tell me who is firing, and what they are firing at," he was heard to ask no one in particular.[162]

At 6:01 he got the next best thing. Through the mist, five miles to the south, appeared Beatty's *Lion*, heavily engaged with an enemy as yet out of sight.[163] "Where is the enemy battlefleet?" a searchlight from the *Iron Duke* flashed out urgently.[164] Finally at 6:14, the *Lion*, having caught a glimpse of Scheer's line through the thickening haze, signaled back. Jellicoe's flag captain, Sir Frederick Dreyer

> was watching the steering of the ship when I heard the signalman calling Beatty's reply: "Have sighted the enemy battlefleet bearing SSW." I then heard the sharp distinctive step of the Commander-in-Chief. He looked in silence at the magnetic compass for about 20 seconds. I watched his keen, brown, weatherbeaten face wondering what he would do. He was as cool and unmoved as ever. Then he looked up and broke the silence with the order to Commander A.R.W. Woods, the Fleet Signal Officer: "Hoist equal speed pendant south east."[165]

It was done. The key move in history's greatest naval game had just been made. The Grand Fleet and all it stood for was irrevocably committed to a certain position on nature's water board. Perhaps Jellicoe felt a sense of relief; he had only to await the results.

But while their battle line was unfolding, the British scouts were destined to meet further misfortune. As the German dreadnoughts drove toward Jellicoe, they cut a swath of destruction through the English screen. Shortly after 6 P.M. Hipper's battle cruisers and Rear Admiral Behncke's Third Battle Squadron loomed out of the haze to find, just 700 yards away, four hostile armored cruisers gathered around the crippled light cruiser *Wiesbaden*. They were *Warrior*, *Defense*, *Black Prince*, and the *Duke of Edinburgh*, all original members of Ernest Troubridge's *Goeben*-avoiding First Cruiser Squadron, now commanded by Rear Admiral Sir Robert Arbuthnot. Those four careful ships had once declined the challenge of just one dreadnought at maximum range; now they were faced with twelve at nearly point-blank. "They were continually hidden by splashes," wrote an officer aboard the dreadnought *Neptune*; "they were being repeatedly hit and must have been going through hell on earth."[166] The *Defense* could be seen to be suffering the most punishment. Then, at 6:15, Lieutenant Langford Smith of the *Warspite* "saw a sight which I shall never forget. Just as we were getting abreast of *Defense* . . . a large salvo fell around her; a terrific flame shot up, and clouds of smoke; her masts and funnels seemed to part all ways, and she was gone. All you could see was a huge column of smoke, on the top of which was a black object, which looked like a gun."[167]

With the ship went Arbuthnot and all 856 of the crew.[168] The rest of the squadron did little better: *Warrior* limped away from the fight with fifteen major-caliber hits, to die the next day of her wounds. *Black Prince* withdrew, her speed reduced to twelve knots by a heavy shell, only to blunder again into the heart of the German line around midnight and be destroyed. The *Duke of Edinburgh* alone escaped serious damage.

Around the same time, on the opposite flank, the three thin-skinned dreadnoughts of Horace Hood's Third Battle Squadron (*Invincible*, *Inflexible*, and *Indomitable*) were racing to join Beatty at the end of the British line, when they suddenly encountered *Lutzow* and *Derfflinger*, the first two ships in the advancing German column. The range was a moderate 9,500 yards, the smoke and haze had momentarily cleared, and both sides began hitting almost immediately. On the bridge of *Invincible* Rear Admiral Hood was increasingly pleased with his men's marksmanship. Phoning *Invincible*'s gunnery officer, Commander H. E.

Dannreuther, in the control top, Hood congratulated him: "Your firing is very good. Keep at it as quickly as you can. Every shot is telling!"[169] These, however, were the last words Horace Hood is recorded to have uttered.

For at practically the same moment, Dannreuther's counterpart on the *Derfflinger*, George von Hase, was watching his own ship straddle *Invincible*, and *Lutzow* do the same.[170] At 6:33 a heavy shell from the German's third salvo struck *Invincible* in the Q turret. Nothing could be observed for about thirty seconds, as the tendrils of flame shot through the loading mechanism down the turret stem and probed the ship's interior. Then they found Q magazine, followed by P, and the ship became a fireball. As the deadly orange blossom bloomed amidship, about to engulf the bridge and quarterdeck, a nearby photographer captured *Invincible's* ascension. An instant later she would break in half and sink in less than 180 feet of water. As her sister ship *Indomitable* passed the scene, one of her officers "saw [her] two ends standing perpendicular above the water . . . each resting on the bottom."[171] The protruding prow and stern looked like grave markers; as well they might, since all but 6 of *Invincible's* 1,062 men were entombed in this dreadnought mausoleum.[172] Having seen the action but dimly through the thickening pall, the men of several ships in the British van had mistaken *Invincible* for a foe and cheered wildly.[173] But if these wrong-headed tars were in for a dreadful surprise, so were the Germans who were about to sail within range of practically every gun in the Grand Fleet.

The moment of truth arrived. More than sixty capital ships had been assembled for the grand finale that was to climax the Jutland extravaganza. Whether by luck or design, John Jellicoe was ready. The last British vessel joined the L-shaped line one minute before the Germans sailed into view, headed directly toward the center of the formation. Not only had the German T been crossed, but the British were positioned between the High Seas Fleet and its home base.[174] It had been a remarkable bit of orchestration by the British commander in chief, the nautical equivalent of checkmate. Had it been played upon a game board, Jellicoe's opponent might have smiled wanly and conceded defeat. This, however, was the North Sea, subject to all the imponderables of fear and confusion that dominate any environment upon which men struggle and die but that were absent from the sterile climate that had spawned the dreadnought. As John Jellicoe prepared to squash the presumably doomed Scheer, he would, for the first time, be made aware of the extent to which conventional naval theory denied reality.

As he watched the action from the *Iron Duke*, Jellicoe hardly fit the stereotype of the omniscient commander in chief. The smoke from hundreds of ships, maneuvering and firing as rapidly as possible, combined to cut visibility to below 8,000 yards.[175] Viewed through this pall, the three or four German ships that could be seen seemed little more than gray smudges, punctuated briefly by bursts of gunfire. "The whole situation was so difficult to grasp," Jellicoe would tell the First Lord of the Admiralty after the battle. "I had no real idea of what was going on, and we hardly saw anything except the flashes of guns."[176] It seemed for a time that the leading German vessels were being pounded, surrounded as they were by a veritable forest of shell splashes. But suddenly, after only nine salvos had been fired, those vessels were gone, fading back into the haze like apparitions. At first Jellicoe did nothing, thinking their disappearance was due "merely to the thickening of the mist, but after a few minutes had elapsed it became clear that there must be some other reason."[177] But how could the High Seas Fleet have turned away so quickly, without exposing each of its ships successively to a merciless British barrage? It seemed impossible; the ships had just vanished.

The answer lay with Germans. As Franz Hipper led the German column chasing the fleeing Beatty, he had a premonition of doom. Turning to *Lutzow*'s captain, he said: "Mark my words, Harder, there is something nasty brewing. It would be better not to get in too deep."[178] Unfortunately it was not customary, even among the pessimistic Germans, to convey such gloomy prognostications to one's commander in chief. Consequently, a few moments past 6:30 Reinhard Scheer got the surprise of his life. The thunder of heavy artillery built to a crescendo, and the sea erupted with shell geysers. It was then that he realized that he had been lured into a deadly trap. "The flash from the muzzles of the guns was distinctly seen through the mist and the smoke on the horizon. The entire arc stretching from north to east was a sea of fire."[179]

The worst had come to pass. It was the entire British battle fleet. Decisively outmaneuvered and outnumbered, Scheer must have felt panic begin to choke his rational processes. Yet he did not let the urge to flee overwhelm him. Instead he coolly considered his alternatives and called out for a *Gefechtskehrtwendung nach Steuerbord* (battle turn to the right), an evolution devised especially for desperate situations. Rather than marching around a common aiming point, each German dreadnought turned along an individual axis, thus reversing the course of the line in less than four minutes.[180] (The fact that the *Gefechtskehrtwendung* had occurred to none of the tacticians of the Royal Navy was itself a pointed commentary on the tunnel vision that line-ahead tactics encouraged.)

The maneuver worked perfectly, and by 6:45 the High Seas Fleet had put an additional six miles between itself and the dreaded British. But as he escaped, Reinhard Scheer's fear was apparently replaced by an equal measure of shame. Germans had run from British capital ships still another time. Gradually his endocrine balance tilted from flee to fight. He would "compel the enemy to fight a second engagement by making another determined advance. The success of the first Battleturn whilst under fire encouraged . . . [him] to try this. It would surprise the enemy, upset his plans and, if the blows fell heavily, facilitate a night escape."[181] Hector had relied on similar reasoning.

Meanwhile Fate was whispering in John Jellicoe's ear, undermining his faith in himself and his ships as he searched for the vanished Hun. First he was reminded of the underwater peril. At 6:45 David Beatty radioed to report a submarine in sight. Twelve minutes later the battleship *Marlborough* indicated that she had just been struck by either a mine or a torpedo. Then at 7:00 Vice Admiral Jerram sent a third unnerving message to Jellicoe: "There is a submarine ahead of you." One minute later, still another of the skulking craft was reported by the *Duke of Edinburgh*.[182] Had it all been part of an elaborate German trap? Was the Grand Fleet about to run into a hail of torpedoes? Such thoughts must surely have passed through the mind of the overburdened British commander in chief. (The *Marlborough's* hit had come from the crippled *Weisbaden*. There were, in fact, no submarines within fifty miles of the battle.)

Then just past 7:00 Jellicoe spied an even more unpleasant omen. The *Iron Duke* steamed past the twin spires of the broken *Invincible*. The destroyer *Badger* was standing by, picking up the few survivors. "Is the wreck one of our own ships?" asked the worried admiral. "Yes, *Invincible*," was the reply.[183] British capital ships must suddenly have seemed as vulnerable above the waterline as they were below. During those last pregnant moments before Scheer reappeared, John Jellicoe's mood could not have been described as aggressive.

Nonetheless, Fate had not deserted him. By 7:12 it was clear that the High Seas Fleet had again run into the middle of the British line and for the second time in a day found its T crossed. "The van of our fleet was shut in by a semicircle of the enemy. We were in a regular death-trap," noted von Hase on *Derfflinger*.[184] For the moment, it looked as if Scheer's unorthodox attempt at surprise would prove to be one of the more colossal blunders in naval history.[185] He promptly ordered another battle turn, but the volume of British fire spread confusion in the German line and the maneuver was botched.[186] The High Seas Fleet was on the verge of falling apart. In a desperate attempt to divert the British

barrage, Scheer ordered his battle cruisers to "Close with the enemy and ram.
. . . Fight to the death."[187] Hipper's *Lutzow*, mortally wounded with twenty
major-caliber hits, had limped off, but her four battered sisters gamely took up
the charge. ("The death ride of the battle cruisers," the Germans would later
call it.) It now seemed certain that the British at the very least would have the
satisfaction of wiping out the German battle cruiser squadron that had claimed
Indefatigable, *Queen Mary*, and *Invincible*.

As a last resort, Scheer unleashed his destroyers, ordering all flotillas to attack
the British line with torpedoes. As a group the German destroyers were peculiarly
well adapted for this task. Unlike their British counterparts, which carried larger
guns and were primarily defensive in intent, the slender Teutonic craft relied on
torpedoes and were designed to attack battleships.[188] Only Flotillas VI and IX
(twenty boats in all) were in a position to respond, but their efforts were
immediately felt.[189] Amid a deluge of secondary fire, the frail craft advanced
beyond the German battle cruisers and moved to within 7,500 yards of the
British line.[190] There, although caught in murderous cross fire, they managed to
launch thirty-one torpedoes.[191] The next move was up to the British.

Poised on the brink of a victory that would have immortalized him, John
Jellicoe spied his nemesis. The massed torpedo boat attack that he had dreaded
for so long was materializing. He was in no mood to take chances. Hadn't he
warned the Admiralty as far back as 30 October 1914 that he would not allow
the Grand Fleet to be subjected to a torpedo barrage, even if it cost him a chance
for a decisive victory? Now he would make good on his promise. Shortly after
7:20, hoping to outrun the deadly fish, Jellicoe ordered his entire line to turn
away from the enemy.[192] By the time he returned, the High Seas fleet was gone.
During the night *Lutzow* sank and the Germans lost the relatively worthless pre-
dreadnought *Pommern*. But Scheer slipped behind the Grand Fleet and made
his way up the Jade about an hour after dawn. The High Seas Fleet had escaped
virtually intact.

The great confrontation was over, and the Royal Navy had come up largely
empty-handed. The mood aboard Beatty's *Lion* as she limped back to Britain
must have summed up the feelings of the fleet. Engineer Commander Randel
wrote:

> The removal of the poor charred bodies from "Q" turret was a very sad sight.
> For the burial, the Admiral, Flag Captain, and all available officers and men
> were on the quarterdeck, the Captain reading the commital prayer. There were

two parties of bearers, and a plank . . . on which bodies were placed in turn under the Union Flag, one each side being slid off on to the sea at the same time. There were 95 poor mutilated forms in their hammocks, shotted [weighted] at the feet, including those of six officers. The band played one or two hymns and the Dead March. . . . We could see other ships similarly engaged.[193]

Earlier that morning a look of anguish had passed over David Beatty's handsome face, and he repeated to his navigator, "There is something wrong with our ships," and added, "and with our system."[194] As the battle-scarred *Lion* steamed slowly into her berth at Rosyth, dockyard workers would boo the weary ship.[195]

Inevitably, there arose a question of who had won and who had lost. Certainly in terms of pure statistics, the Germans had the advantage. They had lost but one dreadnought to the British three. They had sunk over 110,000 tons of British warships, while losing only 62,000 of their own. Six thousand ninety-seven members of the Royal Navy had died at Jutland, whereas only 2,551 Germans had been killed.[196] German capital ships had shown themselves to be superior to those of the British. Their armor was thicker, construction sounder, optical equipment superior, and their loading mechanisms did not conduct flames. Yet it had been the Germans who had run away. In that fact the British could take heart. The Germans had dared to venture forth and had been promptly chased back into port. Without doubt it was a strategic victory for the British. Yet this somehow seemed all very metaphysical to the downhearted men of the Royal Navy. "Never again would American or Japanese sailors be overawed by the powerful, even overwhelming force of British naval tradition," wrote Jutland historian Holloway H. Frost. A long era had ended.

There was, however, one party with not the slightest claim to victory—the dreadnought. No amount of rationalization could erase the fact that twenty tiny boats firing torpedoes had chased the entire British fleet off the field at a critical point in the action. The naval world was at last faced with an apparently irrefutable demonstration of the torpedo's impact. Moreover, the prophet Mahan had been right: The dreadnought was not a decisive weapon. With optical range-finding, the combination of smoke and confusion made accurate firing of the great guns, at the range that torpedoes made necessary, difficult, if not impossible. At Jutland the High Seas Fleet shot 3,597 heavy shells to achieve 120 hits, or 3.33 percent of the total. The Grand Fleet's marksmanship was worse, shooting 4,598 heavy shells to make 100 hits, or a score of 2.17 percent.[197] At that rate no two fleets equipped with optical range finders were ever likely to maintain contact long enough for decisive damage to be inflicted.

Meanwhile, the great armor-piercing shells had done a good deal less damage than expected. At long ranges the British model exploded on contact, largely negating its effect. The German shells did puncture armor up to six inches thick; but it does not appear that any such projectile, simply with its own explosive force, crippled any British capital ship. Secondary explosions caused by flashbacks, not direct shell damage, destroyed the three British battle cruisers. Indeed a cynic might have argued that a dreadnought had only to cease carrying ammunition to become invulnerable to other dreadnoughts. On a more serious note, it is probably true that if the British dreadnoughts had entered the fray with a minimum of ammunition, they might well have done better.

John Keegan[198] recently drew attention to the greater lethality of combat with dreadnoughts in comparison to fights between sailing warships—a total of nearly 9,000 dead at Jutland versus 5,600 at Trafalgar. Given the importance of the latter battle and the inconclusiveness of the former, there is much irony in this assessment. For if the dreadnought was primarily dangerous to itself, the results were no less horrible to the crews involved. As with so many weapons developments in the twentieth century, the true losers in the process were the fighting men. The modern battleship preserved the form and decorum of traditional naval warfare, but the means involved—copious high explosives, huge guns, and the general intensification of potentially lethal forces—were the same as those that turned the Western Front into a charnel house. Although the British battle fleet was the worst example, dreadnoughts in general could very quickly become death traps, prone to sudden explosions (remember the *Maine*) and the possibility of complete destruction. Whereas sailing ships-of-the-line were constructed of inherently buoyant materials and propelled by masts and sails that at worst collapsed on top of their crews, steel dreadnoughts plummeted to the bottom, dragging their crews to horrible deaths amid crushing pressure, secondary explosions, and live steam. This is a side of the modern battleship that should not be overlooked. For if the central lesson of Jutland revealed the dreadnought as a failed offensive instrument, it still remained a prodigious killer of men.

Meanwhile, the respective navies could no longer ignore the truth. The war had gone on for too long. In his final report to the Kaiser, Reinhard Scheer maintained that "it may be possible for us to inflict appreciable damage on the enemy, but there can be no doubt that even the most favorable issue of battle on the high seas will not compel England to make peace in this war. The disadvantages of our geographic position, compared with that of the Island Empire and her great material superiority, cannot be compensated for by our fleet." He then drew the inevitable conclusion that "only the resumption of unrestricted submarine warfare—even at the risk of American enmity" could bring "a victorious conclusion of the war within a measurable time."[199] It marked the official de-emphasis of the battle fleet in the German Navy. With the exception of one short-lived sortie in September 1916, the High Seas Fleet would not again move as a unit until April 1918.[200] Indeed, it would become little more than an honored relic, its best officers transferred to the submarine service, and its high command exerting increasingly more pressure on the Kaiser to unleash the undersea craft.[201] On 9 January 1917 he agreed, and the war at sea entered its ultimate phase.

The Grand Fleet was to meet a similar fate. In late October 1916, John Jellicoe advised the First Lord of the Admiralty that "the very serious and ever-increasing menace of the submarine attack on trade is by far the most pressing question at the present time."[202] That Jellicoe's new realism amounted to more than just words was quickly shown when he released a flotilla of the Grand Fleet's destroyers for antisubmarine work in the south.[203] It was to be the first of a number of such departures from Scapa Flow.[204] As its screen contracted, the Grand Fleet went less and less frequently to sea, seldom venturing south of the Orkney Islands. Quite apparently the British dreadnoughts were not anxious to seek out their quarry. The two fleets would meet only once again, in a strangely appropriate postwar ceremony, in which not a shot would be fired. Only with the coming of peace would the dreadnought's reputation begin to heal.

8

Crisis of Faith: Protecting the North Atlantic

I

The ability of the U.S. Navy to adjust to the traumatic events that transpired in Europe after August 1914 had a great deal to do with the background and technological conceptions of the Annapolites looking on. Yet that ability was also a matter of pure partisanship. The most progressive element among the line officers, the insurgents, led by Sims, Fiske, and Fullam, had never hesitated to enter into civilian politics to get what they wanted, and for a time that strategy worked brilliantly. Yet they had not experienced, or perhaps even thought about, the negative repercussions of becoming too closely associated with one side of the U.S. political process. In their own minds they were essentially interested in naval efficiency and naturally looked to those civilian politicians who were most sympathetic to their ideas. But they did not sufficiently understand that they had branded themselves in the eyes of the other side and when that side came to power, they would suffer accordingly.

So it came to pass that when the great crisis in naval warfare occurred, the group of naval officers most equipped to understand what was really happening were no longer in a dominant position. It was true that certain individuals, through sheer ability, would retain considerable influence, particularly after the United States entered World War I. But from that time, they would have to defer to less-capable, more-conservative Annapolites and a secretary of the Navy like no other they had ever encountered.

Although George Dewey's control of the General Board allowed him to exert a brake on technological development, it was still the insurgents who dominated naval politics during the Roosevelt and Taft administrations. But the election of 1912 brought a Democrat to the White House and Josephus Daniels to the Navy. No one could have been further from the traditionally pliable but dignified mold out of which most naval secretaries seemed to pop. A wily North Carolina newspaper man, Daniels reeked of the kind of showmanship that Annapolites despised. Moreover, he was a reformer and Bible Belt moralist who, as editor of the *Raleigh News and Observer*, had championed prohibition, social democracy, and—perish the thought—the pacifist William Jennings Bryan for president.[1]

As secretary, Daniels viewed the service as primarily a social institution rather than a military mechanism.[2] With precious little regard for Annapolite sensibilities, he banished alcohol from the wardroom.[3] (It was a low blow. Hard drink was the traditional companion of the sailor at sea, but Annapolites had no choice but to go along or face the inevitable charges of debauchery among the seaborne guardians of the republic.) William F. Fullam complained that "it was characteristic of Mr. Daniels that he condemned the 'aristocracy' of the Navy and set about 'democratizing,' by destroying its splendid traditions."[4] The flamboyant secretary instinctively identified with the forgotten enlisted man and devoted a great deal of energy to looking after his welfare. Ritualized obeisance to officers was reduced, and living conditions grew better. But the keynote was self-improvement. During this period the battleship would be advertised as "not merely a fighting machine, but in every sense a complete and splendidly equipped manual training school."[5]

Daniels's idealism was matched by a rare political acumen perfected during long years of service with the Democratic National Committee. He quickly discovered the latent power vested in his office and took to manipulating line officers who opposed his schemes like so many chess pieces. When the officers attempted to retaliate, they found that Daniels's excellent relations with Congress precluded any effective opposition. Among Annapolites such treatment "caused resentment, enmity, permanent resentment, permanent enmity."[6]

The feeling was certainly mutual. To Josephus Daniels the hierarchical world of the naval officer was utterly alien—an aristocratic anachronism in a democratic era.[7] As fair-minded William D. Leahy observed, "I always had the feeling that he did not like naval officers as such and has little sympathy with or understanding of their troubles."[8]

There was, however, one apparent exception to this rule. Josephus Daniels positively adored George Dewey. Upon entering office Daniels referred to the Old Admiral as the "real head of the Navy" and insisted that he preside at the secretary's first meeting with the General Board.[9] The hero of Manila Bay would, in turn, do everything possible to ingratiate himself with his civilian superior. By endorsing Daniels's abolition of the wine mess and even his proposal to replace "port" and "starboard" with "left" and "right," Dewey, sybarite and traditionalist, shamelessly feathered his bureaucratic nest and firmly established himself as the administration's principal naval adviser.

The insurgents found themselves badly outflanked. Although the new secretary inherited a staff that included Bradley Fiske in the key post of aide for operations and William Fullam as aide for inspection, Daniels found it convenient to ignore their recommendations.[10] But it was more than that. As William Fullam concluded, "He did not trust us."[11] They were not just naval officers in the eyes of politically minded Josephus Daniels: They were Republican naval officers. To make matters worse, the insurgents sought to undermine his authority by playing up to his charming and extremely ambitious assistant secretary, Franklin Delano Roosevelt.

Ultimately, this and similar maneuvers accomplished little beyond confirming Daniels's determination to maintain civilian supremacy over the military branch of the service. Moreover, he began to regard the half-finished General Staff, which the insurgents had so laboriously constructed, as a positive threat to that supremacy.

Yet the outbreak of war in Europe prevented a decisive move against the insurgents and their administrative schemes. On 17 December 1914, Bradley Fiske went before the House Naval Affairs Committee and successfully added his arguments for a General Staff to the growing controversy over American naval preparedness.[12] For the moment Daniels could do nothing but bide his time and hope his insubordinate aide for operations took enough rope to hang himself. He did just that. Early in 1915 Fiske and several insurgent underlings, including Harry S. Knapp and Dudley Knox, met with Congressman Richmond P. Hobson, the hero of the ill-fated attempt to block Santiago harbor with the collier *Merrimac*, to plan legislation for a fifteen-member General Staff headed by a chief of Naval Operations.[13] Hobson immediately introduced the bill, and on 6 January it was unanimously approved by the House Naval Affairs Committee.[14] A full-fledged General Staff at last appeared within reach of the insurgents. But at that point the rope snapped taut.

Daniels sprang into action. He nominally supported the measure but insisted that the Senate Naval Affairs Committee amend it to omit the fifteen assistants to the chief of Naval Operations.[15] This act of emasculation served to soothe whatever congressional misgivings still remained, and the bill was quickly passed into law. Now, instead of serving insurgents' purposes, the new office would provide the crafty secretary with a perfect pretext to eliminate their influence. Instead of opinionated Bradley Fiske, William S. Benson, a handsome Georgian of modest reputation and decidedly conservative viewpoint, became the first chief of naval operations.[16] Moreover, Daniels took steps to restore the original relationship between the Navy's civilian head and the bureaus.[17]

With shocking suddenness the insurgents found themselves vanquished. Thoroughly outmaneuvered by Daniels, they were left isolated and removed from the centers of power within the department. From that point they would view U.S. naval policy with the critical eyes of outsiders. Such a stance was not without its compensations, for they would be virtually the only members of the American Navy with the emotional and intellectual freedom to evaluate objectively the performance of the Great War's two main protagonists, the dreadnought and the submarine.

Meanwhile, George Dewey, always a man to know which way the political wind was blowing, rallied to the cause of the secretary. When Fiske's public charges of naval unpreparedness weakened Daniels's position, it was the Admiral of the Navy who provided a refutation. Although aware of the insurgents' intrigues with Hobson, he remained aloof from the scheme. "It has been my opinion for many years," he wrote the secretary in 1915, "that we have in the General Board a better General Staff than the Army."[18] Such loyalty did not go long unrewarded. When, in July 1915, the Wilson administration finally succumbed to the cries of the preparedness advocates, it was to Dewey and his General Board that they looked for advice on naval expansion. The Old Admiral, of course, had never forgotten his Phantom Fleet.

II

Meanwhile, as Annapolites observed the catastrophic events across the Atlantic, they reacted in a predictable manner. During the first days of August 1914 the Navy had been alive with expectation. "The Germans have declared war against England!" wrote Albert Gleaves in his diary. "The great fleet fight will come off within 48 hours, perhaps 24."[19] The General Board had written Secretary Daniels, "earnestly urging that the battleships be brought home and put in perfect readiness."[20] It must have seemed to many that they might be needed at a moment's notice.

But then nothing happened. The days stretched into weeks and the weeks into months, and still the great battle fleets had not fired so much as a shot at each other. Events were making a mockery out of the whole intricate structure of conventional naval strategy. But continued belief in the battleship was an item of faith among Annapolites. When faced with the choice between conviction and actuality, they turned their backs on the real. "The fact of the matter was," wrote Sims's protégé, Lieutenant Tracy B. Kittredge, after the war, "that our naval policy from 1914 to 1917 had ignored altogether the war in Europe, and the Navy had continued the ordinary routine of pre-war years."[21] The battle fleet maneuvered together, regularly shot at targets, and made themselves ready for an action that would never come.

In all of this, they were guided by War Plan BLACK, the latest (completed in the summer of 1913) and best known of a series of documents that foresaw the United States Navy meeting and defeating a European battle fleet in the Caribbean.[22] Apparently, what had been good enough for Admiral Cervera was still good enough for the Germans. It is certainly true that Wilson and Josephus Daniels actively discouraged war planning as incompatible with American neutrality.[23] Yet it also apparent that mainstream Annapolites took the opportunity to avoid thinking too deeply about what was really happening.

It was as if the Navy had fallen into a two-and-a-half-year state of suspended animation. Remembering his experience at the War College, Admiral William V. Pratt wrote, "Europe had for two years been plunged into what we now call the World War. Yet in this Academy of War, everything was quiet. We studied the battles of the Wilderness, and even researched the Mexican campaign, but not one phase of what transpired in Europe injected itself in our work here."[24] The submarine might as well not have fired a torpedo. Only the U.S. entry into the war in the spring of 1917 would snap the spell.

There were some dissenters, of course. By December 1914, the aging prophet Mahan had seen enough to know his time had passed and died quietly. Then there were the insurgents. As political outsiders, they naturally took on the role of iconoclasts. In the fall of 1914 Bradley Fiske, whose relations with Secretary Daniels were rapidly deteriorating, began making increasingly critical statements about the Navy. He claimed that not only was the service understaffed but also its fighting efficiency had dwindled to an alarming degree under the Democratic administration.[25] Such statements could not help but feed the fires of the growing preparedness controversy, a dispute that would soon introduce peaceful Woodrow Wilson to the subtle virtues of the dreadnought.

Sims remained aloof from the quarrel. He was preoccupied with his own conversion experience. In early 1913, he had left the realm of the battleship and had taken command of the destroyer flotilla. After a few weeks on the job, Sims began to notice what he considered to be a curious lack of purpose in his modest armada. His suspicions were confirmed when he asked each of his commanding officers for a written explanation of the flotilla's mission. Besides a vague notion of protecting the battleships, few could find any reason whatever for the destroyers' existence.[26] It was not the sort of subject that they had previously been encouraged to think deeply about. But Sims was different. For him, naval convention counted for little in comparison to naval efficiency. Now that they were his, he would forge the destroyers into an effective force, regardless of the consequences.

As usual, his enthusiasm proved contagious. Soon his young lieutenants were spending their nights talking tactics and their days in formation swooping down on imaginary lines of unsuspecting dreadnoughts. His chief of staff, William V. Pratt, remembered "the era of Sims in the Flotilla as so interesting because it marked the turning point of the destroyer from an individual capable of inflicting damage upon a major craft by its torpedoes (effective but limited in its scope of action), to a coherent body capable of inflicting much damage en masse upon a fleet."[27]

Sims's success became apparent in early 1915 when he was first allowed to conduct a series of nocturnal mock assaults on the battle fleet.

In the first attack all of the screening vessels had their search lights on, covering all the space between the individual ships. The idea was that no destroyers could get through the rays of the search light without being discovered. It turned out to be nearly a total failure as the destroyers got through and delivered a successful attack. On the following night, the experiment was tried again with all the ships of the main body and screen darkened. . . . The attack was nearly as successful as on the preceding night. . . . Of course, the battleship people would not believe we did as successful work as we claimed. They more than implied that we fired many red stars [a surrogate for real torpedoes] when we were outside of torpedo range. I therefore suggested to the Commander-in-Chief that he allow the attack to be repeated, and authorize the vessels . . . to fire actual torpedoes with collapsible heads. This experiment was carried out . . . [and] out of 18 torpedoes fired, 11 sure hits were made, probably 13.[28]

The incident left Frank Fletcher, the commander in chief in question, profoundly embarrassed. He accused Sims of blatantly disregarding the rules of the problem, wrote him an unfavorable fitness report, and asked Secretary Daniels to remove him from his command.[29] Daniels, who respected Sims's competence, if not his politics, refused to do any such thing and the matter was dropped.[30]

The experience would not quickly fade from Sims's mind. Since the beginning of the war, he had become increasingly aware of the rigidity of the average naval officer's conceptual framework. In November 1914, Sims had written fellow dissenter Percy Scott that "victory will be won by the side which springs the most successful surprises on the other."[31] Now, as he observed the conflict, that seemed to be precisely what was happening. But he was perplexed by his colleagues' refusal to admit the truth. Like most Annapolites, Sims still believed in the battleship, but he was beginning to have his doubts.

Scott's letters from Britain did not serve to reassure him. "Submarines are doing pretty well what I foretold," wrote the crusty little Englishman, "and the battleships are doing nothing as I foretold. Why this war goes on for another day I cannot understand."[32] As the conflict lingered, Sims's concern deepened.

In an effort to broaden his outlook, he began corresponding with Lieutenant J. O. Fisher, a young but very clear-headed submariner. To his youthful confidant, Sims frankly admitted worrying about undersea craft, but he still maintained that "the British have control of the sea now to a greater extent than they have ever before exercised it in their history. . . . By the potential power of their battleship fleet, they now 'contain' the German battlefleet."[33]

Fisher had been observing the war from the perspective of a submariner and had little patience with the viewpoint that Sims expressed. He presented Sims with a decidedly blasphemous alternative.

At the present time the submarine is the only active agent in disputing the control of the sea by the English Fleet. . . . In my humble opinion, both battle fleets are passive, not from choice, but because control of the sea can more successfully be disputed with the submarine, using numerous yachts, trawlers and other surface craft. . . . In fact, fleet actions, I believe, are about to be eliminated. . . . Commerce destroying, the control of communications at sea, is the primary object of naval warfare. In the past the opportunity to make naval war along these logical lines has rested with the heaviest gun power. Control of the sea was disputed first by heavier guns, then larger ships, then heavier armor, then more speed, then more ships, which was an entirely logical growth. The gun, the ship and the fleet disputed the control by the gun, the ship and the fleet. Like opposed like. This control is now opposed by the submarine which can accomplish the same result, destruction and deprivation of resources, without using the methods used by the gun, a pitched battle between similar units. . . . The submarine will be the offensive agent in naval warfare, and its antidote is a comparatively light draught, small displacement, submarine destroyer.[34]

The effect of the young lieutenant's tutorial on Sims has not been recorded, but it can be assumed that it did little to settle his mind. As time went on, he would see with increasing clarity that the danger posed by the submarine must ultimately prove the decisive factor in the "Great War at Sea." Fortunately when the American Navy entered the conflict in 1917, it was Sims who would be chosen to direct the campaign.

Meanwhile, the rest of the service continued to interpret the submarine from the perspective of the hierarchy of ships. The war had forced the Navy to admit the submarine's existence, but not a great deal more. Since all the rules reassured Annapolites that those skulking craft could be no real threat to the battle fleet, active defensive measures against them were neglected. Instead, the service concentrated on coping, putting the submarine in its proper place. And the evidence indicates that this effort, not the development of an effective underwater warship, was the object of the Navy's submarine program.

No attempt was made to duplicate the ocean-going 800-ton U-boat that had raised havoc with Allied commerce.[35] Instead the General Board and the Navy confined their efforts to the construction of two much less useful types: one very small and one very large. The diminutive coastal defense submarine dominated the program. Indeed, every military submarine laid down in the United States between 1907 and 1916 (classes B to L) displaced between 350 and 480 tons.[36] That is suggestive. The limited range of the small submarine automatically precluded the possibility of its stalking an ocean-going battle fleet. Nonetheless, the General Board stuck tenaciously to the type, despite numerous warnings that it was relatively worthless.[37] By 1915 even the conservative head of the submarine service, Captain A. W. Grant, and the commander in chief of the Atlantic Fleet, Frank Friday Fletcher, were urging the construction of a long-range 800-ton boat.[38] But Dewey would not budge.

His only concession to the advocates of larger submersibles was the ill-starred fleet submarine. It was to be, as he explained to Secretary Daniels in 1914, "a submarine of an enlarged type with habitability, radius and speed sufficient to enable it to accompany the fleet and act with it tactically, both on offense and defense."[39] Such a submarine would not be free to wander the high seas; it would remain firmly within the chain of command, taking its rightful place in the hierarchy of ships. The insubordinate submarine was to be worked into the system.

What emerged at last in 1925, the year the V-class fleet submarines were finally completed, was a sickly hybrid. Slow to submerge and hard to maneuver, they quickly proved themselves to be operational failures. Like so much in the world of the Annapolites, the fleet submarine served its purpose better as an idea than as a reality. With such a development program it was inevitable that when the United States entered the war in April 1917, the Navy would not have "a single submarine fit for war service."[40]

There would be no similar shortage of battleships. George Dewey would see to that. As the aging Admiral of the Navy sniffed the political climate in late 1914 and early 1915, he must have sensed prosperous times ahead for himself and the Navy. Indeed the seventy-seven-year-old hero of Manila Bay was on the verge of his greatest triumph. The fleet of his dreams was about to materialize.

For world events were closing in on Woodrow Wilson. A scholarly, peace-loving man, he had hoped to dedicate his administration to domestic reform. But it was not to be. Whereas bellicose Theodore Roosevelt had steered a relatively pacific course as president, Wilson would be drawn into international quarrel after international quarrel. There had been the ill-fated intervention into Mexican politics—an episode destined to end ludicrously with General John Pershing in fierce but fruitless pursuit of Pancho Villa. Meanwhile, Europe had erupted with frightening suddenness in August 1914. Wilson was determined to remain clear of the maelstrom. Before the month was out, he officially proclaimed U.S. neutrality and urged Americans to be "impartial in thought as well as action."[41] But then in numbing succession came the German proclamation of the war zone, the sinking of the *Falaba* with the loss of the first American life to the submarine, and then the dramatic end of the *Lusitania*. In June, neutrality received another symbolic blow when pacifist William Jennings Bryan resigned as secretary of state, unable to stomach Wilson's strong note of protest over the *Lusitania*.

Wilson's problems with his cabinet did not end there. The increasingly strident preparedness movement—intent on putting the United States, if not on a wartime footing, then at least in some condition to fight—had focused its attention upon Bryan's friend and admirer, Josephus Daniels. He was an obvious target. Although the secretary proved himself to be a wise judge of men and an excellent administrator, he knew next to nothing about weapons and naval warfare.[42] By his astute maneuvering, Daniels had gotten control of the Navy Department, but he had also inadvertently purged the officers on the forefront of the weapons revolution and surrounded himself instead with technological conservatives like Chief of Naval Operations William S. Benson, the members of the General Board, and George Dewey. Now in the spring of 1915, Daniels found himself challenged by some of the most adroit minds in the service. Moreover, as insurgents like Bradley Fiske moved openly into the role of critics, the inherent shortcomings of U.S. naval policy became increasingly obvious.

Woodrow Wilson did not desert his beleaguered naval secretary, however. In May 1915 a great naval review was staged in the Hudson River to show off the assembled might of the Atlantic Fleet. There, Wilson declared his "confidence . . . admiration and unqualified support" of Daniels.[43]

But presidential and secretarial embarrassment must have become very acute when the results of the fleet's annual war games were published. As one of his last acts as aide for operations, Bradley Fiske had planned the exercise. He had gotten the idea from an article in the *New York World* that suggested that the nation might be shocked into defense-mindedness by a highly publicized war game in which the Atlantic Coast was attacked by a superior battle fleet.[44] Daniels warned Fiske that "he did not want to have any war game in May which included the defeat of the U.S. Fleet" but eventually approved the plan.[45] His misgivings were well warranted. On 22 May the Navy Department announced that the day before a superior Red fleet had eluded the Blue defenders and seized and secured a base along the Chesapeake Bay. The praise heaped upon Red's battle cruisers—a class of ship the Navy lacked, but the General Board wanted— by the fleet umpire, for supposedly crushing Blue's screen, may be taken as an indication of the tenor of the whole exercise. But to a public subjected to a flood of books like Maxim's *Defenseless America* and movies such as *The Fall of a Nation*, the results of this mock invasion had an unpleasant ring of authenticity.

Ever-mindful of the approaching presidential elections, pacifist Woodrow Wilson had, by the latter part of July, reluctantly come to the conclusion that the time had come to shore up U.S. defenses.[46] On 21 July he sent letters to both Secretary of War Lindley Garrison and Josephus Daniels instructing them to begin work on expanding both services. Woodrow Wilson had little knowledge or interest in weapons, but his diplomatic encounters had made it impossible not to become acquainted with the submarine and the strange situation it had created in the North Sea. Therefore, in the message he sent his naval secretary, he made a point of maintaining that he "would be very much obliged if you get the best minds in the Department to work on the subject; I mean the men who have been most directly in contact with actual modern conditions, who have most thoroughly comprehended the altered conditions of naval warfare, and who best comprehend what the Navy must be in the future."[47] Josephus Daniels, the political animal, would turn to George Dewey's bastion of orthodoxy.[48]

The General Board was ready. By July 27 the board had voted seven to one in favor of a navy "equal to the most powerful . . . to be attained not later than 1925."[49] The policy was then quickly reduced to specifics. Three days later Daniels received the General Board's first set of recommendations, calling for a six-year program, costing approximately $1.6 billion and providing for, among other things, forty-eight dreadnoughts.[50] It was George Dewey's Phantom Fleet incarnate.

Not surprisingly, Woodrow Wilson found the proposal unacceptable, and on 12 August told Daniels to instruct the board to lower its sights.[51] There the matter hung until 7 October, when Dewey received Daniels's official request to draw up a building program that would "continue over a period of five years, with an expenditure of about $100 million per annum." Five days later the board produced what it conceived to be a compromise proposal.[52] It called for the construction of ten dreadnoughts, six battle cruisers (the fruits of Bradley Fiske's spring war game), ten scouts, fifty destroyers, nine fleet submarines, and fifty-eight coastal defense submarines. There could be no doubt where the emphasis lay: $293 million of the $460 million total was earmarked for dreadnoughts.

Nearly a month later, almost as an afterthought, the General Board produced an explanation for their projected armada.[53] The document was a blunt, but presumably effective, instrument, the nautical equivalent of a papal bull.

The General Board has noted the progress of the war abroad in order to profit by its lessons in making recommendations . . . as to types and numbers of ships to be laid down. . . . The deeds of the submarine have been so spectacular that in default of engagements between the main fleets undue weight has been attached to them. . . . Its high score was obtained by surprise; it was not due to inherent combat superiority. . . . To hastily form[ed] public opinion, it seemed that submarines were accomplishing great military results. . . . Yet at the present time . . . it is apparent that the submarine is not an instrument fitted to dominate naval warfare. . . . The time has now come to provide for battle cruisers and scouts. As yet the main forces of battleships have not been engaged, [but] control of the sea remains in the hands of the powers having the superior battle fleet.[54]

Surrounded as he was by conservatives, Josephus Daniels had little alternative but to agree. His annual report for 1915 adopted the General Board's plan almost without modification. It was a scheme, he insisted, that had not been pressed "in haste of threatening war or the panic of actual war."[55] That much at least was true.

Whatever Woodrow Wilson's personal feelings about the proposal may have been, political expediency made it imperative that he endorse some form of naval preparedness. Therefore, on 7 December 1915, in his Third Annual Message, he reassured Congress that Daniels's request was based on "plans long matured . . . fitted to our needs and worthy of our tradition."[56] The decision was now in the hands of the legislators.

In spite of the growing sentiment for naval preparedness, the administration's building program did not fare well in the House of Representatives. Hearings before the Naval Affairs Committee dragged on for months, with minority Republicans holding out for an even larger program, and the Democratic majority split by a five-member "little Navy" faction that came to hold the balance of power.[57] The deadlock lasted until the end of May 1916, when the Democrats, on the eve of their national convention, managed to work out a compromise. Instead of a five-year, sixteen-dreadnought program, the bill reported to the House called for the construction of just five battle cruisers and thirty-seven lesser vessels over a period of one year.[58] Yet even this relatively modest proposal provoked sharp floor debate. Representative C. R. Davis of Texas complained:

> When I hear the clamoring call for more . . . stupendous dreadnoughts I cannot resist the feeling it must be the call of the uninformed mind or the plaintive plea of an advocate . . . for the Steel Trust. . . . I am not an expert in matters of war and Navy equipment . . . but I do assume to have common sense and some knowledge of world affairs and one thing above all else that the present war has demonstrated is that the efficient instrument of war is not the great massive battleship.[59]

But in the climate of increasing fear, Davis's remarks went unheeded. On 2 June, two days after Jutland had revealed the battle cruiser's vulnerability, the House passed the compromise measure by a healthy majority.[60]

News of the great battle in the North Sea also had a curious effect upon the deliberations of the upper house. On 3 June, the chairman of the Senate Naval Affairs Committee, the aging "Pitchfork Ben" Tillman, announced that Jutland had demonstrated the necessity of constructing battleships as well as battle cruisers.[61] On 21 June, a subcommittee consisting of Tillman, who was too ill to be of much help, and two outspoken navalists, Democrat Claude G. Swanson and Republican Henry Cabot Lodge, was designated to reframe the House proposal to include several battleships. The next day it was leaked that the subcommittee, after consulting with several members of the General Board, not only planned to restore the entire five-year program but also favored telescoping it into three. Three days later "little Navy" Democrats learned to their consternation that the administration supported the modifications, and on 30 June the enlarged and foreshortened bill was presented to the full Senate.[62]

There it touched off a debate that flared intermittently for three weeks. "Little Navy" advocates attacked the bill as best they could. Senator Charles Thomas of Colorado questioned the logic of building battle cruisers when a number had been sunk at Jutland, "the first time they appeared in any great force in a naval battle." He also complained that the bill

> paid too much attention to craft floating upon the surface of the water and not enough to those which go underneath it and above it. I think this war has demonstrated two things: . . . One is that the submarine is the coming destroyer of the sea . . . and that adequate protection for a country which does not propose to carry on an offensive war can be made by confining the bulk of its expenditures and operations to undersea craft and aircraft.[63]

Senator George Norris also worried that "this bill, though liberal to the degree of extravagance, gives no assurance of a Navy best adapted to new conditions."[64]

But the proposal's sponsors were adamant in its defense. An impassioned Claude Swanson maintained that "the General Board proposed to give us at the completion of the program a well-balanced and efficient Navy in every respect. . . . Higher authority on naval matters than the General Board does not exist in this country."[65] Senator Lodge, for his part, could not "possibly imagine what was operating in the mind of the House committee and of the House in authorizing five battlecruisers and nothing else. It was not in conformity with the recommendations of any board or the Navy Department or of anybody who is best fitted to speak on the subject."[66] The appeal to expertise, combined with Swanson and Lodge's bipartisan approach, proved sufficient to carry the issue, and on 21 July the bill was approved by a vote of seventy-one to four.[67]

The struggle was then transferred back to the House, where support for preparedness had grown stronger and the "little Navy" men more bitter. Representative Rufus Hardy of Texas deplored the "hysteria whipped into a fury" that was "driving Republicans and Democrats in the mad race for shelter in the biggest naval program ever adopted by any nation on earth."[68] Wyoming Republican Frank W. Mondell doubted whether "a third of the membership of the House here present . . . [felt] this increased program . . . [either] justified or justifiable."[69] He may have been correct, but later on the same day, 15 August 1916, his colleagues voted 283 to 53 in favor of the largest dreadnought-construction program the nation and the world had ever seen. With Woodrow Wilson's signature, Dewey's fleet would become law.

There was but a single catch. The sponsors of the bill, in an effort to mollify congressional critics, had incorporated a resolution by Representative Walter L. Hensley whereby "the President is authorized and requested to invite, at an appropriate time . . . all the great Governments of the world to send representatives . . . to consider the question of disarmament." Moreover, the amendment stipulated: "If at any time before the construction authorized by the Act shall have been contracted for, there shall have been established, with the cooperation of the United States of America, an international tribunal . . . [which] shall render unnecessary the maintenance of competitive armaments, then and in that case such naval expenditures . . . may be suspended."[70] At the time of its inclusion, the clause seemed little more than an innocuous gesture. Five years later it would all but sink the Phantom Fleet and mark the true beginning of modern arms control.

Nevertheless, for the present, the naval establishment had won a great victory. Certainly civilian authorities had displayed flashes of insight into what was going on in the North Sea. But when the time for them to decide just how to enlarge the Navy arrived, they lost faith in their own judgment and turned blindly to their military advisers.

George Dewey had less than six months to live, but his retainers on the General Board girded anew for the final herculean task of designing and building the great armada. On 29 August the Naval Appropriations Act went into effect and the board began planning in earnest the characteristics of the sixteen proposed battleships and battle cruisers.[71] The atmosphere of urgency that surrounded the deliberations was underlined by Admiral Charles Badger, the board's perennial spokesman and Dewey's spiritual successor, when he noted, "I believe in getting these ships started while the iron is hot and not waiting."[72] His advice was taken to heart, and by early fall the board had tentatively decided on designs for both types of capital ships. Like purebred horses, each was intended to epitomize a different aspect of the dreadnought stock.

The hefty Clydesdales of the fleet, the ten projected battleships would come in two varieties, both combining armor and big guns in quantities the world had not before seen. The first four of this group (*Colorado, Maryland, West Virginia,* and *Washington*) were to displace 32,000 tons and mount a main battery of eight 16-inch guns, the biggest naval rifles in the world.[73] Those behemoths would, however, be dwarfed by the six projected dreadnoughts of the *North Carolina* class. About 25 percent heavier than the largest previous American capital ships, each of these great vessels would weigh in at a massive 42,000 tons and mount twelve 16-inch guns.[74] In defense of those monsters Admiral Badger explained:

Reliable reports . . . that foreign building programs include battleships mounting ten or twelve 15-inch guns, or guns of possibly larger caliber. Lest our vessels be inferior in power to similar types abroad we must construct battleships carrying more powerful weapons than here-to-fore. . . . The additional weight of such a battery can only be carried either by sacrifice of other military characteristics or by an increase in the size of the vessel. . . . The General Board has arrived at the conclusion that increase in the size of battleships, with the additional cost entailed must be accepted.[75]

In contrast, the six 31,000-ton battle cruisers were intended to be the nautical equivalent of thoroughbreds. Rated at an amazing thirty-five knots, they, like their equine counterparts, sacrificed a great deal for speed. Smaller 14-inch guns were used, underwater protection was cut to a minimum, armor was limited to a mere five inches, and the ship's elongated hull shape and steam-hungry 180,000 horsepower turbines required that half of its boilers be located above the armored deck, leaving the vessel very vulnerable to shell fire.[76] It was quite clear that the lessons of Jutland had been ignored by the planners of the U.S. Navy.

Meanwhile, here and there, glimmers of reality slipped into the naval vista. On July 9 the large merchant-submarine *Deutschland* arrived in Baltimore, after having crossed the Atlantic in sixteen days. Although unarmed and billed as a peaceful attempt to circumvent the British blockade, the *Deutschland* was a potent reminder that American waters would not remain U-boat free should the United States choose to join the Allies.[77] Further warning was given on 17 September when Captain Hans Rose—in *U-53*—arrived unannounced at Newport, virtually in the shadow of the Naval War College, on a mission designed to demonstrate to the Navy's planners that combatant submarines could range as far as large merchant-submarines like the *Deutschland*.[78] Disdaining reprovisioning, *U-53* left port immediately and proceeded directly to the waters off Nantucket, where it sank five British steamers in rapid succession while U.S. destroyers stood by to rescue the crews.[79] Those visitations had little effect on the members of the General Board, who continued their feverish preparations unabated— gathering materials, drawing up contracts, reserving berths in shipyards, and supervising the fabrication of blueprints.

George Dewey would not live to see the paper plans transformed into steel. In January 1917 he was confined to bed and, after a short illness, died in his sleep.[80] He had been a remarkable man. With the exception of George Washington, Andrew Jackson, and Dwight Eisenhower, no officer in U.S. history could match his combination of military ability and political acumen. If Mahan had been the messiah of naval orthodoxy, then Dewey was the rock upon which the church was built. As president of the General Board for sixteen years, he had nurtured the battle fleet like a doting parent and in the process exerted an enormous influence on American naval policy during a critical period. Unfortunately his understanding of naval technology did not match his political skills.

Nor did the Old Admiral's death necessarily mean the end of his influence. George Dewey lived on through the medium of the General Board. Like the shrewdest of prelates, he had carefully screened each and every aspirant to this most exclusive naval synod, blackballing harebrained iconoclasts like Poundstone and smoothing the way for solid establishment types like Hugh Rodman and Dewey's bureaucratic alter ego Charles Badger.[81] What remained of the board after Dewey's departure was a group of men as solidly dedicated as he to the construction of the Phantom Fleet. What was missing was the Old Admiral's political talent and his uncanny ability to ingratiate himself with important politicians and the public. Without those links, the General Board increasingly became a disembodied mechanism, whose liturgical pronouncements for ever-larger numbers of ever-larger capital ships were more a reflection of their own framework of belief than a measured assessment of U.S. defense requirements. So the Navy built dreadnoughts as fast as it could.

III

On 9 January 1917 a decision was made by the German Crown Council at Pless that would rip to shreds the convenient cocoon in which the U.S. Navy and the nation had wrapped themselves. The Kaiser had approved the resumption of unrestricted submarine warfare, and the campaign was scheduled to begin on 1

February.[82] It was a carefully calculated gamble based on Admiral von Holzendorff's figures projecting that a 39 percent reduction in British merchant tonnage coupled with intimidation of neutral shipping would force Britain to sue for peace long before any possible U.S. response could make a difference in the outcome.[83] For an ebbing German Empire, bled white along the Western Front and starved by the shipping blockade, it seemed a good bet. There was little doubt what the reaction of the United States would be. The new policy was initiated "in the certain consciousness that the commencement of an unrestricted U-boat warfare would be followed by war with America."[84]

So the United States and its peace-loving president were to be drawn into the vortex of war. On 31 January, Ambassador Johann von Bernstorff delivered official notification of the decision to Secretary of State Robert Lansing. Four days later, before a joint session of Congress, Woodrow Wilson announced that all diplomatic relations between the United States and Germany were to be severed. On 25 February the president received word of the intercepted Zimmermann note promising Mexico alliance and territorial reparations should it enter the war against the United States. The next day Wilson went before Congress and asked for authority to arm American merchant ships and "employ any other instrumentalities or methods that may be necessary and adequate to protect our people in their legitimate and peaceful pursuits on the seas."[85] By the middle of March eight American vessels had been sunk by U-boats.[86] Then on 2 April word reached Congress that the armed American merchantman *Aztec* had been sunk without warning, with the loss of fifteen U.S. citizens. Two days later it was learned that the unarmed steamer *Missourian* had met the same fate, also with loss of life.[87] On 6 April the United States declared war on Germany. So while the Navy planned dreadnoughts, the submarine succeeded in at last drawing the United States into the great conflict in Europe.

Meanwhile, toward the end of March, the Wilson administration had reluctantly faced the inevitable and began turning its attention to the necessity of fighting a war. What the worried politicians found in the naval arm could hardly have been reassuring. First there was Dewey's death, which had left a potentially disastrous power void in a bureaucracy about to gear up for combat. Then there was the matter of the capital-ship-building program, which to a civilian's eye must have seemed very peculiar in the context of what was actually going on in the Atlantic.

To its credit, the Wilson administration and Secretary Daniels in particular moved both quickly and in the right direction. Anticipating wartime conditions,

Daniels immediately beefed up the newly created Office of Naval Operations and turned to its chief, William S. Benson, as his principal adviser in Washington. Within certain limits, this modest but strong-willed Georgian had been an excellent choice. While lacking the intelligence and technical insights of a Bradley Fiske, he had the happy capacity of commanding top-quality work from brilliant subordinates with whom he personally disagreed.[88]

But there were problems with Benson. He was not a reactionary—in the days of gunnery reform he had stood with the insurgents more often than not. But he was never attracted to the intellectual side of the profession, and the times had passed him by. He still thought basically in terms of surface warfare, as if submarines were a chimera and "airplanes just a lot of noise."[89] Finally, the chief of naval operations was a Catholic and intensely suspicious of the new U.S. ally: Great Britain.

If Benson was something of a plodder, Daniels's choice to coordinate U.S. naval operations in European waters was positively inspired. Casting political differences aside, the North Carolina Democrat magnanimously looked to the most brilliant officer of his generation, William S. Sims, whose grasp of naval strategy had impressed the secretary tremendously on their first meeting at the Naval War College.[90] Anglophile Sims, whose insight often surpassed his modesty, later wrote, "As for my appointment . . . it would seem that I was the logical man considering that my association with the gunnery people over here made me well acquainted with all of the principal men who are now at the top of the British Navy."[91]

Ordered to report without delay to Washington, Sims arrived on 28 March and was immediately subjected to an intense three-day briefing on the administration's interpretation of the crisis. Daniels made it clear at the outset

> that the president believed the British had not taken the necessary vigorous offensive to prevent destruction of shipping by the U-boats, and that he strongly believed two things ought to be done: First, that every effort should be made to prevent the submarines getting into the Atlantic—that the "hornets . . . ought to be shut up in their own nests.". . . Second, that all ships ought to be convoyed. The President had been of this opinion for a long time, and had insisted that it was essential to give protection to shipping.[92]

Admiral Benson, whose relations with Sims were destined to deteriorate steadily, had little to add beyond a pointed warning "not to let the British pull the wool over his eyes."[93]

With that Sims and his chief aide, C. V. Babcock, disguised rather unconvincingly as two gentlemen travelers, boarded the American steamer New York on 31 March. Besides having their false identities exposed by an enterprising steward, they had an uneventful trip until the vessel drew near Liverpool. There, however, the vessel struck a mine, forcing its passengers to be unceremoniously deposited on a rescue steamer and taken ashore.[94] As the somewhat ruffled Sims stepped upon Liverpudlian terra firma, the date was 9 April, three days after the American declaration of war, and the peril beneath the waves must have taken on a new significance.

This was just the beginning. The American admiral was rushed aboard a special train to London, where he met immediately with the First Sea Lord, a post then occupied by the long-suffering John Jellicoe, who had been replaced by David Beatty as commander in chief of the Grand Fleet in December 1916.

After the usual greetings, Admiral Jellicoe took a paper out of his drawer and handed it to me. It was a record of tonnage losses for the last few months. This showed that the total sinkings, British and neutral, had reached 536,000 tons in February and 603,000 in March; it further disclosed that sinkings were taking place in April which indicated the destruction of nearly 900,000 tons. These figures indicated that the losses were three and four times as large as those which were then being published in the press. . . .

I was fairly astounded; for I had never imagined anything so terrible. . . .

"Yes," he said, as quietly as though he were discussing the weather and not the future of the British Empire. "It is impossible for us to go on with the war if losses like this continue. . . ."

"Is there absolutely no solution to the problem?" I asked.

"Absolutely none that we can see now."[95]

Sims soon found out why. The reports that the Admiralty had been publishing for the last several months claiming the destruction of submarines in large numbers were revealed as false. In fact British records showed that since the beginning of the war, only fifty-four German U-boats were positively known to have been sunk. Meanwhile, Sims was informed, enemy submarine production had been geared up considerably.

To top that, it was made clear to the American that the First Sea Lord, his principal advisers (with the notable exception of David Beatty), and service opinion in general were not in favor of convoying merchant ships with military vessels. It was observed that such convoys would be required to proceed at the

German U-boat, a cur among weapons (Courtesy of the U.S. National Archives)

speed of the slowest vessel and thus be relative sitting ducks. Besides, British merchant captains were not trained to maneuver in close formation and collisions were bound to result.[96] But that was not the real reason, and Sims knew it. Convoys would require destroyers, the only torpedo-carrying warship nimble enough to really harass a submarine. But in the Royal Navy, "the one requirement that necessarily took precedence over all others, was that a flotilla of at least 100 destroyers must be continuously kept with the Grand Fleet, ready to go into action at a moment's notice."[97] That was a minimum figure. If the fleet's already-depleted screen was contracted further, the battleships would lose all pretense of being a fighting force.

Sims delayed sending word of what he had learned to Washington for four days, "deterred by a natural reluctance to alter so radically my preconceived views and opinions as to the situation."[98] He was by nature an iconoclast and he had been warned of the submarine's power by the likes of submariner J. O. Fisher, but the news must have still shocked the American profoundly. Like all Annapolites he had been saturated with faith in the Royal Navy and its battleships. Jutland had been bad enough, but this sort of passivity and incompetence made a travesty of the whole naval structure of belief.

Lesser men might have collapsed under the weight of such a revelation, but Sims coolly weighed his options in the harsh light of reality. When he did contact Washington, first by cable on 14 April and then by letter on the 19th, it was clear that he had improvised a plan with at least some chance of success. The first message made it clear that the issue is and must inevitably be decided at the focus of all lines of communication in Eastern Atlantic, therefore I very urgently recommend the following immediate naval cooperation. Maximum numbers of destroyers to be sent, accompanied by small anti-submarine craft. . . . At present our battleships can serve no useful purpose in this area, except that two divisions might be based at Brest for moral effect. . . . The chief other and urgent practical cooperation is merchant tonnage and a continuous augmentation of anti-submarine craft to reinforce our advanced forces.[99]

In his second cable Sims touched upon the issue of the convoy:

It is insistently asked (and was asked by myself) why shipping is not directed to and concentrated at various rendezvous and from these convoyed through the dangerous areas. The answer is the same—the area is too large; the necessary vessels are not available. . . . In the absence of adequate patrol craft, *particularly destroyers* . . . there is but one sure way of meeting the submarine issue upon which there is complete unanimity—increased numbers of merchant bottoms preferably small. "More ships! More ships! More ships!" is heard on every hand.[100]

It was not hard to see what Sims was getting at in the two messages. The U.S. battle fleet should be kept at home and stripped of its destroyers for convoy duty; and the giant capital-ship-construction program should be suspended in favor of an immediate emphasis on destroyers and merchant bottoms.

Sims's advice made a great deal of sense. Reality had rendered War Plan BLACK inoperative. Shortly before war was declared, the battle fleet—instead of massing in the Chesapeake and proceeding to a Caribbean Armageddon—had been herded up the York River and corralled there, like prize bulls, behind steel antisubmarine nets, far out of harm's way.[101] Annapolite Paul Schubert remembered enlisted men aboard the *Texas* asking, " 'Watta we gonna do?' 'My God, who knows? Is this a war or a tea party?' . . . We in the *Texas* chafed. We had always thought that if war was declared, we'd be half-way to the other side in two days."[102]

In Washington William V. Pratt, Sims's former chief of staff in the destroyer days, and a man soon destined to play a key role as assistant chief of naval operations, was suggesting that the battleships be exiled to the Pacific, "where their potential as a fleet in being might be used to the best political advantage."[103] Still crueler cuts were heard from the submarine flotilla, where young Lieutenant Commander Richard Voge was moved to poetry:

Battleships are title B
That's lesson one in strategy
They are the Backbone of the Fleet
Their fighting power can't be beat
They dominate the raging main
While swinging round the anchor chain
And bravely guard your home and mine
While anchored out there all in a line.[104]

In the midst of all of this, the conservative high command of the United States Navy was running true to form. The department's response to Sims's urgent requests for "a maximum number of destroyers" was decidedly unenthusiastic. When the war began, the United States had on its naval lists twenty-nine cruisers, sixty-six destroyers, fourteen ocean-going tugs, and thirteen converted yachts.[105] Of this considerable force of craft suitable for antisubmarine warfare, the Navy at first sent only six ships of Joseph Taussig's Eighth Destroyer Division to the war zone. On 4 May, twenty-one critical days after Sims's first cable arrived, the tiny armada appeared off Queenstown, Ireland, ready for service. By 1 July 1917, three months after the United States had joined the Allies, there were only twenty-eight destroyers and no other antisubmarine craft on duty in the combat zone.[106] The American Navy, it seems, was hardly more anxious than the British to denude their dreadnoughts of destroyers. In 1920 Admiral Badger of the General Board testified: "It looked in April and May very much as though peace would have to be declared by the British and the French. . . . Therefore the men who had a responsibility of that kind considered . . . that we must look out for our own fleet, in addition to the other powers concerned and not strip our battleships of protection against the submarines that might attack them."[107]

As for shifting priority away from the construction of dreadnoughts to destroyers and merchant bottoms, the General Board was equally dubious. On 20 April Badger wrote Secretary Daniels, warning him against allowing the demands of antisubmarine warfare to obscure the possibility of the German and Japanese battle fleets combining after the war in Europe was over, to "operate co-jointly" in the Atlantic and Pacific against the United States. To gain a numerical equality with such an aggressor by 1920, the board felt it would be necessary not only to complete the capital ships already being built but also to begin an additional ten battleships and six battle cruisers.[108]

Meanwhile on both sides of the Atlantic civilian politicians in concert with younger, less-orthodox officers were beginning to take control of naval policy in a desperate effort to yank it into phase with reality before it became too late. In Britain Prime Minister David Lloyd George seized upon the recommendations of Admiral Sims as confirmation of his own faith that the convoy system would work if given the opportunity. By 25 April he had lost all patience with the Admiralty's procrastination on the subject and decided to act himself:

> It was clear that the Admiralty did not intend to take any effective steps in the direction of convoying. . . . I informed the Cabinet that I had decided to visit the Admiralty and there take peremptory action on the question of convoys. . . . Apparently, the prospect of being overruled in their own sanctuary galvanized the Admiralty into a fresh inquisition, and by way of anticipating the inevitable they further examined the plans and figures. . . . They then for the first time began to realize the fact which had been ignored by them since August, 1914, that the figures upon which they had based their strategy were ludicrous, and that therefore protection for a convoy system was within the compass of their resources.[109]

So the Royal Navy, symbol for four centuries of naval competence, had to be coerced by amateurs into trying the one measure that stood some immediate chance of minimizing the depredations of the submarine. Of course, the decision to adopt the convoy and the concomitant increase in the need for destroyers further intensified the pressure on the United States, the one remaining reservoir of Allied naval strength, to modify its naval policies.

It was probably critical. From that point Sims's messages from London became ever more frequent and strident in tone. No fewer than twenty-four times during the months of May and June did he call for more antisubmarine craft to help protect the convoys. "God knows I have said everything which I could say in official communications on this subject," he wrote his protégé in operations, William V. Pratt.[110]

The younger officer had every reason to sympathize with his former commander. For Pratt himself had become embroiled in a controversy with the General Board over the building program. Fortunately for the Navy and the United States, this relatively inexperienced officer proved to be a master service politician and a realist the likes of which was seldom seen in the ranks of Annapolites. A maverick by nature, Pratt's disdain for naval tradition often showed through his smiling, placid outward demeanor. "I dislike salutes and side boys, and never cared much at which angle Johnny wore his white hat. Today, I still spill pipe ashes over choice rugs."[111] As for the fragile reputation of the dreadnought, that meant nothing to him in comparison to winning the war. Consequently, when he found himself in the relatively influential (if unofficial) position of assistant chief of naval operations, he did everything in his power to change the thrust of U.S. building policy. His initiative would lead him to become a major player in the dreadnought's denouement.

The fight began in late May when Major General George W. Goethals, the general manager of the Emergency Fleet Corporation, asked Josephus Daniels to release for transport construction the four giant building ways being readied in private yards for the first of the new battle cruisers.[112] Remembered for his efforts on the Panama Canal, and widely regarded as a managerial wizard, Goethals's request was not to be taken lightly. Nevertheless, when it reached the Navy Department, it was shunted aside, marked with the simple penciled comment: "Can't agree."[113]

Pratt, however, knew about Goethals's proposition and on 7 June wrote his boss, Admiral Benson, a brilliant memorandum in its favor. Arguing that "for the allied purposes, merchant ships are as essential to the successful termination of this war as battleships," Pratt found little basis for the General Board's fears of postwar combination against the United States that would require legions of capital ships. "The counter of the United States, in case of an unsuccessful end to this war lies in: 1. our naval submarines 2. conscription." But whatever the future might hold, "it does not mean that one fraction of the strength of the effort we should put into the successful accomplishment of the immediate mission should be sacrificed to any possible future contingency."[114] Despite his conservative leanings, Benson saw the merit in his assistant's reasoning and dutifully handed his paper over to the secretary of the Navy.

It could not have arrived at a more opportune time, for at that point Josephus Daniels must have felt himself in a tight spot indeed. British requests, after their bumbling performance in the war thus far, were hardly to be looked at uncritically. Yet it had become increasingly obvious that Dewey and the conservatives who cooperated with the secretary politically had been living in a military-technical dreamland. All they seemed to be able to do was beg for battleships. Now he and Woodrow Wilson—two less-likely naval strategists it would have been hard to find—were left to devise somehow a way to win the weird war at sea. Time was growing short: Estimates of the Allied collapse date ranged from August to November. Daniels and Wilson were, to put it mildly, open to suggestions. Under the circumstances, the advice of men like Pratt and Sims took on new meaning.

Consequently, after reading the memorandum, Daniels named Pratt chairman of a Board on Devices and Plans Connected with Submarine Warfare, set up to provide the administration with naval alternatives.[115] This was no council of elders. It was a "board with a lot of youngsters on it," among them Frank H. Schofield, the irreverent inventor of the torpedo dreadnought.[116] The body's membership was immediately reflected in its deliberations, with Pratt, Schofield, and the dominant youthful faction "fighting tooth and nail to get our building modified so that . . . every effort was to be directed at producing anti-submarine craft."[117]

Meanwhile back in the war zone, Admiral Sims was keeping up the pressure. In May, with the first use of the convoy, merchant sinkings had fallen, but the total for the month was still around 600,000 tons. Then in June, with its longer hours of daylight, the Germans made a supreme effort to equal April's rate of transport slaughter. Compared with the eighteen U-boats operating in the North Sea in May, there were twenty-seven in June, and the sinking curve, to Sims's dismay, again began to rise.[118] If this kept up, the end could not be very far away for the Allies. By the last days of June, Sims was on the edge of desperation. Finally, he turned to U.S. Ambassador Walter Hines Page. "Can you not do something to bring our government to an understanding of how serious the situation is?"[119] Page, who knew all too well how badly things were going, immediately cabled an urgent message to the president and secretary of state in complete support of all Sims's recommendations. From the British, the American admiral also obtained and sent to the White House a document to the same effect, signed by Arthur Balfour, the foreign secretary, and Sir Edward Carson, the civilian First Lord of the Admiralty.

Coming simultaneously and at a moment of crisis, the two missives seem to have crystallized the administration's growing inclination to follow the advice of the naval iconoclasts. On 1 July Woodrow Wilson wrote Josephus Daniels: "I think it is time we were making and insisting upon plans of our own, even if we render some of the more conservative of our own naval advisers uncomfortable. What do you think?"[120] The secretary agreed and helped the president prepare a cable to Sims, which was sent on 4 July. The message, which reflected Wilson's continuing dissatisfaction with British naval policy, ended by "begging" the admiral to "give me such advice as you would if you were handling an independent navy of your own."[121]

Sims's reply was intriguing. It made his own position very clear but, at the same time, was carefully framed to avoid antagonizing the still-powerful capital ship enthusiasts. The removal of the battle fleet's screen, he argued, did not have to be interpreted as a sign of its uselessness or disintegration.

> As the fleet, in case it does move, would require a large force of protective Light Craft, and as such craft would delay the Fleet's movement, we should advance to European water all possible craft of such description. . . . Such a force, while waiting for the Fleet to move, should be employed to the maximum degree in putting down the enemy submarine campaign. . . . I would concentrate all naval construction on destroyers and light craft, postpone construction of heavy craft and depend upon the fact, which I believe to be true, that, regardless of any future development we can always count upon the support of the British Navy.[122]

It soon became clear to whom Wilson and Daniels were now listening, and the cable brought almost immediate results. On 6 July Captain Pratt's Board on Devices and Plans Connected with Submarine Warfare recommended the construction of 200 standardized destroyers in addition to the 66 already on the ways. In response, the secretary reacted with record speed, approving the proposal on the very same day.[123]

"They went up in the air when the blow descended—The General Board went up in the air," wrote a rather gleeful Pratt to Sims later in the month.[124] By 13 July the board had protested officially, asking that just fifty destroyers be built, since Pratt's plan was bound to delay the construction of a fleet able to "meet a possible new alignment of power at the end of the war, or the German Fleet if it succeeds in taking the offensive."[125]

But the board's apostolic prophesies of gloom no longer had much effect on the administration. On the same day, 13 July, Woodrow Wilson told Sir William Wiseman of British military intelligence that the war had only demonstrated the battleship's uselessness in comparison to destroyers and submarines. Therefore, he saw no danger in delaying the American capital ship program.[126] Josephus Daniels made it official on 21 July, adopting, with Admiral Benson's consent, a program that called for 50 regular destroyers and 150 of the proposed new standardized type.[127] (Ironically, the importance of the decision to emphasize the construction of destroyers would prove more symbolic than real, since less than a dozen of the 350 new warships would be ready for service prior to the armistice.[128])

Two weeks later, the Navy Department agreed with the Emergency Fleet Corporation that in private yards transports should take precedence over battleships and battle cruisers not yet begun.[129] By late August all new capital ship construction had been postponed indefinitely. Like a great apparition, the Phantom Fleet faded back into the imaginations of its supporters, a dream still unfulfilled.

Although Woodrow Wilson had been convinced that the suspension of dreadnought program would mean little to the Navy militarily, he was apparently not so sure what effect his decision would have upon service morale. Therefore on 11 August, he visited the stationary battle fleet at Yorktown and tried to explain his own actions and the strange war at sea to the dispirited, disoriented Annapolites.

> Here are two great navies . . . our own and the British, outnumbering by a very great margin the navy to which we are opposed and yet casting about for a way in which to use our superiority and our strength, because of the novelty of the instruments used, because of the unprecedented character of this war. . . . The experienced soldier—experienced in previous wars—is a back number so far as his experience is concerned . . . therefore he is an amateur along with the rest of us. . . . Somebody has got to think out a way not only to fight submarines, but to do something different from what we are doing. . . .
>
> The Secretary of the Navy and I have just been talking over plans for putting the planning machinery of the Navy at the disposal of the brains of the Navy and not stopping to ask what rank that brains has. . . . Every time we suggested anything to the British Admiralty the reply has come back . . . that it has never been done that way, and I felt like saying, "Well nothing was ever done so systematically as nothing is being done now." Therefore I would like to see something unusual happen, something that was never done before; and inasmuch as the things that are being done to you were never done before, don't you think it is worth while to try something that was never done before against those who are doing them to you? . . . There is no other way to win.[130]

It was quite a speech, a soliloquy for a tortured century. Picture Woodrow Wilson the scholar—gentle by nature, liberal and humanitarian by inclination—transformed into the warrior-priest haranguing his reluctant Vikings on the virtues of lex talionis, urging them to drop all restraint in this most ceremonial of violent acts, war at sea.

At last it was retribution time: The villainous submarine would get some of its own medicine. For it seemed that the peremptory actions of Lloyd George and Wilson had the effect of loosening, if not removing, the conceptual strait-jacket that had prevented effective action in the face of the submarine crisis. Beginning in the early summer of 1917 the Allied navies began devoting an all-out effort to defeating the submarine campaign. For the first time, really effective countermeasures were being employed against the deadly underwater craft. No one panacea was found; but a combination of new weapons, the convoy system, and fortuitous geographical factors proved sufficient, but just barely, to blunt the German naval offensive.

The U-boats had exerted a maximum effort in June and still had come up 200,000 tons short of April's total of almost 900,000 tons sunk. From June the monthly toll would not exceed the Allied capacity to replace transports.[131] The worst phase had passed. The Germans had waited too long.

For one thing, a submerged U-boat was no longer either invulnerable or undetectable to foes on the surface. In January 1916, the British had developed the depth charge, basically an oil drum filled with 120 pounds of TNT and set to explode at a predetermined depth.[132] But their use and accuracy was limited by the lack of a means to launch them farther than they could be thrown overboard by hand. Consequently, until June 1917, they remained a minor factor, with only two depth charges generally being supplied for each antisubmarine craft.[133]

Then in August 1917 a howitzer-like depth-charge thrower was perfected that could cast the lethal canisters up to forty yards on either side of an attacking surface vessel. Suddenly a destroyer's chances of sinking a submarine caught at or above periscope level appeared much improved—especially if a large number of charges could be fired in a close patter. Consequently, throwers were installed immediately, and antisubmarine vessels were provided with from thirty to fifty charges each.

Soon not even deeply submerged U-boats would be unassailable. For by the beginning of summer 1917, a device called a hydrophone (literally an underwater microphone) had been improved to the point that it could pick up both the propeller beat and general location of craft far below. A submarine might be heard, stalked, and destroyed in a hail of depth charges without its crew even suspecting the danger above.

Actually, neither the depth charge nor the hydrophone was all that physically effective against the submarine. To destroy a U-boat it was necessary to explode a depth charge within fourteen feet of its hull, a very good shot when there was seldom more than a vague idea of the quarry's position. To get even a vague idea of the submarine's position, it was necessary to deal with the inherent inadequacies of the hydrophone. At sea it could only be used from a stationary or nearly stationary vessel; otherwise the noise from the ship's engines and the water rushing against the hull would drown out the sounds made by the submarine.[134] Moreover, the hydrophone's inability to differentiate among sounds meant that it was least effective where the traffic was heaviest, in convoys, the very place it was needed most. Altogether, the new weapons developed to combat the submarine probably accounted for fewer than 40 of the 116 U-boats destroyed between July 1917 and the end of the war.[135]

But statistics did not reflect the psychological damage inflicted by those new developments. If the knowledge that there was no longer any sure way of avoiding surface attack subtly eroded the submarine's morale, the first real experience with depth charges must have had a shattering effect. Waiting, listening in the dank, cramped U-boats, scarcely daring to breath the foul air as the explosions drew closer and closer, the tension must have been nearly unbearable. Within sixty feet of the hull, each detonation produced a miniature earthquake, casting men into bulkheads like rag dolls. Often the electric lights would flicker and die. If charges fell still nearer, plates would sometimes rupture, dousing the crews with high-pressure jets of water and reminding them of the cold, crushing death that must inevitably follow one lucky shot.

Johanne Spiess, one of the German Navy's most durable and successful submariners (Weddigen's second-in-command when the *Cressy*, *Hogue*, and *Aboukir* were sunk), recalled that after a bad depth-charge attack, his crews were listless and unnerved for a week, executing their practice dives with the clumsiness of neophytes. Soon, throughout the U-boat flotilla, men of proven bravery, with thousands of miles of cruising experience behind them, began collapsing at their stations, drained of all will or sense of responsibility.[136] "Shell shock" they called it in the trenches—one of military technology's several gifts to the psychiatric profession.

Conversely, the new antisubmarine devices had an exhilarating effect upon the men who used them. For the first time, surface defenders could do more than gnash their teeth when a submerged U-boat struck. Even if the average depth-charge run accomplished little beyond killing several thousand fish, and perhaps frightening the human prey below, it created the illusion of decisive action. The deep explosive rumble, the parallel pattern of white water boiling to the surface, the occasional oil slick—all spurred the antisubmarine crews to attack their submerged foes vigorously and whenever possible. The war of nerves had turned.

If the new measures against the submarine were more dramatic than effective, the opposite was true of the convoy. Until the system was instituted, U-boats normally scattered widely, picking off individual transports as they approached or left Britain. Now, with the convoy, the German marauders were faced with feast-or-famine conditions. U-boat commanders, who had averaged seven thousand tons a month, cruised for weeks at a time without spotting a single target. (Of the 316 transports joining convoys in June and July 1917—many didn't—only 1 was sunk by a hostile submarine.)[137]

For those Teutonic submersibles that did encounter a convoy, things were not a great deal better. Attacking such a flock entailed difficulties not previously encountered. When merchant vessels still plied the seas unescorted and largely unarmed, U-boats often had only to approach their prey on the surface, demand surrender, and scuttle her with a sachel charge. Should the victim prove recalcitrant, the combination of the U-boat's 105-millimeter deck gun and slim, visible profile was usually decisive against more-heavily armed but easy-to-hit transports. In any case, submerged maneuver (requiring later battery recharge) and torpedoes (of which there was a very limited quantity aboard) were used as a last resort. Now the convoy's fierce watchdogs, the depth-charge-slinging destroyers, made both necessary.[138]

If the experiences of *U-21*'s Captain Hersing with a convoy off Ireland in August can be judged as representative, any U-boat commander intent on surviving the war would think twice about attacking such a body. The convoy, guarded by six destroyers on either flank and one at each end, seemed most vulnerable from the front. The sea was glassy, perfect for spotting the wash of a periscope, so Hersing had to approach cautiously, taking only hurried glances through the telltale tube. Slipping past the lead destroyer, he moved within range, quickly fired off two torpedoes, and crash-dived to 120 feet. After an interval of forty seconds two explosions were heard from the surface—a cleaner kill could hardly be imagined. But before they had time to exult, the crew of *U-21* found itself in the midst of an ordeal by depth charge. Every ten seconds came explosions at 30-, 75-, and 150-foot depths. Relentlessly the tiny submerged craft was thumped and shaken by a seemingly endless string of concussions. Five hours passed before the destroyers finally called off the attack.[139]

Prolonged assault by Allied antisubmarine craft was not merely a product of vindictiveness. The point was to keep the submarines on the defensive and unable to deliver a second and third attack. Under such conditions U-boats were hard-pressed to claim more than a single victim from each of the elusive convoys, and Allied merchant tonnage losses fell off accordingly.

Meanwhile the Germans reacted sluggishly. The submarine's problems with the convoy were largely a product of poor tactics and lack of coordination in the vital western approaches. As early as April 1917, the High Seas Fleet's astute *Führer der U-Boote,* Commander Hermann Bauer, had proposed using the large submarine cruiser 155 (former cargo submarine *Deutschland*) as a radio command boat operating west of the British Isles.[140] With such a midocean wireless relay station, information could have been pooled and submarines deployed in areas of known convoy activity. Moreover, it would have facilitated U-boats operating in groups, or wolf packs, as they came to be known in World War II. In numbers there is strength. And whereas a single submarine could be made to cringe before six or eight destroyers, a coordinated attack by a pack of U-boats would have not only made it difficult to concentrate on any one submerged predator but almost certainly yielded a higher kill ratio per convoy. But the German U-boat command proved incapable of adjusting quickly enough to changing conditions. The plan was rejected, *U-155* dispatched on an independent mission to the Azores, and Bauer himself was summarily relieved of his command in June 1917. With his passing went the best chance of the Germans' integrating and rationalizing their submarine campaign beyond the level of individual initiative.[141] So the convoys remained relatively unscathed.

Finally the submarine's problems with the depth charge and the convoy were compounded by a crucial geographical factor: Britain sat athwart the North Sea in such a way as to reduce the most direct German approaches to the Atlantic to a thin band of water, the English Channel. To reach transport-hunting grounds the departing U-boat commander had the choice of playing it safe and wasting a good deal of fuel by traversing the North Sea and rounding the tip of Scotland or attempting a run through the narrow channel.

Dover, at the narrows of the strait, quickly became the focus of British antisubmarine activities, with a high concentration of destroyers constantly patrolling the surrounding waters for U-boats. To supplement this effort the British dreamed of erecting a permanent barrier across the channel. As far back as the winter of 1914–1915 the British had tried to construct a wooden boom from Folkestone to Gris-Nez (apparently believing the U-boats would not simply dive under it), but it broke up in a storm.[142] In February 1917 a net studded with mines was laid down across the Strait of Dover. The web, however, was only forty to sixty feet deep, and the mines that it used were the standard British model, which ordinarily refused to explode when struck.[143] Therefore not one U-boat was snared before May, when the waves and tide succeeded in fouling the barrier to the point that it became a menace to British patrol vessels. This fiasco did have a silver lining in causing the Admiralty to swallow a bit more of its pride and drop all further efforts to develop a dependable British contact mine. Henceforth they would rely instead on the Herz-horned H-2 model, a replica of the trusty German "E" type that had been sinking Allied ships since the beginning of the war. In November 1917, the H-2 mine became available in quantity and by the end of the month an extensive barrage had been laid across several levels of the shallow strait. It was an immediate success and began to inflict such losses that even Admiral Scheer was compelled to admit that "the straits were actually almost impassable." In February 1917, U-boats were henceforth forbidden to use the English Channel as a route to their Atlantic hunting grounds.[144]

Thrown back on the circuitous detour around Scotland, U-boats for the remainder of the war would have trouble remaining on station in the North Atlantic long enough to dispose of even their limited supply of torpedoes. Yet even that awkward route did not long remain secure.

For if the American Navy could find no way to "crush the hornets in the nest," as their president had suggested, the Navy was at least intent upon confining them to the North Sea. That meant laying an effective mine field across the 240 miles of open water between Scotland and Norway—water that averaged 600 feet deep.[145] In 1915 and again in 1916 the British had considered such a barrier, but the great distance, the depth of the sea, and the estimate that the project would consume 120,000 conventional mines caused the idea to be dropped.[146] But the U.S. Navy rose to the occasion, showing some of the down-home ingenuity and enthusiasm that would eventually make the United States number one in the field of death machinery. At the suggestion of Ralph C. Browne, a New England engineer and inventor, the Navy Department developed a mine that could be detonated by merely brushing a 70-foot electrically charged copper antenna that hung below.[147] When combined with a very long and efficient anchoring mechanism, the antenna principle constituted a revolutionary concept in mining. By arranging the devices—which resembled nothing so much as sperm—in a grid pattern, it became possible to create a mine field considerably denser than the British had contemplated, at a substantial savings in mines. Meanwhile, the deadly grid constituted the first truly tridimensional mine field ever attempted. A passing submarine was in jeopardy anywhere from the surface to its maximum test depth along the entire width of the field.

The ingeniousness of the concept was matched by the promptness with which it was brought to fruition. Having completed the prototype of the new Mark IV mine in mid-July 1917, the Bureau of Ordnance immediately put it in mass production through secret subcontracts with the automobile industry.[148] By late spring 1917 all the necessary Mark IVs had been assembled and shipped to Scotland to await installation. During the summer and early fall a total of 70,263 antenna mines were laid in a network that came to be known as the Great North Sea Mine Barrage.[149]

To reach the Atlantic and open sea, German submarines henceforth had to run a lethal gauntlet, not a pleasant prospect. In full operation slightly more than a month before the armistice terminated hostilities, the barrage accounted for at least six U-boats, and it terrified the crews of every other passing submarine. It was, in short, a very unpleasant antidote to a very unpleasant weapon. In the twentieth century, technology did not just kill, it killed with flair and imagination.

So the Allies, through a fortuitous combination of factors, saved the day at sea. In the final two years of the war, 132 submarines were destroyed, while shipping losses stabilized at or near an acceptable 300,000 tons per month[150] (see Appendix, Table A.4). Once the conflict settled back into its accustomed equilibrium of attrition, it became just a question of endurance, and the Allies with their robust new partner, the United States, had that all on their side. Germany's submarine campaign had failed.

However, it is difficult to conclude that the submarine itself had failed Germany. Rather, the reverse seems to have been closer to what actually happened. As Sims later wrote:

> We know that for every hundred submarines which the Germans possessed they could keep only ten or a dozen at work in the open sea. The rest were on their way to the hunting grounds, or returning, or they were in port being refitted and taking on supplies. Could the Germans have kept fifty submarines constantly at work on the great shipping routes in the winter and spring of 1917—nothing could have prevented her from winning the war. Instead of sinking 850,000 tons in a single month, she would have sunk 2,000,000 or 3,000,000 tons. The fact is that Germany with all her microscopic preparations for war neglected to provide herself with the one instrumentality with which she might have won it.[151]

Sims was right. Despite the obvious advantages of the submersible, the German construction program remained sporadic throughout most of the first three years of war. Even in the crucial period from April 1917 through September 1918, production averaged only eight boats a month.[152] As Admiral Scheer recounted, "When I asked the U-boat Office why in January 1917, when the unlimited U-boat campaign was decided on, more boats were not ordered to be built than was actually the case, I received the following answer: 'As a result of the decision in favor of an intensified U-boat campaign no orders for boats on a large scale were placed.' "[153] Meanwhile, German shipyards still had eight ships-of-the-line under construction.

Only at the last hour, with sneering defeat staring them in the face, did the Germans become irrevocably committed to submarine production. In October 1918, the Scheer Program, intended to produce 376 additional U-boats by late 1919, was inaugurated.[154] It was far, far too late. The time for decisive action had passed, literally, years before.

IV

While the real war at sea was being fought by submarines and destroyers, the dreadnoughts at Scapa tried as best they could to keep up appearances. But it was difficult. As the fleet's screen contracted, any sort of movement became rarer, more difficult, and dangerous. In May 1917 all capital ship maneuvers were curtailed for a month, due to lack of escorts.[155] Things were even worse by July when, of the 100 destroyers and 9 flotilla leaders nominally attached to the Grand Fleet, 46 were away on antisubmarine duty and 29 were being overhauled.[156]

Instead of the intricacies of high-speed maneuver, the operation of delicately synchronized gun-training mechanisms, leading to a grand climax of mortal combat at sea, British officers became preoccupied with the demoralizing effect that enforced idleness might have upon their crews. Consequently, by the latter part of 1917 the Grand Fleet became the subject of a program for filling time so elaborate that even the relentless social directors at upstate New York's resort hotels might have blushed with envy. There were endless bouts of rugby, tug-of-war, and calisthenics to weary the limbs, while the Scapa Flow repertory company regularly dulled the senses of the tired tars. The HMS *Warspite* won some notoriety by presenting a complete light opera based on Edward German's *Merrie England*, whereas Beatty's flagship even put on a Russian ballet to the music of Franz Liszt.[157]

But such froth could not soothe the spirit of the British armada's intrepid commander in chief. David Beatty wrote his wife repeatedly of his unhappiness:

Three months I have been in command of the Grand Fleet and we have not struck the enemy a severe blow yet. . . . I keep on saying to myself "patience, just have patience," but it is hard to act upon that. . . . How many months more do we have to wait? I would not mind how many [months], if I knew at the end we would get them, but it is the haunting fear that we never shall, and the Grand Fleet will never be able to justify itself.[158]

Yet the British dreadnoughts at Scapa would not have to mark time alone. They would be joined in this vigil by their American cousins. After visiting the Grand Fleet with Jellicoe, Admiral Sims sent a telegram on 21 July 1917 requesting the Navy Department to dispatch its four strongest coal-burning battleships to the war zone.[159] Although it was true that the immobile Grand Fleet already outnumbered its stationary adversary by a large margin, the move was meant to be primarily a gesture of goodwill as well as a means of relieving five British pre-dreadnoughts whose personnel was needed for antisubmarine work.[160]

Even in those times of turmoil and impiety, the United States Navy hesitated to break Mahan's "first commandment." Therefore, Admiral Benson informed Sims that a part of the battle fleet could not be sent to Europe, since "the strategic situation necessitates keeping the fleet concentrated."[161] Sims continued to insist on the battleships, and Benson remained adamantly opposed, turning him down again a month later.[162]

By the end of September relations between Sims and Benson, temperamental and intellectual opposites, had deteriorated to the point that the latter wrote the former, "I requested Captain Pratt not to let me read any more of [your letters], as I was afraid that the constant spirit of criticism and complaint that pervaded them . . . would gradually produce a state of mind on my part that was undesirable to say the least."[163]

Nevertheless, the younger officers in Washington continued to press for the division of the capital ships. Both Pratt and Frank Schofield, who was then in charge of war plans at operations, testified before the General Board in favor of sending the capital ships to Britain, arguing that the danger of a later attack by a combined German and Japanese battle fleet would be best removed by doing everything possible to win the present war.[164] Although not convinced by such reasoning, Benson realized that the climate of opinion was shifting against his position, and he withdrew the question of sending the ships from the General Board's consideration. He then made ready for a face-saving trip to London.

Arriving early in November 1917 with the ubiquitous Colonel Edward M. House, Benson conferred with the cream of Allied officialdom, sat in on the various war councils, and subjected Admiral Sims to a series of slights. At the end of this process, however, he acquiesced to the inevitable, recommending that the battleships be sent to "indicate more conclusively and strongly the intentions of the United States."[165] On 12 November, Josephus Daniels ordered that a division of battleships be immediately dispatched to the war zone.[166] Although dreadnoughts were still dreadnoughts, whether anchored in the York River or at Scapa Flow, the decision did serve to mark the origins of a dispute that would eventually rock the naval establishment to its very foundations and become an important factor in the formulation of U.S. foreign policy in the period immediately following the Great War.

Despite the obvious inactivity of European capital ships, the four dreadnoughts of Battleship Division Nine (*New York*, *Wyoming*, *Arkansas*, and *Texas*) left their berths and sailed into the Chesapeake with high hopes. Led by Rear Admiral Hugh Rodman, a conservative to the core and no friend of Sims, the squadron proceeded first to the Brooklyn Navy Yard for provisions and then headed up Long Island Sound toward Britain and adventure.

It came sooner than anyone anticipated. Around midnight the *Texas*, commanded by Benson's friend and ally, Victor Blue, drifted slightly off course and ran into Block Island.[167] After several hours of frantic endeavor to refloat her, it became clear that she was not only stuck fast but that she had also suffered extensive hull damage in the process. Realizing that she would not be able to proceed and worried about submarines, Rodman ordered the three remaining dreadnoughts to resume their journey, leaving their stricken sister to be towed ignominiously back to New York for repairs two days later.

As things turned out, *Texas* missed very little. The American battleships arrived at Scapa on 29 November without further mishap and were immediately incorporated into the Grand Fleet as the Sixth Battle Squadron. For a time the friendly British reception and the thrill of finally being in the war zone sustained the American contingent. "I am sure the captain of each of those ships felt as I did," wrote Henry Wiley of the *Wyoming*. "Not only proud of his command, but lucky to be at Scapa; that he had not only the best job in the world, but had a serious part to play in the greatest war the world has ever seen."[168]

USS Arizona, *passing New York's 96th Street Pier, during World War I. (Courtesy of the U.S. National Archives)*

Every effort was made to perpetuate the illusion. On the Grand Fleet's rare sweeps of the upper North Sea, the Sixth Battle Squadron inevitably occupied a prominent position in the formation. On one occasion David Beatty went as far as to praise the Americans' navigation and seamanship over that of his own officers.[169] Although the Yankee dreadnoughts were destined to fire not a single salvo at a hostile battleship, or at any surface ship for that matter, Admiral Henry T. Mayo would later reassure the public that "our target practice showed us up mighty well."[170] (Ironically, the only American naval rifles to fire at Germans of any sort were the five 14-inch pieces that had been mounted on railway cars and transported to France in hopes of silencing the Krupp works' infamous *Pariskanone*.)

Yet month after inactive month in the dreary, desolate anchorage at Scapa began to wear the veneer of optimism a bit thin. Among the first to grumble were the enlisted men of the repaired *Texas*, who realized the only fighting they were doing was ashore—"long straggling fist fights with stevedores, sailors, Tynesiders." Not very heroic foes, but as one sailor noted, they had little choice. "The only naval war right now is the submarine war, and the submarine is the one thing a battleship's no good at fighting."[171]

At no time was the truth of the remark more apparent than during a farcical sequence that occurred in early February 1918, while the Sixth Battle Squadron was on its way to meet and escort a convoy bound for Norway. As Captain Henry Wiley recalled:

> At about 1:30 PM the *New York* hoisted a green flag, meaning submarine sighted. This was passed along to other ships. Almost immediately, however, the signal was annulled and the *New York* signaled, "destroyer *Valorous* reports porpoises." . . . At this time the lookout on the *Wyoming* reported sighting a periscope, "Unmistakable." We signalled the bearing and had just started to turn four points to starboard when *Florida* broke the black pennant [meaning torpedoes], blew two blasts on her siren and put her rudder hard left. This created a dangerous situation . . . and . . . the two ships cleared by a narrow margin. The *Florida* then signaled the torpedo had passed from right to left ahead. Nobody on the *Wyoming* saw it. . . . While the *Florida* and the *Delaware* went off on their own, a number of destroyers, with them the *Valorous*, were dropping depth bombs. . . . Notwithstanding that the *Wyoming* was a considerable distance away and steaming fast, when the first one exploded it rocked the ships. I certainly thought we had got a torpedo in the stern. And so did the crew evidently . . . [since] they all rushed aft to look over the stern. I quietly called up the steering room . . . and asked how everything was going down there. I was relieved to get the answer, "Fine Sir!" . . . Our alarm was not over, for as the *Florida* reached her position she reported torpedo headed for the *Wyoming* on the port bow, and, as I recall it, a submarine on our starboard. Our people could see no wake of a torpedo. . . . We finally got squared away, however, and settled down and saw no more periscopes.[172]

Dreadnoughts' jumping at their own shadows was hardly the kind of behavior expected from monarchs of the sea. Before the war dragged to its conclusion, the American battleship squadron would report itself attacked by submarines a total of six times.[173] Whether real or imagined, this was the only action in the offing. In the United States a few optimists like Albert Gleaves might still maintain, "The British and American fleets are on watch together, they are maneuvering together, they are drilling together, and when that day comes, when the great battle will be fought, they will win together."[174] But Sims, on the scene, knew better. On 17 September he wrote Benson, "I have found nobody in the Admiralty or outside of it that believes in the probability of the High Seas Fleet giving battle."[175]

Indeed by that time the Kaiser's "Risk Fleet" was in no condition to do much of anything. Since Jutland the German armada had fallen upon evil days. Whereas in 1914 Admiral von Ingenohl, then commander of the High Seas Fleet, had been ordered "to keep this, our main weapon, sharp and bright," by the time unrestricted submarine warfare was resumed, Reinhard Scheer was admitting that "our fleet has become the hilt of a weapon whose sharp blade is the U-boat."[176]

Actually, the nature of the new relationship had become perfectly apparent as early as 4 and 5 November 1916, when two German submarines, U-20 and U-30, ran aground in the fog off Bovsbjerg on the west coast of north Jutland. To cover the stricken submersibles while rescue efforts were under way, the battle cruiser *Moltke*, four dreadnoughts, and a half flotilla of destroyers were dispatched to the scene.[177] Around noon of the second day, after one of the U-boats had finally been freed and the other scuttled, the German heavy forces headed slowly back to port. However, a British submarine had also responded to the distress signals of the stranded U-boats. Moments later the *Grosser Kurfürst* and the *Kronprinz* were each hit with a torpedo. Both ships were seriously damaged and were forced to limp home at a reduced speed.

When the Kaiser learned that a squadron of the dreadnoughts had been risked for the sake of two U-boats and that two capital ships had been torpedoed, he was furious. But when he summoned Scheer to explain himself, the admiral was hardly contrite. He vehemently defended his actions, arguing that in the coming submarine campaign, "the Fleet will have to devote itself to one task— to get the U-boats safely out to sea and bring them home again. Such activities would be on precisely the same lines as the expedition to save the U-20."[178]

Actually, the U-boats were well able to fend for themselves, and the High Seas Fleet spent the submarine campaign in much the same fashion as it had the rest of the Great War, sitting in port. Like a broadsword abandoned to the elements, the Kaiser's armada began to rust, then disintegrate. In August 1917, 600 enlisted men from the dreadnought *Prinzregent Luitpold* spontaneously left their ship and marched off to a local tavern chanting antiwar slogans. The outbreak was harshly suppressed, with ten death sentences and a total of 350 years in prison being passed out in the process.[179] Nonetheless, discontent continued to ferment below decks.

By the fall of 1917 the battle readiness of the fleet had begun to deteriorate drastically. Drills were ignored, target practice neglected, and men carried out their duties sullenly, if at all. When the High Seas Fleet left port at last in April 1918, hoping to find a convoy during a quick sweep of the Norwegian coast, its dilapidated condition became obvious. Twenty-six hours into the mission the battle cruiser *Moltke* lost a propeller, causing a turbine to race and blow to pieces, several of which pierced a main condenser pipe, necessitating the flooding of the entire engine room. The chain reaction left the ship virtually without power— not the sort of accident that befell a well-maintained ship. Franz Hipper ordered the *Moltke* taken under tow and proceeded with his short and unsuccessful search for convoys. Meanwhile, *Moltke* suffered further indignities when she was torpedoed by a submarine forty miles north of Heligoland. Only her stout construction kept the ship afloat until the River Jade and safety could be reached.[180]

During the summer of 1918 the physical condition of the Teutonic dread-noughts continued to deteriorate, while the morale of their men sank to new depths. The High Seas Fleet was a fighting force in name only. Nonetheless, by 15 October Reinhard Scheer, then chief of the Admiralty Staff, was determined that "the fleet must be decisively engaged in battle"; even though it was not expected to "decisively alter the course of events . . . it is a question of honor and of the existence of the Navy to have done its utmost."[181] It was to be a suicide mission, in other words. That, despite the fact that on 20 October the new chancellor, liberal Prince Max of Baden, "implored the Admiral most urgently that the Navy would have to accept the inevitable, since any incident [that] might disrupt the peace negotiations was to be avoided at all costs." In reply Scheer had pledged "the fullest loyalty of the Navy which would be demonstrated by the recall of all submarines."[182] Immediately after the interview, however, he resumed planning the last *Flottenvorstoss* (fleet advance). Later he would declare slyly that "the High Seas Fleet by being relieved of the tasks of [covering] submarine warfare had now regained its operational freedom."[183] On 22 October Franz Hipper, the new commander in chief, received the following order: "High Seas Fleet shall attack and engage in battle the English Fleet."

The men would have none of it. "The idea had taken root in their minds," as Reinhard Scheer innocently put it, "that they were being uselessly sacrificed."[184] When the entire fleet was ordered to assemble at Schilling Roads off Wilhelmshaven to await the death ride, the enlisted ranks became openly rebellious. The crews of *Moltke*, *Derfflinger*, *Von der Tann*, and *Seydlitz* resorted to passive resistance by refusing to board their ships when ordered.[185] Over the next forty-eight hours insurrection spread throughout the battle fleet, and on 29 October Hipper was compelled to cancel his sailing orders. The mutiny spread to the Baltic on 31 October, when the Third Squadron of the High Seas Fleet sailed from Wilhelmshaven up the canal to Kiel. By 4 November bands of sailors began to move inland by truck and train, fomenting revolution as they went. Two days later they reached Berlin and set off a series of events that would topple the government of Prince Max, force the Kaiser to abdicate, and cause Philipp Scheidemann to proclaim the republic. On 9 November 1918 the German Empire was dead. Two days later the armistice was officially proclaimed.

So the extravaganza was over at last. For those in the cast who had dreamed of a naval Armageddon, it must have been the ultimate disillusionment. But like the players in any long-running show that finally closes, they would have to fend for themselves.

In fact they did. On 21 November, long after the house lights had dimmed and the theater had been emptied, something remarkable happened. It was as if the troupe had sneaked back in the playhouse to recreate their roles, this time according to a script of their own making. The occasion was the internment of the German High Seas Fleet.

At first it had been a presentation that both the American and French members of the cast had been inclined to forgo. "As for the German surface fleet, what do you fear from it?" Marshal Foch had pointedly asked. "During the whole war only a few of its units have ventured from their ports."[186] But the British had insisted, and at 4:00 A.M. on 21 November the entire Grand Fleet— 260 ships in all—steamed out of the Firth of Forth in two great lines to meet its elusive adversary once more.

On board the New York, the flagship of the American Sixth Battle Squadron, Lieutenant Francis Hunter wrote: "Each gun is manned. Every man is at his post. The powder bins are filled and shells are up. Range finders scan the horizon. . . . No 'Wooden Horse of Troy' for Admiral Beatty. Not the slightest chance of Hunnish trickery. The destiny of nations is at stake."[187]

The British steamed steadily toward the designated point in the North Sea. By eight bells, men on the New York were beginning to drift up on deck to peer anxiously toward the horizon. For an hour they were left to watch and wonder. Would they come? Would they at last give up without a fight? Then: "Sail Ho!—from the foretop lookout. . . . Dense smoke, Sir, seems to be approaching."[188]

A half hour later the light cruiser *Cardiff,* towing a kite balloon, led a great column of capital ships between the two British lines. First came the battle cruisers, their huge guns trained fore and aft—*Seydlitz, Derfflinger, Von der Tann, Moltke,* and the giant newcomer, *Hindenburg.* Then, after a short pause, came the long line of battleships—led by the flagship *Friedrich der Grosse—Koenig Albert, Kaiser, Kronprinz Wilhelm, Kaiserin, Bayern, Markgraf, Prinzregent Luitpold,* and *Grosser Kurfürst.* "At a prearranged signal," as Admiral Rodman reported, "our forces swung symmetrically through 180 degrees, and, still paralleling the enveloped Germans, conducted them toward a designated anchorage in the entrance of the Firth of Forth."[189]

Aboard the *Texas* Lieutenant Paul Schubert stood within listening distance of several enlisted men. " 'God! Are they just going to take it?' Joking stopped. Talk stopped. They were ours without glory. 'Der Tag,' said an officer. 'Makes you sick.' "[190] "Strangely enough the German surrender lacked the thrill of victory," reported Lieutenant Hunter.[191] Hugh Rodman echoed these sentiments: "Surely no more complete victory was ever won, nor a more disgraceful and humiliating end could have come."[192] This pained ambivalence—the desire to perpetuate the idea that some sort of victory had been salvaged and the realization that it had all been little more than a sham—was nowhere more evident than in David Beatty's farewell to the Sixth Battle Squadron ten days later. "It was a disappointing day. It was a pitiful day to see those great ships coming in like sheep being herded by dogs to their fold without an effort on anybody's part; but it was a day that everybody could be proud of."[193]

The surrender had a meaning all its own. If World War I marked the passing of an age, certainly no ceremony could have been more appropriate—a seance for the prophet Mahan. The battleship had symbolized war by the rules; in the future only lip service would be paid to that way of fighting. Henceforth the dreadnought would survive on sentiment alone.

9

Martyrdom: Dreadnoughts in the Wake of Versailles

I

As the Great War wound down to ashes in the fall of 1918, it became clear that for the second time in a bit over a century an outsider would preside over a general European peace settlement. Like Russia's Alexander I a hundred years before him, Woodrow Wilson was an idealist who had seen the struggle from a vastly different perspective, both geographically and conceptually, from the views of the other belligerents. Millions of his people had not been uselessly slaughtered; the gargantuan hatreds generated by the war were but dimly perceived.

For the United States, the war had come about as a result of a dispute over maritime rights. Similar controversies had precipitated the War of 1812 and had led to grave diplomatic complications during the Civil War. The rights of nonbelligerents on the high seas had become a nagging issue in American diplomatic history.

Yet at the same time that concern betrayed a peculiarly abstract and provincial frame of reference. An absence of fair play, not inevitable conflicts of interests, was viewed as the major stumbling block to peace. The rules of international relations had only to be set right for wars like this to become impossible. Out of this milieu was born the Fourteen Points, Wilson's improved code of geopolitical behavior, and "absolute freedom of navigation upon the seas . . . alike in peace and war" was accorded a prominent place on the list. Indeed after the concept of the League of Nations, the president seems to have considered it his most important point.

To the Allies the Fourteen Points seemed at first little more than a rhetorical device to coax Germany into an armistice, and as such they quickly endorsed them. All of that changed when the Germans accepted the Wilsonian framework as a basis for a cease-fire. Faced with commitments to all sorts of noble principles, the U.S. associates promptly began backing away from the document. "God gave us Ten Commandments and we broke them," suggested French Prime Minister Georges Clemenceau, "Wilson gives us Fourteen Points. . . . We will see." More specifically, the British flatly refused to accept any proposal that would circumscribe their fleet in wartime. Only Colonel House's threat of an American withdrawal and a separate peace with Germany proved sufficient to keep the Allies tethered to the general principles of the Fourteen Points. But Britain remained adamantly opposed to Freedom of the Seas.

Woodrow Wilson was no man to contradict in late 1918. A stern Christian upbringing, a distinguished career as an educator, and manifold triumphs in American politics had combined to imbue him with a profound sense of his own rightness. At the head of a state newly emergent as the most powerful in the world, he was in a position to indulge his didactic tendencies. The British refusal to concede Freedom of the Seas was perceived as an act of an impudence. If they could not see the virtues of cooperation, they would have to be shown. "I want to go to the Peace Conference," he told Josephus Daniels, "with as many weapons as my pockets will hold so as to compel justice."[1] It was at this point that Woodrow Wilson rediscovered the dreadnought.

Since April the ever-persistent planners of the General Board had been clamoring for resumption of the 1916 capital ship program, hoping to breathe life into the stillborn Phantom Fleet.[2] In June, with an admirable touch of bravado, they upped the ante to stratospheric levels, announcing a seven-year program destined to produce twelve battleships and sixteen battle cruisers.[3] But months passed and the naval pleas continued to fall upon deaf ears. Then in mid-fall, when all seemed darkest, the administration began studying the capital ship proposals with renewed interest. If the seven-year program struck Wilson as a bit much, neither was he in the mood to cut corners. The battleship was an ideal diplomatic bludgeon, while peace and the end of submarine depredations had restored at least a measure of its credibility. Consequently, on 15 October he agreed not only to resume work on the half-built battleships but also to support a virtual duplicate of the 1916 program, bringing the total of contemplated capital ships to twenty battleships and twelve battle cruisers.[4] The dreadnought had been launched on a new career, that of a bargaining chip. Woodrow Wilson would journey to France in search of peace and a world safe for democracy with his pockets stuffed full of the largest fleet ever contemplated. Such was the logic of negotiating from strength.

As the liner *George Washington* neared Brest just after dawn on 13 December 1918, she was met by ten American dreadnoughts. Below deck the president of the United States was awakened by a tumultuous rumbling as each of the genial floating fortresses fired a twenty-one-gun salute for their new friend and then fell into a double column behind to escort the steamer into port.

By 1:30 in the afternoon Admirals Sims and Benson had come aboard with a host of other dignitaries to greet their commander in chief. While lighthearted Sims was left to needle the dour General Pershing ("Hello Jack! How the hell did you do it? I didn't know you had it in you."), Benson was taken aside by the president and closely questioned on naval affairs.[5]

This was not accidental. If Wilson wanted to put forward a hard line toward the British, Benson was the officer to do it. An unregenerate Anglophobe, the chief of naval operations had taken care to remind the president that "every great commercial rival of the British Empire has eventually found itself at war with Great Britain—and has been defeated."[6] Spain, Holland, France, and Germany. Now it was the U.S. turn. Postwar security for Benson meant a navy second to none, and that meant a multitude of battleships. Wartime experience had left hardly a mark on his consciousness. Dreadnoughts remained the focal point of seapower, the backbone of the fleet. As such they would act as the primary rudder in Benson's eccentric maneuvers as chief American naval adviser.

From the first day of the armistice the admiral had taken little care to hide his intense suspicion of the British, especially in regard to the eventual fate of the High Seas Fleet. Agreeing only with the greatest reluctance to the internment of the Kaiser's dreadnoughts at Scapa, Benson had fretted ever since over the possibility that they might fall into the hands of the Royal Navy.[7] It did not seem to matter that every gun barrel and shell, every nut and bolt, in the Teutonic warships was based on the metric, and not the English, system, making them almost impossible to integrate into the Grand Fleet. A dreadnought was still a dreadnought, and the admiral continued to send worried cables across the Atlantic warning against distribution of the German vessels lest the British receive the lion's share.[8] The only safe course for the United States lay in their destruction.

It is safe to say that as Woodrow Wilson chatted with his chief of naval operations on the deck of the *George Washington*, the president's concern over the future of the High Seas Fleet was minimal. Battleships were now abstractions to Wilson, instruments of diplomatic coercion, nothing real or tangible like the rusting German hulks marooned in the Orkneys. Yet the admiral's obsession with the German dreadnoughts would not be held against him. Unlike Sims, who the president thought "should be wearing a British uniform,"[9] Benson was an officer who could be trusted not to let the British put anything over on him. As such he would be left with considerable autonomy over naval matters once the peace negotiations got under way at the Paris Peace Conference. It was a serious error. Wilson's own bias blinded him to Benson's. The man's genial but relentless pursuit of his own particularist viewpoint cast a pall of confusion over the entire naval negotiations.

Indeed the dogged chief of naval operations lost little time in making himself a thorn in the side of the Inter-Allied Naval Council. Whereas the British were willing to go along with Benson's insistence on the destruction of the surrendered German warships, the French and the Italians, who did use the metric system, protested vehemently. Meanwhile, the American admiral made himself still less popular by steadfastly refusing to place any restrictions on the future growth of the German Navy.[10] What appeared to Benson as a potential balance wheel against British naval ambitions struck the Europeans as a glaring potential threat to peace. Months passed and the chasm of disagreement only grew wider. "Benson objects to pretty much everything any of the Allies suggest," wrote a dismayed Colonel House, "and he is particularly suspicious of the British."[11] By March nothing had been resolved.

Edward M. House was not about to see the peace evaporate due to one admiral. Once described as a man able to walk on dead leaves and make no more noise than a tiger, this urbane Texan found confrontation alien to his nature.[12] Characteristically, he had chosen the unobtrusive role of alter ego, attaching himself like lamprey to Woodrow Wilson, becoming his friend, confidant, and "second personality." If anyone at the peace conference could claim to speak for the president, it was House. But in one important respect he was a dissenter. He would have none of the administration's John Bull–baiting. The colonel admired the British and sincerely believed that an ironclad Anglo-American naval agreement was imperative to the success of the League of Nations.[13] But this would require tact and compromise, scarce commodities in the U.S. delegation's inner circle.

House's opportunity to strike a more conciliatory note was not long in coming. In early March Woodrow Wilson returned home to defend the League of Nations, leaving his friend virtually in charge. At last he was free to supersede

Benson and take up the matter of the naval impasse directly with Prime Ministers Clemenceau and David Lloyd George. House soon learned that the distribution of the captured battleships was a minor irritant in comparison to the imminent Anglo-American naval race. The British were willing to agree to sink their share of the spoils, but they made that contingent upon a more comprehensive understanding between Britain and the United States.[14] Plainly, they wanted the 1916 program and its duplicate dropped. But a decision of such magnitude would have to await the return of the president.

Woodrow Wilson was less than pleased by the intervention of his alter ego. After meeting with the colonel at Brest, he remarked bitterly, "House has given away everything I had won before we left for Paris."[15] As for the naval stalemate, the president was now willing to see definite limits put on future German fleets and armies. He was also ready to tie the fate of the captured vessels to an Anglo-American naval agreement.[16] But he refused to drop his building program. He knew the British lacked the financial resources to match the United States in competitive building, and he was determined to make the most of the advantage. Apparently the thaw in the naval negotiations was over—the Phantom Fleet lived and House languished in disfavor.

Things grew even worse in mid-March when Lloyd George, realizing he held a weak hand, took the offensive. He not only threatened to retain the German dreadnoughts, but he also informed the Americans that he would sign no league covenant in the absence of a full accord on naval building programs.[17]

To parry the latest thrust, the president turned to Josephus Daniels, who had just arrived in Europe on a mission to study capital ship types. As committed as anyone in the administration to the dreadnought program, the secretary was nonetheless uncertain as to the proper course to steer in the negotiations. "I didn't sleep much that night even though Paris beds were comfortable. I knew that what carried Wilson to Paris was to secure the League. Was it so important that the Navy program must be scrapped to secure Lloyd George's support?"[18] Colonel House, on the one hand, told Daniels on 20 March that "we could afford to have no program of naval construction if others do likewise." Admiral Benson, on the other hand, was equally sure "we could not agree to any limitations on hulls."[19] So Daniels was left to wrestle the matter over with Lloyd George.

The talks did begin on a positive note. The secretary, briefed by his bureau chiefs on the incompatibility of German ships, was fairly sure that the little Welshman's threat to keep the surrendered vessels had been a bluff. Events proved him correct. Lloyd George quickly admitted: "What I would like to see would be to tow all those German ships at Scapa Flow into the middle of the Atlantic and to surround them with the ships of all the Allied countries, and to the music of all our national airs, sink them ostentatiously."[20]

He was, however, much less conciliatory on the subject of the building program. "We have stopped work on our [battle] cruisers, and you ought to stop work on your [battle] cruisers and dreadnoughts if you really believe in the League of Nations."[21] Daniels was apparently impressed by that argument, but he was empowered to do no more than inform the president of the British prime minister's apparent earnestness about dropping the league. Having done what he could, the secretary then departed for Rome to resume his technical mission.

His exit left an opening for House, who began negotiating with Sir Robert Cecil, a fellow member of the league committee and one of the sincerest British advocates of an international organization. On 8 April Cecil wrote House reiterating the importance that the British attached to their naval defenses. He ended, however, on a more abject note, wondering whether it would be possible for the United States to "abandon or modify" its "new naval programme" once the British had ratified the League of Nations.[22] Clearly the British wanted an end to U.S. naval construction even if it meant supporting an international organization ostensibly committed to Freedom of the Seas. Woodrow Wilson's dreadnoughts had apparently won him a considerable victory.

The good tidings did not find the commander in chief in a magnanimous mood, however. Domestic foes of the league were legion. A fleet of paper dreadnoughts might prove as intimidating at home as it had abroad. So the president chose to interpret "new naval programme" as pertaining only to the postwar duplicate of the unbuilt 1916 fleet. That he agreed to abort, but its older twin was to remain alive. It had been voted by Congress. His hands were tied.

It did not take long for the British to pick up the ambiguities in House's reply to Cecil's letter.[23] Lloyd George complained that any agreement that left the original 1916 program in force was tantamount to no agreement at all. But the best that could be wrung from the Americans was a face-saving admission from House that it might be possible to "postpone the commencement of those ships which had not been actually begun until after the Treaty of Peace had been signed."[24] The decisive action in the so-called naval battle of Paris ended with the statesmen still bickering over dreadnoughts. So the great ships remained a viable force in the affairs of men. Like chips at a gambling casino, they were ideal units of measurement and thus eminently useful in scoring the games of politics and diplomacy.

Meanwhile, the pertinacious Admiral Benson must have come to suspect that events had taken a detour around him. Rumors of secret negotiations and an Anglo-American compromise continued to circulate. Yet he was seldom consulted. Undaunted, the admiral kept up the brisk stream of gloomy memoranda warning of the dangers inherent in being the world's second naval power.[25] But they did not seem to have much impact. The president and the senior diplomats were always pleasant, but increasingly vague about their plans.

Worse was yet to come for Benson. The French and the Italians were proving unexpectedly persistent in their opposition to the destruction of the High Seas Fleet, so much so that on 25 April the admiral had gone before the Big Four to argue that the sinking of the offending armada would be an important step toward halting the arms race. But Wilson failed to support his naval adviser, and the council finally voted to omit from the peace treaty any reference to the fate of the surrendered German ships.[26] No longer much of a threat to anybody else, the High Seas Fleet still loomed as a special demon in the imagination of William S. Benson.

Fortunately for the admiral, his ordeal was destined to be a short one. On 21 June 1919 the POW battle fleet committed suicide. The German dreadnoughts had sat at anchor in the gale-swept waters of Scapa Flow for seven months. Their slate-gray hulls were streaked red with rust. Only skeleton crews of officers remained to care for them. Further humiliation was inevitable. There seemed but one way out for their commander, Rear Admiral von Reuter: "It was unthinkable to surrender defenseless ships to the enemy. We officers were bound by a decision of the All Highest to destroy them."[27]

They had to work quickly. Word had arrived that the Treaty of Versailles would be signed on 21 June, ending the armistice and allowing the chief British jailer, Rear Admiral Sydney Freemantle, the right to board the captive vessels and seize them. On the 17th preparatory orders were smuggled through the fleet via a fishing boat.[28] Submerged torpedo tubes and condenser inlets were to be jammed open and watertight doors unhinged. All was made ready for the morning of the 21st when the scuttling was to be accomplished—it was hoped before the British had a chance to intervene.

As fate, forever the lover of spectacles, would have it, the British were nowhere in sight when the moment arrived. On the evening of 20 June the armistice had been extended for forty-eight hours, and Freemantle thought it safe to take his First Battle Squadron out into Pentland Firth for battle practice at dawn.[29] Only two destroyers remained to watch the seventy-four German inmates as the immersion began.

It had seemed at first merely an obscure act of defiance. At 10 A.M. each Teutonic warship had unfurled the ensign of the Imperial German Navy in direct contravention of British orders. Yet it was more than an hour before anyone realized that the ships below the offending flags were slowly disappearing. By that time little could be done. A few shots were fired and the captain of the *Markgraf* was killed. But in general, the guard vessels confined themselves to picking up Germans who had jumped overboard and reporting the bad news to Freemantle. By the time the errant admiral arrived back on the scene, Scapa was littered with the prows and masts of drowning ships. Only the battleship *Baden* and the light cruisers *Emden, Frankfurt,* and *Nürnberg* stood high enough in the water to be beached and saved.

Redistribution was no longer an issue. Water and the high specific gravity of armor plate had succeeded where diplomacy had failed.

The British, of course, were indignant. Once again the Royal Navy had been duped. Von Reuter was hauled off to prisoner-of-war camp, and there was even talk of prosecuting him for war crimes.[30] But when tempers cooled, many officers were willing to admit with Admiral Wester Wemyss that the suicide of the High Seas Fleet had been a "real blessing."[31] It removed one of the two major irritants to Allied naval cooperation. But Wilson's armada remained to haunt the peace.

II

As might be expected, enthusiasm for the dreadnought program fell off rapidly outside the immediate circle of Woodrow Wilson and his naval advisers. Public reaction to the announcement of the virtual doubling of an already-suspect capital ship program, just three weeks after the termination of the most destructive war in history, bordered on the incredulous. The normally staid *New York Times* declared, "The Atlantic Coast is secure as if there were no fleets in Europe" and termed it "grotesque" to even "talk about British aggression today."[32]

It was not simply a matter of alienating the moderates: The chorus of disapproval was joined by some of the Navy's former staunchest allies. From Oyster Bay, Theodore Roosevelt complained that the United States should be satisfied to "have the second navy in the world" and charged the president with wanting "merely . . . to build a spite navy . . . in order to bluff Lloyd George."[33]

Not surprisingly, that general level of hostility was reflected in Congress, where the future of the battleship bill seemed bleak. The Republicans had elected majorities to both houses in the November elections and would assume control on 4 March 1919. If the proposal stood any chance of survival, it would have to be moved expeditiously through the House and Senate in the remaining two months of the lame duck Democratic majority.[34]

Putting up a bold front, Josephus Daniels and a procession of admirals marched before the House Naval Affairs Committee in December and January to defend the program.[35] Calling the measure "a conservative one," the naval secretary warned that "if the Conference at Versailles does not result in a general agreement . . . then the United States . . . must give her men and give her money to the task of the creation of incomparably the greatest Navy in the world."[36] Even more emphatic was Admiral Benson, who cabled from Paris that "no one thing" would more effectively ensure basic principles such as Freedom of the Seas than the evident determination of the United States to build up its naval power as fast as possible, "even if considered desirable to ease up later."[37]

Yet a closer examination of the administration's recommendations revealed a sound basis for avoiding haste. For one thing the duplicate program seemed, even to the public's eye, ill conceived and slipshod. Unlike previous naval lists, which had carefully enumerated the types to be constructed, this plan only specified the 10 battleships and 6 battle cruisers.[38] Just what the remaining 140 proposed warships might turn out to be was apparently not to be divulged to Congress.

Further investigation revealed still more confusion over types. The capital ship, it seemed, was undergoing an identity crisis. By late 1918 both the Navy's technical bureaus and the talented young officers in operations had come to the conclusion that the flimsy battle cruisers and sluggish dreadnoughts of the 1916 program should be curtailed in favor of a single capital ship, the so-called C-type, or fast battleship. Of course, such a vessel was necessarily larger than either of its progenitors; but it was blessed with thick armor plate, twelve 16-inch guns, and a thirty-knot top speed.[39]

Needless to say, it was quick to win influential friends in the naval community. Sims endorsed the C-type in November. Then Benson cabled Daniels from Paris warning against the construction of battle cruisers "already proved a tragic demonstration of error at Jutland."[40] Yet the General Board persisted in backing the battle cruisers it had once shunned,[41] and the secretary chose to avoid the issue simply by asking Congress for a program "substantially like that of 1916." But this facade crumbled on 31 January 1919 when Henry T. Mayo, commander in chief of the Atlantic Fleet, went on record before the House Naval Affairs Committee as favoring the C-type.[42] Nothing about the duplicate program seemed certain. It amounted to asking Congress to authorize the Navy to build as much as they wanted of whatever they liked.

Congress was in no mood for blanket endorsements. Below the level of partisan activity there was a solid bedrock of sentiment against militarism and wartime domination by the executive. The United States was at peace, and the legislative branch wished no longer to be treated as a rubber stamp. "Why this call upon the House by the Naval Department?" asked Democratic Representative Huddleston of Alabama.

> Have they in mind to challenge the naval supremacy of the British Empire? . . . On this floor a gentlemen said yesterday that New York would be an object of attack in case of such a war by that great fleet which never dared venture within sight of . . . the German coast. [Such a prospect] would appear to be nothing but the vain dreams of professional seamen obsessed with their own theories of the importance of their profession.[43]

Representative Currie, Republican from Michigan, asked "whether we were preparing for a test of strength with the British Navy," or was this "one of the meanest, crudest bluffs ever recorded?"[44] Whatever the case, Congress was not likely to christen Wilson's armada any time soon. On 4 March the lame duck session ended with the naval bill still pending before the Senate. Even with the advantage of Democratic congressional majorities, the second Phantom Fleet had not been authorized.

Realizing the administration's naval program was in deep trouble, Josephus Daniels took immediate steps to salvage what he could. All work on the battle cruisers was suspended, and the General Board was ordered to consult Admirals Sims, Mayo, and Rodman on the characteristics of future dreadnoughts.[45] Meanwhile the secretary traveled to Europe to study aircraft and the capital ship question personally.[46] Although this mission did have some impact on the negotiations in Paris, it was to prove no more successful than the General Board's dilatory investigation of dreadnought types. No amount of cosmetics could disguise the basic unsoundness of the program. The times were wrong and the ships were wrong. Only Wilson's agreement with the British to drop the duplicate program saved further embarrassment.

On 27 May 1919 a somewhat relieved Josephus Daniels met with the House Naval Affairs Committee to announce that the Navy, as a gesture of faith in the League of Nations, would withdraw its request for a second battleship program. This left only the original version of the Phantom Fleet to be finished. When asked by Representative Thomas S. Butler if that meant completing the suspect battle cruisers, the secretary hedged, promising an answer in a day or two.[47] In fact the decision to complete all the ships of the 1916 program "as expeditiously as possible" had already been made the previous day by Daniels, his bureau chiefs, and the General Board. The battle cruisers would be modified as necessary.[48]

Nonetheless, the most objectionable portion of the naval bill had been removed, and the legislators responded by passing it quickly through both houses before the end of June. But its passage should not be construed as an endorsement of either the president's naval program or the dreadnought. In truth the bloated construction proposal had aroused congressional ire as few things the administration had done in the past.[49] The dreadnought, in the eyes of many, had become irrevocably associated with waste, militarism, and international blackmail.

Meanwhile Woodrow Wilson would again find it necessary to begin brandishing battleships. Since 10 July, when the president had submitted the Versailles Treaty to the Senate, the pact's Republican opponents had seized upon every opportunity for obstruction. Archenemy Henry Cabot Lodge had stalled the document for two weeks before his Senate Foreign Relations Committee by reading the entire text verbatim in a slow monotone. When the hearings finally did begin, they were carefully orchestrated by the Republican majority to put the treaty in the worst possible light.

So in early September the president took his case to the people. Leaving Washington on a special train, the Mayflower, the frail chief executive traveled almost 10,000 miles, stopping at thirty-seven cities to address the multitudes on the virtues of world cooperation. Repeatedly Wilson resorted to carrot-and-stick tactics, offering the league as the only alternative to weapons construction on a gigantic scale. "The choice is either to accept this treaty or play a long hand. . . . That means that we must always be armed . . . it means we must continue to live under not diminished but increased taxes; it means that we shall devote our thoughts and the organization of our Government to being strong enough to beat any nation. An absolute reversal of all the ideals of American history."[50]

He couldn't have been more clear, and there were signs late in the tour that he was winning public support.

Yet Woodrow Wilson's crusade was destined to end in tragic failure. On 25 September, after warning the people of Pueblo, Colorado, that rejection of the treaty would mean "great standing armies . . . an irresistible navy," the president suffered a stroke and collapsed. Bedridden and partially paralyzed during the waning months of 1919, Wilson watched helplessly as his enemies closed in with knives drawn to maim his beloved league. In the end he killed it himself rather than accept the reservations that Lodge and the others had posted as the price of survival.

It is seldom pleasant to see a man destroyed in the pursuit of an ideal, especially if his cause is to the ultimate benefit of mankind. But it was Wilson's own arrogance and probably his ill health that largely ensnared him. As chief executive during wartime, he had grown used to obedience, come to depend on it. Finally the twenty-eighth president, already a sick man, had fallen victim to the disease of kings. Pride had infected him and crippled his capacity for compromise. Nowhere was this more evident than in his threats to fill U.S. shipyards with dreadnoughts if the world and the nation failed to embrace his master plan. In Wilson's eyes they would either take the league or be made to build battleships endlessly—like rowdies at a blackboard writing the same sentence over and over. But Congress, the nation, and the world were not to be treated like schoolchildren. So in the end the plan failed. All that remained of Wilson's dream were the sixteen half-finished dreadnoughts of the original 1916 program, a bitter legacy for a man of peace.

Woodrow Wilson was not the only victim of his affair with the dreadnought. For the dalliance had set battleships multiplying the world over. Shipbuilding was countered with shipbuilding, as once more the nations of the world found themselves in a pointless arms race.

The Japanese had been the first to react. Having escaped the bloodletting and the prodigal expenditures of the Great War, the Asian power found itself in an unexpectedly strong position as hostilities ended. Although supported by an economy but a fraction of the size of its Western rivals, the Land of the Rising Sun was clearly the dominant force in the Western Pacific. Japan's possessions, including the Mariana and Marshall islands, mandated to it at Versailles, not only outflanked the American outpost in the Philippines but stretched almost to Hawaii. Patrolling this maritime dominion was the third largest navy in the world. Thoroughly modern and as efficient as ceaseless training could make it, the imperial battle fleet was at once the linchpin of empire and the most revered symbol of the nation's meteoric rise to prominence. As such its credibility would be maintained, virtually no matter the cost.[51]

With power had also come danger, for Japan's chief rival for Pacific hegemony was the United States, the strongest and most ambitious nation in the world. Beginning in 1908 with the world cruise of Roosevelt's Great White Fleet, each power had gradually come to accept the other as its most likely adversary in case of war.[52] By 1919, with Germany no longer complicating matters, the mutual enmity had become proverbial. As might be expected, Wilson's armada was an object of great concern to the Japanese. What appeared to others as oriented toward Europe was interpreted by Japan's planners as being aimed directly at the heart of their empire.

Such a challenge did not long go unanswered. In March 1919 word came from Tokyo that its navy had decided to complete its long deferred 8:8:8 program, calling for a construction program aimed at eight battleships and eight battle cruisers, all under eight years of age. The U.S. naval attaché reported that four of the dreadnoughts and all the battle cruisers were to be finished by 1923. Indeed nearly half of the $600 million budget approved by the imperial cabinet in 1919 was devoted to armaments.[53] Before the race was over, Japan's naval expenditures would triple from $85 million in 1917 to $245 million in 1921.[54] Apparently what the oriental power lacked in size, it made up for in determination.

Meanwhile, Japan's increasingly reluctant ally, Great Britain, tried its best to steer a course of moderation. Financially strapped and already in possession of the world's largest herd of dreadnoughts, Britain had every reason to placate the United States. Through patient negotiations at Versailles, Wilson had been persuaded to drop the duplicate fleet, and there was obviously hope within the Foreign Office that the 1916 program also might be disposed of in the same manner.

Consequently, in the early fall of 1919 the urbane Viscount Grey of Fallodon was sent to the United States to do just that. But his mission came to nothing. Arriving in New York the day after Wilson's collapse, Grey waited fully four months without ever being offered the opportunity to present his credentials formally. Finally, after the president became convinced that Grey was working with Lodge, the British diplomat returned home empty-handed.[55]

The British were not about to give up trying to soothe the touchy Americans. Hoping to set an example of restraint, they adopted in 1919 and 1920 what amounted to a unilateral naval holiday. With the exception of the half-finished *Hood*, the entire capital ship program was halted, and the Grand Fleet was ruthlessly pruned of old and obsolete vessels. By May 1920 Admiral Sims would be informed by the Office of Naval Intelligence that twenty-eight British battleships had been marked for the scrap heap.[56]

Also marked for the scrap heap was the Anglo-Japanese alliance. Concluded in 1901 and renewed in 1905 and 1911, the treaty had provided Britain some measure of security in the East, while it had concentrated its battleships in European waters against Germany. But with the High Seas Fleet scuttled and the Americans fretting over the possibility of a combined Anglo-Japanese battle fleet, the British had little interest in renegotiating a strong treaty in 1921.[57] That was made unmistakably clear to Ambassador John W. Davies in June 1920 when he was informed that any new Anglo-Japanese agreement would specifically preclude the possibility of a combination against the United States.[58] However, the Wilson administration's only response to those conciliatory gestures had been to push grimly ahead with the 1916 program.

It was at that point that the British lost their patience. Throughout the naval crisis the diplomats' efforts at moderation had been opposed by pro-Navy politicians like Winston Churchill, who had roared in the House of Commons: "Nothing in this world, nothing you may think of, or dream of, or anyone may tell you; no argument however specious; no appeals however seductive, must lead you to abandon that naval supremacy on which the life of our country depends."[59] As time went on, the pressure to resume construction mounted inexorably. By late 1920 few politicians could afford to ignore David Beatty when he wondered aloud what sort of bargaining leverage Britain's single postwar capital ship, the *Hood*, might command when confronted by Japanese and U.S. programs of sixteen new dreadnoughts apiece. Finally, in the middle of March 1921, Lloyd George's government accepted the inevitable and announced to Parliament that the Navy would lay down four new battle cruisers of an improved *Hood* type. Setting a new standard in capital ship grandeur, the four super-*Hoods* were to displace 52,000 tons, carry twelve 16-inch guns, and ply the seas at a speedy thirty-two knots.[60] Great Britain had joined the race.

In April 1921 the world was faced with the unhappy fact that fully thirty-six capital ships were being brought steadily into existence—1.5 million tons of suspect vessels at a time when sanity demanded that weapons be cast aside. It was a competition apparently without justification.

Closer examination does, however, reveal a certain logic behind the twisted anatomy of the arms race. The Great War had wrecked an international order that had taken centuries to construct. The gargantuan losses and the compromises made by the governing classes to keep their citizens fighting had finally sealed the doom of aristocratic government. Socialism, mass democracy, and revolution were the waves of the future. Meanwhile, in the midst of political chaos, the traditional equilibrium of power relationships had been thrown wildly out of balance. Indeed the focus of power no longer even resided on the European continent. Britain and France had been seriously weakened; Germany, Russia, and Italy were prostrate. Only the United States and Japan had grown stronger. While they tested their might and the world grew accustomed to a new reality, instability was bound to prevail. And the resulting insecurities rather naturally manifested themselves in the most obvious symbol of military power, the dreadnought. Yet as in the political environment that preceded World War I and the climate of the cold war, weapons acquisitions were themselves a major factor in poisoning the international atmosphere. If the air was to be cleared, some peaceful means had to be found to halt the competition.

The postwar race to build dreadnoughts was wasteful, dangerous, and in large measure ridiculous. The time was right to geld the battleship and put it out to pasture. Clearly the initiative lay with the Americans. As the major instigators of the naval arms race, they were the ones who had to make a move to end it. But before that could be done, the battleship's vulnerability would have to be made crystal clear to the people who would do the negotiating. Given the politics of expertise, such information would have to come from within the naval establishment. But as it happened, revelations galore would soon be emanating from the ranks of the United States Navy.

III

The Great War had interrupted the insurgent vendetta against Josephus Daniels. Yet little had been forgiven. All three of the movement's major figures had reason to despise the secretary. Both Bradley Fiske and William Fullam had languished in obscure commands and then had been forced into retirement; Sims felt that he had been consistently undercut as commander of the European zone. "We deliberately chose the better part and refused to utilize our opportunities for professional advancement by playing politics in league with Josephus Daniels," wrote Fiske to Sims. "It would ill-become us to whimper at the results."[61] But there was still the hope of revenge. The sides were clearly drawn; the issues perceived in righteous black and white; the Navy's salvation required the secretary's North Carolina hide.

The first blow came in December 1919 when Daniels published his list of naval decorations to be awarded. Because the list had been formulated by a board composed mostly of retired staff officers, there was immediate grumbling that the line had been shortchanged. There were some unusual judgments on the list. In a number of cases officers whose ships had been torpedoed were slated to receive higher awards than commanders who had successfully attacked submarines.[62] Moreover, the democratic secretary had added the names of numerous enlisted men to the board's list of medal winners.[63] To Sims that was the last straw. Publicly refusing his own Distinguished Service Medal and urging others on the list to do likewise, the admiral moved into open opposition.

As expected, the protest brought forth a burst of public sympathy and provoked the Senate to impanel a subcommittee to investigate the matter. The adroit secretary moved quickly to defend himself. Immediately reconvening the Board of Awards, Daniels was soon maintaining that "all lists published were tentative."[64] Moreover, he further clouded the issue by accusing Sims and his supporters of malicious intent.

The findings, when the congressional panel finally published them, were inconclusive. Although conceding the irregularity of several of Daniels's recommendations, the Republican-dominated subcommittee nevertheless declined to accuse the secretary of impropriety.[65] As for Sims's campaign to convince his fellow war heroes to reject their medals, it met with little success. Had indignation not overcome his good sense, he would have realized that convincing Annapolites to forgo any new medal was a virtual impossibility. So the Navy would keep what decorations Josephus Daniels chose to cast its way, and Sims was left to stalk back to his corner and await the next round.

Once again Daniels had effortlessly boxed the ears of his service opponents. But Sims and his friends were not to be taken lightly. Though retired, Fullam and Fiske both retained wide respect as naval authorities and continued to advise key Republican politicians. Moreover, Fullam had taken to writing a popular column for the *New York Herald* under the nom de plume "Quarterdeck."

Nevertheless, it was Sims who would prove to be the mainstay of the opposition. He was the closest thing to an American naval hero that the war had produced, and his name was already pending in Congress for promotion to

George Dewey's old sinecure—permanent Admiral of the Fleet. More important for the sake of reform was his inauguration as president of the Naval War College. Until October 1922 he would occupy the pulpit that Mahan had made the focal point of the naval world. From here Sims's broadsides would carry the weight of intellectual authority.

The gong for round two sounded on 14 January 1920 when the *Washington Post* published a leaked letter from Sims to Daniels entitled "Certain Lessons of the Great War."[66] Long and biting, it amounted to a blanket condemnation of naval administration prior to and during U.S. participation in World War I. Sims pulled no punches. The Navy's somnolence during the first two and a half years was finally uncovered for all the world to see. Specifically, Sims charged the department with lacking a realistic or "mature" war plan, "not understanding the seriousness of the submarine situation," and being reluctant to supply sufficient destroyer reinforcements to meet the U-boat problem.[67]

Inevitably, controversy boiled up anew. The Navy had been accused of the grossest kind of negligence by one of its most illustrious officers. Charges like these could not go unanswered. Therefore, on 9 March, just two days after publishing its report on the naval awards, the Senate subcommittee found itself back in session, this time charged with investigating the entire conduct of the war by the Navy Department.

Plainly, matters were escalating. Reputations in addition to that of the secretary of the Navy were hanging in the balance. The competence of the high command that had run the Navy for Daniels was being called into question. Officers like William S. Benson, Hugh Rodman, and Charles Badger of the General Board might not have liked the secretary, but they were hardly in a position to desert him. His fight suddenly became their own.

The hearings revealed considerable substance behind the insurgents' charges. Sims alone would require eight days of the subcommittee's time to recount his tale in minute detail. Bradley Fiske remembered bitterly his problems in dealing with a secretary of the Navy who took neutrality seriously: "I found after a while that it was not a good thing to say anything to him about the War. He did not seem to be ready to start on any subject connected with war at all."[68] When the last insurgent stepped off the witness stand, the case against the Navy seemed overwhelming. Leaky submarines, chronic manpower shortages, battleships with no destroyers: The picture they left was a collage of comic mismanagement.

Nor did the Navy's conservative defenders have much luck in refuting the charges. When asked about the status of American war plans prior to April 1917,

Admiral Benson conceded that there were "no definite war plans drawn up on paper."[69] Charles Badger, in contrast, maintained: "We had plans, well considered ones. The trouble is that the plans and the execution of them did not meet with the approval of the critics."[70] But the key critic of those plans in the spring of 1917 was reality itself, which would have nothing to do with War Plan BLACK and its imaginary Caribbean showdown with the German High Seas Fleet. That the admirals could not deny. Nor could they avoid admitting that the Navy had drawn no plans concerning antisubmarine measures prior to entry into the war.

In the end it was only the flamboyant testimony of Josephus Daniels himself that saved the Navy from further embarrassment. Answering none of the charges specifically, he sought instead to bury them in billows of rhetoric. A favorite tactic was entering into the record long lists of the service's accomplishments under his direction, including, at one point, an article from the *Sunday School Times* praising the abolition of the officers' wine mess. After two weeks of grandiloquence Daniels had succeeded in literally boring the life out of the charges. As the testimony mounted, public interest flagged and the story was relegated to the back pages of the nation's newspapers. Little notice was taken when the subcommittee officially closed the hearings. Josephus had won again.

Although the fruits of the insurgent campaign proved meager and bitter, the experience was still instructive. With each successive investigation the insurgents' perspective on naval affairs had grown broader. Finally, the crusade against Daniels led them beyond the Annapolite pale, breaking what amounted to the last psychic bond that had tied them to conventional naval policy. For the first time they began to say the unsayable, to draw the connection between the mistakes of the past and the framework of naval belief dedicated to the preservation of the battleship.

It was a startling reversal of roles, but one that took place on both sides of the Atlantic. In Britain, first Percy Scott and then John Arbuthnot Fisher—the two men most responsible for the HMS *Dreadnought*—declared the battleship finished as a major naval combatant.[71] "All you want is the present naval side of the air force!" Fisher wrote shortly before he died in 1920. "That's the future Navy!"[72] Almost simultaneously the same thing was happening in the United States. The American dreadnought had been conceived in the womb of naval insurgency. Sims's reformed target practices, Bradley Fiske's fire control, these as much as anything had given the U.S. Navy the modern battleship. Now the insurgents proclaimed their backing for newer, more efficient killers, and significantly their choice of successors did not swim below the surface but flew above it.

Insurgent interest in the airplane was no new thing. Bradley Fiske in particular had an early appreciation of its vast potential for military application. As far back as 1911 he had presented the General Board a farsighted plan to defend the Philippines with a fleet of 100 bombers.[73] For his efforts, Fiske was reprimanded for taking up the time of the General Board with "wildcat schemes."[74]

About the same time, it had also occurred to Fiske that if "aeroplanes were large enough, they could launch torpedoes against transports and even battleships."[75] In July 1912 he took out a patent to this effect, making himself officially the inventor of the torpedo plane, a potentially devastating naval weapon. Swift, expendable, and deadly, it took full advantage of all three spatial dimensions—approaching from above and striking from below.

Fiske's idea lay dormant until the coming of the Great War when he realized that a swarm of these aircraft might fly unopposed to Kiel and sink the High Seas Fleet in an afternoon. (Across the Atlantic British Commodore Murray Sueter put the same idea forward in December 1916, suggesting an attack on both the German and Austrian fleets with Sopwith "Cuckoo" torpedo planes. But after receiving some initial Admiralty support, the idea was dropped.[76]) Meanwhile, Fiske's efforts to promote the torpedo plane were blocked at every turn by Josephus Daniels, who had little respect for airplanes and less for Fiske. Having gone to considerable trouble to get rid of the nagging aide for operations, the secretary was not about to embrace any of his visionary schemes.[77] But if the development of an American torpedo plane was forestalled until after the war, Fiske at least succeeded in winning over his brother insurgents to the cause of naval air power.

Exiled to the Asiatic Fleet at Bremerton, William F. Fullam read his friend Brad's enthusiastic letters and watched with growing admiration the young naval aviators practicing overhead. Then on 11 November 1918, the day of the armistice, something happened that convinced him that the era of the dreadnought had passed. To celebrate the occasion the entire Bremerton wing had taken to the air and overflown the base.

They came in waves, until they stretched almost from horizon to horizon, row upon row of these flying machines. What chance, I thought, would any ship, any fleet have against an aggregate such as this? You could shoot them from the skies like passenger pigeons, and still there would be more than enough to sink

The dreadnought and its enemies, the torpedo and the plane. (Courtesy of the U.S. Naval Institute)

you. Now I loved the battleship, devoted my whole career to it, but at that moment I knew the battleship was through.[78]

Sims took longer to convince. No U.S. naval officer had been in a better position to measure the dreadnought's failure in the Great War. Fiske's torpedo plane had impressed him, and he had done what he could to promote naval air power in the European zone.[79] Nonetheless, the armistice found him still clinging to the dreadnought as a vital element of the fleet. A year later, when Fullam sent him a press clipping quoting Percy Scott as saying "that the battleship is dead; that the great fighting machine of the future is the airship," Sims replied, "I should think that he would keep reasonably quiet." But the experience of the naval hearings, combined with the arguments of his friends, were apparently enough to cause Sims to reconsider his position.

During the final months of 1920 the admiral turned the question over in his mind, deciding at last to resolve it in traditional Annapolite fashion, upon the game board.

That is to give each side at the Naval War College a certain amount of money; one side to build sixteen battleships, six airplane carriers and six battle cruisers;

the other to build twenty-two aircraft carriers. . . . The only difficulty is to establish rules for the game. This is a very serious difficulty. This afternoon we had a discussion over the whole matter by the entire staff, and it was easy to see that the question of the passing of the battleship was not an agreeable one to the various members.[80]

Nevertheless, equitable rules were finally formulated, and during the last three weeks in January a series of battles was fought between the two hypothetical fleets. The results of the experiment left Sims with little doubt as to the dreadnought's inferiority.

So by 1921, Fiske, Fullam, and Sims—the three musketeers of naval insurgency—had transferred their allegiance from the battleship to aircraft carriers. It was an understandable choice. For at the core they were naval officers, men committed to a certain outlook, a certain set of rules. The submarine had never really attracted them. They recognized its power, but it had transcended too much that they held dear. War was reduced to a damp, treacherous act.

The plane was different. Seldom had there been a more romantic weapon. The human being as combatant animal was raised to the level of the angels. Visions of aerial acrobatics high above the clouds, of planes soaring toward the sun and hurtling to the ground: They were all part of the mystique that had already come to surround military aircraft. Once again combat became a matter of individuals locked in single mortal strife.

Most important from the Annapolite perspective was the fact that the plane's existence, unlike the submarine's, in no way implied the disappearance of the surface Navy. The warplane was at this point a short-range weapon limited in its strike radius to between one and two hundred miles.[81] Therefore transoceanic aerial operations necessarily required ships to carry, service, launch, and refuel attack planes. All of that took space. So it was clear, even before the first one was built, that the aircraft carrier was destined to be a large, stately vessel, with at least some capability of taking its place at the top of the hierarchy of ships. Fiske struck to the heart of the matter when he wrote Fullam in February: "I think most of the opposition from officers originates in the fear that they may lose their jobs! They do not see that airplane carriers will not only be more powerful than the present slow battleships, but much pleasanter ships to cruise in! And no one will lose his job."[82] The transition might have been, if not exactly that smooth, then at least a great deal less bitter, had it not been for one man.

IV

Brigadier General William Mitchell has come down to us as a minor folk hero. His was a life that might have spilled from the pen of F. Scott Fitzgerald or been produced by some budding Hollywood movie mogul. Wealthy, handsome, arrogant, brilliant, a rider of championship horses, a lover of beautiful women—but most of all, a man with a cause. Like Lindbergh, Billy Mitchell was enraptured by the airplane, projecting the image of a champion locked in mortal combat with reactionaries in its behalf.

However, the man behind this romantic facade was essentially a zealot with a flair for public relations. For years he rode the crest of the headlines, building the plane's reputation with each press release. His was a vision of terror bombing, aerial poison-gas attacks, and the mass strafing of civilians. And he contemplated those things with equanimity. When matched against the growth of air power, the wholesale slaughter of innocents was apparently a matter of minor import to him. As the driving force behind the Army Air Service, he pursued a course dictated only by opportunity and the determination to make the plane look good. It was from that perspective that Billy Mitchell set his sights on the dreadnought.

Ironically, it was an April 1919 meeting of the General Board that seems to have awakened Mitchell's interest in the capital ship. He had been invited to discuss the possibility of testing the effect of aerial bombs on warships and left promising "to get a missile to attack a big ship, whether it takes a ton or two tons."[83] Inadvertently the Navy had handed Mitchell a public relations gimmick beyond comparison. "If I can get the High Command to let me bomb a battleship," he told Major General Mason M. Patrick, "the whole country will understand what all this means. If I send a battleship to the bottom with air bombs . . . perhaps we'll stop wasting billions on these museum pieces and spend the money on planes."[84]

On 3 February 1920, Mitchell officially opened his campaign to secure a sacrificial battleship. Testifying before a House subcommittee on aviation, he unveiled a three-phase plan for shattering an invading battle fleet with air power. Finally, after a pause, he offered to back up his claims: "We would like very much to take the members of the committee down to the Chesapeake Bay, to our airdrome there, and show you these things from the air, which we can do anytime, so that you can judge for yourselves."[85]

Neither the Navy nor its secretary was anxious to take up the gauntlet. Josephus Daniels was so incensed by the proposal that he ordered his staff to keep "Mitchell's ideas" out of his office. "I don't want to hear any more about sinking battleships with air bombs. That idea is so damned nonsensical and impossible that I'm willing to stand bareheaded on the bridge of a battleship while that nitwit tries to hit it from the air!"[86] This was one issue that could not be exorcised with bluster. Mitchell was a public relations genius, and he had powerful allies within the Navy.

William Sowden Sims was one of them. "He [Sims] told me I had done an inestimable service in bringing the controversy of aircraft and seacraft to the surface, and that if I didn't become too impatient I would get the battleship."[87] So Daniels was finally set up for the kill—but not bareheaded on the bridge of a dreadnought—for the secretary's term of office ended on 4 March, long before the tests could be staged. Nevertheless, the campaign to secure a target battleship went forward on its own momentum.

By the final months of 1920 the political tide had turned decisively against the dreadnought. At last the public appeared fed up with arms competition and its symbols. The fall elections had signaled the entry into the body politic of millions of previously disenfranchised women, whose traditional opposition to weapons and war now became a matter of immediate political import.[88] Moreover, the November ballot had produced a new president, Warren G. Harding, a man whose views on foreign policy and defense, if not exactly imaginary, were at least largely unknown. It seemed reasonable to hope that he and his naval secretary–designate, Edwin Denby, might prove less intransigent on the subject of battleships than Wilson or Daniels.

Sensing a popular upheaval, the redoubtable senator from Idaho, William E. Borah, decided to put it into more concrete form. One of the chief executioners of Wilson's treaty, he was now intent on slaying its ugly stepsister, the Phantom Fleet. Harking back to the fateful Hensley amendment to the 1916 bill, Borah introduced a resolution on 14 December calling on the president to establish immediate consultations with Great Britain and Japan aimed at mutual reductions of 50 percent in naval armaments over the next five years.[89]

Popular response to the resolution was enthusiastic. Within the week Borah reported telegrams and letters pouring in from all corners of the nation.[90] Overnight the senator and his resolution became the catalyst for an outpouring of antimilitarism. Membership in organizations devoted to the cause of disarmament swelled rapidly, vast peace rallies were held, Congress began to take notice. The voice of the people had joined the rising chorus against the dreadnought.

The insurgents were not long in getting in touch with Borah. Previously the senator's arguments had been general in nature and oriented toward moral and economic issues. But at that point the naval experts supplemented his indictment with a bill of particulars. On 19 January, William F. Fullam wrote to inform him of the results of the board games at the Naval War College and the tactical case against the dreadnought. The next day Borah replied to thank him. "It is precisely the thing which I have been looking for . . . we are spending millions of dollars which will never represent anything in real defense of the country."[91] Five days later, on 25 January, the senator submitted a motion calling for a six-month suspension of all naval building and a full investigation of "what constitutes a modern fighting navy."[92]

In an attempt to answer this question, Representative Anthony and Senator Harry S. New on 30 January introduced a joint resolution before Congress directing the secretary of the Navy to place certain German warships that had not been scuttled at Scapa at the disposal of the Army Air Service for experimental purposes.[93] Before the matter could be brought to a vote, Daniels acquiesced, inviting the Air Service to join in a bombing test scheduled to begin in late June. Among the vessels designated as targets was the German dreadnought *Ostfriesland*, recently turned over to the U.S. Navy as a war prize.

Meanwhile, the months that preceded the trial in the Chesapeake were not to be happy ones for the dreadnought. In early February the House Naval Affairs Committee opened hearings on U.S. naval policy and was promptly greeted with a barrage of evidence against the battleship. Both Admiral Sims and Admiral Fiske testified that the aircraft carrier and not the dreadnought was the capital ship of the future, and Mitchell entertained the committee with extravagant claims of what his bombers could do to a battleship.[94]

In reply conservatives could muster little more than sour rejoinders. "We want 10 battleships so we can have a properly balanced Navy," the new chief of naval operations, Robert E. Coontz, told Representative Hicks. "In 1916 we at last got started so that we could secure a Navy of some importance and equality. We had waited all our lives. Now the propaganda comes to stop it."[95]

Meanwhile, the new president, Warren G. Harding, took stock of the situation and began edging away from the dreadnought. Basically a friend of the Navy, Harding had entered the White House on record as favoring the completion of the 1916 program. But his astute secretary of state, Charles Evans Hughes, had argued strongly in favor of some kind of disarmament.[96] Then on 23 June Congress passed the Borah amendment, and the president found himself practically under instructions to convene an arms conference. Never one to stand fearlessly in the face of overwhelming odds, the Man from Marion accepted the inevitable, and wrote the House majority leader to praise the measure as "wholly desirable."[97] As for the tactical future of the dreadnought, Harding seemed resigned to its being settled at the forthcoming bombing trials. "Denby thinks the whole idea is crazy," he told his friend Benedict M. Holden. "But I notice he hasn't offered to stand on deck under the bombs as Daniels did."[98]

As the president spoke, Billy Mitchell was probably at Langley Field, Virginia, practicing. It was not going to be easy. The Navy had insisted that the tests be staged sixty miles off the Virginia coast, necessitating a long over-water flight to the target area in heavily laden planes.[99] Once there, the aviators would find a 27,000-ton veteran of Jutland, minutely subdivided into eighty-five watertight compartments, and equipped with a triple bottom. Like all German dreadnoughts, *Ostfriesland* was tough, and there would be no munitions on board to cause secondary explosions. She would not be sunk easily.

Mitchell was not a man to be put off by a few obstacles. At Langley he had assembled the best pilots in the country and was welding them together into a crack tactical-bombing unit. Daily, from dawn to dusk, they practiced bombing runs against battleship-shaped targets. Navigators trained by flying in the worst possible weather conditions. Photography planes were rigged with still and movie cameras to capture the moment. No detail of preparation was overlooked.

Meanwhile Army Ordnance was busy building for the general what would prove to be the biggest bombs in the world. These 2,000-pound ship breakers, half their weight in TNT, were critical to his plans. For Mitchell grasped that a vessel's Achilles heel lay below the surface, that it was best attacked from below, not above. His monster bombs were equipped with pressure-sensitive fuses set to explode at a depth of thirty feet. There the entire explosive force of 1,000 pounds of TNT would be channeled up through the hull, creating what he liked to call a "water hammer."[100] In practical terms, it was like exploding ten torpedoes in one spot against the side of a ship. A very big hole was likely to result.

The trials began on 21 June and ran through a month of preliminaries, during which time the Army bombers systematically slugged their way up through the lower divisions of the hierarchy of ships. First three U-boats, then the destroyer *G-102*, and then the cruiser *Frankfort* fell prey to the bombardment from above.[101] Finally, all attention shifted to the main event, the 20 July title match between the *Ostfriesland* and Billy Mitchell.

Newspaper coverage was heavy, and bets of all sorts were laid down. Fights and arguments erupted over the relative merits of the dreadnought and the general. But this was not merely a stunt to amuse the public. The wielders of power took careful measure of the contest. When the Navy's public relations transport *Henderson* left for the target area, she was packed with eminent observers. On board were Secretary of Agriculture Henry Wallace, Secretary of War John W. Weeks, Secretary of the Navy Edwin Denby, Assistant Secretary of the Navy Theodore Roosevelt, Jr., nine U.S. senators, including the influential Eugene Hale of Maine and King of Utah, ten representatives, William F. Fullam, General Pershing, and an assortment of top Army and Navy brass, three foreign naval attachés, and the cream of the Washington press corps—three hundred notables in all.[102] Yet missing from the crowd was perhaps the most important guest, Secretary of State Charles Evans Hughes. Hughes had received and accepted an invitation but had canceled at the last moment to meet with Japanese Ambassador Baron Shidehara.[103] However, Hughes's interest in the tests should not be discounted, for Billy Mitchell's moment of truth was likely to have a considerable influence on the course of the forthcoming arms negotiations.

From the first the Navy had been concerned about the rules governing the ship bombings. It was the Navy's contention that this was a scientific experiment that should be interrupted frequently so that construction experts might assess the damage.[104] In other words, the trials were to be conducted as methodically and undramatically as possible. Should the planes, after two days, fail to dispatch the *Ostfriesland*, then the new dreadnought *Pennsylvania* would be standing by with twelve 14-inch guns to do the job in the good old-fashioned way.[105] Also in the great circle of warships anchored two miles from the target was the USS *Olympia*, Dewey's flagship at Manila Bay. If the Old Admiral had a ghost, he was probably on the bridge watching.

So the trial began with Mitchell's Martin bombers dropping single 230-pound projectiles on the German dreadnought. Six hits were scored, but only half the bombs exploded, inflicting very superficial damage on the ship. In the afternoon, the aviators switched to 600-pound bombs, which ripped holes in the *Ostfriesland*'s deck and left her with a slight list to stern. Nevertheless, at 4:00 P.M., after the ship had been subject to a full day of punishment, observers who came aboard could find no evidence of serious, much less mortal, injury.[106] All things considered, it was not an impressive display of air power.

To the observers on the *Henderson*, the battleship seemed once again invincible. "The Navy was content with the day's work," reported *Washington*

Post correspondent Clinton Gilbert. "High officers sniggered cheerfully."[107] Mitchell's bombers had seemed like so many gnats attacking the great gray hulk. "I doubt if I shall waste more time on this croquet game tomorrow," General Pershing remarked to Secretary of War Weeks. Shortly thereafter, the two were seen departing on a destroyer to await the results on land. Later in the afternoon the commander in chief of the U.S. Fleet, Hilary P. Jones, held a reception for fifty honored guests on the *Pennsylvania*. Likely the *Ostfriesland* was the subject of at least one toast. The Navy had reason to celebrate.

But for Billy Mitchell fuming back at Langley Field, tomorrow was another day. At dawn his bombers were finally armed with the 2,000-pound ship wreckers. Amid the roar of the warming motors and cheers of his men, he gave final instructions. "Bomb low," he told them, and "get into this thing as if we had to sink an enemy ship attacking one of our ports."[108] Plainly the object was to sink the *Ostfriesland* and not to follow the Navy's complicated rules.

Led by Mitchell's two-seat command plane, all the Martin bombers were in the air by 11:20 A.M. and circling over the target by 12:15.[109] Three minutes later one maneuvered into position at an altitude of 1,700 feet and let loose with the first of the giant projectiles. "It blazed in the sunshine as it tumbled over and over in its course, landing on the crest of a wave one hundred feet off the starboard bow of the warship," wrote a *New York Herald* reporter. "There was a muffled roar and a great splash of water, which let out black and white smoke.[110] One by one, the other Martins followed, raining ship breakers on the *Ostfriesland*. The fourth and fifth struck within twenty-five feet of the port side, causing eruptions that left the vessel "rolling uneasily, plainly hurt."[111] Then at 12:31 a sixth bomb landed a few feet off starboard and its detonation threw the stern high in the air. When the dreadnought settled back, she was listing heavily, her bow thrust out of the water to reveal a mortal gash in the rusted hull. The water hammer had done its work. Deeper and deeper she sank, until only the extended prow remained above the surface. That too disappeared when the last of the Martins unloaded its payload over the wreckage. It had taken but twenty-one minutes.[112]

Aboard the *Henderson* William Fullam noted the increasing dismay registered on the faces of the battleship advocates. "Their anxiety was painful to behold. When a bomb hit they all but fainted. A miss was like a whiff of smelling salts. And when the *Ostfriesland* joined Mr. McGinty's Navy their emotions were indescribable."[113] Former secretary of war Benedict Crowell, standing near Fullam, saw numerous captains and admirals sobbing, while others hid their faces behind handkerchiefs.[114] Such emotions may have been difficult for civilians to fathom. But the ship that sank before them dragged a great deal of baggage down with it. For years Annapolites had clung to their maxims and their dogma despite all evidence to the contrary. Now their faith was being rewarded with public humiliation at the hands of this sneering impresario Mitchell, who even now buzzed the *Henderson* in a final act of derision. No wonder they hated him.

10

Requiem: The Washington Naval Conference

The chorus of naval protest that arose over Mitchell's disregard of the rules could not drown out the test's stark, simple lesson. A plane had sunk a battleship. Those were the words spoken by the public after reading their morning papers. That was the rationale behind Senator's King's 25 July bill to terminate work on the new dreadnoughts.[1] That was the message that pierced the ornate gray facade of the State Department building and found the ear of Charles Evans Hughes.

The secretary of state was nobody's fool. He was, in fact, the only first-class man in a third-class administration. He would have been president himself had Wilson not capitalized on U.S. neutrality in the election of 1916. Now Charles Evans Hughes was the next best thing, secretary of state to a cipher chief executive.

Hughes deserved it. His was a career so distinguished as to be almost a parody of success. College at fourteen, Phi Beta Kappa, wealthy commercial lawyer, celebrated law professor, reform governor of New York, associate justice of the U.S. Supreme Court, presidential nominee, now the State Department. Totally a man of the system; its virtues and limitations were his own.

A case in point was his attitude toward arms limitation. Reared in a stable, agricultural United States isolated by two oceans from natural enemies, Hughes and his generation had developed an acutely bifurcated outlook toward power in international affairs. Overtly, it was denied any role at all. War became an aberration, weapons development anathema. Yet tacitly Hughes accepted a state system ruled by force and remained acquiescent to the really revolutionary aspects of the arms race. It was for those reasons that the upcoming disarmament

261

conference, the Washington Conference on the Limitation of Armaments, was to be largely preoccupied with symbols. Battleships would be limited, but submarines and airplanes remained untouched. As for the world's vast postwar power disequilibriums, they would not be resolved, merely shrouded with a patched-up agreement that meant little.[2]

Although formal invitations went out on 11 July, preparations for the 12 November conference in Washington were postponed until Mitchell had successfully dispatched the *Ostfriesland*. Finally on 27 July Assistant Secretary of the Navy Theodore Roosevelt, Jr., got the ball rolling by directing the General Board to report on the naval power of the various guests and on an "equitable relativity of strength."[3] (Roosevelt was the third member of the clan to occupy the post in less than twenty-five years. A sort of caricature of his father, he was nonetheless energetic and intelligent and was destined to serve as the key link between Hughes and the Navy Department.)

It soon became clear, however, that the General Board was in no mood for straight answers. It presented instead a collection of essays on arms limitation written by individual members, along with two dozen similar questionnaires from former high-ranking naval planners.

After a month, having received little more than a formidable pile of papers, Charles Evans Hughes apparently decided on a more directive course of action. His next move was brilliant. On 1 September he wrote the Navy Department asking it for "a yardstick by which to measure existing armaments and which can also be applied as a standard of measurement in any general plan of reduction."[4] It was a foregone conclusion that the Navy would designate tonnage in dreadnoughts as the single best criterion of naval strength, thus inadvertently lending official sanction to capital ship limitation.[5] Nevertheless, it was also clear that the Navy's idea of limitation was vastly different from the secretary's. By 8 October the board had delivered a "basic plan" that would allow the United States to complete all fifteen of its unfinished dreadnoughts, Britain to build four super-*Hoods*, and Japan to finish seven of its sixteen planned capital ships.[6] Creating a ratio of 10:10:6 among the three powers, the program would leave both the United States and Great Britain with huge battle fleets aggregating more than one million tons apiece.

As might be expected, the secretary of state was not impressed by that rather brazen set of figures. The conference was scheduled to open in just over a month, and still he had nothing resembling a reasonable proposal. Two high civilian officials (probably J. Reuben Clarke, Hughes's legal adviser, and Theodore Roosevelt, Jr.) soon met informally with members of the General Board to warn them that unless radical reductions were made, "we will cut the heart out of the Navy."[7] The board took the hint and went back to work. On 14 October the body submitted the so-called modified plan, its version of compromise. Although it did cut British and U.S. battle lines to 820,000 tons apiece and the Japanese to half of the other two, or 410,000 tons, the modified plan did very little to curtail new construction. Eleven of the fifteen members of the Phantom Fleet were still to be completed along with all four super-*Hoods*. Only the Japanese were shortchanged, with an allotment of but two new dreadnoughts.[8] Hughes found the proposal completely unacceptable but was informed by the General Board that they were rock-bottom figures below which they would not stray.[9]

The secretary of state was in no mood for ultimatums. He simply turned to a new set of naval advisers more likely to give him what he wanted. The men composing this group of three were Chief of Naval Operations Robert E. Coontz, Theodore Roosevelt, Jr., and Sims's friend William V. Pratt, the officer who had so much to do with the curtailment of the wartime battleship program. From the first, the team worked swiftly and effectively to provide Hughes with realistic naval data.

A prime opportunity came on 25 October, when the secretary of state formally asked the Navy Department the question that would become the basis for the Five Power Agreement: "Assuming that it were proposed to abandon our entire building program for capital ships . . . what would be entirely fair to propose as a condition for such action on our part, with respect to the reduction of capital ship tonnage by the British and Japanese?"[10] The very next day Hughes's new naval experts provided him with a plan that would halt all capital ship construction and stabilize the ratio of weights among the three powers at 10:10:6. Calling for battle lines a bit over half the size of the General Board's "basic plan," the proposal actually specified a reduction of contemporary tonnage through the selective scrapping of obsolescent vessels.[11]

Accompanying the so-called stop now proposal to the State Department was a letter of protest from William Rodgers, chairman of the General Board. Calling the plan "fraught with danger," the admiral warned that "the loss of these fifteen new powerful and up-to-date capital ships, the chief element of our naval strength, would without doubt, seriously affect the influence which the United States today has in the world."[12]

The prospect did not overly concern the secretary of state, who told Roosevelt, Jr., and Pratt to begin working on a final draft of the new plan. When the assistant secretary delivered it on 4 November, Hughes told him he was going to lock it up in his safe and show it to no one. Through the next week the two of them worked in secret on the secretary's opening speech. It was an important document, for, as Roosevelt wrote in his diary on 10 November, "The plan is to spring everything, including our definitive naval program, on the opening day."[13]

"The first meeting of the Washington conference this morning will be merely of a formal character," predicted the *New York Times* on 12 November. It was a sensible prediction. The bland amenities of diplomacy took time. Nothing ever happened at plenary sessions. The real bargaining went on behind the scenes. Wilson's dream of "open covenants, openly arrived at" had quickly faded from the minds of most. Consequently, there was little precedent for what happened that morning in Continental Hall, the headquarters of the Daughters of the American Revolution.

The galleries filled quickly with a throng that included, it seemed, everybody who was anybody in Washington political circles. From Alice Roosevelt Longworth to William Jennings Bryan to Justice Oliver Wendell Holmes, they had all come. Yet they had come more to be a part of a ceremony than to witness anything significant actually occur. To H. G. Wells it seemed "like a very smart first night in a prominent London theatre."[14] The delegates appeared equally nonchalant as they strolled in to take their places at the great green U-shaped table set in the middle of the hall. The appearance of the president of the United States did nothing to dispel the mood. Indeed Warren G. Harding's claims of "wanting less of armaments and none of war" seemed but a preface to still-more-platitudinous effusions.

Then the secretary of state got up to speak. At first nothing appeared extraordinary. He began stiffly with a review of previous disarmament attempts. But as he turned to contemporary matters, his voice became heavy with emotion and the audience was nudged into an awareness that the American secretary of state was no longer mouthing bromides.[15] Addressing the question of naval competition, Hughes stated flatly, "There is only one adequate way out and that is to end it now."[16] Then, to the amazement of practically everyone in the hall, he began setting out concrete proposals to do just that. At the core of the U.S. proposition were four principles: first, that all capital ship construction either actual or projected be suspended for not less than ten years; second, that further reduction be made through the scrapping of older ships; third, that all reduction be based on the existing naval strength of the powers involved; and last, that capital ships be used as the yardstick of that naval strength.[17]

Applying his formula to the U.S. Navy, the secretary specified the sacrifice of all fifteen new capital ships plus the entire pre-dreadnought fleet, for a total reduction of 845,740 tons. The British were expected to follow suit, scrapping 583,375 tons of capital ships, including the four proposed super-*Hoods*. Finally, the Japanese were asked to cease work on their entire 8:8:8 program, for a net sacrifice of 448,928 tons. Since France and Italy had no dreadnoughts under construction, they were to be dealt with once the three main powers reached agreement. In a bit over half an hour the U.S. secretary of state put 1,878,043 tons of dreadnoughts on the block and seized the initiative for the entire conference. Still more important, his speech marked a watershed in the history of the human species. For the first time a major political entity had offered a clear and specific proposal to limit what was perceived to be a key weapon system. Many in the audience must have thought a new day had arrived. As Hughes sat down, pacifist William Jennings Bryan led a cheer from the press gallery that swept the hall.

People in one group, however, probably clapped without much enthusiasm, if they clapped at all. To be sure it was not a good moment for the world's naval officers. David Beatty's face seemed to register the feelings of all the naval representatives at the conference. To reporter Mark Sullivan he looked "like a bull dog sleeping on a sunny door step, who had been poked in the stomach by an itinerant soap canvaser."[18] Yet there was little he or his brother officers could do to salvage the situation. For the plan was fair and practical and came close to meeting the naval requirements of all the major powers.

Immediate response was almost completely favorable. In the United States the press was nearly unanimous in praising Hughes's plan. An informal poll of the Senate indicated that the body would surely ratify a treaty drawn along those lines.[19] From London came word of approval and relief at the possibility of an honorable end to the shipbuilding race. In Tokyo the response was restrained, though generally agreeable to such a proposal.[20]

In all cases, however, details would have to be worked out. That presented problems. For enough remained of the dreadnought's reputation and the diplomats' respect for specialists to allow for the negotiation of specifics to be delegated to a technical committee composed almost entirely of naval officers. The sole exception was Theodore Roosevelt, Jr., who was installed as chief American naval adviser at Hughes's insistence.[21]

From the beginning, the naval advisory council's work went badly. At the very first meeting on 16 November, supernationalist Admiral Kato Kanjii, a firm believer in the "principle of huge battleships and big guns," cast a pall over the negotiations.[22] He announced that Japan wanted a 10:10:7 ratio in capital ships, equality in aircraft carriers, and the retention of the 98 percent–completed *Mutsu*, which had been paid for with voluntary gifts and contributions.[23]

To make matters worse, British-American cooperation in bringing the Japanese around was being disrupted by David Beatty. The admiral was evasive and obviously dissatisfied with the course the negotiations were taking. Moreover, he refused to sanction limitations on the tonnage of individual units, and Theodore Roosevelt, Jr., began worrying that the competition would simply be switched from numbers to sheer size. "Beatty will have to be talked to by those over him," Roosevelt, Jr., wrote angrily.[24] On 23 November, at Hughes's request, Beatty was called to the office of Arthur James Balfour, the head of the British delegation, and informed that Britain and the United States would stand together on capital ships.[25] When Beatty continued to balk, he was removed from his post and sent back to Britain.[26]

Nevertheless, the problem of accommodating the Japanese still remained, and the naval experts, buried in calculations of gun sizes, armor distribution, and the other esoteric details of naval orthodoxy, seemed incapable of producing a reasonable compromise. Things got so bad by 27 November that Roosevelt, Jr., had come to "believe, in the very near future, Hughes should fire both barrels and take the matter out of the hands of the naval experts."[27] Three days later the exasperated Hughes did just that, and the meetings of the naval advisers were terminated, with the Japanese apparently still adamant in their desire to gain at least a 10:10:7 ratio with the two English-speaking powers.

However, the representatives of the oriental power were not nearly so intransigent as they appeared. Even while his naval representative, Admiral Kato Kanjii, was stoutly maintaining Japan's claims, Naval Minister Kato Tomosaburo was cabling Foreign Minister Uchida in Tokyo informing him of the necessity of reaching an agreement before word of the impasse caught the ear of the public.[28] Since few in Tokyo seriously believed that Japan, with its small industrial base, could actually keep up in an all-out building race, a rupture of the conference spelled disaster for the island empire's nautical credibility.[29]

Consequently, Uchida authorized Kato Tomosaburo to make such concessions as were necessary for an accord, with two significant qualifications. If Kato accepted Hughes's 5:5:3 ratio, it was to be with the understanding that the Japanese would be able to preserve the *Mutsu,* and that the Americans would cease fortification of their bases in the Philippines, Guam, and Hawaii. It was an excellent maneuver, and one that would make it extremely difficult for the U.S. Navy to wage a campaign against Japan in the Western Pacific.[30] In essence, the Japanese were offering to refrain from building useless ships they could ill afford in return for concessions of real strategic value.

Ironically, their coup was largely accidental. Not having experienced the frustrations of the Great War, the Japanese, of all the major naval powers, had the most confidence in the dreadnought.[31] If the death of the 8:8:8 program was the price they had to pay to end a competition they had no hope of winning, then it would be duly served up. But with the exception of Kato Tomosaburo and the moderate faction, they were mortified by the sacrifice.[32]

Hughes was basically agreeable, but also determined to extract a price for the *Mutsu.* After consulting with Roosevelt, he produced a counterproposal that had the Americans retaining the almost-completed *Colorado* and *Washington* (later replaced by the *West Virginia*), and the British building two of its four proposed capital ships—all in return for allowing Japan to retain the newest member of its fleet. To keep relative tonnages within the 5:5:3 ratio, several additional older battleships were to be scrapped. Finally, all new battleships, both now and after the ten-year holiday, were to be limited to 35,000 tons apiece and could carry guns no larger than sixteen inches. The British—not exactly anxious to build more dreadnoughts, especially when Hughes's plan required cutting the super-*Hoods* from 52,000 to 35,000 tons—nevertheless reluctantly agreed to the American counterproposal. The Japanese had little choice but to acquiesce.[33]

With the three major naval powers in accord over capital ships, it was necessary to draw the French and Italians into the compact. Because neither of the two had dreadnought construction programs worth taking seriously, the 1.75 tonnage ratio to be allotted to each seemed fair, even generous to the American planners.[34]

For their part, the Italians were pleasantly surprised with their share, which would give them instant equality with France. The same could not be said for the Gallic representatives, whose response to Hughes's offer bordered on the hysterical. Shocked at being rated inferior to the Japanese, Admiral de Bon and his cohorts complained bitterly to Hughes, Balfour, and even Roosevelt, Jr.

USS Maryland, *sister to* Colorado *and* West Virginia—*all that would remain of the Phantom Fleet after the Washington conference. (Courtesy of the U.S. Naval Institute)*

"They said it was unthinkable. They spoke of their honor and the honor of France every two words. They finished up by explaining to me that they were now placed with their backs to the wall."[35]

Hughes reacted as he had throughout the negotiations. When military representatives proved intransigent, he simply went over their heads. On 18 December, Ambassador George Harvey delivered a special message from the American secretary of state to French Premier Aristide Briand in London, where the latter was conferring with David Lloyd George. In it Hughes argued that the limit of 175,000 tons on French capital ships would double the real strength of their navy and that France would gain because of the sacrifices the United States, Great Britain, and Japan were prepared to make.

Briand, basically a politician dedicated to guiding France out of the trauma of war, was not anxious to draw upon himself and his country the onus of having wrecked the arms limitation conference. Therefore, he agreed to instruct the French delegation to accept Hughes's formula in so far as capital ships were concerned.[36] However, the French statesman also made it clear that his country would not accept "corresponding reductions" in auxiliary classes and submarines. After ten days of fruitless debate, the powers agreed first to accept France's acknowledgment of the 175,000-ton limit and then to discuss the tonnage ratio of the auxiliary classes.

So the conference's major aim had been accomplished. The scandalous reproduction of the dreadnought would be stopped. For Theodore Roosevelt, Jr., it seemed "like the end of an era." At the funeral of an old admiral he watched the tired remnants of the men who had helped his father build dreadnoughts shuffle in, "white haired, decrepit, and feebly wandering to the pews assigned them. . . . I couldn't help thinking that to them the world of airplanes and submarines, and the problems which are confronting us, must be as strange . . . as the day of the colonies would be to us."[37]

As much of a turning point as it was, the agreement to limit the construction of dreadnoughts was shot through with irony. Foreshadowing a favorite technique of the nuclear arms negotiator, the diplomats at Washington approached armament limitation by setting ceilings above current force levels. Consequently, the agreement sanctioned the commissioning of a total of five new dreadnoughts in the fleets of the three major naval powers. Like some giant sausage machine, the momentum of the process squeezed out a few more ships even though the power had been turned off.

In this, there is also irony. Had any of the civilian principals possessed the courage or cynicism to utterly disregard military advice and accept a drastically lower allotment of dreadnoughts in return for other concessions, his nation might have reaped a diplomatic windfall. The Japanese had even managed to do that by accident. The potential was there. Yet the Washington agreement, like all such treaties of this type (except the 1987 U.S.-Soviet treaty on intermediate nuclear forces [INF] pact), was primarily aimed at arms control, not disarmament. And if further proof of that point is required, it is only necessary to look at the treatment of the aircraft carrier and the submarine.

Prior to the conference, there had been some talk of limiting the military applications of the airplane. But Charles Evans Hughes's choice of representatives to the aviation subcommittee made that seem highly unlikely. Brigadier General William Mitchell had not been forgotten by the secretary of state. It was quite apparent that the sinking of the *Ostfriesland* had been a major factor in the decision to go ahead with the dramatic dreadnought proposal. The general was a man who could be trusted not to tether the future development of the airplane.

It must be said that as a diplomat Billy Mitchell proved no easy touch. He sat through twelve inconclusive meetings of the Military Aviation Subcommittee alternately scowling and staring blankly at the paneled walls of the chamber. Finally, smiling broadly, he suggested that "the only practicable limitation as to the number of aircraft that could be used for military purposes would be to abolish the use of aircraft for any purpose."[38] The sarcasm of the proposal was not lost on the other delegates who shortly produced a final report declaring military aviation limitation dangerous, futile, and prone to "shut the door on the process."[39]

But if the plane was not easily limited, its transporter, the aircraft carrier, could be and was—if this class's eventual tonnage allotment can remotely be considered a limitation. Theodore Roosevelt, Jr., proved to be the pivotal figure in the maneuvers leading up to an agreement. Believing the ships to be vital, he met with Hughes on 30 December and recommended limits of 135,000 tons apiece for the United States and Great Britain, 81,000 tons for Japan, and 54,000 tons each for France and Italy.[40] All of those figures vastly exceeded the current carrier-tonnage levels of the respective nations. Nonetheless, the secretary of state was encouraging enough for Roosevelt, Jr., to begin meeting with Admirals Coontz and Pratt to work out the details. The idea of converting the huge half-built battle cruisers *Lexington* and *Saratoga* into carriers soon found its way into their discussions.[41] Rated at thirty-three knots, those huge hulls were ideal candidates for conversion—in fact, they constituted the basis for virtual super-carriers—fully developed capital ships capable of attacking and easily outrunning entire battle lines.

Significantly, the two ships were far larger than any carrier the U.S. Navy wanted or even contemplated. To the General Board and the majority of the naval high command, the aircraft carrier was to be strictly an auxiliary ship designed to provide air cover for the dreadnoughts. Thus, after the *Lexington* and *Saratoga*, the U.S. Navy's interwar aircraft carrier construction program would concentrate exclusively on much smaller ships, such as the 14,500-ton *Wasp* and *Ranger* and the 20,000-ton *Yorktown* and *Enterprise*. Meanwhile, the two giants would remain almost like orphans in the fleet, unwanted prototypes of the true attack carrier, capital ship of the future.

After firming up the aircraft carrier proposal, Roosevelt, Jr., submitted it to Hughes, who in turn presented it to the other delegates. Since both the British and Japanese had carrier conversion plans of their own, there were no serious objections.[42] By the end of January the powers had settled upon a clause that defined aircraft carriers as ships larger than 10,000 tons, built exclusively to carry planes, and whose guns did not exceed eight inches. The United States and Britain were each to be allotted five units, Japan three, and France and Italy two apiece.[43] So under the rubric of arms control, an agreement was reached at Washington that would underwrite the development of naval air power in the period between the two world wars. In this case, tonnage limitations became targets to which the individual services could aspire.

Of course, the aircraft carrier was an attractive weapon, a relatively inoffensive successor to the dreadnought. Its good fortune at the hands of diplomats can be explained at least partly in those terms. But what of the submarine, universally despised and a prime candidate for outright prohibition? As things turned out, its fate was not significantly worse.

Prior to the opening of the conference, such a conclusion might have seemed highly unlikely. In both the United States and Great Britain large segments of the public expressed hatred and disgust at the weapons that, just a few years prior, had plunged thousands of innocents into the North Atlantic and a cold, dark death.[44] Moreover, the British government had come to consider the submarine a lethal threat to the security of its empire, and its delegation went to Washington under official instructions to press for its total abolition. Yet Hughes and the U.S. delegation were not about to be carried away with humanitarian sentiment. Again revealing the pragmatic side of arms control, the Americans at the first plenary session unveiled a proposal to allot 90,000 tons of submarines to themselves and the British and 54,000 to Japan.[45] The British were bitterly critical of the offer, complaining especially of its failure to limit the large cruising submarine, whose whole purpose was "attack . . . probably . . . by methods which civilized nations would regard with horror."[46] The American public seemed to agree and by early in January had bombarded Hughes and his colleagues with over 40,000 letters and telegrams urging abolition.

The dispute between the two English-speaking nations soon began to seem minor compared with the rift that had developed when it became known that the French were demanding no less than 90,000 tons of submarines for themselves. Taking this as a calculated affront, the British openly spoke of Gallic blackmail and treachery. On 22 December, the British, against the advice of the U.S. delegation, launched a frontal attack on the French position by publicly calling for total abolition of the submarine. Lest anyone catch a whiff of self-interest, the civilian head of the Admiralty, Lord Lee, "wished to make it clear that the British Empire delegation had no unworthy or selfish motives." Means of combatting the submarine were now so advanced, he maintained, that it could no longer be considered an especially valuable weapon.[47]

It is unlikely that many believed him. Hanihara, of the Japanese delegation, spoke up for the submarine, calling it a "relatively inexpensive yet effective" instrument of defense for an insular country.[48] Italy's Senator Schanzer agreed, terming it an "indispensable weapon for the defense of the Italian coasts."[49] This too was essentially the position of the special committee advising the U.S. delegation. "It will be impossible for our fleet to protect our two long coast lines properly at all times. . . . Submarines are therefore necessary."[50] Seeing the British isolated, the French on 28 December coupled their acceptance of the 175,000-ton limit on battleships with an absolute refusal to consider any submarine quota under 90,000 tons.[51] That announcement killed all further hope of abolishing the submarine or limiting its size and tonnage. The grip of technology over human destiny proved stronger than the diplomats' resolve. Like many before and after, the men in the frock coats deferred to the shrouded figure whose skeletal hand was always pointed toward the future.

Appearances had to be preserved, however. Millions around the globe expected their leaders to do something about the submarine. It was for just such contingencies that Charles Evans Hughes had included Elihu Root in the U.S. delegation. An elder statesman among elder statesmen, the venerable Root took a fervent belief in international law to his deathbed. Such men are always useful to politicians on ceremonial occasions. Accepting the Gallic logic that inhuman use of a weapon was not valid grounds for condemning the weapon, only its user, Root set to work on a code of conduct for submarines. Although that was analogous to trying to teach wolves table manners, after a suitable interval, the desired document was produced. Prohibiting all but the most ceremonious of attacks on merchant vessels, it would turn submarine captains into veritable Lancelots.[52] Of course, the idea of postponing an attack until a victim refused visit and search was nothing less than ridiculous, given what had happened during the Great War. The submarine's vulnerability, the existence of effective depth charges, and the fact that merchant ships were now sure to travel in convoys constantly guarded by destroyers during wartime made it practically a certainty that any commander who endeavored to live up to the Root resolution would quickly meet his death in the attempt. It is difficult to believe that the delegates who unanimously signed the declaration were not aware of its fantastic nature. Nonetheless, it did serve to obscure the fact that the Washington naval treaty failed to deal effectively with the hated submarine. Meanwhile the illusion of disarmament was preserved, at least until France's failure to ratify made the Root resolution a dead letter.[53]

So too would the mirage of peace in the Far East be sustained, for as a replacement of the offending Anglo-Japanese alliance, Hughes carefully orchestrated a four-power nonaggression pact covering the entire Pacific area. Maintaining the slogan of the Open Door in Asia, the four-power pact provided not even the mildest of sanctions for enforcement. It was merely an agreement not to press matters until France and Britain had a chance to recover from their war wounds and until the United States and Japan had a chance to settle their differences "by other means." But to the grateful world it looked like peace.

But it soon became apparent that the glossy facade of verbiage now known as the Washington naval treaties concealed a rather less imposing structure of accomplishment. Throughout the episode Charles Evans Hughes performed brilliantly, but shallowly. Apparently a sincere devotee of peace and disarmament, the U.S. secretary of state lacked fundamental insight into the nature of the problem. To Hughes and the great majority of arms controllers, the essence of the problem was individual weapons, not the systematic application of technology to destructive purposes. The dreadnought, for so long the symbol of world weapons competition, was an obvious target for restriction.

Yet the equation of its limitation with the end of arms racing in general was naïve. Indeed the evidence indicates that Hughes was aware of the dreadnought's tactical weakness, and that this knowledge was the basis of his decisiveness at Washington. Certainly his tolerance of the aircraft carrier and submarine contrasted strongly with his sternness toward the battleship. However, that can be assumed to be less a manifestation of cynicism than an example of the peculiar bifurcation that allowed American diplomats and policymakers during the interwar period to mouth the highest idealism, while acting in a basically pragmatic fashion. And Americans were not alone in doing so: Virtually all the participants in the Great War occupied themselves at one level with messianic schemes of disarmament while at the same time made realistic plans for renewed warfare—frequently emphasizing the very weapons they most deplored or had been victimized by during World War I. So it was that the United States quietly prepared to wage unrestricted submarine warfare, the British acquired the aircraft to stage massive bombing raids on civilian population centers, and the Germans learned to fight with tanks.

Nevertheless, all this should not be allowed to obscure the fact that the Washington naval conference was the first such gathering to succeed in limiting a major weapon system. That was no mean accomplishment, for increasingly it was arms developments and deployments that became the primary factors in destabilizing relations between major powers. And it is in that context that the Washington conference is best viewed. Although some interesting precedents had been set at the two Hague conferences, the proceedings at Washington can be said to have given birth to the first of the modern arms control treaties. And as such, the naval agreements provided a prospectus for the future, outlining both the possibilities and limitations of that form of diplomacy. Clearly the events of late 1921 demonstrated the importance of relatively simple, comprehensive proposals, originating from the highest levels of government. When negotiations were allowed to devolve to the level of military experts, endless wrangling over technical issues ensued. The results of the Washington conference also revealed that negotiated arms control was generally far more successful at limiting weapons that did not work or were unwanted for other reasons. In 1921 the focus was on the dreadnought; the Stategic Arms Limitation Talks (SALT) would deal with similarly suspect antiballistic missile systems; Ronald Reagan and Mikhail Gorbachev would agree to eliminate the very dangerous INFs; and Strategic Arms Reduction Talks (START) negotiations would concentrate on the provocative heavy ICBMs. Conversely, arms controllers would prove far less successful in curbing so-called sweet technologies—the submarine and aircraft carrier at Washington and MIRV and advanced cruise missiles in the later context.

Nonetheless, for the world in 1922 it was enough. No sarcastic snickers were heard in the Senate chamber when the report of the American delegation stated that "the limitation of capital ships, substantially meets the existing need, and, its indirect effect will be to stop the inordinate production of any sort of naval craft."[54] Congress was satisfied. Within weeks all clauses would be ratified by overwhelming majorities. So it was with all the other signatories. In Britain, France, Italy, and Japan the Washington agreements were received as a major foreign policy accomplishment and the dawn of a new age.

Only from within the world's naval establishments came howls of dismay, and perhaps the most anguished cries emanated from the U.S. Navy. Like no other event since the collapse of the Civil War armada, the Washington naval treaties demoralized Annapolites and made them fear for the future. Hardly consulted during the negotiations, officers complained bitterly that Japan had received too high a ratio and that the nonfortification agreement needlessly sacrificed American interests.[55] Yet there was a more fundamental reason for their despair. As William F. Fullam later wrote Sims: "They are opposed to the Treaties and the conference simply because they all wanted the 1916 program— more battleships! That is the gist of the matter."[56] Undeniably the naval conference dealt a crushing blow to the battleship. Nonetheless, Annapolites would manage to resuscitate the victim and keep it breathing until the final debacle at Pearl Harbor twenty years later. For the dreadnought there would truly be life after death.

11

Life After Death:
Rehabilitating the Dreadnought

I

The U.S. Navy steamed into the interwar period with its course set to rehabilitate the battleship. But its bearings were askew: Those charting the passage were enshrouded in a fog of their own making, heavy with illusions of both past and future. Fortunately it was a multinational overcast, similarly dimming the vision of the British and Japanese naval leadership, leaving all three of the world's great fleets steering nearly equally eccentric paths across the 1920s and 1930s. Certainly there were dissenters within each of the three services, but until the very end of the period their voices were generally muffled by the liturgical chants of the orthodox and the manifest thunder of the sacred vessels. And appropriately enough that chapter ended with a massive slaughter of dreadnoughts, a massacre that, though perceived initially as a great victory, would prove tactically and strategically irrelevant to the conduct of the war it had provoked.

The leaders of the U.S. Navy may have been headed in the wrong direction, but bureaucratically they proved steadfast and resourceful in their campaign to restore the battleship's good name. Initially they had to work under considerable handicaps: Not only had the great ships been publicly branded as obsolete and symbols of uncontrolled militarism, but also the Navy was prohibited by treaty from producing any more of them for at least a decade. Nonetheless, those obstacles were viewed as temporary and capable of being overcome.

The first item on the Navy's agenda was to reverse the perceived results of Mitchell's bombing test. The approach was twofold: denunciation and counter-demonstration. Almost immediately naval officers of nearly all stripes launched what amounted to a verbal assault on the *Ostfriesland* tests, arguing that they were essentially meaningless because the battleship was sitting dead in the water and unable to defend itself (but failing to note that the German vessel was also empty of ammunition likely to cause lethal secondary explosions).[1] There was also a general concern expressed that Mitchell's hurried sinking of the ship compromised the "scientific" nature of the tests, the implication being that naval professionals could do better. They would certainly try.

Between 1921 and 1924 the Navy staged a series of its own tests, experimenting with torpedo planes against the *Arkansas*, and sinking the old battleships *Alabama* and *Iowa*, along with the partially completed *Washington*, scheduled to be eliminated under the Washington treaty. To say these trials were "controlled" understates the case. In the first instance, although aircraft succeeded in hitting the *Arkansas* with nine out of eighteen torpedoes as she steamed along at fifteen knots, the Navy apparently paid little attention to the results.[2] Similarly, although the *Alabama* was attacked with apparently devastating results, using explosive and phosphorus bombs as well as tear gas, no member of the General Board nor, for that matter, any officer above the rank of commander managed to be among the observers.[3]

That was certainly not the case in the *Iowa*'s destruction, which amounted to almost a parody of the *Ostfriesland* test. In March 1923 Secretary Denby filled the public relations ship *Henderson* with high-ranking officers along with as many senators, congressmen, and reporters as he could gather aboard and transported them to the Caribbean, where the electrically controlled *Iowa* awaited them. It was to be sunk in the grand naval manner, using heavy gunfire from the USS *Mississippi*.[4] As if the *Iowa*'s demise had not made it perfectly clear that a battleship could also sink a battleship, the exercise was essentially repeated in 1924, using the much more modern *Washington*, which succumbed after two and one-half hours of shelling from turret guns. But from the sidelines of retirement Admiral Fullam wondered, "Why were naval bombers deprived of the opportunity to drop heavy bombs upon the *Washington*? . . . Why were not naval airmen permitted to fire live torpedoes at the *Washington* with torpedo planes? . . . Why has the Navy refused or failed to carry out any important tests if it is so anxious to know what airplanes can do against a hostile fleet?"[5]

Meanwhile the plane had already captured the people's imagination. Prompted by Billy Mitchell's relentless cheerleading, the public had come to view aircraft as a panacea for national defense. Cheap, versatile, and demonstrably powerful, planes were seen as promising not simply to revolutionize warfare, but also potentially to eliminate the expensive and man-consuming activities that made traditional combat unattractive. And thanks to Mitchell, the battleship had been branded as symbolic of the old approach. So when the public sensed that the progress of air power was being stymied, they tended to blame the Navy and demand prompt remediation.

During the mid-1920s that syndrome resulted in a series of highly publicized government hearings, which, although their focus was on aeronautics, also featured extended discussion of the usefulness and future of the battleship. Thus both the House Inquiry into the Operations of the United States Air Service, or Lampert Board, and the still more prestigious Morrow Board became forums for the likes of Billy Mitchell, Sims, and Fullam on one side and, on the other, conservative admirals like Robert Coontz and Hilary Jones arguing the relative merits of the *Ostfriesland* tests, gun-based air defenses, and what would constitute a "well-balanced" fleet in the future.[6] In actual fact the net effect of the hearings was beneficial to the service, since it contributed to a decision allowing the Navy to develop its own air arm, rather than having this element consolidated into the independent air force envisioned by Mitchell.[7] Nonetheless, as the Navy was essentially on the defensive and both the service and the battleship were clearly in public disfavor, the admirals emerged from the experience feeling somewhat less than vindicated.

Their response was characteristic. At the prompting of Naval Secretary Curtis D. Wilbur the General Board set up its own panel headed by Chief of Naval Operations Edward W. Eberle, who was an ordnance specialist, to consider "recent developments in aviation, . . . listen to" the advice of experienced officers, and recommend "a policy with reference to the development and upkeep of the Navy."[8] Packed with conservatives, the panel included three other members of the General Board besides Eberle and no naval aviators.[9] Most of the witnesses, exemplified by Admirals C. C. Bloch and C. F. Hughes, were of an equally orthodox orientation and testified accordingly. Those exhibiting iconoclastic tendencies, even slight ones, like Captain W. H. Standley and Admiral T. P. Magruder, were marched through a line of questioning calculated to reveal the battleship as still the backbone of the fleet.[10] Only Fullam refused to knuckle under, exclaiming at one point, "I love the surface navy, I hate everything else, and I would gladly see [the battleships modernized], if you can get the money without taking away the money necessary to get airplanes."[11]

In the end the Eberle Board's recommendations were predictable, though not entirely divorced from reality. "Aviation," noted the board, "has introduced a new and highly important factor in warfare," but one essentially limited to "accurate control of fire at long ranges . . . and scouting."[12] Even the hated submarine was conceded a future role, though a decidedly domesticated one "accompanying the fleet in an overseas campaign for its protection." But the board agreed with Admiral Hughes that at the center remained the battleship, "the basis or nucleus around which the fleet must be formed."[13] Moreover, Eberle and his colleagues concluded that "the battleship of the future can be so designed as to distribution of her armor on decks and sides . . . that she will not be subject to fatal damage from the air."[14]

The jury had spoken, and in the eyes of the Navy the battleship was exonerated, acquitted of obsolescence. And in line with that judgment Eberle and his colleagues produced seven basic recommendations for future naval investment, which, at President Calvin Coolidge's request, the board subsequently listed as follows: first, modernization of the six oldest battleships; second, completion of the aircraft carriers *Saratoga* and *Lexington;* third, modernization of the remaining battleships; fourth, construction of eight 10,000-ton cruisers; fifth, the acquisition of aircraft; sixth, construction of six fleet submarines, and last, the building of an additional aircraft carrier.[15] Considering the source, one could say that this was not a totally reactionary program. But it clearly reflected the continuing centrality of the dreadnought, and in line with the program, the dreadnought would remain at the heart of the Navy's planning until the mid-1930s.

In theory, and in the absence of actual combat to test it, the Navy's agenda must have seemed reasonable enough. Certainly it did not reject new technology out of hand. Rather it attempted to do what the naval establishment had always done when faced with dramatic change—accommodate it within a familiar framework. Just as Admiral Aube's torpedo boat had been transformed from attacker to protector of the battle fleet, the submarine and the aircraft carrier would be brought into the naval fold as "auxiliaries." The problem was that both represented much more legitimate challenges than the torpedo boat had been to the battleship's primacy and did so at a time when technology and its possibilities were evolving considerably faster than in the day of the Jeune Ecole. But if the Navy's objective was ultimately unattainable, the service was not alone in pursuing it. Both the British and the Japanese navies were equally intent on deploying fleet submarines and using the carrier and its aircraft to scout for and defend the all-important battle line.[16] For not only was the natural course of weapons development symmetrical, but also all three services, having sprung from the same traditions, remained committed to the same Mahanite body of belief. However, there remained a gaping chasm between mutual reinforcement and making such concepts work in actual fact.

In that regard the U.S. Navy's experience with the fleet submarine can be judged as characteristic. From the beginning it was clear that such a vessel would not be easy to build. In order to accompany the battle fleet and successfully scout and run interference for it, a fleet submarine would need a very long range and much improved habitability, a surface speed of around twenty knots, combined with a relatively high submerged speed, and heavy torpedo armament. Given the state of submarine technology, particularly that of diesel engineering, those were extremely challenging requirements.[17] The situation was not improved by the fact that the Navy had failed to make complete plans of the very advanced German submarines surrendered after World War I and subsequently destroyed in tests. But even in the absence of clear technical solutions, it was readily apparent that a fleet submarine would be, by necessity, a large submarine. After initially considering and rejecting steam propulsion, the General Board foresaw a boat around 330 feet long with a top speed of eighteen knots (the highest attainable using existing diesel engines) and a cruising range of 12,000 miles—all of which was expected to add up to a displacement in excess of 1,500 tons.[18] The resulting V-class proved to be very expensive and time-consuming to build, each example requiring from three to four and one-half years in the yards. Consequently just six would be completed by 1930, the entire U.S. submarine production during the decade. And they proved to be slow divers, unwieldy, and unstable—all characteristics exaggerated by the Navy's insistence upon mounting guns of up to six inches on the decks. Not surprisingly, their record in exercises with the fleet proved uniformly dismal.[19]

By the late 1920s it was clear that U.S. naval planners considered the fleet submarine concept a failure.[20] On that basis the General Board recommended that submarines in general be abolished during the next round of arms control negotiations.[21] For the Navy had not bothered to develop any alternative submarines to the fleet type. Unlike other areas covered under the Washington treaty, the naval establishment had interpreted the agreement and also U.S. public opinion literally, assuming that under no circumstances would the United States resort to a submarine campaign waged primarily against commerce. It followed that there was simply no need for alternative submarines—a conclusion so out of phase with reality that it would be countermanded within the Navy even as the

United States sought to abolish the submarine at Geneva in 1927 and at the London Naval Conference in 1930.[22]

Meanwhile parallel British and Japanese efforts to generate an effective fleet submarine encountered similar technical difficulties, though in the latter case the institutional response was both different and highly suggestive. The Royal Navy was the first to give vent to the urge for a fleet submarine and also the most innovative in this regard. As far back as 1915 the British service introduced the first of the breed, the K-class, whose steam turbines ensured both a high surface speed and a very slow diving rate, which led to their disappearance by the mid-1920s.[23] Subsequently, the British experimented with the M-type mounting a single 12-inch gun, the very large XI with four 5.2-inch guns, and even a modified M carrying a small seaplane in a watertight hangar.[24] Yet technical problems with each, combined with the invention and deployment of ASDIC—a primitive sonar device in which the British placed great and unjustified faith—led to the near total de-emphasis of the submarine by the Royal Navy and the ultimate atrophy of the fleet sub concept.

The Japanese, however, proved more persistent. Despite serious technical problems, the Imperial Navy in 1932 laid down the first of the Fleet Type 6s, 2,000-ton boats with a cruising range of 20,000 miles.[25] In line with the submarines' anticipated role as scouts and skirmishers for the battle fleet, technicians succeeded in grafting first observation aircraft and then midget attack submarines onto the commodious Type 6s, which remained at the heart of Imperial Navy's submarine planning. Significantly, the Japanese never wavered in their determination to use underwater craft to decimate naval assets rather than commerce. For among the three major naval powers the Japanese would remain most rigidly loyal to the battle fleet ideal and the concomitant determination to interpret and integrate new naval technology within this context. And it was this orientation that would go far to counteract the significance of the otherwise very robust Japanese effort to build up its naval power during the interwar period and pave the way for defeat in the Pacific.

The submarine was by nature an outsider among naval combatants, and that basically is why the fleet sub concept was doomed. Yet the aircraft carrier, on the face of it, promised much more adaptability to the traditional hierarchy of ships. Nonetheless, like the submarine, the carrier had the tactical-technical potential, even in a relatively undeveloped form, to displace the battleship from the top of the pyramid of ships. Because the carrier was inherently a large surface vessel and therefore much more in sync with traditional naval values, its future and use inevitably became key questions in naval planning. And it was in the U.S. Navy that the potential of carrier aviation was most quickly and thoroughly explored.

In part this was purely a matter of politics. Archenemy Billy Mitchell and his relentless campaign for an independent air force had the net effect of forcing the Navy's hand, acting as a sword of Damocles threatening to sever aviation from the Navy unless steady progress was made within the service. Moreover, the man in charge of naval air, Rear Admiral William A. Moffett, was a master of service politics, deftly carving a narrow path between Mitchell and the Navy, taking advantage of every bit of leverage the situation presented.[26] Yet the difficulty of his position was reflected in the results of the so-called Second Taylor Board, which, although it did include a modicum of less-orthodox officers, still concluded in April 1927 that the central role of the carrier was to defend the battle fleet and engage in "scouting and offensive operations at a distance from the battle line."[27] This judgment was followed that November by the General Board's guidance for future carrier construction, recommending five relatively small 13,800-ton ships capable of less than thirty knots. Although the board's program to some degree reflected a desire to build as many carriers as possible under the Washington treaty's tonnage limitations, it was also clear that this class (only one of which was ever finished, the unsuccessful USS *Ranger*) was configured strictly to protect the battle fleet.[28]

There were alternatives, however. By 1928 the giant converted battle cruisers *Lexington* and *Saratoga* were completed as carriers and ready to join the fleet. Those 888-foot-long vessels, listed at 33,000 tons apiece but actually more than 3,000 tons heavier, were the biggest ships in the Navy and constituted true attack carriers, with top speeds of thirty-four knots and a capacity for around eighty aircraft.[29] To conservatives they were something of an embarrassment, accidentally so large only because of their original hulls and basically unsuited for the designated role of fleet auxiliaries. But in certain quarters there was enthusiasm for letting the two big ships live up to their potential.

Moffett and his aviators had important allies in the surface Navy. The original naval insurgents had been replaced by a second generation of technological progressives. Although a looser amalgam and less consistently partisan in its politics, this group was similarly committed to innovation within the Navy. At its head was a triumvirate analogous to that of Fullam, Fiske, and Sims, this one being made up of Harry E. Yarnell, Frank Schofield (the inventor of the heretical torpedo dreadnought), and the remarkable William V. Pratt. The key transitional figure between the first and second generation, Pratt had assumed Sims's position

The old battle line. The Pennsylvania *and* Colorado *followed by three cruisers.* (*Courtesy of the U.S. National Archives*)

The new battle line—domesticating the carrier. The aircraft carriers Langley *and* Ticonderoga *in line with the* Washington, North Carolina, *and* South Dakota, *followed by cruisers.* (*Courtesy of the U.S. National Archives*)

as chief instigator but proved far less acerbic, rising to the very pinnacle of naval responsibility.[30] From there he supported the proponents of carrier aviation represented by J. M. "Billy Goat" Reeves and Moffett himself, giving them their first real opportunity to show what the new weapons could do.[31]

The occasion was the 1929 naval maneuver known as Fleet Problem IX, one of a series of war games conducted in southern waters during the interwar years. In prior fleet problems, carrier aviation had been represented by the USS *Langley*—a plodding converted transport known not entirely affectionately as the "Covered Wagon"—which was normally tethered to the battle line in a strictly subordinate role.[32] Number IX would be different, however, for the *Lexington* and *Saratoga* were included for the first time, and the *Langley* was left behind at Mare Island for overhaul.[33] The scenario called for Pratt's Black Force, consisting of the battle fleet including the *Saratoga*, to attack the Panama Canal, defended by Admiral Taylor's Scouting Force, reinforced by the *Lexington*. Out of the Black contingent, Pratt designated a force of four battleships, the cruiser *Omaha*, and the *Saratoga* to stage the assault. Almost immediately, however, *Saratoga* and *Omaha* cut loose from the dreadnoughts and swept toward the target area at twenty-five knots. When they reached a point 140 miles from the canal, Admiral Reeves launched the *Saratoga's* planes, which then easily found their way to the target and bombed the Miraflores Locks in two waves.[34] Only the mission requirement for the *Saratoga* to head toward her own battleships (which never found her) and pick up the returning aircraft near the target area caused the *Saratoga* to be located and notionally destroyed by the defenders.

Nonetheless, it was clear to many involved that something extraordinary had taken place. The promise of Sims's ground-breaking games with carriers at the War College had been fulfilled at sea with real ships—a naval star was born. In his post mortem Pratt looked to the future, saying, "I believe that when we learn more of the possibilities of the carrier we will come to an acceptance of Admiral Reeves' plan which provides for a very powerful and mobile force . . . the nucleus of which is the carrier."[35] In all but name, this was a carrier task force. Momentarily at least it seemed as if there might be a new focal point of seapower. "I am not one who believes that we are in a position to abolish the battleship," ventured the *Lexington's* Captain Berrien, "but my eyes have been opened."[36] As for Pratt, he flew his flag from the *Saratoga* on the return cruise, "partly as a badge of distinction, but mostly because I want to know what makes the aircraft squadrons 'tick.'"[37]

The issue was far from resolved. Undoubtedly many officers continued to agree with Admiral Henry Wiley that Fleet Problem IX only confirmed "the battleship as the final arbiter of naval destiny."[38] Even those with more-open minds could be expected to demand a good deal more evidence before they might be willing to consider scrapping the battle fleet concept. And Pratt himself seems to have longed for additional proof of the carrier task force's superiority. Consequently, in the spring of 1930, upon returning from the London Naval Conference (where he proved no friend of the battleship), Pratt, as commander in chief of the U.S. fleet, approached Chief of Naval Operations C. F. Hughes for permission to carry out further comparative tests. He was so rudely rebuffed, however, that he left vowing to use his influence to get Hughes's job.[39] Within months Pratt was named chief of naval operations, and suddenly the way was clear for a true inquiry into the naval future. Symbolic of this resolve, Pratt quit the General Board shortly after assuming his new post. But more important, he had begun laying plans for a direct confrontation between the battle line and the carrier task force.[40]

Fleet Problem XII was set to take place in January 1931. It would consist of a Blue Force made up of both big carriers, *Lexington* and *Saratoga*, surrounded by light cruisers and destroyers—all dedicated to stopping a Black invading force supported by virtually the entire battle fleet, with the carrier *Langley* attached. Rather than attacking Black's battleships with everything, Blue split its force into two carrier groups and attempted to find and bomb the convoy carrying the actual landing force. Through a combination of bad luck and inexperience, Blue failed, and Black managed a landing. Reeves warned, "There is a grave possibility that these lessons may be incorrectly interpreted and that the strength and power of certain weapons may be incorrectly estimated."[41] Very likely no one was listening.

This had been meant to be the acid test. The General Board had been brought down to observe.[42] Even though Number XII had essentially consisted of two ships against the entire navy, probably no one was counting. All that mattered was that the dreadnoughts had lumbered into the invasion site with the convoy still in existence. Whatever Pratt's real feelings, he accepted the results: "The battleship is the backbone of the Fleet. No clearer demonstration of the value of the battleship to the Fleet could be shown than was done in this problem."[43]

Fleet Problem XII was a critical moment. The carrier task force would be practiced again, but not with the idea of replacing the battle line. However, had the dreadnoughts done poorly in XII, it might have spelled the end. Instead, their position as the focal point of naval power was now secure until Pearl Harbor. The vindication of the battleships was virtually complete. Only one item remained. Pratt would be directed to use the results of XII to help secure dreadnought modernization.[44]

There is a saying in the construction business: "In good times folks build houses; in bad times they renovate." So it was with U.S. battleships. Precluded from building more of them until 1936 by two naval holidays, the Navy chose the next best thing. And although a good deal of the naval history of the 1920s and early 1930s was focused on the service's efforts to build cruisers and the resultant arms control implications, it is important to remember that the first priority remained the modernization of the dreadnoughts.[45]

The program had two basic aspects: defensive and offensive. First there was an underlying assumption that the dreadnought could be made invulnerable to its enemies above and below. Torpedoes and mines would be dealt with by reinforcing the hulls internally and through the addition of external "blisters"— welded steel false sides running along the length of the vessel and intended to form a void to blunt the force of submarine explosions.[46] Similarly, the detonation of aerial bombs and plunging shells was to be counteracted through the addition of armored decks.[47] Unfortunately, the logic behind both "blisters" and thicker decks failed to account for the greater ease with which the destructive power of torpedoes and bombs could be increased to defeat them—the basic fallacy of the unsinkable ship. Considerable faith was also placed in antiaircraft guns, grafted onto the dreadnoughts with increasing frequency at convenient locations. But there again the Navy underestimated the inherent difficulty of shooting down an attacking plane and therefore failed to place sufficient emphasis on antiaircraft in terms of both numbers and quality.

American officers were not alone. The British and Japanese navies were also enthralled by the illusion of the unsinkable ship. Both made similar mistakes, betting too heavily on passive measures like "blisters," and only gradually realizing the many obstacles to effective antiaircraft fire.[48] Consequently, until the late 1930s, it is likely that a majority of all three services would have agreed with Captain W. D. Puleston that "it is a conservative statement to say the danger from enemy aircraft has been greatly reduced."[49]

Modernizing the dreadnoughts was not simply a matter of protecting them. Perhaps even greater emphasis was placed on enhancing their perceived offensive capabilities, particularly in the United States, where plans to project power across

A dreadnought visits the Big Apple. Modernized USS Colorado *(note catapult-launched spotter aircraft) off lower Manhattan in the early 1930s. (Courtesy of the U.S. Naval Institute)*

the vast expanses of the Pacific drove efforts to increase the battleships' reach. In a strategic sense that meant the wholesale conversion to oil fuel, a change that was very attractive to sailors everywhere, since the filthy and arduous task of coaling was universally hated. Moreover, because oil contained more energy per unit volume, it not only added to top speed but very significantly increased range. The latter was of real importance to Americans, who lacked bases in the Pacific. But for the British and Japanese, who had no domestic sources of petroleum, it also meant a strategic dependency. In the end it was the need for oil to run its ships that led directly to the Japanese decision to wage a disastrous war with the United States.[50]

Tactically, offensive modernization focused on the dreadnoughts' great guns. Although sights and fire control were improved, ironically, those moves also entailed the attachment of catapult-launched aircraft intended as spotters for the even-longer-range firing contemplated during the interwar years—air power domesticated in the grand naval tradition. Judging from the reception given pilot J. J. Clark by the USS *Mississippi*'s commander, Thomas C. Hart, flyers were still not all that welcome: "We've got too many aviators on this ship already! Why, I can take you up on my quarterdeck and show you oil marks where aviators have spilled oil."[51] But the key element in extended-range fire focused on the big guns themselves, and that proved controversial. As far back as December 1922, the General Board recommended that the Navy begin increasing the elevation of the battleships' turret guns to 30 degrees, arguing that the British had already done so—a measure that translated into a theoretical British range advantage of 30,000 yards to the Americans' 21,000 yards.[52] Problems surfaced almost immediately. Not only did the British deny making any such modifications, but they argued that the modifications constituted a violation under the Washington treaty.[53] While the General Board continued to maintain that elevation was legal, Secretary of State Hughes publicly apologized for the Navy's false statements, and in January 1925 the Senate froze funding for further modifications to the turret guns.[54] Yet the Navy refused to give up and eventually succeeded in elevating the guns of thirteen of its eighteen battleships (the remainder already having been built to those specifications.)[55] The British and the Japanese soon followed suit, as did most other navies around the world.

Battleship modernization was not without its critics. Fullam, for example, characterized it as "attempting to resuscitate a dying gladiator by vainly adding to the thickness of his shield or to the length of his lance."[56] Nor were the battleships popular with civilian politicians, particularly among the economy-minded Congresses of the late 1920s and early 1930s. There the great ships were seen as excessively expensive to maintain—consuming fully 20 percent of the Navy's enlisted strength—and quite possibly obsolete.[57] Therefore, modernization was viewed skeptically. Consider, for example, an April 1930 dialogue between Representative McClintic and Admiral Rock, the chief of the Bureau of Construction: "'Admiral Rock, those battleships, before they are modernized, are comparatively useless, are they not?' Rock: 'They are not as efficient as they should be.' McClintic: 'How many battleships did we use in the World War? . . . Did we fire a single shot from a battleship?' Rock: 'I think you are getting out of my specialty.'"[58]

Rock's reply may have been disingenuous, but it was not entirely irrelevant. Having successfully blocked further dreadnought construction through arms control, civilians were loath to ignore the advice of the Navy's experts totally.

Consequently, on four separate occasions between 1925 and 1931, Congress authorized the funds necessary to complete the refurbishment of U.S. dreadnoughts.[59] So even in the face of the Great Depression and two naval holidays, the Navy was able to keep its herd of battleships sleek and well groomed.

II

In fact battleship modernization would prove to have almost no tangible military significance. But it set an important arms control precedent. In return for the military's grudging cooperation with quantitative limitation, it typically was left free to pursue qualitative advantage. And in an environment of ever-increasing technological sophistication, that proved highly destabilizing. For example, once the first SALT treaty placed ceilings on the numbers of U.S. and Soviet long-range rockets, the military on both sides responded with programs to provide individual launchers with up to ten guided warheads, or MIRVs. Not only did this undermine verification and greatly increase the potential levels of damage, but in certain circles it also called into question the whole arms control process. Nonetheless, virtually all participants were eventually forced by the logic of events to admit that their was no viable policy alternative to negotiated arms control.

So it was in the 1920s and 1930s, when the string of naval negotiations that followed the Washington treaties provided the most practical means available to civilian politicians for limiting and channeling warship construction and circumscribing the ambitions of the international naval fraternity. The naval negotiations were at times chaotic, generally dominated by a very conventional view of seapower, and increasingly suffused with cynicism, so their tangible achievements were not great. But they provided an intricate and in many ways accurate blueprint for the future of arms control.

Just as in the nuclear era, there was a general conviction, especially in the United States, that arms control was a continuing process. Therefore, it was generally expected that subsequent negotiations would broaden and deepen the limits on warships initiated by the Washington treaties. As Robert Gordon Kaufman has recently pointed out, that outlook was reinforced by the antinaval sentiment prevalent in the democracies, particularly in the United States, where the orientation of Congress and the Coolidge and Hoover administrations was to minimize naval spending while maintaining the relative position of the U.S.

fleet through arms limitation.[60] Therefore, nearly every major appropriations bill during the 1920s called for another naval conference to be convened.[61] Meanwhile, the country cut back dramatically on construction, authorizing a mere thirty-one warships from 1922 to 1930, and only ten of them were even begun by the end of the decade.[62]

Although this approach was basically in consonance with that of the British, who also had reason to want to cut back on naval expenditures, it was sorely out of phase with the Japanese agenda. Spurred on by the "fleet faction," Japanese political opinion steadily came to view the 5:5:3 ratio established by the Washington treaties as a national affront and set out to readjust the nautical power equation—at first through negotiation and finally through intimidation and sheer self-sacrifice. Meanwhile, like the Soviets during the 1970s, the Japanese pursued an aggressive construction program, building up to and even beyond treaty limits. Thus during the last eight years of the 1920s the Japanese began 123 warships, completing almost all of them before the first London conference in 1930.[63] The net effect did not simply undermine the bargaining position of the democracies; it put them directly at odds with the Japanese in terms of negotiating objectives. And when that became obvious, it would spell the end of this chapter of arms control.

The Japanese were not the only reluctant players. The U.S. Navy and to a lesser extent the Royal Navy were disgruntled hostages to the arms control policies of their respective countries. But the only alternative to participation was standing aside while civilians savaged their future. So in the United States the Navy grudgingly took part, though the role played by its preferred representative, the General Board, was less than constructive.

This became immediately apparent during the first post-Washington attempt at arms control, the ill-fated 1927 Geneva Naval Conference, which was expected to extend the tonnage ratio system to auxiliary warships, particularly cruisers.[64] Instead the British and Americans came to Geneva with vastly differing proposals: the former desiring more than fifty-five light cruisers to protect its far-flung trade and empire, and the latter wanting an agreement that would allow them to emphasize heavy cruisers.[65] To complicate matters further, the British favored extending the life span of battleships six years beyond the twenty years established at Washington and lowering the tonnage and armament limits of future dreadnoughts—all of which was flatly rejected by the Americans, who wanted big ships for the contemplated trans-Pacific campaign.[66]

As Kaufman noted, both countries viewed Geneva as essentially a technical endeavor and staffed their delegations accordingly. On the U.S. side that meant the absence of a major political figure and a heavy representation from the General Board, most notably the recalcitrant Admiral Hilary Jones, its senior member. As for the British, their delegation was similarly dominated by naval officers.[67] The net effect was diplomatic permafrost, with both sides wrangling fruitlessly over technical issues and items of naval theology. Finally, with the talks completely deadlocked, Hugh Gibson, the titular head of the U.S. delegation and conference chairman, mercifully called a halt to the proceedings—the bickering between the erstwhile allies having essentially masked the still-wider chasm that separated the objectives of the democracies from those of the Japanese.

The reaction in the United States to the proceedings in Geneva was highly suggestive in light of the future dynamics of arms control. In late 1927, the president abruptly shifted his heretofore parsimonious position on naval building, asking Congress to approve a seventy-one-ship program, including twenty-five heavy cruisers. "We know now," he explained, "that no agreement can be reached which is inconsistent with a considerable building program on our part."[68] Yet negotiating from strength was just one lesson to be derived from Geneva. In November 1928 Coolidge told Sir Esme Howard: "The trouble with these discussions for naval disarmament lies really in the fact that they have hitherto been conducted mainly by naval technical experts. . . . They jealously compare and weigh ton against ton and gun against gun. . . . What we need in these discussions is men taking the broader and more statesmanlike view."[69] Those words undoubtedly would have found a sympathetic ear in the person of Coolidge's successor, Herbert Clark Hoover.

Hoover entered the White House in virtually complete agreement with the premises behind the era's commitment to naval arms control. His Quaker background and abhorrence of international violence combined with his business experience to convince him that weapons building not only "breeds suspicion, fear, [and] counterarmament" but was a serious drag on the domestic economy.[70] Not surprisingly, he had very little sympathy with the Mahanite outlook of Annapolites (if indeed he even knew who Mahan was) or the sacred postulates that governed their view of naval technology. "The days of the battleship are numbered owing to the development of aircraft," he told British Prime Minister Ramsay MacDonald in 1929.[71]

Firm in those convictions, Hoover rapidly set out to repair the damage done at Geneva. And almost immediately his campaign received an unexpected boost, with revelations in the summer of 1929 that the American shipbuilding industry had hired lobbyist William Shearer to sow discord at the failed naval conference. Hoover skillfully orchestrated public outrage to build support for a formal arms conference in the near future and to further preliminary talks already in progress with the British.[72]

The conduct of those prior negotiations not only would set the stage for the meeting in London the following January but also clearly indicated that both sides understood what had gone wrong in Geneva. Not accidentally, the negotiations transpired at the highest levels, with Hoover, his secretary of state, Henry Stimson, and Ramsay MacDonald all personally participating in an intense effort to reach prior agreement so as to avoid pointless squabbling at the actual naval conference.

The course of the talks also convinced the civilian leaders of the need to strictly subordinate military advice. Critical on the American side was Stimson and Hoover's experience in trying to induce the General Board to formulate a universal "yardstick" of naval power capable of measuring the relative value of different types of warships. Not surprisingly, after its disastrous experience with Charles Evans Hughes and "yardsticks" at the Washington conference, the General Board proved reluctant to cooperate, finally producing a formula so qualified by ambiguity as to be nearly useless.[73] In fact it was probably impossible to create such a "yardstick," but Stimson and Hoover were left profoundly annoyed and ready to accept a British request that naval officers be denied delegate status at the forthcoming London conference, relegated instead to the role of advisers. And when the time came to choose the naval advisers, the administration further revealed its orientation by turning to Pratt and Moffett, including Hilary Jones only as an afterthought.[74]

Although agreement on specifics, particularly the central issue of cruisers, would not be reached until later, the preliminary talks did indicate that the British and Americans were thinking along parallel lines in two other key areas: battleships and submarines. As far as dreadnoughts were concerned, it was clear that both sides were interested in further arms control, although their approaches differed. MacDonald essentially repeated the British proposal at Geneva—this time calling for a reduction in individual dreadnought tonnage from 35,000 to 25,000, a decrease in main armament from 16- to 12-inch guns, and an extension of ship life span from twenty to twenty-six years. Hoover, however, wanted to avoid building any battleships at all, suggesting that the construction holiday be extended to 1936 and that several older ships be scrapped.[75]

Not unexpectedly, the General Board was in total opposition, warning repeatedly that an extended naval holiday would prove ruinous to industry. If anything, the board was more negative about the possibility of shrinking the fleet's backbone even slightly, predicting that any reduction in the size of individual capital ships "would seriously jeopardize the national defense."[76] Whereas the naval conservatives' proverbial stance of not giving an inch on battleships probably served to undermine their credibility with the civilians further, their views on the submarine exactly paralleled that of the administration and the consistent position of the British. With the failure of the V-class fleet submarine, the General Board now concluded the submarine had no future—or at least none board members were willing to endorse.[77]

While differences over specifics certainly remained, the Anglo-American preliminary talks were successful in that they had the effect of establishing a political condominium that would smooth the way for cooperation during the actual conference. There again the civilians on both sides appear to have grasped the necessity in arms control negotiations for basic prior agreement at the highest political levels. Of course, naval limitation in this era was not bilateral but encompassed the entire naval world, and one key member of that community was essentially marching to a different drummer.

Japan's naval and foreign policies were already in the midst of a profound transition, motivated in part by a fundamental split in the Imperial Navy. On one side was the "administrative faction," moderates who feared a weapons competition with the industrial giant, the United States, and saw arms control as the best means of improving Japan's naval position; on the other side was the "fleet faction," who favored national aggrandizement whatever the cost. The moderates were responsible for Japanese accession to the Washington treaties and had maintained the upper hand through most of the 1920s, but they were losing their grip and gradually being supplanted by the "fleet faction."[78] Soon Japan would be committed to aggression and untrammeled naval expansion, but as the London conference approached, there was still some common ground to be exploited. Both sides entered the negotiations agreeing that any treaty must leave the Japanese predominant in the Western Pacific, and that this would require a 70 percent ratio in auxiliaries and nearly 80,000 tons of submarines.[79] As it happened, virtually all this would prove possible.

The London Naval Conference itself proved to be something of an anticlimax. The bipartisan U.S. delegation, led by Stimson, worked purposefully and consistently for compromise. On the cruiser issue, without consulting the

General Board, the delegates produced a tentative plan that forged the basis for agreement largely on British terms, but that preserved essential parity between the two.[80] This was eventually followed by a compromise between U.S. delegate Senator David Reed and Ambassador Matsudiara, which technically gave the United States a 10:6 ratio in heavy cruisers, but actually allowed the Japanese around 70 percent of U.S. tonnage in this class over the life of the treaty.[81] In addition, the Reed-Matsudiara agreement also granted the Japanese a 7:10 ratio in light cruisers and destroyers and parity in submarines, for a total ratio of 69.25 percent of the American navy, only 0.75 percent lower than their original goal.

The U.S. delegation proved equally purposeful in generating an acceptable position on battleships. At the heart of the matter was Hoover's proposal to extend the battleship holiday until 1936. In addition, the Americans, British, and Japanese agreed to scrap enough old dreadnoughts to leave them with fifteen, fifteen, and nine capital ships respectively. Only the French and Italians would be allowed to build up to Washington treaty limits.[82] Not only did this compromise effect significant savings, but it neatly sidestepped the issue of shrinking the dreadnought by deferring construction—thereby tossing a bone to the General Board. Although most historians now consider cruisers to be at the heart of the London agreements, Ernest Andrade noted that at the time the battleship provisions were "hailed as one of the most important parts of the Treaty."[83] All parties save the dreadnought profited from the extension of the battleship holiday.

The lone element of true controversy at London was supplied by the submarine. With the British behind him, Stimson himself made a direct appeal for the submarine's abolition, pointing to its high cost per ton and calling it a "weapon particularly susceptible to abuse."[84] Elaborating on this theme from an Annapolite perspective, Hilary Jones argued that abolition would not be complete until "all plans and drawings of submarines throughout the world were destroyed."[85] Such schemes fell on deaf ears among the Italians, Japanese, and particularly the French. "Must it disappear, because it disturbs the habits and the honored traditions of surface ships?" wondered one French delegate, whose country had invested heavily in submarines and believed them to be ideal for smaller navies.[86] The French would not even agree to qualitative limits on submarines, while the Japanese achievement of parity with the U.S. simply ratified what in fact already existed.[87] In the end consensus was reached through cosmetics. Submarines over 2,000 tons, which nobody wanted anyway, were banned, and the Washington treaties' code of underwater chivalry was modified to make it somewhat less absurd.[88] Once again realism and euphemism intervened on the side of the useful but unsavory submarine.

The London conference marked the high tide of naval arms control during the interwar years. Dreadnought procreation had been curbed again, and at least among the three navies that truly counted, relatively equitable and realistic tonnage ratios had been established in all major warship categories. Unfortunately, the agreement did not rest on solid political bedrock. Rather it simply marked a point of coincidence among powers moving in opposite directions—Japan toward militarism, aggression, and a massive arms buildup, and the United States and Great Britain toward isolationism and appeasement respectively. By the time the participants met again five years later in London for a final attempt at naval arms control, that would be obvious. So the necessity of linkage was affirmed.

Meanwhile, the United States Navy was not happy over the results of the proceedings in 1930. Of the twenty-five officers who testified before Senate panels on the London treaty, only four favored it, all carrier advocates—Harry Yarnell, Arthur Hepburn, Moffett, and Pratt himself, who placed special emphasis on the money saved by scrapping old battleships and extending the construction holiday.[89] That was very much in line with Pratt's behavior during the actual negotiations, where he had demonstrated a flexibility bordering on cynicism over issues such as gun size and capital ship replacement. But he was also aware that his views on the relative value of ship types, in part derived from Fleet Problem IX, represented only a minority opinion within the Navy.[90] Nor was this about to change, especially after the results of Fleet Problem XII. In fact the dreadnought was headed for better days: Modernization would be completed, and the Navy would bide its time until the day when new battleships could be built. Meanwhile, civilians had only to play the last hands in a losing game of arms control.

First came the 1932 Geneva Conference on the Reduction and Limitation of Armaments, which had as its goal the abolition of "offensive weapons." Unfortunately it foundered on a methodological shoal, the inability to define what precisely constituted such an armament.[91]

This left only the second London Naval Conference, of 1935–1936, a negotiation based on form rather than substance if there ever was one. The root of the problem was, as it had been throughout the 1930s, Japan. By 1933 army hard-liners and the "fleet faction" were finally dominant in that country, and the 10:10:7 ratio had joined the Washington treaties' 5:5:3 tonnage allotment as a symbol of national humiliation. Military spending was projected at 45 percent of total government outlays; Manchuria had been seized; and further incursions into China were being contemplated.[92] By early 1934, the Imperial Navy confirmed its decision to end any sincere efforts toward disarmament, and in July, Foreign Minister Hirota told Prince Saonji that Japan would soon abrogate and break out of both the Washington and London naval treaties regardless of "how much other powers agree with our proposals."[93] There would be precious little to agree with, since the Japanese delegation went to London under instructions to seek absolute naval parity with the democracies and the abolition of both battleships and aircraft carriers—the latter proposal having been included because it was presumed unacceptable to all parties.[94] In fact the real mission of the Japanese delegation was to manipulate public opinion and shift the blame for the collapse of arms control away from themselves.

Nor were the democracies taken by surprise. Even before Japan's formal announcement, in late December 1934, that it intended to abrogate the Washington treaties, both the Americans and the British presumed that the oriental power would play a less-than-constructive role at the forthcoming conference.[95] Yet each continued to have its own reasons for preserving the possibility of at least the semblance of arms control.

In the United States President Franklin D. Roosevelt was a true friend of the Navy. Having already served in the family bailiwick of the assistant secretary-ship nearly two decades earlier, now as chief executive he was predisposed to act as his own naval secretary to do what he could to build up the service. But Roosevelt was also a consummate politician, very much aware of the popularity of arms control and the reciprocal unpopularity of naval building among Americans during the 1930s. Moreover, although he was undeniably suspicious of Japanese objectives and willingness to use force, Roosevelt was not ready to believe that they were ready to start a full-blown naval arms race with the United States.[96] Consequently, the president held out some hope for the second London conference and authorized his delegation to seek a reduction of up to 20 percent in total tonnage, some new qualitative limits on battleships, and abolition of submarines, but no change in the fleet ratios.[97] Should the Japanese refuse to cooperate, then the onus for the collapse of the negotiations would be placed squarely on their shoulders. In the end, that would prove the only feasible objective.

The British had still more reason to be forthcoming negotiators. Hostages to a domestic pacifism bred of three-quarters of a million dead in World War I, and mired in economic depression, the British could have hardly picked a less propitious moment to contemplate rebuilding the Royal Navy. Nonetheless, the threat was undeniably growing. In home waters the Germans were once again expanding their navy, whereas in the Pacific the relentless expansion of the Japanese fleet was steadily eroding the security of the British Empire's Asian possessions. Between these poles, east and west, Britain's seapower was being stretched to the breaking point.

Under those circumstances, arms control, no matter how insubstantial its basis, was bound to be perceived as a significant component of imperial defense policy. So it was that in June 1935 the British were willing to sign a naval treaty with Hitler's Germany that promised to set upper limits on Teutonic naval expansion. Even disregarding the questionable political wisdom of such an agreement, the treaty still stands as a trenchant commentary on a naval frame of reference that scrupulously allowed the Germans only a 30 percent ratio in capital ships but granted them potential parity in submarines in return for German cooperation in seeking the abolition of submarines and a promise not to resort to unrestricted submarine warfare.[98] The results would speak for themselves.

The British were also anxious to strike a bargain with the Japanese. But they had little to offer. Basically the British approach to arms control remained based on qualitative limitation (particularly the reduction of battleships to 25,000 tons and 12-inch guns), a large number of light cruisers to protect lines of trade and communication, and essentially the same naval ratios—though they held out some hope of an increase for Japan in return for a substantial quid pro quo.[99] It was simply a nonnegotiable position. Not only did it undermine Anglo-American trust, but events would show that the Japanese had absolutely no interest in compromise, particularly when it came to shrinking battleships.[100]

The second London Naval Conference opened in December 1935 on a less than propitious note, with the French, unwilling to accept naval equality with Italy, having recently abrogated the Washington treaties. That was simply a prelude to the Japanese performance. The conference had barely begun when Admiral Nagano detailed the Japanese position, which included fleet parity among the three major naval powers, great reductions in overall tonnage, no qualitative limitation before quantitative agreement, and, as a last nail in the arms control coffin, the abolition of battleships and carriers.[101] There was something in this proposal for all the other participants to hate, and when it was dismissed, the Japanese delegation simply withdrew from the conference. In a real sense the date of that withdrawal, 15 January 1936, marked the end of naval arms control.

But form would triumph over substance, and the Americans, British, and French lingered to hammer out a meaningless, but cosmetic, agreement. In the first portion, the guns of future battleships were to be reduced to fourteen inches and their life span increased to twenty-six years, carriers would be limited to 23,000 tons, and the original London treaty's worthless prohibition on submarines exceeding 2,000 tons was extended.[102] All of that was then negated by "escalator clauses," which allowed any party, upon prior notification, to build up to the dimensions of any ship undertaken by a nonparty. Finally, there was a procès-verbal renewing the 1930 London treaty's chivalric rules of submarine warfare, which even the Japanese ratified. Truly, this was arms limitation as fig leaf.

There was considerable irony attached to the end of the interwar period's experiment with naval arms control. A case can be made that partly because so much of the process was concerned with limiting battleship size and proliferation, the end of the naval "holiday" augured the opposite—more and bigger dreadnoughts. Whatever the exact causes, it remains indisputably true that the major naval powers marched toward war in lockstep, each with a shipbuilding program that featured as its centerpiece weapons destined to do it little good in combat and for which there had been ample warning of obsolescence. Naval tradition and sheer persistence had triumphed over good sense. As unlikely as it might have seemed in 1921, once again it was springtime for dreadnoughts.

III

The resurrection of the battleship was in part contingent on the kind of notional wars the various chapters of the international naval fraternity were planning to fight as the real thing approached. Despite the farsighted American experiments with carrier task forces undertaken during the late 1920s and early 1930s, the mainstream of the naval world remained preoccupied with dreadnought Armageddon. So it was that at least until late 1937, the high commands of both the U.S. and the Japanese navies were contemplating what amounted to the same campaign: the Pacific "bad trip."[103] In the United States this was premised on the defense of the Philippines and was the object of a series of planning exercises known collectively as War Plan ORANGE. Essentially, ORANGE called for the U.S. battle fleet, screened by its auxiliaries, to advance across the Pacific in the event of war with the aim of engaging and destroying the Imperial Japanese Navy, thereby thwarting an invasion of the U.S.-held archipelago. From the Navy's point of view there were two essential prerequisites for War Plan ORANGE, continued possession of the Philippines and a large fleet—each being necessary to justify the other. But both presented problems. For there was increasing political pressure during the 1930s to grant the islands their independence and, as a corollary, a general reluctance to fortify them or provide the Navy with the numbers and kinds of ships necessary to undertake a campaign in their defense.[104] Arms control complicated matters still further, particularly measures that threatened to limit ship size or range, for the United States also lacked intermediate bases west of the Hawaiian Islands.

Like War Plan BLACK, ORANGE was ridiculous as strategy but excellent as fantasy. As Louis Morton explained, not only was it highly questionable whether the Philippines were worth defending with the cream of the American Navy, but also the advantages of time and distance were all on the side of Japan.[105] As events would show, a Japanese expeditionary force could reach the Philippines far faster than the islands could be reinforced by the United States. Therefore, it was highly probable that the American battle fleet would arrive after its long journey without even a base at which to replenish itself and be forced instead into battle under the most disadvantageous circumstances.[106] Indeed the strategic reasoning behind ORANGE was so flimsy that it is far better explained at the level of fantasy—as the most plausible rationale for a dreadnought showdown.

Perhaps the most graphic example was provided by Hector Bywater, a highly respected British naval correspondent who frequently lectured the General Board. In his 1925 book *The Great Pacific War* (later incorporated into the curriculum of the Naval War College), Bywater described a campaign mirroring ORANGE and culminating in the climactic Battle of Yap—best characterized as Jutland made right. Not only were submarines and aircraft shown to be basically irrelevant ("How different now were the circumstances from those which aviation enthusiasts, deceived by peace tests against helpless targets, had pictured!"[107]), but American dreadnoughts confronted with the approach of darkness were also able to plunge forward in the spirit of "damn the torpedoes, full speed ahead" to inflict a complete defeat upon the Japanese battle fleet. Nor had things changed much eleven years later when Sutherland Denlinger and Lieutenant Commander Charles Gary published *War in the Pacific:* "The men and the ships of the Mikado, aware that our advance was imminent, need nothing more. Guns manned, personnel as tense as ours, the Japanese battle fleet charges north at full speed." Once again the U.S. dreadnoughts emerged victorious, though "death and destruction exact the usual percentage from those who gamble at this sea-green table."[108] Admittedly they were only books, but their scenarios and imagery so accurately reflected the bulk of U.S. Navy war planning and fleet problems prior to 1938 that it seems reasonable to assume that they were representative of the American naval imagination.

Meanwhile the members of the Imperial Japanese Navy were entertaining similar fantasies, though with a different outcome. Until shortly before the outbreak of World War II, Japanese naval planning was dominated by a reciprocal version of ORANGE. It too assumed the inevitable advance of the U.S. battle fleet, culminating in a single decisive battle—the central difference being that the Japanese were designated victors, not victims. In some respects the oriental version was more plausible. There was certainly precedent: The Russians had obligingly sailed halfway around the world only to offer themselves up for complete defeat at Tsushima. Moreover, the Japanese plan, *Zengen Sakusen*, took full account of distance, lack of U.S. bases, and the possibilities of attrition. The campaign was to begin with an attack on the Philippines, with the aim of luring the main body of the American Navy to the Western Pacific. The advancing U.S. fleet would then be weakened by stages, first with the large Type 6 submarines, then island-based bombers and torpedo planes, followed by destroyers launching very-long-range torpedoes, and finally a carrier air attack—the last being intended solely to prevent scouting.[109]

Blinded and suitably softened up, the American battle fleet would then be engaged by the Japanese capital ships, which, using superior speed and gun power, would inflict a defeat so crushing that recovery would require five to eight years of naval reconstruction. But rather than build a new bevy of super battleships, it was assumed the Americans would sue for peace.[110]

As superficially plausible as that may have sounded, and despite American planning along the same lines, it all hung on a single shaky assumption—that in actual warfare the combined leadership of the United States really would be willing to send the bulk of its fleet on what amounted to a suicide mission to defend the indefensible. Other than within the confines of Mahanite logic, that was simply not reasonable. But it said a good deal about the nature of war planning in general. As the experience with BLACK had demonstrated, until hostilities are actually imminent, war plans are frequently more reflective of the institutional needs of the military services doing the planning than they are of strategic reality. Thus ORANGE and its Japanese reciprocal were primarily significant as outlets for the naval imagination and as rationales for armament.

A good deal has been written about the prescience of Japanese naval-weapons development during the 1930s.[111] The extremely powerful very-long-range Type 93 torpedo, the Type 96 Mitsubishi bomber (in 1932 the fastest plane in the world), the first carrier-based monoplane (the Claude), midget submarines, and very advanced torpedo planes—all constituted significant technical innovations. However, each was undertaken within the larger context of *Zengen Sakusen*, and the centerpiece of everything was a weapon so excessive and flamboyant, but so steeped in naval orthodoxy, that it must be interpreted at least partly in symbolic terms.

For behind Japanese uninterest in qualitative limitations on battleships at the second London conference were plans to build dreadnoughts so large as to dwarf anything even contemplated by the other powers.[112] By 1934 naval architects had begun work on blueprints for the *Yamato*-class battleships—to be armed with and armored against 18-inch guns (no ship in the world possessed anything larger than 16-inch main armament), having three separate layers of protection plus three-foot blisters below the waterline to counter torpedoes, and driven forward by giant engines capable of propelling it at nearly thirty knots—all adding up to a combined displacement of approximately 70,000 tons.[113] It was a ship roughly twice the size of any dreadnought then in existence. And in November 1937, amid great secrecy, work began on the huge *Yamato*—its very name symbolic of the spirit of the Japanese people—soon to be followed by its sister, *Musashi*.

These ships were at the heart of the Japanese plans for victory. One-third faster, firing shells one-third heavier, 10,000 yards farther than their American equivalents, they were intended to shatter the U.S. battle line in the climax of the great Pacific showdown—all the while remaining impervious to damage— invincible. The ghosts of Cuniberti and John Fisher might have been amused, but the Japanese were dead serious. By 1940 two more of the monsters were laid down.[114] There were also plans for subsequent dreadnoughts with 20-inch guns and "a battlecruiser strong enough to destroy the value of the American Navy's existing heavy cruisers."[115]

The Japanese Navy had succeeded in breaking cleanly out of the treaty structure constraining its expansion, and as war approached, that navy's total tonnage reached 81 percent of its American adversary.[116] Nonetheless, its leadership remained prisoners of their Mahanite frame of reference, and too much of the nation's precious industrial resources were channeled in conventional directions. For a brief moment as the war began, the leaders staged a sort of escape. But then the old ethic reasserted itself. For in a real sense the Imperial Navy had sold its soul to dreadnoughts, which in combat could do little more than die bravely.

Meanwhile, the United States Navy had set a similar, though less extreme, course. However, in the American context, beginning to rebuild the fleet was an agonizing process, able to proceed no faster than political routines would allow. And at the nadir of the Great Depression that was slow indeed. In January 1932 Representative Carl Vinson, the new chairman of the House Naval Affairs Committee, introduced a bill aimed at authorizing the Navy to build to treaty limits, only to see the proposal withdrawn for lack of support.[117] Worse would come. In the spring of 1933 it was announced that as an economy measure one-third of the fleet and its personnel would have to go on rotating reserve.[118] But almost immediately Franklin Roosevelt came to the rescue with the remarkable discovery that warships constituted public works and therefore deserved funding through an executive order under the National Industrial Recovery Act.[119] The corner had been turned, and from that point the attitude of the Congress and monetary prospects would improve steadily. Of particular note was the 1934 Vinson-Trammel Act, which constituted a commitment finally to build the Navy to treaty levels and allowed the president to replace over-age ships in all classes. Among other things it cleared the way for the construction of new battleships.[120] And this was critical. For although the building program authorized by a succession of congressional measures prior to Pearl Harbor encompassed literally hundreds of ships, dreadnoughts were at its heart.

Long frustrated by naval holidays, Annapolites by 1937 finally saw new dreadnoughts on the horizon and were determined that they would not prove to be a mirage. Since 1935 the General Board had been involved in intense planning for the new ships, examining no fewer than eleven alternative configurations.[121] After due deliberation, the board settled on a 35,000-ton model, sacrificing around three knots of top speed to take advantage of the second London treaty's "escalator clause" to increase gun size from fourteen to sixteen inches—"thank the Lord it is 16-inches," wrote Admiral Harold Stark, echoing traditional Annapolite sentiments with respect to bigger guns.[122] But an even more important issue was ensuring that the ships were actually built. "Whether or not great fleets will ever again meet in battle is beside the point," wrote the commander of the battle fleet's battleships. "So long as a fleet engagement exists as a potentiality, no naval power is justified in sacrificing the requirements of the battle line in the desire to meet other military requirements."[123] And the General Board was equally insistent in its recommendations to the secretary of the Navy: "The battleship is the basic instrument of naval warfare. . . . We have not built a capital ship for more than 15 years. . . . An orderly program of replacement must be instituted . . . to prevent our battle line strength from falling to a third rate status."[124]

This sense of urgency was not feigned. All over the world navies were building battleships. Besides the Japanese, by January 1937 Great Britain had begun five 35,000-ton dreadnoughts of the *King George V* class; the Germans had completed four 12,000-ton pocket battleships, nearly finished the 31,000-ton battle cruisers *Scharnhorst* and *Gneisenau*, and were working on the 42,000-ton *Bismarck* and *Tirpitz*; the French were nearly through with the 26,500-ton *Dunkerque* and *Strasbourg* and had begun work on the 38,500-ton *Richelieu*, *Jean Bart*, and *Clemenceau*; and the Italians had commenced work on four 35,000-ton ships of their own.[125] Nevertheless, American dreadnought construction had yet to begin.

The prospects were excellent; however, the U.S. Navy was firmly in the hands of a group known to the service as "the ordnance gang,"[126] and their building program was not likely to be countermanded or even questioned from above. Septuagenarian Secretary of the Navy Claude Swanson, who owed his position to his general decrepitude, was not exactly at the cutting edge of weapons development, and his immediate superior, the president, was disinclined to buck the naval mainstream. Roosevelt certainly loved running the Navy—hence his choice of naval secretaries—but this did not really extend to radical opinions with respect to ship types. Although a good friend of Pratt's—bringing him out of retirement during World War II—it was apparent that Roosevelt had not been deeply influenced by the former's heretical views on naval weaponry. Instead, the president cheerfully presided over the battleship buildup, writing Admiral Leahy in December 1937 that the Navy's model of the first of the new dreadnoughts, the USS *North Carolina*, was "the nicest Christmas present I have had."[127] As with many things, the president's loyalty was deceptive, and when the time came he would switch allegiances almost instantly. But until Pearl Harbor, Roosevelt stood squarely behind building battleships.

Like the Japanese, the planners of the U.S. Navy were certainly interested in obtaining bigger dreadnoughts. In fact each of the four classes of battleships

USS North Carolina, *first of the U.S. posttreaty battleships, lets loose a full broadside.* (*Courtesy of the U.S. National Archives*)

ordered prior to World War II (*North Carolinas*—35,000 tons, *South Dakotas*—35,000+ tons, *Iowas*—45,000+ tons, and *Montanas*—58,000 tons) was progressively larger than the previous one.[128] Nonetheless, there was considerable support for even larger battleships, ones in excess of 70,000 tons. W. F. Gibbs, of the naval architecture firm of Gibbs and Cox, proposed such a ship in 1939, and he was echoed a month later by the House Subcommittee for Naval Appropriations, which requested that the General Board study such a superdreadnought.[129] A poll of the high command revealed that although such vessels were attractive, the weight of opinion was against them.[130] Given the traditional Annapolite orientation toward size, that was surprising. However, there were two basic explanations. First, the Navy lacked accurate information on the new Japanese dreadnoughts, having received reports from Naval Intelligence that the ships did not exceed 43,000 tons.[131] Second, it was understood that building

70,000-ton capital ships would necessitate some sacrifice in numbers. "The old adage of too many eggs in one basket would seem to have some bearing here," explained Admiral Kalbfus, president of the Naval War College.[132]

At that point the Navy was in no mood to sacrifice numbers. By October 1937 the *North Carolina* had been laid down, with the *Washington* soon to follow. But that was just the beginning. In April 1938 the Navy Department projected a construction program lasting nine years and leading to the replacement of all the dreadnoughts.[133] The first of these, the four-ship *South Dakota* class, was commenced in July 1939. Meanwhile, plans were being formulated for six ships of the *Iowa* class, the first of which would be begun in June 1940. That same month, however, the chairman of the General Board wrote Admiral Stark, chief of naval operations, "Due to the long holiday experienced in the building of battleships . . . it is necessary that the United States go further in the building of this type than the existing laws allow."[134] That led directly to the approval of five more dreadnoughts of the *Montana* class, for a total projected battleship strength of thirty-two battleships, seventeen of them being new.[135]

That was still not the end of it. In October 1935 the president of the Naval War College had written the General Board recommending that three of the battleships be replaced by a similar number of battle cruisers.[136] Although the General Board clearly liked the idea of battle cruisers, it was unwilling to sacrifice battleships. So there the matter stood until October 1939, when the chairman of the General Board hit upon an ingenious scheme. The 26,000-ton ships would simply be called "cruisers," thereby obviating the necessity of charging them against mandated capital ship strength limits.[137] There were to be six of these "cruisers," the first of which, the *Alaska*, would be laid down in December 1941. However, the addition of these dreadnought "cruisers" on top of everything else apparently prompted concern on the General Board that they all could not be built promptly. Citing estimates that the Japanese would hold a numerical lead in battleships by 1942, Chairman Sexton urgently requested the secretary of the Navy in April 1940 to expedite capital ship construction through continuous shifts and the expansion of armor plants.[138] Plainly it was no easy thing to build twenty-three dreadnoughts as quickly as possible. As to the wisdom of doing such a thing, it seemed self-evident. "The Department probably feels that as soon as the new battleships are finished we will be ready to meet all comers," wrote Admiral Harry E. Yarnell sarcastically.[139] But he was part of only a small naval minority questioning the soundness of the building program. As Admiral Yates Stirling wrote at the time: "We are to lay down soon 45,000 ton battleships with twelve 16-inch guns each, costing probably 70 million apiece, a staggering sum for one ship. Certainly we would not waste so much money if we thought that type of ship was becoming obsolete."[140] Only Pearl Harbor would reveal this judgment to be a colossal error.

IV

The dominant elements of the world's great navies sailed toward combat, furiously building capital ships, but that was not the whole story. In the days of Sims and Fisher proponents of radical armaments constituted true splinter groups, operating (if they survived at all) on a shoestring. But by the fourth decade of the twentieth century, major navies had grown into huge institutions, so big and so accustomed to a modicum of technological change that they were perfectly capable of accommodating alternate channels of weapons development on a scale sufficient to allow them to shift perspectives and on short notice prosecute very different kinds of operational plans. All that was required was an event or motive of sufficient magnitude to set the process of metamorphosis in motion.

Consequently, a service like the U.S. Navy really existed as three possible navies—encompassing a preeminent battleship theme, along with two alternative and subordinate themes, that of the carrier and the submarine. However, from the perspective of arms technology this was less a question of mutual exclusivity than it was of focus and emphasis—which system would dominate? Indeed, to a certain degree the weapons were interchangeable. Thus the battle line used carriers for air cover and with less success, the fleet submarine for scouting and attrition, just as carrier task forces would later recruit fast battleships for escort duty and antiaircraft protection. There were clearly limits to this versatility, particularly with the submarine. Nonetheless, the perceived, or at least hoped-for, usefulness of subordinate weapons in dominant schemes provided a ready rationale for their continued development, even in spite of their subversive possibilities. As long as tactical and institutional obeisance was paid to the battleship as the backbone of the fleet, the proponents of the air and submarine arms were left relatively undisturbed to improve further and, to a limited extent, proliferate their respective craft. Moreover, as war grew closer, particularly after it came to Europe in 1939 and France fell a year later, there was increasing realism on the part of even conservative officers, in terms of both weapons and war plans. In the case of the U.S. Navy that did not halt the reproduction of dreadnoughts, but it did further the service's ability to make a rapid transition to a very different style of war.

Relatively speaking, U.S. naval air power thrived during the mid- and late 1930s. Although the results of Fleet Problem XII and the untimely death of Admiral Moffett in the 1933 crash of the dirigible *Akron* left the Navy's air arm somewhat adrift, it quickly regrouped and forged ahead. In part its success can be attributed to the attractiveness of the carrier/aircraft combination and the sheer romance of flying. Thus by the mid-1930s young Annapolites in significant numbers were signing up for flight training, forming a cadre of excellent pilots, many of them versed in the new and lethal techniques of dive-bombing and aerial torpedo delivery. Meanwhile, the planes they flew were not only improving rapidly but also becoming steadily more numerous. Partly this was a product of the very dynamic young American aviation industry, but ironically it was also fostered by the General Board, which, if it proved highly conservative with regard to ships, did consistently recommend the acquisition of large numbers of aircraft. Consequently, in 1934 steps were taken to increase the Navy's combat planes to 750 before 1940.[141] By 1938 the fleet's air arm already had 670 planes, with approximately 350 being added yearly. Then in May of that year, with the passage of the second Vinson bill, Congress committed the nation to the acquisition of naval aircraft literally by the thousands.[142]

Adequate carriers, however, were not so readily accumulated. As late as 1934 the Navy continued to favor carriers no larger than necessary to protect the battle line, laying down the *Yorktown* and *Enterprise* with a planned displacement of 13,800 tons, and only increasing this figure to 20,000 tons after the troubles encountered with the diminutive *Ranger* made such a move obvious.[143] However, with its next carrier, the 14,500-ton *Wasp*, the Navy reverted back to the smaller type.[144] Moreover, in the spring of 1938, just as the battleship program was picking up steam, the Navy proposed a temporary halt in carrier construction until either the larger or the smaller type was shown to be superior.[145] Finally, in January 1940, the Navy settled on a new standard, a 27,000-ton vessel truly suitable to perform the role of attack carrier pioneered almost two decades before by the *Lexington* and *Saratoga*.[146] By June there were plans to build at least eighteen carriers, but no keels for the big new ships of the *Essex* class woAH be laid down until 1941.[147] Consequently, when Pearl Harbor came, the Navy was building the ships it would need to win the air war in the Pacific, but they were far from ready.

The dynamics of the American submarine program were somewhat different. Although it was a far smaller effort than naval air, the inherent lethality of the weapon and the relative rapidity with which submarines could be constructed led to very substantial results. Those results, however, were achieved in direct opposition to doctrinal guidance. By the early 1930s the concept of the fleet boat had been discarded and the Navy was willing to see the submarine banned. To most naval officers, if the submarine had any use at all, it was strictly against enemy warships, and as late as May 1941 the General Board remained unequivocally opposed to the use of American submarines as commerce raiders.[148]

Nonetheless, technological evolution led in an entirely different direction. During the early 1930s a group known as the Submarine Officers Conference began making recommendations for a general-purpose boat of something over 1,000 tons, mounting a large number of torpedo tubes, and having a range on the order of 12,000 miles. What this boat would do, beyond attacking Japanese naval assets in the Western Pacific, was not stipulated. But the submariners knew what they wanted, and they got it. The General Board endorsed the development of a series of general-purpose submarines of gradually increasing displacement, under the vacuous rubric "long-range patrol boat." These culminated in the ten-tube, 1,475-ton *Tautog*.[149] At the time of Pearl Harbor *Tautog* constituted the most advanced long-range submarine in the world and was rapidly reproduced as the basis for the American construction program during World War II. (Ironically, torpedo development was much less successful, resulting in the Mark-14 model. For lack of testing, the Mark-14 refused through nearly two years of combat to explode when it hit something. Similarly lacking, as Michael Gannon has recently shown, were U.S. capacity and willingness to wage antisubmarine warfare against the German U-boats that ravaged coastal shipping during 1942 in the vital Atlantic sector.) Nonetheless, at least one key piece was in place when the eight-word order went out to the fleet on 7 December 1941: "Execute unrestricted air and submarine warfare against Japan."[150]

Operationally, this order proved to be the penultimate step in the journey toward strategic reality begun officially when U.S. war planners issued a new ORANGE plan in February 1938. For the first time the Navy compromised its position on an early movement of the fleet toward the Philippines, though most Annapolites still remained committed to sending the battle line west at some point.[151]

Meanwhile, one doubter, Admiral Harry E. Yarnell, early recognized the "Pacific bad trip" for what it was—a fantasy to build battleships by—and did his best to convince his peers in the naval high command. In October 1937 he wrote Chief of Naval Operations Leahy that, "it may not be necessary for the Battle Fleet, as such, to proceed west of Pearl Harbor." Three months later he was even more direct with C. C. Bloch, the new commander in chief of the U.S. fleet: "When we began this idea of moving the Fleet to the Far East seventeen years ago, Japan then had few submarines and practically no aircraft. . . . At present the situation is entirely different. . . . I commend the whole subject to your earnest consideration."[152]

Yet Yarnell's concerns were not simply derived from a lack of adequate bases and the possibilities of attrition. It was apparent that he had an entirely different view of how naval war might transpire and what arms were likely to be most important. In early 1937 he wrote Admiral C. F. Snyder, president of the Naval War College, "New weapons are going to have a great influence on the character and outcome of the next war, and the nation which recognizes their possibilities and is prepared to use them in the most efficient manner will have a great advantage."[153] Yarnell spoke from some experience. He had been placed in charge of developing carrier doctrine in the early 1930s and had become a firm believer in the task force concept.[154]

In fact, by March 1938 the Navy was once again ready to let the carriers loose, this time for a notional attack on Hawaii. Commanding the designated task force for Fleet Problem XIX was the irascible E. J. King, one of Yarnell's most capable subordinates during the formative days of carrier doctrine. He was accompanied aboard the *Saratoga* by soon-to-be chief of naval operations, Harold R. Stark,[155] who was anxious to observe carrier operations firsthand. King gave him quite a show. He swept far to the northwest of Oahu, and concealing his force in a weather front moving slowly eastward, he ran with it for approximately a thousand miles without being discovered by the defending force. When he was in range, he launched a successful air strike on Pearl Harbor, recovering all his planes in the process.[156] It was a prophetic moment.

Gradually the message contained in Yarnell's admonitions began to have an impact on planning. During the spring of 1939 monolithic ORANGE was replaced by RAINBOW, consisting of an array of contingencies besides a Pacific advance.[157] And although Admiral J. O. Richardson, commander in chief of the U.S. fleet, apparently remained committed to a sortie into the Western Pacific, further complications soon arose.[158] In May 1940, after completing Fleet Problem XXI in Hawaiian waters, the battle fleet was ordered to remain at Pearl Harbor until further notice. While this certainly constituted forward basing, the inadequacies of facilities there as a staging area cast further doubt on a Pacific advance.[159] "You are there," Chief of Naval Operations Stark later told Richardson, "because of the deterrent effect which it is thought your presence may have on the Japs going into the East Indies."[160]

Things would get worse. As the criticality of the struggle to keep the Atlantic sea-lanes open grew, so did the pressure to increase the U.S Navy's presence in this theater, even though the United States was not yet at war. Finally, after one transfer had been countermanded, in May 1941 Stark ordered three battleships, one carrier, and four cruisers—a quarter of the U.S. fleet—to leave Pearl Harbor and head toward the Atlantic.[161] Mahan's "first commandment" had been broken. Then in the late summer of 1941 several squadrons of B-17 bombers were transferred to the Philippines to act as the prime American striking force and deterrent in the Far East, bringing to fruition after three decades Bradley Fiske's farsighted suggestion.[162] At that point the "Pacific bad trip" officially became a memory. The remaining dreadnoughts in Pearl Harbor effectively had no mission—except the unintended one of targets. Nonetheless, had a poll been taken of the Navy at the time, it seems certain that a comfortable majority of Annapolites would have still maintained that the battleship was the backbone of the fleet. That too would soon change.

Meanwhile, a similar evolutionary process had been taking place in the Japanese Navy. Though continuing as a battleship-oriented force, its technological policy was increasingly progressive. That was particularly true of carrier-based aviation, which, because of the vast expanses of the Pacific and the correspondingly heavy requirements for reconnaissance, was inherently attractive to the high command of the Imperial Navy. Between 1933 and 1939 the Japanese built five carriers, adding several more before entering the war with a total of ten—seven more than were initially available to the United States in the Pacific.[163]

But an even greater strength was the Navy's pilots and planes. At the time of Pearl Harbor, Japanese naval aviators were quite probably the best in the world. Hardened by a Spartan and comprehensive training program, by 1941 pilots averaged in excess of 300 hours of flight time before joining the fleet, far more than their American counterparts. Moreover, a good many had combat experience in China. In addition, the aircraft they flew were excellent. Of particular note were the torpedo planes—the long-range Type 95 and the tactical "Kate," both being superior to their U.S. competitors.[164] But most remarkable was the Zero, in 1940 the world's most advanced fighter aircraft, carrier based or otherwise. Designed by Jiro Horikoshi and rushed into production at the insistence of Admiral Yamamoto (the Harry E. Yarnell of the Japanese Navy), approximately 30 early Zeros scored 266 confirmed kills in China.[165] Nevertheless, the Zero's performance, like that of the other planes and the pilots of the Imperial Navy, was ignored by the Americans and the British, who preferred shibboleths like "Japanese pilots are inevitably near-sighted and lack initiative," or "the wings of their planes fall off in dives."[166] That was a serious mistake. At nearly 500 combat planes, the Imperial Navy's First Air Fleet constituted the most powerful ship-borne air force then in existence. But how to use it?

Although the carriers had been administratively grouped together since 1938, the dominance of the battleship admirals precluded their independent use, despite some rumblings from aviators. Things began to change in 1940, however. Sometime late that year the Imperial Navy's leading carrier tactician, Commander Genda Minoru, watched a newsreel showing four American carriers operating together, a formation he would not soon forget.[167] Then in early November 1940, on the opposite side of the world, the Royal Navy carrier *Illustrious* launched an air strike against virtually the entire Italian fleet assembled in the harbor of Taranto. The next day a spotter plane surveyed the damage wrought by *Illustrious*'s twenty-one attacking aircraft—two battleships beached, a third down at the bow and leaking oil, a cruiser bombed out of commission, two destroyers damaged, two supply vessels sunk, and the Taranto oil depot reduced to a charred wreck.[168] Less than two months later, aboard his flagship *Nagato*, Admiral Yamamoto turned to his chief of staff, Admiral Fukudome Shigeru, and remarked, "An air attack on Pearl Harbor might be possible now, especially as our air training has turned out so successfully."[169]

Yamamoto Isoroku is frequently referred to as a "moderate,"[170] which for the Japan of 1940 must be taken as a relative term. He was certainly ready to fight and die for his country. But he had also studied in the United States and knew it well: "Anyone who had seen the auto factories in Detroit and the oil-fields of Texas knows Japan lacks the national power for a naval race with America."[171] War would be worse. And it was not just a matter of size and industrial strength. Yamamoto had little sympathy with the orientation and building program of the Japanese Navy, particularly as it related to the huge symbolic dreadnoughts *Yamato* and *Musashi:* "These ships are like elaborate religious scrolls which old people hang up in their homes. They are of no proved worth. They are purely a matter of faith—not reality."[172] For Yamamoto was the leader of a small group in the upper echelons of the Imperial Navy who truly believed in the possibilities of air power. And as such his sympathies lay with his friend and colleague Admiral Inoue Shigeyoshi, chief of Aviation Section of the Navy General Staff, who foresaw a war in the South Pacific revolving almost entirely on carriers and planes and consequently told the Navy minister in early 1941 that Japan's "ratio neurosis" had led it to build the wrong fleet for the wrong conflict.[173] If that was the case, then something dramatic would have to be done quickly to even the odds.

Yamamoto was in a position to make it happen. In spite of his moderate politics and his unorthodox weapons orientation, he had risen on sheer ability to commander in chief of the combined fleets. Formulating battle plans was part of his job. It is unclear if Yamamoto understood that War Plan ORANGE had been superseded, and that he would therefore have to come and get the U.S. fleet. But it is apparent that he was immersed in specific plans for a carrier-based air strike on Pearl Harbor during January 1941. On 1 February he outlined his concept to Rear Admiral Onishi Takijiro, chief of staff of the Eleventh Air Fleet, who in turn passed it on to Genda Minoru for study.[174] Although Genda's testimony after the war was somewhat contradictory, it did appear that he considered the general scheme as risky, but standing a reasonable chance of success.[175] Very probably Genda was impressed with the kind of force designated to carry out the attack. At any rate he and Captain Kuroshima Kameto, an eccentric operations officer, began working out the tactical details, while the Navy took up training and the modification of its torpedoes to operate in the shallow waters of Pearl Harbor. In essence, the plan—soon to be named Operation Z in honor of the famous signal given by Admiral Togo at Tsushima— called for a strike force (*Kido Butai*) of six carriers plus escorts to steam across half the Pacific in the rough and deserted winter seas of latitude forty degrees north, approaching Oahu much in the manner of Ernest King during Fleet Problem XIX.

There was certainly opposition to Operation Z. Through the summer of 1941 the General Staff resisted it as too dangerous and removed from the attrition strategy that had been the basis of planning for years. But the U.S. oil embargo and Japan's gradually dwindling reserves forced their hand; if they didn't fight soon they wouldn't be able to. And Yamamoto's plan was really the only one promising to cripple the American fleet long enough to allow the Japanese military time to secure vital supplies of oil and raw materials in Southeast Asia and the Dutch East Indies. So in the end the General Staff acceded.

Pearl Harbor, the end of the Arizona. *(Courtesy of the U.S. National Archives)*

The scheme was certainly audacious, risking six of Japan's ten carriers—the very ships Yamamoto knew he couldn't afford to lose—and demanding almost total surprise. Nevertheless, planning and training were meticulous, and the attacking force (360 planes: 81 fighters, 135 dive bombers, 104 high-level bombers, and 40 torpedo planes), large enough to ensure very substantial results. But Yamamoto appears to have missed one very elemental point: The targets in Pearl Harbor were mostly battleships, the very class he scorned in his own navy. That was symptomatic of a larger irrationality that ensured that Pearl Harbor would be remembered as a terrible mistake.

As the Japanese pilots flew away from the smoking ruins of Battleship Row on 7 December they undoubtedly believed they had won a great victory. Their execution had been almost perfect; like a flashing samurai sword they had decapitated the U.S. fleet. The *Arizona* had blown up, *Oklahoma* had capsized, *Nevada* was beached, *West Virginia* had sunk, and *California* was sinking. Counting the old *Utah*, a target ship that had been mistakenly attacked, six dreadnoughts had been sunk.[176] Only *Tennessee, Pennsylvania,* and *Maryland* escaped. For the first time a battle fleet had been destroyed from the air; on paper Pearl Harbor was as great a victory as Tsushima.

But in reality it was no victory at all. The dreadnoughts of Battleship Row were hollow symbols of national power, not effective fighting machines. With the exception of the men who died in them and the blow to national pride, the loss of these vessels hardly constituted any setback at all. Indeed a good case could be made that the ultimate result of Pearl Harbor was a net gain for the United States, in that it allowed the warship construction program to be reorganized in a more rational direction, and it freed the Navy of the line-of-battle concept once and for all. For if the dreadnought was a hollow symbol, it was certainly a potent one, requiring a truly humiliating drubbing to dispel.

It has been frequently said that if the American carriers had been in port, or if the Japanese pilots had bothered to destroy the fuel reserves stored in the local tank farms, or if they had simply launched a second strike to mop up, then the Pearl Harbor attack would have been truly devastating to the U.S. war effort in the Pacific. Perhaps that is so. But it also misses a central point. The American battleships were the primary targets,[177] and their destruction constituted mission success. Other targets would have been perceived as useful, but serendipitous. The Japanese were essentially satisfied with the results of Pearl Harbor, just as the sinking of the British dreadnoughts *Repulse* and *Prince of Wales* two days later off the east coast of Malaysia by the torpedo planes of the Eleventh Air Fleet would be seen as a similarly important success.

There would be a heavy price attached, however. As Sir George Sanson noted, it was a strategic blunder of the first magnitude, an attack that would steel the American people for a fight to the finish—exactly the kind of war Japanese planners had counted on avoiding and knew they could not win.[178] Pearl Harbor also would have a significant effect on the way that war would be fought. The U.S. naval high command would be quickly shifted from ordnance specialists to people with more varied backgrounds, who would then destroy the Imperial Navy and the Japanese transport fleet with carrier task forces and submarines. In contrast, the battleship would retain an important role in Japanese naval planning. Although the Imperial Navy would certainly emphasize carrier operations in the future, the *Kido Butai* would be broken up immediately after Pearl Harbor, never to be reconstituted in that strength. As for the submarine, it would remain tied to military operations and prove only marginally useful to the Imperial Navy. So it seems that what the attack on Pearl Harbor did for the

Americans, it could not do for the Japanese. They remained worshippers at the shrine of the sacred vessels, while their enemies were at last free to pursue a more agnostic course.

Not surprisingly, there was some effort to rehabilitate the dreadnought in the U.S. Navy. Twenty days after the Japanese raid, Admiral Rowcliffe, of the General Board, generated a memorandum arguing that the attack at Taranto, the sinking of the *Bismarck*, the destruction of *Repulse* and *Prince of Wales*, and "the Pearl Harbor affair" were all "the result of special circumstances. . . . The strongest argument for the battleship is that in each one of these cases it was made the objective of a major planned operation."[179] But the time had come when that sort of argument ceased to have much resonance. The Navy was in other hands, and the commander in chief was a notably pragmatic sort. In late July 1942 Admiral King informed the chairman of the General Board that henceforth submarine construction would be granted first priority and battleships sixth.[180] Only four of the six *Iowa*-class battleships and two of the six *Alaska*-class battle cruisers would be completed, while the entire *Montana* class would be canceled. The battle line would never again practice together as a unit. For the American Navy the day of the dreadnought had finally passed.

12

Conclusion:
Vampires of Seapower

The day of the dreadnought may have passed, but the individual ships lived on
. . . and on. Considering how it had begun, World War II proved to be something
less of a debacle for battleships than might have been expected, but their role in
the American Navy remained definitely a secondary one. After Midway—the
first naval battle when the warships involved didn't come within sight or gunshot
of one another—it was utterly apparent that the carrier was the new capital ship.
For their part, dreadnoughts would subsequently engage hostile surface-vessels
only four times during the course of war, the high point coming when the new
battleships *Washington* and *South Dakota* sank the Japanese *Kirishima* in
November 1942 off Guadalcanal. However, battleships did prove useful for shore
bombardment in support of amphibious operations, as antiaircraft platforms to
protect carriers, and still less heroically as oilers. All in all, it was a modest but
positive performance, although other, far cheaper ships could have approximated
most of these services, including shore fire mimicked by massed rocket barrages.
Nonetheless, when the shooting stopped, it was a dreadnought that steamed into
the spotlight at the moment of victory. For on 2 September 1945, Japanese
representatives signed the instrument of surrender, not on the flight deck of a
battle-scarred aircraft carrier, but aboard the dreadnought *Missouri*. Old loyalties
die hard.

Yet the cessation of the global conflict brought the gradual retirement of
America's battleships, until only the *Missouri* remained in service. The onset of
the Korean War, however, brought them still another lease on life, drawing the
three other hefty sisters of the *Iowa* class out of storage for shore bombardment
duty. But that adventure proved short-lived. Peace in 1953 spelled more hard

USS Washington, *which (with the help of the* South Dakota*) was the only American dreadnought to sink an enemy battleship in combat. (Courtesy of the U.S. Naval Institute)*

times, and the *Iowa* headed one by one for mothballed purgatory at Bremerton, Washington, and the Philadelphia Navy Yard, until in 1958 the USS *Wisconsin*, the final American battleship, was decommissioned. At last the end seemed to have come.

But no! In the summer of 1966, as the United States found itself sinking deeper and deeper into the Vietnam quagmire, Marine Corps Brigadier General James D. Hittle, addressing a group of battleship veterans in San Diego, delivered a heartfelt plea for the return of the dreadnought to provide artillery support to his troops. The American Battleship Association needed no more prompting, immediately launching a publicity campaign to bring the sacred vessels out of retirement. Significantly, the chief of naval operations and most of the naval hierarchy were opposed on the grounds that carrier aviation was perfectly capable of performing this sort of close support. But Senator Richard Russell, chairman of the Senate Armed Services Committee, fervently believed in battleships, and in April 1968, amid much fanfare, the modernized USS *New Jersey* was recommissioned and sent to Vietnam. The results were less than startling. During her single cruise off the coast, *New Jersey* fired 5,688 16-inch shells and succeeded in inflicting 113 confirmed enemy deaths and blowing up a small island in the process. With that the battleship was returned again to her

Japanese surrender on the deck of the USS Missouri. *(Courtesy of the U.S. National Archives)*

slumbers—at a total mission cost of around $100 million. Once again the career of the dreadnought seemed over.

But time in the grave wrought a remarkable transformation: The once-sacred vessels had become nautical vampires, rising over and over to drink deeply at the public trough. The next visitation began in the late 1970s when lobbyist Charles Myers, Jr., came to believe that battleships were the perfect substitute for many of the dangerous close-air-support missions that had destroyed so many planes and pilots in Vietnam. With visions of great guns pounding a variety of Third World targets into dust, Myers set about gathering backing for the return of the *Iowas.* But support in Congress was lukewarm; the Navy was clearly opposed, fearing that recommissioning would undermine plans for more of the now-sacred carriers; and Annapolite Jimmy Carter decreed that it was "inefficient to apply hundreds of millions of dollars to resurrect 1940s technology."

Back from the grave, the USS New Jersey *in the 1980s. Note cruise missile launchers. (Courtesy of the U.S. Naval Institute)*

There the matter stood until the landslide election of 1980 swept into office Ronald Reagan, determined to finance the greatest military-hardware shopping spree in U.S. history. Meanwhile, the death-defying dreadnought had won over an important new friend, the chairman of the Republican party's Committee on Defense and soon-to-be naval secretary, John Lehman, who dreamed of equipping the great ships with Harpoon and Tomahawk cruise missiles to transform them from naval antiques to formidable fighting platforms. Ageless Ronald Reagan loved the idea. And at a cost of approximately $2 billion, all four of the *Iowas* were returned to service. It took a while for the Navy to get used to the idea, but soon war gamers at the Naval War College were happily generating all manner of new missions for the born-again dreadnoughts—showing the flag to Third World thugs, forcing entry into heavily defended straits, and making cameo appearances in outbreaks of U.S.-Soviet nonnuclear global conflict. As usual, however, the resurrected battleships proved less versatile and effective in reality than in the naval imagination.

In 1983–1984, off the coast of Lebanon, the *New Jersey* sought to suppress hostile Syrian and Druse militia artillery positions in the hills. Lacking forward spotters, the great guns proved wildly inaccurate, on one occasion decimating a herd of goats rather than the 23 mm antiaircraft guns against which they were targeted. As the *New Jersey* finally withdrew, Lebanese civilians and militia alike shook their fists in contempt at the great ships. So much for showing the flag. Soon, as the cold war wound down, the idea of dreadnoughts engaging aggressive Russian surface vessels with cruise missiles or anything else grew daily more improbable.

Then in 1989, as if to remind the world that dreadnoughts remained a significant danger to themselves, a turret of the USS *Iowa* blew up during routine firing practice, killing more than forty sailors. The ship was hastily withdrawn from service, and it seemed that her sisters would soon follow.

But just as the future grew dim again for the battleship, Saddam Hussein invaded Kuwait, and *Wisconsin* and *Missouri* were sent to the Middle East. They were among the most visible members of the multinational naval task force, subject of numerous television reports that extolled their size, their dignity, their Harpoon and Tomahawk cruise missiles, and, above all, their 16-inch guns. Great things were expected of the dreadnoughts.

On 16 January, when the Gulf War began, the *Wisconsin* was among the first to launch a Tomahawk against Iraq—a spectacular photo opportunity duly recorded and subsequently aired worldwide. There is every reason to believe that the *Wisconsin's* Tomahawks worked exceedingly well, but not necessarily better than those launched from other ships. Unlike crews of the other ships, however, an intelligence unit aboard the *Wisconsin* immediately broadcast news of the launch over a special war-warning network, thereby overriding all other communications and setting off the alarms on military Teletypes all over the world. "Why did those dumb bastards do that?" one key general in the Pentagon is reliably reported to have complained. Had he known more about dreadnoughts, he might not have asked such a question. And no sooner had the shooting stopped when the *Proceedings of the U.S. Naval Institute* took up the chant for sacred vessels: "Battleships have the following capabilities: major-caliber, long-range, relatively inexpensive weapons; rapid and sustained all-weather response; relatively invulnerable to countermeasures; and can either outrange counterbattery fire or accept counterbattery fire and continue to fight. The requirement for these capabilities will not go away. . . . The surface warfare successors to the battleship should be under serious, active, funded development now for employment in the next century."[1] In other words, new dreadnoughts. Here was an idea whose time had come—and gone, long ago.

The modern battleship has never lived up to expectations. But its sheer attractiveness, the degree to which it fulfilled people's conceptions of what a weapon *should be,* caused it to generate tremendous respect, loyalty, and unwarranted longevity. As I promised in the introduction, the story of the modern battleship is a cautionary tale, chosen precisely because of the wild divergence between performance and reputation. But if the readers leave this story convinced only how foolish and stubborn naval officers were to cling to the battleship, they will have largely missed the point. The members of the U.S. Navy and the rest of the international naval fraternity were not selfish fools but men trying their hardest to defend their respective countries with the best weapons available. But their view was also a narrow one, conditioned by their past, their daily lives, and misperceptions about power shared by many ashore. The aim of this book was to make these elements overt, to show how they worked and why.

In a future of severe cost constraints and dramatically changing threats, we will have to choose our weapons with extreme care, considering the full range of their implications. Psychological impact and sociological compatibility are exceedingly important, as the tale of the battleship should show. If we are to choose wisely, we will have to take them carefully into account. Meanwhile the dreadnought lives on to remind us that our fantasies are as real as anything else.

Appendix

TABLE A.1 Summary of Pre-Dreadnought Construction in the United States, 1893–1905

Description	Name	Year Launched	Main Guns	Displacement (tons)	Top Speed (knots)
Prototypes	*Maine*	1890	4-10″	6,682	17.0
(really armored	*Texas*	1893	2-12″	6,300	17.0
cruisers)					
Designed prior	*Oregon*	1893	4-13″, 8-8″	10,250	16.0
to the	*Indiana*	1893	4-13″, 8-8″	10,250	16.0
Spanish-American	*Massachusetts*	1893	4-13″, 8-8″	10,250	16.0
War	*Iowa*	1896	4-12″, 8-8″	11,340	16.5
	Kearsarge	1898	4-13″, 8-8″	11,520	16.5
	Kentucky	1898	4-13″, 8-8″	11,520	16.5
	Alabama	1898	4-13″, 14-6″	11,550	16.0
	Illinois	1898	4-13″, 14-6″	11,550	16.0
	Wisconsin	1898	4-13″, 14-6″	11,550	16.0
Designed	*Maine*	1901	4-12″, 16-6″	12,500	18.0
afater war:	*Missouri*	1901	4-12″, 16-6″	12,500	18.0
Longer-range	*Ohio*	1901	4-12″, 16-6″	12,500	18.0
ships necessary	*Virginia*	1904	4-12″, 8-8″	14,950	19.0
to reach	*Nebraska*	1904	4-12″, 8-8″	14,950	19.0
Philippines	*Georgia*	1904	4-12″, 8-8″	14,950	19.0
	New Jersey	1904	4-12″, 8-8″	14,950	19.0
	Rhode Island	1904	4-12″, 8-8″	14,950	19.0
	Connecticut	1904	4-12″, 8-8″	16,000	18.0
	Louisiana	1904	4-12″, 8-8″	16,000	18.0
	Vermont	1905	4-12″, 8-8″	16,000	18.0
	Kansas	1905	4-12″, 8-8″	16,000	18.0
	Minnesota	1905	4-12″, 8-8″	16,000	18.0
	Mississippi	1905	4-12″, 8-8″	13,000	17.0
	Idaho	1905	4-12″, 8-8″	13,000	17.0
	New Hampshire	1906	4-12″, 8-8″	16,000	18.0

Source: Author's compilation.

TABLE A.2 Comparison Between U.S. and Spanish Ships Engaged at Manila Bay

	U.S.				Spanish		
Ship	Year Completed	Displacement (tons)	Main Battery	Ship	Year Completed	Displacement (tons)	Main Battery
Olympia	1890	5,870	4-8", 10-5"	Reina Christina	1890	3,520	6-6"
Baltimore	1888	4,413	4-8", 6-6"	Castilia	1881	3,260	4-5", 2-4"
Boston	1888	2,000	2-8", 6-6"	Isla Cuba	1886	1,045	4-4"
Raleigh	1892	3,213	1-6", 10-5"	Isla Luzon	1887	1,045	4-4"
Concord	1889	1,710	6-6"	Don Antonio de Ulloa	1887	1,060	4-4"
Petrel	1888	892	4-6"	Marquis del Duero	1884	500	2-4"

Source: Author's compilation.

TABLE A.3 Shipbuilding Programs, 1904-1914: Recommendations and Congressional Approval

| | Recommendations of | | Congressional Approval |
	General Board	Navy Department	
1904	2 battleships, 4 scout cruisers, 1 armored cruiser, 3 destroyers, 3 protected destroyers	not published	1 battleship, 2 armored cruisers, 3 scout cruisers, 4 submarines
1905	3 battleships, 3 protected cruisers, 4 scout cruisers, 3 destroyers	not published	2 battleships
1906	3 battleships, 3 scout cruisers, 4 destroyers, 4 torpedo boats, 4 submarines	2 battleships, 2 cruisers, 4 destroyers, 2 submarines	1 battleship, 3 submarines, 3 destroyers
1907	2 battleships, 2 scout cruisers, 4 destroyers, 4 submarines	General Board program published with no recommendations	1 battleship, 2 destroyers,
1908	4 battleships, 4 scout cruisers, 10 destroyers	General Board program published with no recommendations	2 battleships, 8 submarines, 10 destroyers
1909	4 battleships, 4 scout cruisers, 10 destroyers, 4 submarines	2 battleships, 1 repair ship	2 battleships, 4 submarines, 6 destroyers
1910	4 battleships, 4 scout cruisers, 10 destroyers	2 battleships, 1 repair ship	2 battleships, 4 submarines, 6 destroyers
1911	4 battleships, 4 scout cruisers, 16 destroyers, 5 submarines	2 battleships	1 battleship, 8 submarines, 6 destroyers

Source: Author's compilation.

TABLE A.4   Monthly Total of Merchant Tonnage Sunk by German Submarines and Mines, Mid-1917 to Armistice

	1917	1918
January	—	356,600
February	—	318,900
March	—	342,500
April	—	274,700
May	—	295,500
June	687,500	255,500
July	557,900	260,900
August	511,700	283,800
September	351,700	187,800
October	458,500	118,500
November	289,200	17,600
December	399,100	—

Source: R. H. Gibson and Maurice Prendergast, *The German Submarine War 1914–1918* (New York: 1931), p. 352.

Notes

Chapter One

1. Elting Morison, *Men, Machines, and Modern Times* (Cambridge, Mass., 1966), pp. 217–218.
2. Richard Hough, *The History of the Modern Battleship: Dreadnought* (New York, 1964), p. 3.

Chapter Two

1. Elting Morison, *Admiral Sims and the Modern American Navy* (Cambridge, Mass., 1942), p. 101.
2. Letter William S. Sims to Albert Niblack, 21 May 1902, Sims Papers, Naval Historical Foundation, Library of Congress; Letter William S. Sims to Theodore Roosevelt, 17 November 1901, Sims Papers.
3. The disgusted admiral of the squadron made a general signal of "melancholy" and ordered the target sunk with six-pounders at point-blank range. Albert Gleaves, "Unfinished Autobiography," chap. 9, Gleaves Papers, Naval Historical Foundation, Library of Congress.
4. Letter Roosevelt to Sims, 12 December 1901, Sims Papers.
5. Morison, *Sims*, p. 144.
6. Letter A. P. Niblack to Albert Gleaves, 25 July 1917, Gleaves Papers.
7. Morison, *Men, Machines, and Modern Times*, p. 32.
8. Letter Sims to Henry C. Mustin, 13 April 1923, Sims Papers.
9. Letter C. V. Babcock to Henry Reuterdahl, 4 March 1919, Sims Papers.
10. Letter Seaton Schroeder to Sims, January 1910, Sims Papers.
11. It should be noted that Sims's admission of the dreadnoughts' fatal weaknesses took place twenty years before it dawned on the vast majority of naval officers.
12. Letter Bradley A. Fiske to Frank Friday Fletcher, 14 March 1915, Frank Friday Fletcher Papers, Alderman Library, University of Virginia.
13. Sutherland Denlinger and Charles B. Gary, *War in the Pacific: A Study of Peoples and Battle Problems* (New York, 1936), pp. 16–17.
14. Peter D. Karsten, "The Naval Aristocracy: U.S. Naval Officers from the 1840s to the 1920s: Mahan's Messmates" (Ph.D. Dissertation, University of Wisconsin, 1968),

p. 123. Later published in book form as *The Naval Aristocracy: The Golden Age of Annapolis and the Emergence of Modern American Navalism* (New York, 1972). Dissertation cited with author's permission.

15. Yates Stirling, *Sea Duty: The Memoirs of a Fighting Admiral* (New York, 1939), pp. 116–117.

16. See for example David Howarth, *Sovereign of the Seas: The Story of Britain and the Sea* (New York, 1974), pp. 12–13; 331–332.

17. Reinhard Scheer, *Germany's High Seas Fleet in the World War* (London, 1920), p. 3; John Toland, *The Rising Sun in the Pacific: The Decline and Fall of the Japanese Empire 1936–1945* (New York, 1970), p. 477.

18. Charles Carlisle Taylor, *The Life of Admiral Mahan* (New York, 1920), pp. 63–64.

19. Letter C. F. Sperry to wife, 15 November 1884, cited in Karsten, "Naval Aristocracy," p. 135.

20. Letter Sims to wife, 20 December 1910, Sims Papers.

21. Letter Captain G. W. Steele to Admiral H. T. Mayo, cited in Stephen Roskill, *Naval Policy Between the Wars* (London, 1968), vol. 1, p. 244, n. 4.

22. Morison, *Men, Machines, and Modern Times*, pp. 19–20.

23. Vincent Davis, *The Admiral's Lobby* (Chapel Hill, 1967), p. xxi.

24. Kenneth J. Hagan, ed., *In Peace and War: Interpretations of American Naval History, 1775–1978* (Westport, Conn., 1978), pp. 86–87.

25. Karsten, "Naval Aristocracy," pp. 11–12. Morris Janowitz notes that after this date alumni of the Naval Academy continued to dominate the naval high command. "As of 1950, the Navy was, in effect, completely inbred at the top level. In the elite cadre the post of fleet admiral, admiral, and vice admiral were reserved for graduates of Annapolis. Among the one hundred and fifty-four rear admirals of the line, 95.5 percent were graduates of Annapolis. Thirty-seven rear admirals with technical specializations were listed in the annual register after ensigns of the line as dual status hierarchy. Only four of this group were Academy graduates." Morris Janowitz, *The Professional Soldier: A Social and Political Portrait* (New York, 1960), pp. 57, 59–60.

26. Janowitz, *Professional Soldier*, p. 127.

27. "You'll Never Get Rich," *Fortune*, March 1938, p. 67.

28. W. D. Puleston, *Annapolis: Gangway to Quarterdeck* (New York, 1942), p. 223.

29. Karsten, "Naval Aristocracy," p. 51.

30. *Army-Navy Journal*, September 1913, cited in William R. Braisted, *The United States Navy in the Pacific, 1909–1922* (Austin, Tex., 1971), p. 124.

31. Janowitz, *Professional Soldier*, pp. 98–99.

32. Letter F. A. Todd to D. F. Sellers, 19 July 1937, Sellers Papers, Naval Historical Foundation, Library of Congress.

33. Park Benjamin, *The United States Naval Academy* (New York, 1900), p. 272; Puleston, *Annapolis*, pp. 107–108.

34. Paul Foley, "The Naval Academy Practice Cruise," *Proceedings of the United States Naval Institute* (henceforth, *USNIP*) 36 (1910), p. 246.

35. Ernest J. King and Walter M. Whitehall, *Fleet Admiral King: A Naval Record* (New York, 1952), p. 148.

36. Benjamin, *United States Naval Academy*, p. 362.

37. Puleston, *Annapolis*, p. 202.

38. Ridgely Hunt, "Education at the Naval Academy," *USNIP* 42 (May 1916), p. 736.

39. W. S. Sims, "Minority Report" to "Report of the Board of Visitors to the United States Naval Academy, 1933," Sims Papers.

40. Karsten, "Naval Aristocracy," p. 154.

41. Denlinger and Gary, *War in the Pacific*, p. 12.

42. Theodore C. Mason, *Battleship Sailor* (Annapolis, Md., 1982), p. 68.

43. Benjamin, *United States Naval Academy*, pp. 93, 97.

44. J. O. Hoffman, "Tact in Relation to Discipline," *USNIP* 46 (1920), p. 1206.

45. Arthur J. Marder, *Anatomy of British Sea Power* (New York, 1940), p. 68; William Hovgaard, *Modern History of Warships: Comprising a Discussion of Present Standpoint and Recent War Experiences* (New York, 1920), pp. 69–72.

46. See for example Admiral William D. Leahy, Diary, 30 March 1936, Papers of William D. Leahy, Library of Congress.

47. Janowitz, *Professional Soldier*, p. 196.

48. Letter Lieutenant R. G. Turpin to W. S. Sims, 4 July 1904, Sims Papers.

49. Alfred T. Mahan, *From Sail to Steam: Recollections of Naval Life* (New York, 1907), p. 69.

50. William V. Pratt, "Autobiography" (unpublished), chap. 11, pp. 3–4, Pratt Papers.

51. Gleaves, "Autobiography," chap. 4.

52. C. H. Davis, *USNIP* (1901), p. 276, cited in Karsten, "Naval Aristocracy," p. 399.

53. A. T. Mahan, "Some Recollections of Alfred T. Mahan," Papers of Alfred T. Mahan, Library of Congress.

54. Henry A. Wiley, *An Admiral from Texas* (New York, 1934), pp. 67–68.

55. W. W. Phelps, *USNIP* 39 (1913), p. 526.

56. Morison, *Sims*, pp. 167–169.

57. "Selectionist" (Sims), "Promotion by Selection in the Navy," 27 August 1906, Sims Papers; see also Wiley, *An Admiral from Texas*, p. 293; Memorandum from Albert Gleaves to the Secretary of the Navy, 26 July 1919, Gleaves Papers.

58. Karsten, "Naval Aristocracy," p. 460.

59. Robert A. Hart, *The Great White Fleet: Its Voyage Around the World: 1907–09* (Boston, 1965), pp. 168–169.

60. Janowitz, *Professional Soldier*, p. 244.

61. Karsten, "Naval Aristocracy," p. iv.

62. See for example Robert E. Coontz, *From Mississippi to the Sea* (Philadelphia, 1930), chap. 1; William F. Halsey and J. G. Briant, *Admiral Halsey's Story* (New York, 1947), chap. 1; and Stirling, *Sea Duty*, p. 3. "I did have many fights though . . . I believe that my evident desire to keep out of physical combats actually brought me into fights with other boys, that with more of a show of assertiveness, might have been avoided."

63. Address by Rear Admiral William L. Rodgers, 12 December 1927, Papers of William L. Rodgers, Naval Historical Foundation, Library of Congress.

64. Bradley A. Fiske, *The Navy as a Fighting Machine* (New York, 1917), pp. 5–6.

65. William F. Fullam, *USNIP* 16 (1890), William F. Fullam Papers, Naval Historical Foundation, Library of Congress.

66. Leahy, Diary, pp. 94–95.

67. Richard W. Unger, *The Ship and the Medieval Economy: 600–1600* (Montreal, 1980), p. 192; T. C. Lethbridge, "Shipbuilding," in *History of Technology*, vol. 2, ed. Charles Singer et al. (Oxford, 1954), p. 587.

68. Garrett Mattingly, *The Armada* (Boston, 1959), p. 89; G. B. Naish, "Ships and Shipbuilding" in *History of Technology*, vol. 3, ed. Singer et al., p. 474.

69. Michael Lewis, *The Spanish Armada* (New York, 1968), pp. 62–63; Peter Padfield, *Armada* (Annapolis, Md., 1988), p. 34.

70. Lewis, *The Spanish Armada*, pp. 62–63.

71. Colin Martin and Geoffrey Parker, *The Spanish Armada* (New York, 1988), p. 52; Padfield, *Armada*, p. 27; Roger Whiting, *The Enterprise of England: The Spanish Armada* (New York, 1988), pp. 87–91.

72. Geoffrey Parker, "Why the Armada Failed," *MHQ: Quarterly Journal of Military History* 1, no. 1 (1988), pp. 18–27; Whiting, *Enterprise of England*, p. 223.

73. Mattingly, *The Armada*, p. 277.

74. Padfield, *Armada*, pp. 150–155.

75. David Howarth, *The Voyage of the Armada: The Spanish Story* (New York, 1981), pp. 97–98; Mattingly, *The Armada*, pp. 367–370.

76. Marvin Harris, *Our Kind: Who We Are; Where We Came From; Where Are We Going?* (New York, 1989), p. 471.

77. John Keegan, *The Price of Admiralty* (New York, 1988), p. 6.

78. Ibid.

79. Theodore Ropp, *War in the Modern World* (Durham, N.C., 1959), p. 48; Michael Lewis, *A Social History of the Navy: 1793–1815* (London, 1960), p. 344.

80. Julian S. Corbett, *Some Principles of Naval Strategy* (London, 1960), p. 344.

81. Alfred T. Mahan, *The Influence of Sea Power upon History, 1660–1783* (Boston, 1890), p. 30.

82. E.H.H. Archibald, *The Wooden Fighting Ship in the Royal Navy: 897–1860* (New York, 1968), pp. 25–36.

83. Ibid., pp. 33–40.

84. Ropp, *War in the Modern World*, p. 54.

85. Howarth, *Sovereign of the Seas*, p. 116.

86. John Ruskin, cited in Lewis Mumford, *Technics and Civilization* (New York, 1934), pp. 208–209.

87. Corbett, *Principals of Naval Strategy*, pp. 98–103.

88. Michael Lewis, *The History of the British Navy* (Englewood Cliffs, N.J., 1957), pp. 106–107; Mahan, *Influence of Sea Power*, pp. 132–136.

89. Mahan, *Influence of Sea Power*, p. 109.

90. P. K. Kemp, *History of the Royal Navy* (New York, 1969), p. 84; E. B. Potter et al., *The United States and World Sea Power* (Englewood Cliffs, N.J., 1955), pp. 49–50.

91. J. Charbaud-Arnault, *Revue Maritime*, 1889, cited in Mahan, *Influence of Sea Power*, pp. 115–116.

92. Lewis, *History of the British Navy*, p. 84.

93. De Guiche cited in Kemp, *History of the Royal Navy*, p. 39.

94. Ropp, *War in the Modern World*, p. 53; Michael Lewis, *The Navy of Britain* (London, 1948), chap. 4.

95. Keegan, *Price of Admiralty*, p. 45; Robert L. O'Connell, *Of Arms and Men: A History of War, Weapons and Aggression* (New York, 1989), pp. 180, 182; Ropp, *War in the Modern World*, p. 97; Oliver Warner, *Nelson's Battles* (Newton Abbot, UK, 1971), pp. 50–64.

96. Lewis, *Navy of Britain*, p. 432.

97. Ropp, *War in the Modern World*, p. 55.

98. Lewis, *Social History*, p. 370.

99. Keegan, *Price of Admiralty*, pp. 87–88.

100. O'Connell, *Of Arms and Men*, pp. 164–165.

101. Lewis, *History of the British Navy*, p. 203.

102. Archibald, *The Wooden Fighting Ship*, p. 76.

103. Lewis, *Navy of Britain*, p. 86.

104. Corbett, *Principles of Naval Strategy*, p. 100.

105. Kemp, *History of the Royal Navy*, p. 120.

106. Potter et al., *United States and World Sea Power*, p. 104.

107. Ropp, *War in the Modern World*, p. 54; Keegan, *Price of Admiralty*, p. 95.

108. Andrew Lambert, *Battleships in Transition: The Creation of the Steam Battle-fleet, 1815–1860* (Annapolis, MD, 1984), p. 101.

109. Howarth, *Sovereign of the Seas*, p. 187; Archibald, *The Wooden Fighting Ship*, p. 59.

110. Mahan, *Influence of Sea Power*, p. 259; Archibald, *The Wooden Fighting Ship*, pp. 33, 66.

Chapter Three

1. William Hovgaard, *Modern History of Warships: Comprising a Discussion of Present Standpoint and Recent War Experiences* (New York, 1920), p. 4.

2. James P. Baxter, *The Introduction of the Ironclad Warship* (New York, 1920), p. 16.

3. Hovgaard, *Modern History of Warships*, p. 3.

4. Harold and Margaret Sprout, *The Rise of American Naval Power: 1776–1918* (Princeton, 1959), p. 225; Frank M. Bennett, *The Monitor and the Navy Under Steam* (Boston, 1900), pp. 23–24.

5. A. Angas, *Rivalry on the Atlantic* (New York, 1939), pp. x–xi, 75, 88, 90, 100.

6. Baxter, *Introduction of the Ironclad Warship*, pp. 13–14; Sprout and Sprout, *Rise of American Naval Power*, p. 126.

7. Edgar C. Smith, *A Short History of the Naval Engineer* (Cambridge, Mass., 1937), p. 14.

8. Alfred T. Mahan, *From Sail to Steam: Recollections of Naval Life* (New York, 1907), pp. 26–27.

9. This discovery and Benjamin Franklin Isherwood's struggle to disprove Mariotte's Law in relation to steam engines provide almost archetypical examples of the collision between human and technological logic. See Elting Morison, *Men, Machines, and Modern Times* (Cambridge, Mass., 1966), pp. 101–102; Edward William Sloan, *Benjamin Franklin Isherwood: Naval Engineer* (Annapolis, 1966), chap. 4.

10. Smith, *History of the Naval Engineer*, p. 174.

11. Hovgaard, *Modern History of Warships*, pp. 367–370.

12. E. B. Potter et al., *The United States and World Sea Power* (Englewood Cliffs, N.J., 1955), p. 393.

13. Richard Humble, *Before the Dreadnought* (London, 1976), p. 113; Hovgaard, *Modern History of Warships*, pp. 15, 71.

14. Baxter, *Introduction of the Ironclad Warship*, pp. 18, 24.

15. Michael Lewis, *The Navy of Britain* (London, 1948), p. 575; Bernard Brodie and Fawn Brodie, *From Crossbow to H-Bomb* (Bloomington, Ind., 1972), pp. 115–116.

16. Walter Millis, *Arms and Men* (New York, 1960), p. 90.

17. The most famous incident of this kind was the explosion of the "Peacemaker," a 12-inch gun on board the USS *Princeton*, on 28 February 1844. The blast killed

Secretary of State Abel P. Upshur, the secretary of the Navy, and a New York state senator and severely wounded twenty others, including Senator Thomas H. Benton. See Samuel E. Morison, Henry S. Commager, and R. Leuctenburg, *The Growth of the American Republic* (New York, 1968), pp. 543–544.

18. J. D. Scott, *Vickers: A History* (London, 1962), p. 25.

19. William A. McNeill, *The Pursuit of Power: Technology, Armed Forces, and Society Since 1000 AD* (Chicago, 1982), p. 238, n. 27.

20. Potter et al., *United States and World Sea Power*, p. 267; Lewis, *Navy of Britain*, p. 575.

21. Lewis, *Navy of Britain*, p. 581; Peter Hodges, *The Big Gun: Battleship Main Armament: 1860–1945* (Annapolis, Md., 1981), p. 14.

22. Hovgaard, *Modern History of Warships*, p. 456.

23. Ibid., p. 464.

24. "Modern armor is relatively little improved over the famous Krupp Cemented or K. C. armor which revolutionized ballistic standards 45 years ago." Bernard Brodie, A *Layman's Guide to Naval Strategy* (Princeton, 1942), pp. 25–26.

25. John Keegan, *The Price of Admiralty* (New York, 1988), p. 104.

26. Bernard Brodie, *Sea Power in the Machine Age* (Princeton, 1941), p. 222.

27. R. A. Fletcher, *Warships and Their Story* (London, 1911), p. 283.

28. Hovgaard, *Modern History of Warships*, pp. 415–416.

29. Andrew Lambert, *Battleships in Transition: The Creation of the Steam Battlefleet, 1815–1860* (Annapolis, Md., 1984), p. 101; Keegan, *Price of Admiralty*, p. 99.

30. William D. Puleston, *The Life of Admiral Mahan* (New Haven, 1939), p. 272.

31. Frank Friday Fletcher, "Guns, Armor, and Speed," Fletcher Papers; E. J. King, "Some Ideas About the Effect of Increasing the Size of Battleships," *USNIP* 45 (March 1919); Richard Hough, *The History of the Modern Battleship: Dreadnought* (New York, 1964), p. 105; see also Hovgaard, *Modern History of Warships*, chap. 2, for the general evolution of pre-dreadnoughts.

32. Robert A. Hart, *The Great White Fleet: Its Voyage Around the World: 1907–09* (Boston, 1965), pp. 50–51; Millis, *Arms and Men*, p. 172, n. 17; Hovgaard, *Modern History of Warships*, chap. 2; Alfred T. Mahan, "Reflections, Historic and Other, Suggested by the Battle of the Sea of Japan," *USNIP*, June 1906.

33. Lee J. Levert, *Fundamentals of Naval Warfare* (New York, 1947), p. 253.

34. Ibid.

35. King, "Some Ideas," p. 396; Bradley A. Fiske, *From Midshipman to Rear Admiral* (New York, 1919), p. 389.

36. Fletcher, *Warships*, p. 262.

37. Oscar Parkes, *British Battleships* (London, 1956), p. 531; Keegan, *Price of Admiralty*, p. 120.

38. Archibald, *The Wooden Fighting Ship*, p. 62; Hovgaard, *Modern History of Warships*, p. 393.

39. Winston Churchill, *The World Crisis* (New York, 1923), vol. 1, p. 129.

40. Bradley A. Fiske, "Compromiseless Ships," *USNIP,* September 1905, p. 549.

41. Letter Rear Admiral C. F. Goodrich to Secretary of the Navy, 31 January 1908, Sims Papers.

42. King, "Some Ideas," p. 390.

43. Hough, *Dreadnought*, p. 105.

44. Letter Alfred T. Mahan to Secretary of the Navy, 31 January 1900, Mahan Papers.

45. "Substance of Remarks of Rear Admiral Joseph Strauss Before the Executive Committee of the General Board," 25 May 1915, General Board Papers, pp. 420–426.

46. Admiral George Dewey, "Introduction to a Book by N. L. Stebbings, 12 March 1912, Dewey Papers.

47. The recent development of so-called Chobham armor and the inclusion of depleted uranium powder in U.S. tanks raise some interesting possibilities for ship defenses. Yet metallurgically the statement remains basically correct.

48. Memo to Theodore Roosevelt from Naval Constructor Bowles, 22 October 1902, Study File 420-6, General Board Papers.

49. Potter et al., *United States and World Sea Power*, p. 250; Baxter, *Introduction of the Ironclad Warship*, pp. 30–32; Sprout and Sprout, *Rise of American Naval Power*, pp. 113–116.

50. Mahan, *From Sail to Steam*, p. 39.

51. Sloan, *Isherwood*, p. 4.

52. Harold G. Bowen, *Ships, Machinery, and Mossbacks: The Autobiography of a Naval Engineer* (Princeton, 1954), pp. 16–17.

53. B. F. Isherwood, 38th Congress, 2nd Session, House Executive Document No. 1, pp. 1214–1215.

54. Pamphlet by anonymous naval engineer, *Strictly Private and Confidential* (n.p., ca. 1880), pp. 22–26, Lawrence Letters, cited in Peter D. Karsten, "The Naval Aristocracy: U.S. Naval Officers from the 1840s to the 1920s: Mahan's Messmates" (Ph.D. Dissertation, University of Wisconsin, 1968), p. 73.

55. Letter A. T. Mahan to Samuel Ashe, 27 January 1876, Ashe Papers, cited in Karsten, "Naval Aristocracy," p. 73.

56. Sloan, *Isherwood*, p. 194.

57. Letter W. F. Fullam to Mr. Hapgood, 3 November 1908, Sims Papers: "Compare the experience, training, and life of the line officer with that of a staff officer. The former begins at the bottom of the ladder, does the duty of an enlisted man in all essential respects while at the Naval Academy, and takes the hard knocks, night watches, exposure,

and responsibilities in every grade. The young staff officer comes in from civil life . . . comparatively speaking he has a soft easy job with little hardship and few responsibilities all his life. And yet he demands to be called a 'Commander,' 'Captain,' and 'Admiral' just the same though he never . . . performs any of the functions of command—he cannot do so because he is not trained for it."

58. Sloan, *Isherwood*, p. 27.

59. Potter et al., *United States and World Sea Power*, p. 303.

60. Theodore Ropp, *War in the Modern World* (Durham, N.C., 1959), p. 175.

61. Official records of the Union and Confederate Navy, Ser. II, vol. 2, pp. 67, 69; Letter Stephen Mallory to C. M. Confrad, Chairman of Committee on Naval Affairs, C. S. House of Representatives, 8 May 1861; Sprout and Sprout, *Rise of American Naval Power*, p. 156.

62. Baxter, *Introduction of the Ironclad Warship*, p. 233.

63. The board's report printed in full in Senate Executive Document No. 1, 37th Congress, 2nd Session, pp. 152–156.

64. Baxter, *Introduction of the Ironclad Warship*, p. 285.

65. Potter et al., *United States and World Sea Power*, p. 322.

66. Bennett, *Monitor and the Navy*, p. 117.

67. Baxter, *Introduction of the Ironclad Warship*, p. 293.

68. Bennett, *Monitor and the Navy*, pp. 132–133.

69. Karsten, "Naval Aristocracy," p. 75; Sloan, *Isherwood*, p. 133.

70. 40th Congress, Second Session, House Executive Document No. 1, pp. 179–180.

71. Sloan, *Isherwood*, pp. 192, 209.

72. Ibid., p. 209.

73. Morison, *Men, Machines, and Modern Times*, pp. 98–99; Sloan, *Isherwood*, p. 177.

74. Annual Report of the Secretary of the Navy, 1864, 38th Congress, 2nd Session, House Exec. Doc. No. 1, vol. 6, p. xxii.

75. Millis, *Arms and Men*, p. 134; Potter et al., *United States and World Sea Power*, p. 393.

76. Caspar F. Goodrich, *Rope Yarns from the Old Navy* (New York, 1931), p. 65.

77. Potter et al., *United States and World Sea Power*, 394.

78. W. D. Puleston, *Annapolis Gangway to Quarterdeck* (New York, 1942), p. 104.

79. Sloan, *Isherwood*, p. 232.

80. Morison, *Men, Machines, and Modern Times*, pp. 116–119.

81. Ibid.

82. Letter Vice Admiral David Porter to Henry A. Wise, 20 December 1967, Wise Papers, New York Historical Society; Karsten, "Naval Aristocracy," p. 72.

83. Sprout and Sprout, *Rise of American Naval Power*, pp. 92, 118.

84. Vincent Davis, *The Admiral's Lobby* (Chapel Hill, 1967), p. 17.

85. R. G. Albion, "Makers of Naval Policy," Washington, 1950, p. 347. (An unpublished typescript in Office of Naval History, Washington, D.C.)

86. Gideon Wells, Diary, vol. 2, p. 233, vol. 3, p. 559, cited in Sloan, *Isherwood*, pp. 198, 225.

87. Letter "Survey" to *New York Evening Post*, 13 March 1868, cited in Sloan, *Isherwood*, p. 200.

88. Karsten, "Naval Aristocracy," pp. 72–73.

89. Sloan, *Isherwood*, p. 231.

90. Karsten, "Naval Aristocracy," p. 75.

91. Elting Morison, *Admiral Sims and the Modern American Navy* (Cambridge, Mass., 1942), p. 19.

92. Hovgaard, *Modern History of Warships*, p. 96; Sprout and Sprout, *Rise of American Naval Power*, p. 170.

93. *Report of the Secretary of the Navy* (Washington, 1881), p. 62.

94. Karsten, "Naval Aristocracy," p. 343.

95. Frank V. McNair, "Report on Fleet Maneuvers," *USNIP*, pp. 162–176.

96. Richard West, *Admirals of the American Empire* (New York, 1948), p. 93.

97. Karsten, "Naval Aristocracy," p. 345.

98. Bradley A. Fiske, *Wartime in Manila* (Boston, 1913), p. 235.

99. Fiske, *From Midshipman to Rear Admiral*, p. 18; Morison, *Sims*, pp. 17, 93.

100. Lambert, *Battleships in Transition*, p. 101.

101. Ibid.

102. Keegan, *Price of Admiralty*, p. 98.

103. Humble, *Before the Dreadnought*, pp. 113, 121–123.

104. Lambert, *Battleships in Transition*, p. 111.

105. Keegan, *Price of Admiralty*, p. 99.

106. Humble, *Before the Dreadnought*, pp. 116–117.

107. Millis, *Arms and Men*, p. 146.

108. Report of the Naval Advisory Board, Exec. Doc. No. 2016, 47th Congress, First Session, p. 28; Benjamin Franklin Cooling, *Grey Steel and Blue Water Navy: The Formative Years of America's Military-Industrial Complex: 1881-1917* (Hamden, Conn., 1979), pp. 28–29.

109. Hovgaard, *Modern History of Warships*, p. 97; Cooling, *Grey Steel*, pp. 43–45.

110. Hovgaard, *Modern History of Warships*, p. 395; Cooling, *Grey Steel*, pp. 43–45.

111. Hovgaard, *Modern History of Warships*, p. 97.

112. Brayton Harris, *The Age of the Battleship: 1880-1920* (New York, 1965), pp. 13-14.

113. Cooling, *Grey Steel*, chaps. 3-5.

114. Walter LaFeber, *The New Empire: An Interpretation of American Expansion: 1860-1898* (Ithaca, 1963), p. 60.

115. Charles A. Beard, *The Navy: Defense or Portent?* (New York, 1932), pp. 38-40; Karsten, "Naval Aristocracy," pp. 371-372.

116. William E. Livezy, *Mahan on Seapower* (Norman, Okla., 1947), p. 6.

117. Mahan, *From Sail to Steam*, p. xiv.

118. Livezy, *Mahan on Seapower*, p. 6; Robert Seeger II, *Alfred Thayer Mahan: The Man and His Letters* (Annapolis, Md., 1977), p. 171.

119. West, *Admirals of the American Empire*, p. 20; Seeger, *Alfred Thayer Mahan*, pp. 22-24.

120. Charles Carlisle Taylor, *The Life of Admiral Mahan* (New York, 1920), p. ix; Philip A. Crowl, "Alfred Thayer Mahan the Naval Historian," in *Makers of Modern Strategy: From Machiavelli to the Nuclear Age*, ed. Peter Paret (Oxford, UK, 1986), p. 445.

121. Karsten, "Naval Aristocracy," p. 428.

122. "Blockading was desperately tedious work, make the best one could of it. The largest reservoir of anecdotes was sure to run dry; the deepest vein of original humor to be worked out. . . . I have never seen a body of intelligent men reduced so nearly to imbecility as my shipmates were." Mahan, *From Sail to Steam*, pp. 174-175.

123. Letter Mahan to William C. Church, 29 November 1876, Church Papers, Library of Congress.

124. Mahan, *From Sail to Steam*, p. 197.

125. Letter Mahan to Ashe, 2 February 1886, Ashe Papers, cited in Karsten, "Naval Aristocracy," p. 417.

126. Keegan, *Price of Admiralty*, p. 169; Puleston, *Mahan*, p. 68.

127. William V. Pratt, "Autobiography" (unpublished), chap. 11, pp. 1-2, Pratt Papers; John B. Stapler, "The Naval War College: A Brief History," *USNIP* 58, no. 8 (August 1932), pp. 1157-1158.

128. Sprout and Sprout, *Rise of American Naval Power*, pp. 424-5; Millis, *Arms and Men*, p. 114.

129. Alfred T. Mahan, *The Influence of Sea Power upon History: 1660-1783* (New York, 1890), p. 2.

130. Louis M. Hacker, "The Incendiary Mahan," *Scribner's*, April 1934, p. 313; Sprout and Sprout, *Rise of American Naval Power*, p. 205.

131. Mahan, *Influence of Sea Power*, pp. 136, 535.

132. Crowl, "Mahan the Naval Historian," p. 450.

133. Letter A. T. Mahan to T. Roosevelt, 16 October 1902, Study File 420-6, General Board Papers. Ronald Spector, "The Triumph of Professional Ideology," in *In Peace and War: Interpretations of American Naval History, 1775–1978*, ed. Kenneth J. Hagan (Westport, Conn., 1978), p. 176.

134. In answer to Mahan's hypothesis, technologically oriented Naval Constructor A. T. Bowles wrote an interesting and charactistic criticism that began, "Any conclusion upon the features of modern battleships deduced from the experience of the sailing navies of the world prior to 1850 should be critically examined on account of the fact that there is little or no basis for comparison." Memorandum, Naval Constructor A. T. Bowles to T. Roosevelt, 1 October 1902, Study File 420-6, General Board Papers.

135. Mahan, *Influence of Seapower* p. 86.

136. Sprout and Sprout, *Rise of American Naval Power*, pp. 251–252.

137. A. T. Mahan, "The United States Looks Outward," *Atlantic Monthly*, December 1890.

138. Although Mahan indicated in *The Influence of Seapower* (pp. 87–88) that the restoration of the transport fleet was imperative to the growth of maritime power, Walter LaFeber noted (*New Empire*, pp. 89–90), that this was one of the few times in the decade that Mahan stressed the indispensibility of this aspect of his program. Such an omission, Peter Karsten believed, is indicative of Mahan's whole motivation and outlook. He was not so much the economic theorist interested in the formulation of sound policy as he was the naval officer determined to provide a rationale for the construction of a battleship fleet. "Mahan's interest in the merchant marine will be understood to survive only so long as an interest served to support his arguments for a stronger Navy." Karsten, "Naval Aristocracy," p. 429, n. 40B.

139. Mahan, *Influence of Seapower*, p. 26.

140. LaFeber, *New Empire*, p. 91.

141. Livezy, *Mahan on Seapower*, p. 157.

142. Mahan, *Influence of Seapower*, p. 33.

143. Sprout and Sprout, *Rise of American Naval Power*, p. 251.

144. Mahan, *Influence of Seapower*, p. 83.

145. A. T. Mahan, "The Isthmus and Sea Power," originally published in the *Atlantic Monthly*, September 1893, cited in Julius W. Pratt, *The Expansionists of 1898* (Baltimore, 1936), p. 15.

146. LaFeber, *New Empire*, pp. 91–92; Seeger, *Mahan*, pp. 395–396.

147. Mahan, *Influence of Sea Power*, p. 83.

148. Millis, *Arms and Men*, p. 161. A number of scholars have noted the circular nature of Mahan's arguments, without having attributed it to what would appear to be the most obvious of motives, the advancement of the service per se (Davis, *Admiral's Lobby*, p. 112; Sprout and Sprout, *Rise of American Naval Power*, p. 203;

LaFeber, *New Empire*, pp. 85–94). However, when the writings of the scholar/officer Mahan are examined in the context of the overwhelming influence that membership in the naval aristocracy exerted, they begin to take on quite a different cast. It seems significant that the historian whose sociolocial and psychological insights into the nature of the fin de siècle Navy are most acute, Peter D. Karsten, wrote: "Mahan was, first and foremost, a navalist. Everything else followed in the wake of his devotion to the service. Like the later proponents of an independent Air Force, who justified their appeal for independence with a strategy ('strategic bombing') before they had a weapon capable of carrying the strategy out, Mahan 'discovered' historic and strategic principles to justify a bigger navy." Karsten, "Naval Aristocracy," p. 428.

149. William R. Braisted, *The United States Navy in the Pacific, 1897–1909* (Austin, Tex., 1958), p. 6; Beard, *The Navy: Defense or Portent?* p. 18.

150. Letter Lieutenant Commander Richard Rush to Mahan, 12 June 1893, Mahan Papers.

151. Letter C. F. Goodrich to Mahan, 14 May 1892, Mahan Papers.

152. Letter William L. Rodgers to Mahan, 12 July 1894, Mahan Papers.

153. Livezy, *Mahan on Seapower*, pp. 40–50.

154. Davis, *Admiral's Lobby*, p. 113.

155. Ibid.

156. Taylor, *Mahan*, p. 127.

157. The 1893 cruise of the *Chicago*, Mahan's last command, was little more than a triumphal tour of the European naval banquet circuit. The prophet was wined and dined to the point that his immediate superior, Admiral Erban, accused him of neglecting his shipboard duties. (Puleston, *Mahan*, pp. 137–148.)

158. Taylor, *Mahan*, p. 114; Harris, *The Age of the Battleship*, p. 18.

159. Puleston, *Mahan*, p. 149; Hacker, "The Incendiary Mahan," p. 318; Jonathan Steinberg, *Yesterday's Deterrent: Tirpitz and the Birth of the German Fleet* (London, 1965), pp. 20, 125–127; George T. Davis, *A Navy Second to None* (New York, 1940), p. 74; Alfred P. von Tirpitz, *My Memoirs*, 2 vols. (New York, 1919), vol. 1, pp. 143–145.

160. Livezy, *Mahan on Seapower*, p. 51.

161. Arthur J. Marder, *Anatomy of British Sea Power* (New York, 1940), p. 47.

162. Ropp, *War in the Modern World*, p. 192.

163. Millis, *Arms and Men*, p. 163.

164. Alfred T. Mahan, *The Problem of Asia* (Boston, 1890).

165. Letter Theodore Roosevelt to Mahan, 12 May 1890, Mahan Papers.

166. Ernest R. May, *American Imperialism* (New York, 1968), pp. 198, 201–202.

167. Howard K. Beale, *Theodore Roosevelt and the Rise of America to World Power* (New York, 1956), p. 50; Arthur M. Johnson, "Theodore Roosevelt and the Navy," *USNIP* 84, no. 10 (October 1958), p. 76.

168. LaFeber, *New Empire*, pp. 84–94.

169. Gerald K. Wheeler, *Prelude to Pearl Harbor: The United States Navy in the Far East* (Columbus, Mo., 1963), p. 64.

170. Alfred Vagts, *History of Militarism* (New York, 1937), p. 324; Letter W. F. Fullam to Sub-Committee of U.S. Senate investigating the conduct of the War, 24 May 1920, Fullam Papers; Davis, *Admiral's Lobby*, p. 17.

171. Sprout and Sprout, *Rise of American Naval Power*, p. 207; Millis, *Arms and Men*, p. 157; West, *Admirals of the American Empire*, p. 147.

172. Annual Report of the Secretary of the Navy, 1889, 51st Congress, 1st Session, House Exec. Doc. No. 1, pt. 3, pp. 3–4.

173. Letter Hilary A. Herbert to Mahan, 4 October 1893, Mahan Papers.

174. Livezy, *Mahan on Seapower*, pp. 165, 171.

175. 51st Congress, 1st Session, House Report No. 1178, p. 16, to accompany HR 8909 Appropriations for the Naval Service, 1 April 1890, p. 26.

176. 64th Congress, 4th Session, *Congressional Record*, p. 3113.

177. Hart, *Great White Fleet*, p. 51; John C. Reilly and Robert L. Scheina, *American Battleships: 1886–1923* (Annapolis, Md., 1980).

Chapter Four

1. W. V. Pratt, "The Naval War College," *USNIP* 53, no. 9 (September 1927), p. 939; Burke Davis, *The Billy Mitchell Affair* (New York, 1967), p. 274.

2. A. P. Niblack, "The Tactics of Ships-of-the-Line of Battle," *USNIP* 22, no. 2, p. 28.

3. "History of the United States Naval War College: 1884–1954" (Newport, prepared in accordance with OpNav Instructions 5750.9 of 5 May 1959), p. 3. On file in the Operational Archives, Washington Naval Yard.

4. Francis J. McHugh, "Gaming at the Naval War College," *USNIP*, March 1964, pp. 49–50; Bradley A. Fiske, *The Navy as a Fighting Machine* (New York, 1917), pp. 152–153; A. P. Niblack, "The Jane Naval Game," *USNIP* 29, no. 3 (September 1903), p. 581.

5. Edwin Baumgarten, "Strategic War Gaming," *Naval War College Review* 13, no. 10 (June 1961), p. 19.

6. Fiske, *Navy as a Fighting Machine*, p. 201.

7. Caspar F. Goodrich, "Closing Address, Session of 1897," *USNIP* 23, no. 4, p. 682.

8. Fiske, *Navy as a Fighting Machine*, pp. 126–127.

9. A. P. Niblack, "The Tactics of the Gun," *USNIP* 28 (December 1902), p. 925.

10. William Hovgaard, *Modern History of Warships: Comprising a Discussion of Present Standpoint and Recent War Experiences* (New York, 1920), p. 146; Fiske, *Navy as a Fighting Machine*, pp. 38–39; E. J. King, "Some Ideas About the Effect of Increasing the Size of Battleships," *USNIP* 45 (March 1919), pp. 400–401.

11. Thomas Johnson, "Large vs. a Greater Number of Smaller Battleships," *USNIP* 42, no. 4 (July-August 1916), pp. 1080–1081.

12. Niblack, "The Tactics of the Gun," p. 925.

13. Sutherland Denlinger and Charles B. Gary, *War in the Pacific: A Study of Peoples and Battle Problems* (New York, 1936), pp. 133–135.

14. Stephen B. Luce, "Our Future Navy," *USNIP* 21, no. 2 (1895), p. 257.

15. Richard Wainwright, "Tactical Problems in Naval Warfare," *USNIP* 21, no. 2 (1895), p. 257.

16. Alfred T. Mahan, *Sea Power in Its Relations to the War of 1812* (New York, 1905), p. 316.

17. Fiske, *Navy as a Fighting Machine*, pp. 54–58, 94–95.

18. Niblack, "Tactics of Ships-of-the-Line of Battle," p. 17.

19. Wainwright, "Tactical Problems," p. 254.

20. Ibid., p. 243.

21. After 120 plays of one particular game, the War College concluded that "the value of 20 percent superior speed to a fleet of ships of the line of battle is less than one-twelfth of its total tactical force." McHugh, "Gaming at the Naval War College," p. 50.

22. Arthur J. Marder, *From Dreadnought to Scapa Flow*, 4 vols. (London, 1961), vol. 1, p. 397; Franklin Percival, "Fisher and His Warships," *USNIP*, August 1939, pp. 1099, 1101.

23. Wainwright, "Tactical Problems," p. 221.

24. J. Cameron Dierks, *A Leap to Arms* (New York, 1970), p. 39.

25. Fiske, *Navy as a Fighting Machine*, pp. 54–58.

26. Wainwright, "Tactical Problems," p. 70.

27. Niblack, "Tactics of Ships-of-the-Line of Battle," p. 12.

28. Letter Mahan to Secretary of the Navy Long, 31 January 1900, Mahan Papers.

29. Letter George Dewey to Secretary of the Navy, 26 July 1905, General Board Papers.

30. "Results to Be Achieved by Squadron Work," ca. 1902, Dewey Papers.

31. How much good all of this did is open to question. In 1904 Admiral J. B. Coughlan wrote Admiral Dewey that "the solutions of the tactical situations submitted by some of our Flag Officers and Captains, showed an almost childish grasp, or lack of grasp, of the idea of tactics. Officers who have commanded squadrons and others . . .

proposing to maneuver our squadrons by assuming that the enemy will adopt the worst thing possible for himself and the best moves possible for us." Letter J. B. Coughlan to Admiral Dewey, 28 August 1904, Dewey Papers.

32. Henry C. Taylor, "The Fleet," *USNIP* 24, no. 4 (December 1903), p. 803.

33. Vincent Davis, *The Admiral's Lobby* (Chapel Hill, 1967), p. 129, n. 45; John B. Stapler, "The Naval War College: A Brief History," *USNIP* 58, no. 8 (August 1932), p. 1160.

34. Fiske, *Navy as a Fighting Machine*, pp. 102, 120.

35. Davis, *Admiral's Lobby*, pp. 104–105.

36. E. B. Potter et al., *The United States and World Sea Power* (Englewood Cliffs, N.J., 1955), p. 550.

37. Theodore Roscoe, *On the Seas and in the Air* (New York, 1970), p. 63; Walter Millis, *Arms and Men* (New York, 1960), p. 172, n. 17; Robert A. Hart, *The Great White Fleet: Its Voyage Around the World: 1907–09* (Boston, 1965), p. xi.

38. Davis, *Admiral's Lobby*, p. 33.

39. Elting Morison, *Admiral Sims and the Modern American Navy* (Cambridge, Mass., 1942), p. 292.

40. Henry A. Wiley, *An Admiral from Texas* (New York, 1934), p. 46.

41. Yates Stirling, *Sea Duty: The Memoirs of a Fighting Admiral* (New York, 1939), pp. 194–196.

42. Harris Laning, "Big Navy," *Fortune*, March 1938, p. 54.

43. "Position of the Navy Department Relative to Each Article of the Draft Convention," Geneva Conference, 1932, Series X, General Board Report to Secretary of the Navy, 1932–1934, pp. 49–57.

44. Stirling, *Sea Duty*, pp. 187–188.

45. Robert A. Hart recounted the reactions of a number of New York and Philadelphia reporters when invited into the cabin of an admiral or captain: "These were homey apartments, more spacious than one might have guessed. Rugs were thick, and chairs and footstools were covered with velvet or soft leather. There might be a walnut desk . . . and certainly a drop-leaf table which could be set for private parties of eight or ten. One admiral kept at least six large urns of plants which transformed his cabin into a pleasant grove." Hart, *Great White Fleet*, pp. 67–68.

46. Letter Charles J. Badger to W. S. Sims, 11 June 1912, Sims Papers.

47. Letter W. S. Benson, to Sims, 14 March 1903, Sims Papers.

48. Wiley, *An Admiral from Texas*, p. 143.

49. Norman Mailer, "Ego," *Life*, 19 March 1971, p. 19.

50. Letter Poundstone to Sims, 15 August 1905, Sims Papers.

51. Letter Albert L. Key to Theodore Roosevelt, 23 January 1909, Sims Papers.

52. King, "Some Ideas," p. 398.

53. Theodore C. Mason, *Battleship Sailor* (Annapolis, Md., 1982), p. 5.

54. Sutherland Denlinger and Charles B. Gary, *War in the Pacific: A Study of Peoples and Battle Problems* (New York, 1936), p. 35.

55. H. M. LeFleming, *The ABC Warships of World War I* (London, 1962), p. 11.

56. Thomas Beyer, *The American Battleship in Commission, as Seen by an Enlisted Man* (Washington, 1906), p. 47.

57. Paul Schubert, *Come on Texas* (New York, 1930), pp. 43, 46–47.

58. Bradley A. Fiske, "If Battleships Ran on Land," *Popular Science Monthly*, October 1915, p. 24.

59. Schubert, *Come on Texas*, p. 4.

60. Mason, *Battleship Sailor*, p. 5.

61. Denlinger and Gary, *War in the Pacific*, p. 160.

62. Lowell Tozer, "American Attitudes Toward Machine Technology: 1893–1933" (Ph.D. Dissertation, University of Minnesota, 1953), p. 235. Henry Kissinger reached a similar conclusion when he noted that the reply of each service to technological change "will be an effort to treat new weapons by analogy to familiar functions." Henry A. Kissinger, *Nuclear Weapons and Foreign Policy* (New York, 1957), p. 63.

63. Vincent Davis suggested that the response of officers to early threats against the battleship "was additionally important because it set a pattern for their reaction to all subsequent developments." Davis, *Admiral's Lobby*, p. 63.

64. Henry Cabot Lodge, *The War with Spain* (New York, 1899), p. 28.

65. Dierks, *A Leap to Arms*, p. 17; Sigsbeen quoted in Henry Watterson, *History of the Spanish-American War* (St. Louis, 1898), p. 3.

66. Narrative of Lieutenant Blandin of *Maine*, Watterson, *History of the Spanish-American War*, pp. 4–5.

67. Out of a complement of 26 officers and 328 men, 260 were eventually reported dead or missing. John Edward Weems, *The Fate of the Maine* (New York, 1958), p. 33.

68. Ibid.

69. Joseph Wisan, *The Cuban Crisis as Reflected in the New York Press, 1895–98* (New York, 1934), pp. 21–38.

70. A. T. Mahan, "The War on the Sea and Its Lessons," *McClure's* 3 (December 1898-April 1899), pp. 111–112; Albert K. Weinberg, *Manifest Destiny* (Baltimore, 1935), pp. 398–399.

71. Nevertheless, the Navy Department did hold a court of inquiry presided over by Captain William T. Sampson, soon to lead the Atlantic Fleet against the Spanish. After an intensive four-week investigation, the court "was unable to obtain evidence fixing responsibility for the destruction of the *Maine* upon any person or persons. It did, however, hold the inward bend of the wrecked battleship's keel plates as conclusive proof that the disaster was caused by the external explosion of a submarine mine. (Findings of

the *Maine* Court of Inquiry, Appendix to the Report of the Chief of the Bureau of Navigation, 1898, p. 17). During this period, as J. C. Dierks noted, the Spaniards had initiated their own investigation. Although refused permission to examine the hulk, they did produce some thought-provoking questions. Why, for instance, had no one on board nearby ships either seen the geyser or felt the shock wave that an underwater explosion inevitably produced? Why had no one noticed any of the dead fish that ordinarily accompany this type of detonation? (Dierks, *A Leap to Arms*, p. 21.) Quite recently H. G. Rickover (*How the Battleship Maine Was Destroyed*, Washington, D.C.: 1976, pp. 91, 104) established, on the basis of expert testimony and careful engineering analysis, that "in all probability, the *Maine* was destroyed by an accident which occurred inside the ship," likely caused by spontaneous combustion in a coal bunker, which then led to the explosion of several forward magazines.

72. John D. Long, *The New American Navy*, 2 vols. (New York, 1903), vol. 2, p. 141.

73. Dierks, *A Leap to Arms*, p. 38.

74. Mahan, "The War on the Sea and Its Lessons," p. 240.

75. Scheme for War with Spain, 1896, Lieutenant W. W. Kimball, RG 42, Records of the North Atlantic Station, cited in William R. Braisted, *The United States Navy in the Pacific, 1897–1909* (Austin, Tex., 1958), pp. 21–22; Walter Millis, *The Martial Spirit: A Study of Our War with Spain* (Boston, 1931), p. 147.

76. Letter Roosevelt to John D. Long, 20 September 1897, in Elting Morison, *Letters of Theodore Roosevelt* (Cambridge, 1951), vol. 1, pp. 684–685.

77. Letter Roosevelt to B. H. Diblie, 16 February 1898, in Morison, *Letters*, vol. 1, p. 774.

78. Long, *New American Navy*, vol. 1, p. 145.

79. Millis, *Martial Spirit*, p. 111.

80. Lawrence Shaw Mayo, ed., *America of Yesterday in the Diary of John D. Long* (New York, 1923), p. 36.

81. Long, *New American Navy*, vol. 1, p. 147; Braisted, *Navy in the Pacific, 1897–1909*, p. 25.

82. Robley D. Evans, *A Sailor's Log* (New York, 1911), pp. 408–409.

83. Long, *New American Navy*, vol. 1, p. 162.

84. William D. Puleston, *The Life of Admiral Mahan* (New Haven, 1939), p. 186; Richard West, *Admirals of the American Empire* (New York, 1948), p. 214. Apparently, the prophet was somewhat offended at being asked to share with other officers the mantle of strategic authority over the crusade. After his second day on the job, he proposed that the War Board be replaced by a single authority individually responsible for advising the secretary. "Professional opinion," he wrote, "should come to him, not as the result of a majority vote, but with the far weightier sanction of a single competent authority, acting

under his high sense of personal responsibility." (Letter Mahan to Long, 9 May 1898, cited in West, *Admirals of the American Empire*, p. 214.) The suggestion was ignored and the prophet continued on the board.

85. Telegram Theodore Roosevelt to Dewey, in Morison, *Letters*, vol. 1, pp. 784–785.

86. Theodore Roosevelt, *Theodore Roosevelt, An Autobiography* (New York, 1915), pp. 784–785.

87. Ronald Spector, *Admiral of the New Empire: The Life and Career of George Dewey* (Baton Rouge, 1974), pp. 3, 67–68, 123.

88. George Dewey, *The Autobiography of George Dewey* (New York, 1913), p. 188.

89. Ibid., p. 180; Long, *New American Navy*, vol. 1, p. 180.

90. Lodge, *War with Spain*, p. 52.

91. Dewey, *Autobiography*, p. 192; Spector, *Admiral of the New Empire*, p. 49.

92. Watterson, *History of the Spanish-American War*, p. 48.

93. "Official Report of Admiral Montojo," Dewey, *Autobiography*, Appendix C.

94. Brayton Harris, *The Age of the Battleship: 1880–1920* (New York, 1965), pp. 66–67.

95. Millis, *Martial Spirit*, p. 189.

96. Dewey, *Autobiography*, p. 213.

97. Ibid., p. 214.

98. Long, *New American Navy*, vol. 1, p. 342.

99. Dewey, *Autobiography*, p. 216.

100. Carlos G. Calkins, "Historical and Professional Notes on the Naval Campaign of Manila in 1989," *USNIP* 25, no. 2 (January 1899), p. 276.

101. Millis, *Martial Spirit*, p. 190; Bradley A. Fiske, *From Midshipman to Rear Admiral* (New York, 1919), p. 250.

102. "Official Report of Admiral Montojo," p. 46; Lodge, *War with Spain*, p. 57.

103. Dewey, *Autobiography*, p. 219.

104. Long, *New American Navy*, vol. 1, p. 198.

105. Dierks, *A Leap to Arms*, p. 43; Harold and Margaret Sprout, *The Rise of American Naval Power: 1776–1918* (Princeton, 1959), p. 234; Mahan, "The War on the Sea," p. 358.

106. Millis, *Martial Spirit*, p. 202.

107. Long, *New American Navy*, vol. 1, p. 206.

108. Lodge, *War with Spain*, p. 86.

109. Letter Cervera to Ministry of Marine, 15 April 1898, cited in Long, *New American Navy*, vol. 1, p. 226.

110. Letter Cervera to Ministry of Marine, 12 April 1898, cited in Long, *New American Navy*, vol. 1, p. 226.

111. Millis, *Martial Spirit*, p. 168.

112. Herbert H. Sargent, *The Campaign of Santiago de Cuba* (Chicago, 1907), vol. 1, p. 64.

113. Millis, *Martial Spirit*, p. 231.

114. Charles H. Brown, *The Correspondent's War* (New York, 1967), p. 255.

115. Frank Friedel, *Splendid Little War* (New York, 1956), p. 52.

116. Evans, *Sailor's Log*, p. 439.

117. Millis, *Martial Spirit*, p. 241.

118. Harris, *The Age of the Battleship*, p. 90.

119. Dierks, *A Leap to Arms*, p. 36.

120. Friedel, *Splendid Little War*, p. 195.

121. Cervera's reply to Governor-General Blanco's letter of 28 June 1898, quoted in Long, *New American Navy*, vol. 2, p. 28.

122. Potter et al., *United States and World Sea Power*, p. 410.

123. Dierks, *A Leap to Arms*, p. 120.

124. Brown, *Correspondent's War*, pp. 377–378.

125. George E. Graham, *Schley and Santiago* (Chicago, 1902), pp. 287–290.

126. Watterson, *History of the Spanish-American War*, p. 152.

127. Long, *New American Navy*, vol. 2, pp. 30–31.

128. Ibid., vol. 2, p. 36.

129. Narrative of Lieutenant Gomez Inas reported to interrogators aboard USS *St. Louis*, published in *New York Sun*, 23 September 1898.

130. Dierks, *A Leap to Arms*, p. 142.

131. Dierks, *A Leap to Arms*, p. 153.

132. Millis, *Martial Spirit*, p. 311.

133. Phrase from Admiral Sampson's battle communiqué, 3 July 1898; Captain Concas's estimate of the dead (cited in Friedel, *Splendid Little War*, p. 229.)

134. Graham, *Schley and Santiago*, pp. 313–314.

135. Dierks, *A Leap to Arms*, pp. 160–164.

136. West, *Admirals of the American Empire*, pp. 49–56.

137. Dierks, *A Leap to Arms*, pp. 177–180.

138. Robert Brinkerhoff, "Naval Lessons of the War with Spain," *New York Commercial Advertiser*, 16 July 1898.

139. Evans, *Sailor's Log*, p. 448.

140. W. I. Chambers, "Naval Lessons of the War," *USNIP*, May 1900, p. 242.

141. Evans, *Sailor's Log*, p. 448.

142. Dewey, *Autobiography*, pp. 220–221; Dierks, *A Leap to Arms*, p. 176.

143. Chambers, "Naval Lessons of the War," p. 244.

144. Generally the American line had to close to within 2,000 yards of the Spaniards before their fire became effective, and at Santiago the range had occasionally dropped below 1,000 yards. (Long, *New American Navy*, vol. 1, p. 195; Friedel, *Splendid Little War*, p. 214; Evans, *Sailor's Log*, p. 441.

145. Long, *New American Navy*, vol. 1, p. 162; J. Butler, "The General Board of the Navy," *USNIP* 56 (August 1930), pp. 701–702; West, *Admirals of the American Empire*, p. 221.

146. Charles Carlisle Taylor, *The Life of Admiral Mahan* (New York, 1920), p. 167; Richard Wainwright, "The General Board," *USNIP* 48, no. 2 (February 1922), p. 190.

147. Braisted, *The Navy in the Pacific, 1897–1909*, p. 73.

148. Dierks, *A Leap to Arms*, p. 201.

149. William R. Braisted, *The United States Navy in the Pacific, 1909–1922* (Austin, Tex., 1971), pp. 7–8, 465–466; Gerald K. Wheeler, *Prelude to Pearl Harbor: The United States Navy in the Far East* (Columbus, Mo., 1963), pp. 75–90.

150. Sprout and Sprout, *Rise of American Naval Power*, pp. 233–234.

151. Dierks, *A Leap to Arms*, p. 52; Dewey, *Autobiography*, p. 290.

152. Dewey, *Autobiography*, p. 286.

153. Josephus Daniels, *The Wilson Era: Years of Peace, 1910–1917* (Chapel Hill, 1944), p. 505; Braisted, *Navy in the Pacific, 1897–1909*, p. 23.

Chapter Five

1. Elting Morison, *Admiral Sims and the Modern American Navy* (Cambridge, Mass., 1942), p. 78.

2. Letter Sims to Theodore Roosevelt, 11 March 1907, Sims Papers.

3. Hearings before Select Committee of Inquiry into Operations of the United States Air Service, H. R. 68th Congress, Pt. 4, 1925, pp. 2977–2978, Sims Papers.

4. "Arrangement of the Magazine, Ammunition Supply, and Installation of Batteries, USS *Kentucky*," 2 February 1901, Sims Papers.

5. Sims's marginal note on Letter to Office of Naval Intelligence, 29 June 1901, Sims Papers.

6. Sir Percy Scott, *Fifty Years in the Royal Navy* (London, 1919), p. 149.

7. Arthur J. Marder, *Anatomy of British Sea Power* (New York, 1940), p. 422.

8. Morison, *Sims*, p. 83.

9. Bernard Brodie, *Sea Power in the Machine Age* (Princeton, 1941), p. 229.

10. Elting Morison, *Men, Machines, and Modern Times* (Cambridge, Mass., 1966), p. 23.

11. W. S. Sims, "The Remarkable Record Target Practice of the HMS *Terrible*," Sims Papers, p. 19.

12. Letter W. S. Sims to A. P. Niblack, 21 May 1902, Sims Papers.

13. W. S. Sims, "Protection of Gun Positions, HMS *Canopus* Class Compared with That of the *Kentucky* and *Kearsarge*," 19 May 1901, Sims Papers.

14. Henry F. Pringle, *Theodore Roosevelt* (New York, 1931), p. 4; Harold and Margaret Sprout, *The Rise of American Naval Power: 1776-1918* (Princeton, 1959), pp. 225-226.

15. Letter Sims to Homer Poundstone, 9 November 1901, Sims Papers.

16. Pringle, *Theodore Roosevelt*, p. 92; Arthur M. Johnson, "Theodore Roosevelt and the Navy," *USNIP* 84, no. 10 (October 1958), p. 760.

17. Morison, *Men, Machines, and Modern Times*, p. 4.

18. Brayton Harris, *The Age of the Battleship: 1880-1920* (New York, 1965), p. 111; quote cited in Gordon C. O'Gara, *Theodore Roosevelt and the Rise of the Modern Navy* (Princeton, 1943), p. 7.

19. Calling Roosevelt's "ardor" for the Navy "a passionate affair," naval historian W. R. Braisted noted that "his half-dozen naval secretaries were able men, but with one or two excetpions, they seemed to regard the naval secretaryship as a comfortable resting place en route to a more attractive assignment." (William R. Braisted, *The United States Navy in the Pacific, 1909-1922* (Austin, Tex., 1971), pp. 4-5.

20. Letter Roosevelt to George Foss, 11 January 1907; Elting Morison, *Letters of Theodore Roosevelt* (Cambridge, 1951), vol. 5, p. 545.

21. Alfred P. von Tirpitz, *My Memoirs*, 2 vols. (New York, 1919), vol. 1, p. 128; Walter Gorlitz, ed., *The Kaiser and His Court: Notebooks and Letters of Admiral George Alexander von Muller* (London, 1961), p. xxi; O'Gara, *Roosevelt and the Rise of the Navy*, p. 46.

22. Letter Roosevelt to W. S. Cowles, 21 December 1901, in Morison, *Letters*, vol. 3, pp. 206-7.

23. Morison, *Sims*, p. 115.

24. Letter Roosevelt to H. C. Taylor, 22 April 1902, *Letters*, vol. 3, p. 253.

25. Morison, *Sims*, pp. 126-128.

26. Letter Sims to A. P. Niblack, 13 January 1903, Sims Papers.

27. Morison, *Sims*, p. 144.

28. Ibid., p. 132; Letter A. P. Niblack to Sims, 10 March 1902, Sims Papers.

29. Morison, *Sims*, p. 133.

30. W. S. Sims, "The Defects in Gun Gear, Gun Sights, etc. at Pensacola," May 1903, Sims Papers.

31. W. S. Sims, "Roosevelt and the Navy," *McClure's*, November 1922, p. 37.

32. "Report of the Chief of the Bureau of Ordnance" in *Report of the Secretary of the Navy* (Washington, 1907), p. 484, cited in Morison, *Sims*, p. 137.

33. Morison, *Sims*, pp. 145-146.

34. Homer Poundstone, "Plan for Fire Control," 6 February 1904, Sims Papers; Lieutenant Commander Mark L. Bristol, "Lectures on Fire Control," delivered at the Naval War College, 27–28 August 1906, Mark L. Bristol Papers.

35. Bradley Fiske, *From Midshipman to Rear Admiral* (New York, 1919), pp. 124–126; Paolo E. Coletta, *Admiral Bradley Fiske and the American Navy* (Lawrence, Kan., 1979), pp. 72–74.

36. "Report of Board on Fire Control," in "Report of Autumn Target Practice," 1905, Sims Papers.

37. Letter George Dewey to the Secretary of the Navy, 30 September 1905, Study File 420-6, General Board Papers.

38. A. J. Marder, "Fisher and the Genesis of the Dreadnought," *USNIP,* December 1956, pp. 1310–1311; Marder, *Anatomy of British Sea Power,* p. 537; Reginald Bacon, *The Life of Lord Fisher of Kilverstone,* 2 vols. (Garden City, 1929), vol. 1, p. 254; W. L. Rodgers, "Notes on the Design for a Battleship Proposed by Lieut. Homer Poundstone," 22 May 1905, Rodgers Papers.

39. Memorandum signed by W. L. Chambers referring to G. B. 420 of 17 October 1903, Study File 420-2, General Board Papers; W. S. Sims "Memorandum on Fire Control at Long Ranges."

40. Letter Poundstone to Captain H. A. Baldridge, 8 January 1940, Poundstone Papers.

41. Letter Roosevelt to H. Poundstone, 27 December 1902, Poundstone Papers.

42. Letter Poundstone to Sims, 13 August 1903, Sims Papers.

43. Letter H. S. Knapp to Sims, 9 July 1908, Sims Papers.

44. Memorandum W. I. Chambers, 17 October 1903, Study File 420-2, General Board Papers.

45. Letter George Dewey to Secretary of the Navy, 26 January 1904, File 420-6, General Board Papers.

46. Letter Sims to Poundstone, 15 July 1904, Poundstone Papers.

47. Letter Sims to Poundstone, 24 July 1904, Poundstone Papers.

48. Memorandum from Board on Construction and Repair to the Secretary of the Navy, 7 October 1904, File 420-6 General Board Papers.

49. Endorsement, W. L. Capps, Chief Constructor, to Secretary of the Navy, 4 October 1904, General Board Papers.

50. Memorandum of Board on Construction, 17 October 1904, Secretary's File, Naval Archives.

51. Letter Spencer S. Wood (Secretary of the General Board) to A. T. Mahan, 30 September 1910. In this letter is contained the contents of the General Board's letter of 28 October 1904, Mahan Papers.

52. Naval Appropriations Act, 3 March 1905, General Board Papers No. 17, 221-E.5.

53. General Board Papers, No. 17221-E.7.

54. Stephen Howarth, *The Fighting Ships of the Rising Sun: The Drama of the Imperial Japanese Navy, 1895–1945* (New York, 1983), pp. 82–86.

55. Robert A. Hart, *The Great White Fleet: Its Voyage Around the World: 1907–09* (Boston, 1965), pp. 14–15.

56. William R. Braisted, *The United States Navy in the Pacific, 1897–1909* (Austin, Tex., 1958), p. 180.

57. Letter Lieutenant Robert W. McNeely to Sims, 30 May 1905, Sims Papers.

58. Letter Dewey to Fred A. Hobbs, 12 June 1905, Dewey Papers.

59. Letter Poundstone to Sims, 15 August 1905, Sims Papers.

60. William Hovgaard, *Modern History of Warships: Comprising a Discussion of Present Standpoint and Recent War Experiences* (New York, 1920), p. 443; Charles Domville-Fife, *The Submarine and Seapower* (New York, 1923), p. 198.

61. E. B. Potter et al., *The United States and World Sea Power* (Englewood Cliffs, N.J., 1955), p. 444; Brodie, *Sea Power in the Machine Age*, p. 281.

62. Vitorio Cuniberti, "An Ideal Battleship for the British Fleet," *Jane's Fighting Ships* (London, 1903), p. 407.

63. Bacon, *The Life of Lord Fisher*, vol. 1, pp. 248–251; vol. 2, p. 71.

64. Arthur J. Marder, ed., *Fear God and Dreadnought*, 3 vols. (London, 1959), vol. 3, p. 480.

65. Letter Poundstone to W. Sims, 15 August 1905, Sims Papers.

66. Ibid.

67. Letter H. Poundstone to W. Sims, 15 August 1905; Letter George Dewey to Commander Nathan Sargent, 29 August 1905, Dewey Papers.

68. Letter George Dewey to Secretary of the Navy, 30 September 1905, File 420-6, General Board Papers.

69. Endorsement from Board on Construction, 23 November 1905, File 420-6, General Board Papers.

70. Marder, *Anatomy of British Sea Power*, p. 535.

71. Arthur J. Marder, *From Dreadnought to Scapa Flow*, 4 vols. (London, 1961), vol. 1, p. 44; Richard Hough, *The History of the Modern Battleship: Dreadnought* (New York, 1964), p. 84.

72. Letter H. Poundstone to Bureau of Construction and Repair, 6 February 1905, W. L. Rodgers Papers; Letter Poundstone to Sims, 15 August 1905, Sims Papers; Hough, *Dreadnought*, p. 25.

73. Morison, *Sims*, p. 181.

74. Arthur M. Johnson, "The USS *Delaware*: 'The Skeered O'Nuthin,'" *USNIP* 83, no. 8 (August 1937).

75. Park Benjamin, "The Shout for Big Ships," *Independent*, January 1909, p. 264.

76. Walter Millis, *Arms and Men* (New York, 1960), p. 189.

77. William Hovgaard, "Transactions of the Society of Naval Architects and Marine Engineers," 1906, p. 14.

78. Benjamin, "The Shout for Big Ships," p. 268.

79. William D. Puleston, *The Life of Admiral Mahan* (New Haven, 1939), p. 334.

80. A. T. Mahan, "Reflections, Historic and Other, Suggested by the Battle of the Sea of Japan," *USNIP*, June 1906, p. 451.

81. Ibid., pp. 452, 461–462.

82. Ibid., p. 468.

83. Letter Loeb to W. S. Sims, 30 August 1906, Sims Papers.

84. Letter Sims to T. Roosevelt, 24 September 1906, Sims Papers; W. S. Sims, "The Inherent Tactical Qualities of All-Big-Gun, One-Calibre Battleships of High Speed and Large Displacement and Gun Power," *USNIP*, December 1906, p. 1360.

85. Letter Sims to Roosevelt, 24 September 1906.

86. Letter T. Roosevelt to W. S. Sims, 27 September 1906, in Morison, *Letters*, vol. 5, p. 427.

87. Letter T. M. Kinkaid to Sims, 18 December 1906, Sims Papers; Letter W. F. Fullam to Sims, 2 March 1907, Sims Papers; Letter H. Poundstone to Sims, 12 January 1907, Sims Papers.

88. Letter T. Roosevelt to W. S. Sims, 23 October 1907, in Morison, *Letters*, vol. 5, p. 821.

89. Millis, *Arms and Men*, p. 190.

90. Theodore Roosevelt, *Theodore Roosevelt, An Autobiography* (New York, 1915), p. 563.

91. Braisted, *The Navy in the Pacific, 1897–1909*, p. 206; Howard K. Beale, *Theodore Roosevelt and the Rise of America to World Power* (New York, 1956), p. 285; Hart, *Great White Fleet*, p. 23.

92. Millis, *Arms and Men*, p. 192; Hart, *Great White Fleet*, p. 25.

93. Millis, *Arms and Men*, p. 195.

94. Letter Sir Frederick Richards to Admiral Lord Beresford, 1909, cited in Marder, *Anatomy of British Sea Power*, p. 515.

95. Marder, *From Dreadnought to Scapa Flow*, vol. 1, p. 515.

96. Admiral Sir Reginald Custance, "The Fighting Power of Capital Ships," Sims Papers.

97. Ibid.

98. W. W. White, "The Cult of the Monster Warship," *Nineteenth Century and After*, June 1908, pp. 918–919.

99. Winston S. Churchill, *The World Crisis* (New York, 1923), vol. 1, p. 33.

100. Hough, *Dreadnought*, p. 24.

101. Tirpitz, *Memoirs*, vol. 1, p. 263.

102. John Keegan, *The Price of Admiralty* (New York, 1988), p. 101.

103. Barbara Tuchman, *The Guns of August* (New York, 1962), p. 6.

104. Keegan, *Price of Admiralty*, p. 101.

105. Letter Baron Friedrich von Holstein to Paul Harzfield, 9 April 1897, cited in Jonathan Steinberg, *Yesterday's Deterrent* (London, 1965), p. 117.

106. Lewis Elkind, "The Kaiser's Dream of Sea Power," *The Nineteenth Century and After*, August 1900, p. 222.

107. Ibid., p. 218.

108. Marder, *Anatomy of British Sea Power*, p. 457.

109. Steinberg, *Yesterday's Deterrent*, p. 330.

110. Tirpitz, *Memoirs*, vol. 1, p. 345.

111. "Statement of Captain William S. Sims," Committee on Naval Affairs, H. R. 19 December 1916, Sims Papers.

112. Lee J. Levert, *Fundamentals of Naval Warfare* (New York, 1947), pp. 76, 313, 315.

113. Harold G. Bowen, *Ships, Machinery, and Mossbacks* (Princeton, 1954), p. 146.

114. Custance, "The Fighting Power of the Capital Ship."

115. Bernard Brodie, *A Layman's Guide to Naval Strategy* (Princeton, 1942), p. 251.

116. Letter Sims to Ridley McLean, 24 April 1910, Sims Papers.

117. John J. Sumida, *In Defense of Naval Supremacy: Finance, Technology, and British Naval Policy, 1898–1914* (London, 1989); Stephen Roskill, *Admiral of the Fleet Earl Beatty, the Last Naval Hero: An Intimate Biography* (New York, 1981), pp. 63–67. See also Ronald Spector, "Passage to Jutland," *MHQ: Quarterly Journal of Military History*, Spring 1989, pp. 116–117.

118. Fiske, *From Midshipman to Rear Admiral*, p. 621.

119. Peter D. Karsten, "The Naval Aristocracy: U.S. Naval Officers from the 1840s to the 1920s: Mahan's Messmates" (Ph.D. Dissertation, University of Wisconsin, 1968), p. 357.

120. Ibid.

121. W. S. Sims, "Memorandum on Fiske's Work," 1907, Sims Papers; Coletta, *Admiral Bradley A. Fiske*, pp. xiii–ix, 9–13, 40–41.

122. "Quarterdeck" [Fullam], "A Navy of Three Planes," *New York Herald Tribune*, 24 January 1919, p. 36, Fullam Papers.

123. Karsten, "Naval Aristocracy," p. 365.

124. S. W. Perry, *USNIP*, 1890, p. 523.

125. Letter W. F. Fullam to Fiske, 11 January 1912, Sims Papers.

126. Morison, *Sims*, p. 179.

127. Letter Rear Admiral William A. Moffett to Captain Powers Symington, 16 February 1925, cited in Edward Arpee, *From Frigates to Flat-tops* (private publication, 1953), p. 100.

128. Fiske, *From Midshipmen to Rear Admiral*, p. 88.

129. Letter A. L. Key to Sims, 29 November 1922, Sims Papers; Morison, *Sims*, p. 183.

130. Letter Frederick Winslow Taylor to Secretary of the Navy George von L. Meyer, 10 April 1910, Sims Papers.

131. Karsten, "Naval Aristocracy," p. 367.

132. Memorandum Wims to T. Roosevelt, 1909, Sims Papers.

133. Morris Janowitz, *The Professional Soldier: A Social and Political Portrait* (New York, 1960), p. 64.

134. Letter Fullam to Bradley Fiske, 8 September 1904, Fullam Papers.

135. Richard Wainwright, "The General Board," *USNIP* 48, no. 2 (February 1922), p. 193.

136. Ibid.

137. W. S. Sims, "Memorandum of Fiske's Work: 1904–1907," 1907, Sims Papers.

138. Memorandum W. S. Sims to Roosevelt, 1909, Sims Papers.

139. Richard Wainwright, "The New Naval Academy," *World's Work* 4 (1902), pp. 2275–2280.

140. Karsten, "Naval Aristocracy," pp. 400–401.

141. Letter C. H. Davis to W. F. Fullam, April 1896, Fullam Papers.

142. Park Benjamin, "The United States Naval Academy" (New York, 1900), p. 342; Bowen, *Ships, Machinery, and Mossbacks*, pp. 16–17.

143. Harris, *The Age of the Battleship*, p. 135.

144. Memorandum W. S. Sims to T. Roosevelt, 25 November 1908, Sims Papers.

145. Memorandum Mahan to T. Roosevelt, 16 October 1902, Mahan Papers.

146. Letter Rodgers to W. S. Sims, 23 October 1904, Rodgers Papers.

147. W. L. Rodgers, "Lecture Delivered to the Post-Graduate Class of the Naval Academy, 6 October 1923, on Duties of the General Board," Rodgers Papers; Memorandum from General Board to the Secretary of the Navy, 12 October 1900, Dewey Papers.

148. Morison, *Sims*, p. 183.

149. Henry Reuterdahl, "The Needs of Our Navy," *McClure's*, January 1908, pp. 260, 263.

150. Morison, *Sims*, p. 184.

151. Letter W. S. Fullam to W. S. Sims, 25 February 1908, Sims Papers.

152. W. S. Sims, Marginal Note on Memorandum, "Suggestion for Board on Design," Sims Papers; Letter Sims to M. deWolfe Howe, 25 September 1919, Sims Papers.

153. H. Poundstone, "Remarks on the Reorganization of the Navy," Poundstone Papers.

154. Yates Stirling, *Sea Duty: The Memoirs of a Fighting Admiral* (New York, 1939), p. 139.

155. Letter Sims to T. Roosevelt, 10 August 1908, Sims Papers.

156. "Certain Needs of the Navy: Message from the President," 25 February 1909, Mahan Papers. The membership consisted of ex-secretaries Dayton, Moody, and Morton, and retired admirals Luce, Mahan, William N. Folger, William S. Cowles, and Robley D. Evans.

157. Morison, *Sims*, pp. 228–9.

158. Letter Dewey to Henry C. Taylor, 29 October 1900, Dewey Papers.

159. Stirling, *Sea Duty*, p. 199.

160. "Selectionist" [Sims], "Promotion by Selection in the Navy," 27 August 1906, Sims Papers.

161. Morison, *Sims*, p. 68.

162. "Selectionist" [Sims], "Promotion by Selection in the Navy."

163. Morison, *Sims*, p. 322.

164. Memorandum, Albert Gleaves to the Secretary of the Navy, 26 July 1909, Gleaves Papers.

165. Ronald Spector, *Admiral of the New Empire: The Life and Career of George Dewey* (Baton Rouge, 1974), p. 123.

166. Letter George Creel to Secretary of the Navy Josephus Daniels, 23 July 1916, Dewey Papers.

167. Fiske, *From Midshipman to Rear Admiral*, p. 475; Spector, *Admiral of the New Empire*, pp. 123, 127; Braisted, *The Navy in the Pacific, 1909–1922*, p. 4; Bowen, *Ships, Machinery and Mossbacks*, p. 54; Letter Dewey to H. Poundstone, 27 September 1907, Dewey Papers; Letter Bradley Fiske to Dewey, 13 August 1914, Dewey Papers; Secretary of the Navy Daniels to Dewey, 7 July 1915, Dewey Papers; 23 July 1915, Dewey Papers; Letter L. C. Lucas to Admiral Johnson, 23 December 1916, Papers of Hilary P. Jones, Naval Historical Foundation, Library of Congress.

168. Wainwright, "The General Board," p. 194.

169. Thadius V. Tuleja, *Statesmen and Admirals: Quest for a Far Eastern Policy* (New York, 1968), p. 34; Warner R. Schilling, "Admirals and Foreign Policy, 1913–1919" (Ph.D. Dissertation, Yale University, 1955), pp. 106–108.

170. Letter Senator George Perkins to Mahan, 7 January 1911, Mahan Papers.

171. F. E. Chadwick to Dewey, 10 October 1903, File 420, General Board Papers.

172. Braisted, *The Navy in the Pacific, 1897–1909*, p. 174.

173. Dewey to Secretary of the Navy Metcalf, 25 April 1907, Navy Department, General Board letter press.

174. Braisted, *The Navy in the Pacific, 1897–1909*, p. 239; George Dewey to Secretary of the Navy Meyer, 6 November 1910, Navy Department General Board letter press.

175. Hovgaard, *Modern History of Warships*, pp. 106–107; Braisted, *The Navy in the Pacific, 1909–1922*, p. 59.

176. Tuleja, *Statesmen and Admirals*, p. 43.

177. Sprout and Sprout, *Rise of American Naval Power*, pp. 251–252; Braisted, *The Navy in the Pacific, 1897–1909*, p. 171.

178. Braisted, *The Navy in the Pacific, 1909–1922*, p. 20.

179. Ibid., pp. 58, 521.

180. Extract from *Washington Herald*, 12 April 1913, Study File 420-2, General Board Papers.

181. Letter Dewey to Secretary of the Navy, 9 February 1903, Study File 420-2, General Board Papers.

182. Karsten, "Naval Aristocracy," p. 449; John D. Long, *The New American Navy* (New York, 1903), vol. 2, pp. 163–164; Spector, *Admiral of the New Empire*, p. 151.

183. Letter Dewey to Hayne Davis, 29 October 1910, Dewey Papers.

184. "Confidential Memorandum for the Information of the Secretary of the Navy in Connection with Building Programs for Fiscal Year Ending 30 June 1912," 15 October 1910, Study File 420-2, General Board Papers.

185. Letter from Senior Member of the General Board to the Secretary of the Navy, 1 July 1914, Study File 420-2, General Board Papers.

186. Wainwright, "The General Board," pp. 195–196; Braisted, *The Navy in the Pacific, 1909–1922*, p. 5.

187. Naval Constructor R. D. Gatewood, "Memorandum on Battleships Design," 16 September 1913, Study File 420-2, General Board Papers.

188. Letter Dewey to Naval Constructor Francis T. Bowles, 17 February 1903, Dewey Papers.

189. W. D. Puleston, *Annapolis: Gangway to Quarterdeck* (New York, 1942), p. 12.

190. Memorandum from the President of the General Board to the Secretary of the Navy, 3 May 1916, Study File 420-2, General Board Papers.

191. Letter Dewey to C. F. Goodrich, 17 November 1905, Dewey Papers.

192. Hough, *Dreadnought*, pp. 244–246; Randal Gray, ed., *Conway's All the World's Fighting Ships: 1906–1921* (London, 1985), pp. 112–116.

193. Resolution, Senator Tillman, Committee on Naval Affairs, Senate, 16 July 1912, Study File 420-6, General Board Papers.

194. Letter Acting Secretary Beekman Winthrop to Chairman of Committee on Naval Affairs (Tillman), 18 July 1912, Study File 420-6, General Board Papers.

195. Letter Tillman to Beekman Winthrop, 19 July 1912, Study File 420-6, General Board Papers.

196. Memorandum for the General Board from Bureau of Construction and Repair, 23 July 1912, Study File 420-6, General Board Papers.

197. Braisted, *Navy in the Pacific, 1909–1922*, p. 508. With the advent of the supercarrier, the U.S. Navy would indeed build ships too large to transit the canal.

198. Charles J. Badger to the Secretary of the Navy, 31 July 1920, Study File 426-1, Serial 1010, General Board Papers.

199. Fiske, *From Midshipman to Rear Admiral*, p. 478.

200. Memorandum from General Board to the Navy Department, 14 December 1910, Study File 420-6, General Board Papers.

201. Letter President of the General Board to Navy Department, 17 January 1912, Study File 420-6, General Board Papers.

202. Memorandum from General Board to Secretary of the Navy, 29 August 1911, Study File 420-6, General Board Papers.

203. Letter Sims to Admiral H. B. Jackson, RN, 2 November 1911; Letter H. I. Cone to Sims, 16 April 1912; Letter Sims to H. I. Cone, 22 April 1912, Sims Papers.

204. Letter Schofield to General Board, 3 January 1907, Study File 420-6, General Board Papers.

205. Ibid.

206. Letter President of the Naval War College to the President of the General Board, 29 March 1907, Study File 420-6, General Board Papers.

207. Endorsement George Dewey to Secretary of the Navy, 27 March 1908, Study File 420-6, General Board Papers.

208. Memorandum from Commander Frank H. Schofield to the President of the Naval War College, 21 September 1911, Study File 420-6, General Board Papers.

209. Memorandum from the President of the General Board to Secretary of the Navy, 17 October 1911, "Subject: Bureau of Construction and Repair's Suggestion that a Torpedo Battleship be Included in Building Program of 1913," Study File 420-6, General Board Papers.

Chapter Six

1. Edward MacCurdy, *The Notebooks of Leonardo da Vinci* (New York, 1939), p. 33.

2. Alex Roland, *Underwater Warfare in the Age of Sail* (Bloomington, Ind., 1978), p. 33.

3. William Hovgaard, *Modern History of Warships: Comprising a Discussion of Present Standpoint and Recent War Experiences* (New York, 1920), p. 439.

4. Roland, *Underwater Warfare*, pp. 70–71.

5. Bernard Brodie and Fawn Brodie, *From Crossbow to H-Bomb* (Bloomington, Ind., 1972), p. 118.

6. Ibid.

7. Charles Domville-Fife, *The Submarine and Seapower* (New York, 1923), pp. 202.

8. Hovgaard, *Modern History of Warships*, p. 440.

9. Stephen Roskill, *The Strategy of Sea Power* (London, 1962), p. 105; Julian S. Corbett, *Some Principles of Naval Strategy* (London, 1960), p. 181.

10. Richard Hough, *The Death of the Battleship* (New York, 1963), p. 6.

11. Hovgaard, *Modern History of Warships*, p. 452; Richard Compton-Hall, *Submarine Boats: The Beginning of Underwater Warfare* (New York, 1984), pp. 128–129.

12. Hovgaard, *Modern History of Warships*, p. 452.

13. E. B. Potter et al., *The United States and World Sea Power* (Englewood Cliffs, N.J., 1955), p. 391.

14. Hovgaard, *Modern History of Warships*, p. 452.

15. Potter et al., *United States and World Sea Power*, p. 391.

16. "Report of Bombing Maneuvers Drawn from 1923 Bombing, Hatteras," 5 September 1923, Papers of William D. Mitchell, Library of Congress.

17. Theodore Ropp, "Continental Doctrines of Sea Power," in *The Makers of Modern Strategy*, ed. Edward M. Earle (Princeton, 1943), p. 447.

18. Ibid., p. 449.

19. Hough, *The Death of the Battleship*, p. 8.

20. Potter et al., *United States and World Sea Power*, p. 392; Hovgaard, *Modern Hisory of Warships*, p. 263.

21. Letter Babcock to Sims, 28 April 1903, Sims Papers.

22. Letter Keit to Admiral George Dewey, 24 December 1902, Sims Papers.

23. Letter Sims to Lieutenant R. A. White, 22 July 1910, Sims Papers; see also Letter Sims to Commander T. R. Griffin, August 1906, Sims Papers.

24. Domville-Fife, *Submarine and Seapower*, p. 8; John P. Holland, "The Submarine Boat and Its Future," *North American Review*, December 1900, p. 54.

25. Compton-Hall, *Submarine Boats*, pp. 43–44.

26. Richard Knowles Morris, *John P. Holland* (Annapolis, Md., 1966), pp. 14, 20, 37.

27. J. P. Holland, "Notes on the Fenian Ram," pp. 5–6, Memoirs, in the Patterson [N.J.] Museum, cited in Morris, *Holland*, p. 42.

28. Compton-Hall, *Submarine Boats*, pp. 56–57.

29. Morris, *Holland*, p. 42.

30. Ibid., p. 64.

31. Hovgaard, *Modern History of Warships*, p. 291.

32. Wilbur Cross, *Challengers of the Deep* (New York, 1959), p. 53; Morris, *Holland*, p. 70.

33. Morris, *Holland*, p. 79.

34. Hovgaard, *Modern History of Warships*, p. 291.

35. Morris, *Holland*, p. 89.

36. Cross, *Challengers of the Deep*, p. 52; Compton-Hall, *Submarine Boats*, p. 96.

37. Testimony of Admiral George Dewey taken by House Committee on Naval Affairs, 23 April 1900, Dewey Papers.

38. *Daily Times* [Troy, N.Y.], 22 December 1900, cited in Morris, *Holland*, p. 116.

39. Lee J. Levert, *Fundamentals of Naval Warfare* (New York, 1947), p. 187.

40. Bernard Brodie, *A Layman's Guide to Naval Strategy* (Princeton, 1942), p. 252.

41. Donald G. Macintyre, *The Thunder of the Guns: A Century of Battleships* (New York, 1959), p. 47.

42. "Report of the Reconciling Committee on Question 21," U.S. Naval War College, 21 August 1909, Sims Papers.

43. Lieutenant D. C. Bingham, "The Military Value of the Submarine," a paper delivered to the Naval War College, 30 September 1910, Sims Papers.

44. Arthur Hezlet, *The Submarine and Sea Power* (New York, 1967), p. 23; Hovgaard, *Modern History of Warships*, p. 310; Philip K. Lundeberg, "Undersea Warfare and Allied Strategy in World War I, Part I, to 1916," *Smithsonian Journal of History* 3 (1966), p. 6.

45. Randal Gray, *Conway's All the World's Fighting Ships: 1906–1921* (London, 1985), p. 87.

46. Ibid., p. 176.

47. Ropp, "Continental Doctrines of Sea Power," p. 453.

48. Arthur J. Marder, *The Anatomy of British Sea Power* (New York, 1940), p. 358.

49. Bernard Brodie, *Sea Power in the Machine Age* (Princeton, 1941), p. 267.

50. Bingham, "The Military Value of the Submarine."

51. Arthur J. Marder, *From Dreadnought to Scapa Flow*, 4 vols. (London, 1961), vol. 1, p. 332.

52. Yates Stirling, *Sea Duty: The Memoirs of a Fighting Admiral* (New York, 1939), p. 154.

53. Sutherland Denlinger and Charles B. Gary, *War in the Pacific: A Study of Peoples and Battle Problems* (New York, 1936), p. 76.

54. Memorandum from Naval Constructor E. S. Land to General Board, 9 February 1916, Sims Papers.

55. Morris, *Holland*, p. 7.

56. Denlinger and Gary, *War in the Pacific*, p. 76.

57. John Arbuthnot Fisher, *Memories and Records*, 2 vols. (New York, 1920), vol. 2, p. 170.

58. Ibid., vol. 1, p. 175.

59. Lundeberg, "Undersea Warfare and Allied Strategy," p. 6.

60. Alfred P. von Tirpitz, *My Memoirs*, 2 vols. (New York, 1919), vol. 1, pp. 196–197.

61. Louis M. Hacker, "The Incendiary Mahan," *Scribner's*, April 1934, p. 318.

62. *Conway's All the World's Fighting Ships*, p. 173.

63. Stirling, *Sea Duty*, p. 154.

64. Ridley McLean, "Submarines, Their Function in War: Types and Numbers Required, Value and Training," 21 December 1910, Sims Papers.

65. Bingham, "The Military Value of the Submarine."

66. McLean, "Submarines, Their Function in War."

67. Richard Wainwright, "The General Board," *USNIP* 48, no. 2 (February 1922), p. 197.

68. Harold and Margaret Sprout, *The Rise of American Naval Power: 1776–1918* (Princeton, 1959), p. 269, n. 70.

69. Letter George Dewey to Henry H. Ward, 23 November 1914, Dewey Papers.

70. Vincent Davis, *The Admiral's Lobby* (Chapel Hill, 1967), pp. 60–61; Archibald D. Turnbull and Clifford L. Lord, *History of United States Aviation* (New Haven, 1949), p. 7, n. 10.

71. Turnbull and Lord, *United States Aviation*, p. 7, n. 10.

72. Edward Arpee, *From Frigates to Flat-tops* (private publication, 1953), p. 72.

73. Turnbull and Lord, *United States Aviation*, pp. 12–13.

74. Ibid., p. 62.

Chapter Seven

1. Letter King George V to Admiral Sir John Jellicoe, 5 August 1914, cited in Geoffrey Bennett, *The Battle of Jutland* (Philadelphia, 1964), p. 29.

2. Arthur J. Marder, *From Dreadnought to Scapa Flow*, 4 vols. (London, 1961), vol. 2, p. 4; Alfred P. von Tirpitz, *My Memoirs*, 2 vols. (New York, 1919), vol. 1, p. 345.

3. Richard Hough, *The Great Dreadnought: The Strange Story of the HMS Agincourt* (New York, 1967), p. 13; Winston S. Churchill, *The World Crisis* (New York, 1923), vol. 2, p. 222.

4. Churchill, *The World Crisis*, vol. 2, p. 545.

5. Thomas G. Frothingham, *The Naval History of the World War*, 2 vols. (Cambridge, Mass., 1924), vol. 1, p. 77.

6. Marder, *From Dreadnought to Scapa Flow*, vol. 2, p. 21.

7. Geoffrey Bennett, *Naval Battles of the First World War* (New York, 1969), p. 27.

8. Frothingham, *Naval History of the World War*, vol. 1, p. 84; Dan van der Vat, *The Ship that Changed the World: The Escape of the Goeben to the Dardanelles in 1914* (Bethesda, Md., 1986), p. 76.

9. Telegram, Tirpitz to Souchon, 4 August 1914, cited in Bennett, *Naval Battles of the First World War*, p. 30.

10. Wray's testimony, "Proceedings of the Troubridge Court Martial," p. 42, cited in Marder, *From Dreadnought to Scapa Flow*, vol. 2, p. 26.

11. van der Vat, *Ship that Changed the World*, Ch. 9.

12. Alfred P. Tirpitz, *My Memoirs*, 2 vols. (New York, 1919), vol. 2, p. 82.

13. van der Vat, *Ship that Changed the World*, pp. 187–190.

14. Jonathan Steinberg, *Yesterday's Deterrent: Tirpitz and the Birth of the German Fleet* (London, 1965), pp. 28, 328.

15. Marder, *From Dreadnought to Scapa Flow*, vol. 3, p. 189.

16. Sir Percy Scott, *Fifty Years in the Royal Navy* (London, 1919), p. 196.

17. Steinberg, *Yesterday's Deterrent*, p. 37.

18. Tirpitz, *Memoirs*, vol. 2, p. 396.

19. Marder, *From Dreadnought to Scapa Flow*, vol. 2, p. 19.

20. Reinhard Scheer, *Germany's High Seas Fleet in the World War* (London, 1920), p. 11.

21. Marder, *From Dreadnought to Scapa Flow*, vol. 3, p. 19.

22. Ibid., vol. 3, p. 18.

23. Scott, *Fifty Years in the Royal Navy*, p. 198.

24. Marder, *From Dreadnought to Scapa Flow*, vol. 2, p. 40.

25. Franklin Percival, "Fisher and His Warships," *USNIP*, August 1939, p. 1109.

26. Marder, *From Dreadnought to Scapa Flow*, vol. 2, p. 47.

27. Scheer, *Germany's High Seas Fleet*, p. 11.

28. Tirpitz, *Memoirs*, vol. 2, p. 93.

29. Marder, *From Dreadnought to Scapa Flow*, vol. 2, p. 42.

30. Scheer, *Germany's High Seas Fleet*, p. 25.

31. Bennett, *Jutland*, p. 35.

32. Ibid., p. 36.

33. Bennett, *Jutland*, p. 38.

34. Marder, *From Dreadnought to Scapa Flow*, vol. 2, p. 62.

35. Reginald Bacon, *The Life of Lord Fisher of Kilverstone*, vol. 1 (Garden City, 1929), p. 191.

36. Marder, *From Dreadnought to Scapa Flow*, vol. 2, p. 48.

37. Arthur J. Marder, *Portrait of an Admiral: The Life and Papers of Sir Herbert Richmond* (London, 1952), p. 121.

38. Marder, *From Dreadnought to Scapa Flow*, vol. 2, p. 55.

39. John Jellicoe, *The Grand Fleet, 1914–1916: Its Creation, Development, and Work* (New York, 1919), pp. 397–398; A. Temple Patterson, *Jellicoe: A Biography* (London, 1969), p. 44; John Winton, *Jellicoe* (London, 1981), pp. 154, 171.

40. John Arbuthnot Fisher, *Memories and Records* (New York, 1920), vol. 1, p. 51.

41. Hough, *Dreadnought*, p. 147.

42. A. A. Hoeling, *The Great War at Sea* (New York, 1965), p. 107; Stephen Roskill, *Admiral of the Fleet Earl Beatty, the Last Naval Hero: An Intimate Biography* (New York, 1981), pp. 46–47.

43. Marder, *From Dreadnought to Scapa Flow*, vol. 2, p. 11.

44. Ibid., vol. 2, p. 398.

45. Letter David Beatty to Lady Beatty, 21 May 1915, cited in Marder, *From Dreadnought to Scapa Flow*, vol. 2, p. 413.

46. Letter Scott to *London Times*, 15 December 1913 (printed 5 June 1914, p. 9).

47. Marder, *From Dreadnought to Scapa Flow*, vol. 1, p. 333.

48. Scheer, *Germany's High Seas Fleet*, p. 58.

49. Frothingham, *Naval History of the World War*, vol. 1, p. 68.

50. Hoeling, *Great War at Sea*, p. 45.

51. Weddigen quoted in ibid., p. 48.

52. Marder, *From Dreadnought to Scapa Flow*, vol. 2, p. 55.

53. Hoeling, *Great War at Sea*, p. 52.

54. Marder, *From Dreadnought to Scapa Flow*, vol. 2, p. 56; Richard Compton-Hall, *Submarine Boats: The Beginning of Underwater Warfare* (New York, 1984), p. 174.

55. Richard Hough, *The Great War at Sea: 1914–1919* (Oxford, 1983), p. 62.

56. Jellicoe, *The Grand Fleet*, p. 207; Hoeling, *Great War at Sea*, p. 59.

57. Kenneth Edwards, *We Dive at Dawn* (London, 1924), p. 369.

58. Archibald Hurd, *The British Fleet in the Great War* (New York, 1918), p. 193.

59. Marder, *From Dreadnought to Scapa Flow*, vol. 2, p. 349.

60. Ibid., vol. 2, p. 349.

61. W. F. Fullam, "What is a Strong Navy?" *New York Tribune*, 16 June 1919.

62. Frothingham, *Naval History of the World War*, p. 102.

63. H. M. LeFleming, *The ABC Warships of World War I* (London, 1962), p. 312.

64. Jellicoe, *The Grand Fleet*, p. 77.

65. Letter Jellicoe to Winston Churchill, 30 September 1914, Jellicoe Papers, cited in Marder, *From Dreadnought to Scapa Flow*, vol. 2, p. 67.

66. Marder, *From Dreadnought to Scapa Flow*, vol. 2, pp. 66–67.

67. Ibid., vol. 2, pp. 67–68.

68. Letter R.A.R. Plunkett to Herbert Richmond, 21 October 1914, Richmond Papers, cited in Marder, *From Dreadnought to Scapa Flow*, vol. 2, p. 69.

69. Frothingham, *Naval History of the World War*, vol. 1, pp. 150–151; William S. Sims, *Victory at Sea* (Garden City, 1920), p. 205.

70. Letter Tyrwhitt to A. Beauchamp, 9 August 1914, Tyrwhitt Papers, cited in Marder, *From Dreadnought to Scapa Flow*, vol. 2, p. 72.

71. Letter Jellicoe to Admiralty, 30 October 1914, Admiralty Papers, cited in Bennett, *Naval Battles of the First World War*, p. 152.

72. A. Conan Doyle, *Danger* (London, 1913), p. 16.

73. Ibid., p. 40.

74. Ibid., pp. v–vi.

75. Tirpitz, *Memoirs*, vol. 2, p. 415; Ernest R. May, *The World War and American Isolation* (Chicago, 1959), p. 115.

76. Marder, *From Dreadnought to Scapa Flow*, vol. 2, p. 343.

77. Memorandum by Hugo von Pohl, 7 November 1914, cited in Scheer, *Germany's High Seas Fleet*, p. 222.

78. May, *The World War and American Isolation*, p. 118.

79. Tirpitz, *Memoirs*, vol. 2, p. 142; Scheer, *Germany's High Seas Fleet*, p. 225.

80. *Foreign Relations of the United States*, Supplement 1915 (Washington, 1916), pp. 96–97.

81. Marder, *From Dreadnought to Scapa Flow*, vol. 2, p. 345.

82. Ibid.

83. May, *The World War and American Isolation*, p. 132; Marder, *From Dreadnought to Scapa Flow*, vol. 2, p. 345.

84. Colin Simpson, *The Lusitania* (Boston, 1972).

85. Charles Seymour, "American Neutrality: The Experience of 1914–1917," *Foreign Affairs*, October 1935.

86. Letter Wilson to Senator William J. Stone, 24 February 1916, in Ray Stannard Baker, *Woodrow Wilson: Life and Letters*, 6 vols. (Garden City, 1937), vol. 6, p. 168.

87. Marder, *From Dreadnought to Scapa Flow*, vol. 2, p. 345.

88. Arthur S. Link, *Woodrow Wilson and the Progressive Era* (New York, 1954), p. 168.

89. Ibid.

90. Samuel Dumas and K. O. Vedel-Petersen, *Losses of Life Caused by War, Part II, the World War* (London, 1923), p. 139.

91. George von Muller, Diary, 9 February 1916, cited in Walter Gorlitz, ed., *The Kaiser and His Court: Notebooks and Letters of Admiral George Alexander von Muller* (London, 1961), pp. 133–134.

92. Scheer, *Germany's High Seas Fleet*, p. 218.

93. Commander Bartenback to Admiral Z. D. Dick, 10 April 1916, cited in Tirpitz, *Memoirs*, vol. 2, p. 424.

94. Tirpitz, *Memoirs*, vol. 2, p. 202.

95. Frank G. Percival, "The Tirpitz Technique," *USNIP*, April 1937, p. 1255.

96. Bennett, *Naval Battles of the First World War*, pp. 86–87, 91.

97. Jack Sweetman, "Coronel: Anatomy of a Disaster," in *Naval Warfare in the Twentieth Century, 1900–1945: Essays in Honor of Arthur Marder*, ed. Gerald Jordan (London, 1977), pp. 70–89.

98. Hoeling, *Great War at Sea*, p. 61; Ronald Bassett, *Battle Cruisers: A History, 1908–1948* (London, 1981), p. 63.

99. Frothingham, *Naval History of the World War*, vol. 1, pp. 180, 182.

100. Marder, *From Dreadnought to Scapa Flow*, vol. 2, p. 120; Hough, *Great War at Sea*, p. 105.

101. Frothingham, *Naval History of the World War*, vol. 1, p. 172.

102. Marder, *From Dreadnought to Scapa Flow*, vol. 2, p. 121; Hough, *Great War at Sea*, p. 113.

103. Hoeling, *Great War at Sea*, p. 74.

104. Bennett, *Naval Battles of the First World War*, pp. 115, 117.

105. Edward Bingham, *Falklands, Jutland, and the Bight* (London, 1919), p. 47.

106. Bennett, *Naval Battles of the First World War*, p. 120.

107. Hans Pochhammer, *Before Jutland* (London, 1931), p. 68.

108. Bennett, *Naval Battles of the First World War*, p. 112.

109. Fisher, *Memories and Records*, vol. 2, pp. 231–232.

110. Marder, *From Dreadnought to Scapa Flow*, vol. 2, p. 123.

111. Bennett, *Naval Battles of the First World War*, p. 118.

112. Marder, *From Dreadnought to Scapa Flow*, vol. 2, p. 12; Bennett, *Naval Battles of the First World War*, p. 112.

113. Bennett, *Jutland*, p. 43.

114. Churchill, *The World Crisis*, vol. 2, p. 131.

115. Marder, *From Dreadnought to Scapa Flow*, vol. 2, p. 159; Hough, *Great War at Sea*, p. 133; Bassett, *Battle Cruisers*, p. 80.

116. Scheer, *Germany's High Seas Fleet*, p. 81; Bennett, *Naval Battles of the First World War*, p. 161; E. B. Potter et al., *The United States and World Sea Power* (Englewood Cliffs, N.J., 1955), p. 492.

117. Bennett, *Naval Battles of the First World War*, p. 162.

118. Marder, *From Dreadnought to Scapa Flow*, vol. 2, pp. 160–161; Potter et al., *United States and World Sea Power*, pp. 492–493; Hough, *Great War at Sea*, p. 137.

119. Bennett, *Naval Battles of the First World War*, p. 165.

120. Narrative by two of *Blucher's* survivors, cited in Fisher, *Memories and Records*, vol. 1, pp. 127, 153.

121. Marder, *From Dreadnought to Scapa Flow*, vol. 2, p. 164.

122. Hough, *Great War at Sea*, p. 139.

123. Marder, *From Dreadnought to Scapa Flow*, vol. 2, pp. 160, 170.

124. Hough, *Great War at Sea*, p. 141.

125. Donald G. MacIntyre, *Jutland* (New York, 1958), p. 94.

126. Bennett, *Naval Battles of the First World War*, pp. 164–165.

127. Bennett, *Jutland*, p. 51.

128. MacIntyre, *Jutland*, p. 100; Bennett, *Jutland*, p. 52.

129. Scheer, *Germany's High Seas Fleet*, pp. 134–135.

130. Hough, *Great War at Sea*, p. 203.

131. Jellicoe, *The Grand Fleet*, pp. 200–201.

132. Hough, *Dreadnought*, p. 149.

133. Ibid., p. 149.

134. Bennett, *Jutland*, p. 52.

135. Ibid., p. 63.

136. Ibid., pp. 59–60.

137. According to the logic of the game board, the Grand Fleet's advantage went considerably beyond simple numbers of ships. Fully 344, 12- to 15-inch English pieces could be brought to bear on 244 German 11- and 12-inch guns. As if this were not enough, progressively increasing projectile weights produced a collosal 401,260 pound to 167,320 pound British advantage in the supposedly critical weight of broadside.

138. Potter et al., *United States and World Sea Power*, p. 520.

139. Bennett, *Jutland*, p. 69.

140. Holloway H. Frost, *The Battle of Jutland* (Annapolis, 1936), p. 147.

141. Bennett, *Jutland*, p. 72; Hough, *Great War at Sea*, p. 217.

142. Frost, *Jutland*, p. 175.

143. Hough, *Great War at Sea*, p. 220.

144. Bennett, *Jutland*, p. 77.

145. W. S. Chalmers, *The Life and Letters of David Earl Beatty* (London, 1951), p. xxi.

146. Frost, *Jutland*, p. 203.

147. Hough, *Great War at Sea*, p. 222.

148. Bennett, *Jutland*, p. 78.

149. MacIntyre, *Jutland*, p. 138; Frost, *Jutland*, p. 213; George von Hase, *Kiel and Jutland* (London, 1921), p. 148; Bassett, *Battle Cruisers*, p. 113.

150. Von Hase, *Kiel and Jutland*, p. 161.

151. Francis's narrative cited in Bennett, *Jutland*, p. 83; Hoeling, *Great War at Sea*, p. 117.

152. Hoeling, *Great War at Sea*, p. 117.

153. Roskill, *Admiral of the Fleet Earl Beatty*, p. 160.

154. Marder, *From Dreadnought to Scapa Flow*, vol. 2, p. 438.

155. Hough, *Dreadnought*, p. 87.

156. From a series of lectures on Jutland by Admiral Sir William Tennant, cited in Bennett, *Jutland*, p. 86.

157. Bennett, *Jutland*, pp. 87–88.

158. Jellicoe, *The Grand Fleet*, p. 330.

159. MacIntyre, *Jutland*, pp. 143–144; Bennett, *Jutland*, p. 50.

160. Hough, *Great War at Sea*, p. 236.

161. Marder, *From Dreadnought to Scapa Flow*, vol. 3, pp. 77, 79.

162. Ibid.

163. Frost, *Jutland*, p. 299; MacIntyre, *Jutland*, p. 155.

164. Patterson, *Jellicoe*, p. 119.

165. Frederick Dreyer, *The Sea Heritage* (London, 1936), p. 146.

166. Bennett, *Jutland*, p. 10.

167. Frost, *Jutland*, p. 310.

168. Hough, *Great War at Sea*, p. 245.

169. From a post-Jutland interview with Dannreuther, cited in Hoeling, *Great War at Sea*, p. 125.

170. Von Hase, *Kiel and Jutland*, p. 371; Frost, *Jutland*, pp. 326–327.

171. Bennett, *Naval Battles of the First World War*, p. 204.

172. Hoeling, *Great War at Sea*, p. 125; Hough, *Great War at Sea*, p. 247; Bassett, *Battle Cruisers*, p. 123.

173. Marder, *From Dreadnought to Scapa Flow*, vol. 3, p. 99.

174. Bennett, *Naval Battles of the First World War*, p. 78.

175. Frothingham, *Naval History of the World War*, vol. 2, p. 148.

176. Marder, *From Dreadnought to Scapa Flow*, vol. 3, p. 104.

177. Ibid.

178. Hoeling, *Great War at Sea*, p. 135.

179. Scheer, *Germany's High Seas Fleet*, p. 153.

180. Frost, *Jutland*, p. 328; MacIntyre, *Jutland*, p. 173; Bennett, *Jutland*, p. 113.

181. A fortnight after the battle, Scheer remarked to an Austrian naval attaché, "If I had fought such an action in peacetime, I should have lost my command—but it was necessary to escape!"

182. Jellicoe, *The Grand Fleet*, pp. 354–355; Frost, *Jutland*, pp. 340–341.

183. Frost, *Jutland*, p. 348.

184. Von Hase, *Kiel and Jutland*, p. 286.

185. Frost, *Jutland*, p. 354.

186. MacIntyre, *Jutland*, pp. 184–185.

187. Von Hase, *Kiel and Jutland*, p. 289.

188. MacIntyre, *Jutland*, pp. 51–52; Marder, *From Dreadnought to Scapa Flow*, vol. 2, p. 440.

189. Scheer, *Germany's High Seas Fleet*, p. 156; Bennett, *Jutland*, p. 121.

190. Frost, *Jutland*, p. 369.

191. Bennett, *Naval History of the Great War*, p. 209.

192. Bassett, *Battle Cruisers*, p. 126; Frost, *Jutland*, p. 384.

193. Bennett, *Jutland*, p. 153.

194. Oscar Parkes, *British Battleships* (London, 1956), p. 141; Chalmers, *Beatty*, p. 262.

195. MacIntyre, *Jutland*, p. 250.

196. Marder, *From Dreadnought to Scapa Flow*, vol. 3, p. 203; Bennett, *Jutland*, p. 203; Hough, *Great War at Sea*, p. 296.

197. Marder, *From Dreadnought to Scapa Flow*, vol. 3, p. 167.

198. John Keegan, *The Price of Admiralty* (New York, 1988), pp. 142, 151–153.

199. Scheer cited in Hoeling, *Great War at Sea*, pp. 150–151.

200. Arthur Hezlet, *The Submarine and Sea Power* (New York, 1967), pp. 59–60; Marder, *From Dreadnought to Scapa Flow*, vol. 3, p. 256.

201. MacIntyre, *Jutland*, p. 273; Frost, *Jutland*, p. 529.

202. Memorandum to the First Lord of the Admiralty from John Jellicoe, 20 October 1916, cited in Marder, *From Dreadnought to Scapa Flow*, vol. 3, p. 279.

203. Ibid.

204. Jellicoe, *The Grand Fleet*, pp. 215, 276–277.

Chapter Eight

1. William R. Braisted, *The United States Navy in the Pacific, 1909–1922* (Austin, Tex., 1971), pp. 124–125.

2. Tracy B. Kittredge, *Naval Lessons of the Great War* (Garden City, 1921), p. 212.

3. Braisted, *Navy in the Pacific, 1909–1922*, pp. 124–125.

4. Testimony of W. F. Fullam before 1920 Naval Hearings, quoted in Kittredge, *Naval Lessons of the Great War*, p. 250.

5. Robert W. Nesser, *The Battleship as an Educational Institution* (Washington, 1913), p. 3; Paolo Coleta, *Admiral Bradley A. Fiske and the American Navy* (Lawrence, Kan., 1979), p. 160.

6. Testimony of Fullam, 1920 Naval Hearings, in Kittredge, *Naval Lessons of the Great War*, p. 250.

7. Ronald Spector, *Admiral of the New Empire: The Life and Career of George Dewey* (Baton Rouge, 1974), p. 191.

8. William D. Leahy, Diary, p. 210, Leahy Papers, Library of Congress.

9. Josephus Daniels, *The Wilson Era: Years of Peace, 1910–1917* (Chapel Hill, 1944), p. 501.

10. Ibid., p. 239.

11. Kittredge, *Naval Lessons of the Great War*, p. 212.

12. Bradley A. Fiske, *From Midshipman to Rear Admiral* (New York, 1919), pp. 565–566; Letter Ridley McLean to W. S. Sims, 30 December 1914, Sims Papers.

13. Bradley Fiske, Diary, 3–7 January 1915, Fiske Papers.

14. Ibid.

15. Fiske, *From Midshipman to Rear Admiral*, p. 560; Ernest J. King and Walter M. Whitehall, *Fleet Admiral King: A Naval Record* (New York, 1952), pp. 102–103.

16. Stephen Roskill, *Naval Policy Between the Wars* (London, 1968), vol. 1, pp. 53–55; King and Whitehall, *A Naval Record*, p. 103; Braisted, *Navy in the Pacific, 1909–1922*, p. 183; Coleta, *Fiske*, pp. 158–159.

17. Daniels, *The Wilson Era*, p. 239.

18. Letter Dewey to Secretary of the Navy Daniels, 5 March 1915, Dewey Papers.

19. Albert Gleaves, Diary, 4 August 1914, Gleaves Papers.

20. Memorandum from the General Board to Secretary of the Navy, 1 August 1914, Dewey Papers.

21. Kittredge, *Naval Lessons of the Great War*, p. 267.

22. Spector, *Admiral of the New Empire*, p. 187; Warner R. Schilling, "Admirals and Foreign Policy, 1913–1919" (Ph.D. Dissertation, Yale University, 1955), p. 16; David F. Trask, "In a World at War," in *In Peace and War: Interpretations of American Naval History, 1775–1978*, ed. Kenneth J. Hagan (Westport, Conn., 1978), pp. 205–207.

23. Edwin Bickford Hooper, *United States Naval Power in a Changing World* (New York, 1988), p. 124; Coleta, *Fiske*, pp. 117, 132–133.

24. William V. Pratt, "Autobiography" (unpublished), chap. 14, p. 1, Pratt Papers.

25. Braisted, *Navy in the Pacific, 1909–1922*, pp. 171–172; Letter Ridley McLean to W. S. Sims, 30 December 1914, Sims Papers.

26. Memorandum from Commander, Destroyer Flotilla, Atlantic Fleet to Commander-in-Chief, 11 November 1915, Sims Papers; Elting Morison, *Admiral Sims and the Modern American Navy* (Cambridge, Mass., 1942), p. 295.

27. Pratt, "Autobiography," chap. 2, p. 4.

28. Letter Sims to W. F. Fullam, 24 February 1917, Fullam Papers.

29. Memorandum from Commander, Destroyer Flotilla, Atlantic Fleet, to Commander-in-Chief, Atlantic Fleet, 11 November 1915, Sims Papers; Morison, *Sims*, pp. 306–310.

30. Letter Daniels to F. F. Fletcher, 23 January 1915, Frank Friday Fletcher Papers.

31. Letter Sims to Percy Scott, 12 November 1914, Sims Papers.

32. Letter Scott to W. S. Sims, 15 October 1914, Sims Papers.

33. Letter Sims to J. O. Fisher, 19 August 1915, Sims Papers.

34. Letter Fisher to Sims, 22 August 1915, Sims Papers.

35. Kittredge, *Naval Lessons of the Great War*, pp. 187–188.

36. Figures taken from Fletcher Pratt, *The Navy: A History* (Garden City, 1941), pp. 448–449.

37. See for example Memorandum from Naval Constructor E. S. Land to General Board, 9 February 1916, Sims Papers.

38. Kittredge, *Naval Lessons of the Great War*, pp. 187–188; Letter Fletcher to Secretary of the Navy, 14 June 1915, Fletcher Papers.

39. Letter Dewey to Secretary Daniels, 17 November 1914, Study File 420-2, General Board Papers.

40. Testimony of A. W. Grant before Senate Naval Affairs Committee, March 1920, cited in Kittredge, *Naval Lessons of the Great War*, p. 187.

41. Woodrow Wilson, "August 17 Appeal,"cited in Arthur S. Link, *Wilson: The Struggle for Neutrality* (Princeton, 1960), p. 65.

42. Kittredge, *Naval Lessons of the Great War*, p. 212.

43. Ray Stannard Baker and William E. Dodd, *The Public Papers of Woodrow Wilson*, 6 vols. (New York, 1925), vol. 3, pp. 329–332.

44. Bradley A. Fiske, Diary, 24 February 1915, Fiske Papers; Letter Fiske to Frank Friday Fletcher, 14 March 1915, Fletcher Papers.

45. Braisted, *Navy in the Pacific, 1909–1922*, p. 184.

46. Arthur S. Link, *Woodrow Wilson and the Progressive Era* (New York, 1954), p. 179; Ernest Andrade, "United States Naval Policy in the Disarmament Era: 1921–1937" (Ph.D. Dissertation, Michigan State University, 1966), p. 5.

47. Letter Wilson to Josephus Daniels, 21 July 1915, cited in Letter Daniels to George Dewey, 23 July 1915, Dewey Papers.

48. Ibid.

49. The sole dissenter, Captain Harry S. Knapp, would have committed the board to an armada larger than even the British by striking out the word "equal"; entry dated 27 July 1915, *Proceedings*, 7, p. 199, General Board Papers; "Confidential Memorandum . . . in connection with General Board's confidential letter to Secretary of the Navy, 30 July 1915," Study File 420-2, General Board Papers; Braisted, *Navy in the Pacific, 1909–1922*, p. 188.

50. General Board's 30 July report was published in the *New York Times*, 25 December 1915, cited in Arthur S. Link, *Wilson: Confusion and Crises* (Princeton, 1964), p. 15.

51. Ibid.

52. Letter Daniels to Dewey, 7 October 1915, cited in Letter Dewey to Daniels, 12 October 1915, Study File 420-2, General Board Papers.

53. Letter Chairman of the General Board to the Secretary of the Navy, 9 November 1915, Study File 420-2, General Board Papers.

54. Ibid.

55. Annual Reports of the Navy Department, 1915, p. 5.

56. Annual Message, 7 December 1915, cited in Link, *Wilson: Confusion and Crises*, p. 36; Braisted, *Navy in the Pacific, 1909–1922*, p. 193.

57. Harold and Margaret Sprout, *The Rise of American Naval Power: 1776–1918* (Princeton, 1959), p. 337.

58. Armin Rappaport, *The Navy League of the United States* (Detroit, 1962), pp. 58–59.

59. Representative C. R. Davis, *Congressional Record 53*, 64th Congress, First Session, 31 May 1916, pp. 8963–8964.

60. Braisted, *Navy in the Pacific, 1909–1922*, p. 197.

61. Sprout and Sprout, *Rise of American Naval Power*, p. 340.

62. Ibid., p. 341; Braisted, *Navy in the Pacific, 1909–1922*, pp. 199–200.

63. Senator Thomas, Colorado, *Congressional Record 53*, 17 July 1916, pp. 11, 165–166.

64. Senator Norris, *Congressional Record 53*, 18 July 1916, pp. 11, 173.

65. Claude G. Swanson, *Congressional Record 53*, 13 July 1916, pp. 10, 924.

66. Senator Lodge, *Congressional Record 53*, 13 July 1916, pp. 10, 931.

67. Braisted, *Navy in the Pacific, 1909–1922*, p. 201.

68. Representative Rufus Hardy, *Congressional Record 53*, 15 August 1916, pp. 12, 672–673.

69. Representative Mondell, *Congressional Record 53*, 15 August 1916, pp. 12, 679–680.

70. Hensley Amendment, cited in George T. Davis, *A Navy Second to None* (New York, 1940), p. 228.

71. Thadius V. Tuleja, *Statesmen and Admirals: Quest for a Far Eastern Policy* (New York, 1968), pp. 22–24.

72. Hearings of Chief Constructor Taylor and Naval Constructor Stocker on the Characteristics of Battleships and Battle Cruisers, September 1916, Study File 420-6, General Board Papers.

73. Memorandum from the President of the General Board to the Secretary of the Navy, 3 May 1916, Study File 420-6, General Board Papers.

74. Memorandum 11 September 1916, Study File 420-6, Serial 687, General Board Papers; Braisted, *Navy in the Pacific, 1909–1922*, p. 202.

75. Letter Chairman of the Executive Committee to Secretary of the Navy, 16 October 1916, Study File 420-6, General Board Papers.

76. Letter George Dewey to Secretary of the Navy, 16 October 1916; Lieutenant Commander H. C. Dinger, "Comments and Suggestions as to the Characteristics for Battle Cruisers," 1 September 1916, Study File 420-6, General Board Papers.

77. R. H. Gibson and Maurice Prendergast, *The German Submarine War, 1914–1918* (New York, 1931), p. 103.

78. Ibid., pp. 110–111.

79. William S. Sims, *Victory at Sea* (Garden City, 1920), p. 310.

80. Daniels, *The Wilson Era, 1910–1917*, p. 509; Spector, *Admiral of the New Empire*, p. 203.

81. Letter Dewey to Badger, 18 June 1914, Dewey Papers; letter Daniels to Dewey, 7 July 1915, Dewey Papers; Letter Dewey to Poundstone, 7 June 1908, Poundstone Papers; Letter Daniels to Dewey, 22 August 1916, Dewey Papers.

82. Josephus Daniels, *The Wilson Era, Years of War and After: 1917–1923* (Chapel Hill, 1946), p. 18; Ernest R. May, *The World War and American Isolation* (Chicago, 1959), pp. 413–415; Paolo Coletta, *The American Naval Heritage*, 3rd ed. (New York, 1987), p. 243.

83. Arthur Hezlet, *The Submarine and Sea Power* (New York, 1967), p. 85.

84. From "Report of the Second Subcommittee of the Committee of Inquiry," 18 June 1920, Official German Documents, I, p. 150.

85. Baker and Dodd, *The Public Papers of Woodrow Wilson*, vol. 2, pp. 428–432.

86. Daniels, *The Wilson Era, 1917–1923*, p. 19.

87. Arthur S. Link, *Wilson: His Compaigns for Progress and Peace, 1914–1917* (Princeton, 1947), vol. 5, p. 429.

88. Braisted, *Navy in the Pacific, 1909–1922*, p. 183; Roskill, *Naval Policy Between the Wars*, vol. 1, pp. 53–55.

89. Letter Bradley Fiske to Sims, 7 February 1920, Sims Papers, cited in Isaac Don Levine, *Mitchell: Pioneer of Air Power* (New York, 1943), p. 183.

90. Letter Daniels to Sims, 15 December 1917, Sims Papers.

91. Letter Sims to Ridley McLean, 17 July 1917, Sims Papers.

92. Daniels, *The Wilson Era, 1917–1923*, pp. 67–68.

93. Braisted, *Navy in the Pacific, 1909–1922*, p. 290.

94. Sims, *Victory at Sea*, p. 4.

95. Ibid., p. 9.

96. Arthur J. Marder, *From Dreadnought to Scapa Flow*, 4 vols. (London, 1961), vol. 4, pp. 115–137.

97. Sims, *Victory at Sea*, p. 36.

98. Ibid., p. 378.

99. "First Detailed Report on Allied Naval Situation," 14 April 1917, Sims Papers.

100. Letter W. S. Sims to Josephus Daniels, 19 April 1917, Sims Papers.

101. Fiske, Diary, 3 April 1917, Fiske Papers.

102. Paul Schubert, *Come on Texas* (New York, 1930), p. 68.

103. Plan from Pratt, undated, U.S. Congress, Senate Committee on Naval Affairs, Naval Investigations, I, p. 1320; Braisted, *Navy in the Pacific, 1909–1922*, p. 292.

104. Theodore Roscoe, *On the Seas and in the Air* (New York, 1970), p. 63.

105. Morison, *Sims*, p. 355.

106. Kittredge, *Naval Lessons of the Great War*, p. 118.

107. Testimony of Admiral Charles Badger Before the Senate Naval Affairs Committee, 1920, cited in ibid., pp. 303–304.

108. Letter Badger to Daniels, 20 April 1917, Confidential Records of the Secretary of the Navy, 1917–1919; Braisted, *Navy in the Pacific, 1909–1922*, pp. 293–294.

109. David Lloyd George, *The War Memoirs of David Lloyd George* (London, 1926), vol. 3, pp. 1162–1163.

110. Letter Sims to Pratt, 3 July 1917, Sims Papers.

111. Pratt, "Autobiography," chap. 20, p. 12.

112. Letter Goethals to Josephus Daniels, 28 May 1917, Secretary of the Navy's General Records, No. 28789/1, NA+ RG 80; Braisted, *Navy in the Pacific, 1919–1922*, pp. 295–296.

113. Braisted, *Navy in the Pacific, 1909–1922*, pp. 295–296.

114. Letter Pratt to Chief of Naval Operations, 7 June 1917, Sims Papers.

115. Letter Pratt to Sims, 22 July 1917, Sims Papers.

116. Ibid.

117. Ibid. Also see letter Pratt to Sims, 2 July 1917, Sims Papers.

118. Gibson and Prendergast, *The German Submarine War*, p. 186.

119. Letter Sims to W. H. Page, 26 June 1917, cited in Morison, *Sims*, p. 357.

120. Letter Wilson to Daniels, 2 July 1917, cited in Ray Stannard Baker, *Woodrow Wilson: Life and Letters* (New York, 1939), vol. 7, p. 140.

121. Cable Wilson to Sims 4 July 1917, in Baker, *Woodrow Wilson* vol. 7, p. 147.

122. Telegram Sims to Wilson 5 July 1917, Sims Papers.

123. Board on Devices and Plans Connected with Submarine Warfare to Secretary of the Navy, 6 July 1917; Daniels to Department Bureaus, 6 July 1917, Secretary of the Navy's General Records.

124. Letter Pratt to Sims, 22 July 1917, Sims Papers.

125. Memorandum Badger to Secretary of the Navy, 13 July 1917, U.S. Congress, Senate Committee on Naval Affairs, *Naval Investigations*, vol. 1, pp. 1218–1219.

126. Interview between W. Wilson and William Wiseman, 13 July 1917, in Charles Seymour, ed., *The Intimate Papers of Colonel House* (New York, 1926), vol. 3, pp. 70–72.

127. Letter Pratt to Sims, 22 July 1917, Sims Papers.

128. Kittredge, *Naval Lessons of the Great War,* p. 308.

129. W. L. Capps to Secretary of the Navy, 7 August 1917, Records of the Secretary of the Navy; Braisted, *Navy in the Pacific, 1909–1922,* p. 300.

130. Daniels, *The Wilson Era, 1917–1923,* pp. 43–45.

131. Gibson and Prendergast, *The German Submarine War,* pp. 161–191.

132. John Jellicoe, *The Crisis of the Naval War* (New York, 1921), pp. 59–60.

133. Marder, *From Dreadnought to Scapa Flow,* vol. 4, p. 71.

134. Ibid., vol. 4, pp. 75–76.

135. See Gibson and Prendergast, *The German Submarine War,* Appendix 3.

136. Ibid., p. 189; Sims, *Victory at Sea,* pp. 95–96.

137. Marder, *From Dreadnought to Scapa Flow,* vol. 4, p. 258.

138. Hezlet, *The Submarine and Sea Power,* p. 93.

139. The incident is described in Gibson and Prendergast, *The German Submarine War,* pp. 201–202.

140. Philip K. Lundeberg, "Undersea Warfare and Allied Strategy in World War I, Part II, 1916–1918," *Smithsonian Journal of History,* Winter 1966-1967, pp. 62–63.

141. Ibid.

142. Gibson and Prendergast, *The German Submarine War,* pp. 116–117.

143. Marder, *From Dreadnought to Scapa Flow,* vol. 4, pp. 73–74, 88.

144. Ibid., vol. 4, p. 88; Lundeberg, "Undersea Warfare, Part II," p. 62; Reinhard Scheer, *Germany's High Seas Fleet in the World War* (London, 1920), p. 314; Gibson and Prendergast, *The German Submarine War,* pp. 223, 289.

145. Brayton Harris, *The Age of the Battleship: 1880–1920* (New York, 1965), p. 174.

146. Jellicoe, *The Crisis of the Naval War,* p. 167.

147. Sims, *Victory at Sea,* p. 272.

148. Lundeberg, "Undersea Warfare, Part II," p. 65.

149. Letter Reginald R. Belknap to wife, November 1918, Reginald R. Belknap Papers.

150. Gibson and Prendergast, *The German Submarine War,* p. 352.

151. Sims, *Victory at Sea,* p. 29.

152. Marder, *From Dreadnought to Scapa Flow,* vol. 3, p. 54.

153. Scheer, *Germany's High Seas Fleet,* p. 334.

154. Lundeberg, "Undersea Warfare, Part II," p. 67.

155. John Jellicoe, *The Grand Fleet, 1914–1916: Its Creation, Development, and Work* (New York, 1919), p. 215.

156. Marder, *From Dreadnought to Scapa Flow*, vol. 4, p. 42.

157. Richard Hough, *Death of the Battleship* (New York, 1963), p. 15.

158. Letters Beatty to Lady Beatty, 1 March 1917, 24 May 1917, 21 May 1917, cited in W. S. Chalmers, *The Life and Letters of David Earl Beatty* (London, 1951), p. 289.

159. Telegram Sims to Secretary of the Navy, 21 July 1917, Sims Papers.

160. Braisted, *Navy in the Pacific, 1909–1922*, p. 302.

161. Operations to Sims 19 August 1917, Naval Records Collection Telegrams, vol. 57, O-L-194, NA, RG 45; Braisted, *Navy in the Pacific, 1909–1922*, p. 302.

162. Letter Benson to Sims, 24 September 1917, U.S. Congress, Senate Committee on Naval Affairs, Naval Investigations, vol. 1, p. 76.

163. Letter Benson to Sims, 24 September 1917, cited in Morison, *Sims*, p. 401.

164. Testimony of Captain Pratt and Captain Schofield Before the General Board, 19 October 1917, General Board Papers.

165. Telegram Chief of Naval Operations to the Secretary of the Navy, 9 November 1917, General Board Papers.

166. Telegram Daniels to Benson, 12 November 1917, Area D File, Papers of the Secretary of the Navy, cited in *Navy in the Pacific, 1909–1922*, p. 304.

167. Schubert, *Come on Texas*, p. 140.

168. Henry A. Wiley, *An Admiral from Texas* (New York, 1934), p. 194.

169. Daniels, *The Wilson Era, 1917–1923*, p. 119.

170. Mayo quoted in the *New York Times*, 4 December 1917, p. 5.

171. Wiley, *An Admiral from Texas*, pp. 198–202.

172. Ibid.

173. Harris, *The Age of the Battleship*, p. 168; Josephus Daniels, *Our Navy at War* (New York, 1922), pp. 154–155.

174. Albert Gleaves, Diary, 10 June 1918, Gleaves Papers.

175. Letter Sims to Benson, 17 September 1918, Sims Papers.

176. Ingenohl cited in Scheer, *Germany's High Seas Fleet*, p. 40; Scheer cited in Lundeberg, "Underseas Warfare, Part II," p. 68.

177. Scheer, *Germany's High Seas Fleet*, pp. 191–192; Marder, *From Dreadnought to Scapa Flow*, vol. 3, p. 256.

178. Scheer, *Germany's High Seas Fleet*, p. 194.

179. Daniel Horn, *The German Naval Mutinies of World War I* (New Brunswick, N.J., 1969), pp. 93–97.

180. Scheer, *Germany's High Seas Fleet*, pp. 318–323.

181. Horn, *German Naval Mutinies*, p. 206.

182. Ibid., p. 207.

183. Scheer, *Vom Segelschiff zum U-Boot* (Leipzig, 1925), p. 356.

184. Scheer, *Germany's High Seas Fleet*, p. 355.

185. Horn, *German Naval Mutinies*, p. 222.

186. Charles Seymour, ed., *The Intimate Papers of Colonel House* (New York, 1928), vol. 4, p. 128.

187. Francis T. Hunter, *Beatty, Jellicoe, Sims, and Rodman* (New York, 1919), p. 174.

188. Ibid., p. 175.

189. Daniels, *Our Navy at War*, p. 158.

190. Schubert, *Come on Texas*, p. 195.

191. Hunter, *Beatty, Jellicoe, Sims, and Rodman*, p. 176.

192. Daniels, *Our Navy at War*, p. 158.

193. "Address of David Beatty to the Sixth Battle Squadron of the U.S. Fleet on the Day of Their Leaving for New York," 1 December 1918, Sims Papers.

Chapter Nine

1. David Cronin, ed., *The Cabinet Diaries of Josephus Daniels, 1913–1921* (Lincoln, 1963), p. 342.

2. Benson to Sims, 19 April 1918, Telegram, Naval Records Collection, Area File, NA RG 45.

3. Letter Senior Member (Badger) General Board to Secretary of the Navy, 15 June 1918, Study File 420-2, General Board Papers.

4. Cronin, *Cabinet Diaries*, p. 341.

5. John Dos Passos, *Mr. Wilson's War* (Garden City, 1962), p. 447.

6. Memorandum Benson to Wilson, 4 November 1918, cited in Ray Stannard Baker, *Woodrow Wilson and the World Settlement* (New York, 1922), vol. 3, p. 211.

7. Stephen Roskill, *Naval Policy Between the Wars* (London, 1968), vol. 1, p. 74.

8. Telegram Benson to Secretary of the Navy, 27 November 1918, Naval Records and Library Collection, VM File, NA, RG 45.

9. William R. Braisted, *The United States Navy in the Pacific, 1909–1922* (Austin, Tex., 1971), p. 430.

10. Telegram Benson to Operations, 8 March 1919, Mission #318, 319, Naval Records Collection, VM File, NA, RG 45.

11. Braisted, *Navy in the Pacific, 1909–1922*, p. 432.

12. For an accurate, though hostile, view of House, see Josephus Daniels, *The Wilson Era, Years of War and After: 1917–1923* (Chapel Hill, 1946), pp. 535ff.

13. Charles Seymour, ed., *The Intimate Papers of Colonel House* (New York, 1928), vol. 4, p. 181.

14. David Lloyd George, *Memoirs of the Peace Conference* (New York, 1922), p. 187.

15. Thomas A. Bailey, *Woodrow Wilson and the Lost Peace* (Chicago, 1944), p. 209.

16. Braisted, *Navy in the Pacific, 1909–1922*, p. 433.

17. Ibid.

18. Daniels, *The Wilson Era, 1917–1923*, p. 433.

19. Cronin, *Cabinet Diaries*, pp. 380–381.

20. Daniels, *The Wilson Era, 1917–1923*, p. 371.

21. Ibid.

22. Letter Cecil to House, 8 April 1919, cited in Seymour, *The Intimate Papers of Colonel House*, vol. 4, p. 419.

23. Letter House to Cecil, 9 April 1919, cited in ibid., vol. 4, pp. 420–421.

24. Memorandum of Conversation between House and Cecil, 10 April 1919, cited in ibid., vol. 4, p. 422.

25. For example see Memorandum from Naval Advisory Staff, 7 April 1919, cited in Ray S. Baker, *Woodrow Wilson and the World Settlement*, vol. 3, pp. 207–217.

26. Braisted, *Navy in the Pacific, 1909–1921*. I am indebted to W. R. Braisted for his interpretation of this portion of the negotiations at Paris.

27. Geoffrey Bennett, *Naval Battles of the First World War* (New York, 1969), p. 307.

28. "Scapa Flow Twenty Years Ago," *Memphis Commercial Appeal*, 28 July 1939.

29. Bennett, *Naval Battles of the First World War*, p. 307.

30. Roskill, *Naval Policy Between the Wars*, vol. 1, pp. 93–94.

31. Lady Wester Wemyss, *The Life and Letters of Lord Wester Wemyss: Admiral of the Fleet* (London, 1935), p. 432.

32. *New York Times*, 11 December 1919, p. 12.

33. *New York Times*, 11 December 1919, p. 14.

34. Braisted, *Navy in the Pacific, 1909–1922*, p. 422.

35. See letter Charles Badger to Representative Lemuel Padgett, Chairman of the House Naval Committee, 2 December 1918, Study File 420-2, General Board Papers.

36. Press release of Secretary of the Navy's Testimony before the House Naval Committee, 26 December 1918, Sims Papers.

37. Telegram Benson to Operations, 21 November 1918, Daniels Papers.

38. Harold and Margaret Sprout, *Toward a New Order of Sea Power* (Princeton, 1943), p. 55.

39. Letter General Board to Secretary of the Navy, 6 July 1918, Study File 420-6, Serial 844, General Board Papers; Letter Mayo to Secretary of the Navy, 20 January 1919, Study File 420-6, General Board Papers.

40. Benson to Operations for Secretary of the Navy, 5 January 1919, Benson Papers; Braisted, *Navy in the Pacific, 1909–1922*, p. 421.

41. Letter Charles Badger to Representative Padgett, 2 December 1918, Study File 420-6, General Board Papers.

42. *New York Times*, 31 January 1919, p. 1.

43. Representative Huddleston, *Congressional Record* 57, 65th Congress, 3rd Session, 1919, p. 2771.

44. Representative Currie, *Congressional Record* 57, 65th Congress, 3rd Session, 1919, p. 3085.

45. General Board to Sims, 21 March 1919, Sims Papers.

46. Letter Daniels to Badger, 14 March 1919, Josephus Daniels Papers; Braisted, *Navy in the Pacific, 1909–1922*, p. 455.

47. Braisted, *Navy in the Pacific, 1909–1922*, p. 453.

48. Senior Member Present to Secretary of the Navy, 28 May 1919, Study File 420-6, General Board Papers.

49. C. L. Hoag, *Preface to Preparedness: The Washington Conference and Public Opinion* (Washington, 1941), p. 22.

50. Woodrow Wilson, Speech at Billings, Montana, 11 September 1919, cited in David Cronin, ed., *The Political Thought of Woodrow Wilson* (New York, 1965), p. 508; see also speeches at St. Louis, Kansas City, Seattle, Portland, and Denver.

51. Stephen Howarth, *The Fighting Ships of the Rising Sun: The Drama of the Imperial Japanese Navy, 1895–1945* (New York, 1983), pp. 140–148.

52. Gerald E. Wheeler, *Prelude to Pearl Harbor: The United States Navy in the Far East* (Columbia, Mo., 1963), p. 37.

53. Braisted, *Navy in the Pacific, 1909–1922*, pp. 468–469.

54. George T. Davis, *A Navy Second to None* (New York, 1940), p. 252.

55. Daniels, *The Wilson Era, 1917–1923*, pp. 454–455.

56. Director of Naval Intelligence to President of the Naval War College, 2 June 1920, Sims Papers.

57. Howarth, *Ships of the Rising Sun*, pp. 148–149.

58. John W. Davies to Secretary of State, 7 June 1920, *Papers Relating to the Foreign Relations of the United States, 1920* (Washington, 1922), vol. 2, pp. 680–682.

59. Benjamin H. Williams, *The United States and Disarmament* (New York, 1931), p. 137.

60. Braisted, *Navy in the Pacific, 1909–1922*, p. 553.

61. Letter Fiske to Sims, 24 November 1921, Sims Papers.

62. Tracy B. Kittredge, *Naval Lessons of the Great War* (Garden City, 1921), p. 42.

63. Daniels, *The Wilson Era, 1917–1923*, p. 43.

64. Memorandum Daniels to Admiral Knight, 26 December 1919, Daniels Papers.

65. Kittredge, *Naval Lessons of the Great War*, p. 65.

66. Letter cited in Elting Morison, *Admiral Sims and the Modern American Navy* (Cambridge, Mass., 1942), p. 446; Brayton Harris, *The Age of the Battleship: 1880–1920* (New York, 1965), p. 193.

67. Letter "Certain Lesson of the Great War," Sims to Secretary of the Navy, 7 January 1920, Sims Papers.

68. Kittredge, *Naval Lessons of the Great War*, p. 215.

69. U.S. Congress, Senate Subcommittee on Naval Affairs, *Hearings on the Naval Policy of the United States* (Washington, 1920), pp. 1825, 1887.

70. Kittredge, *Naval Lessons of the Great War*, p. 299.

71. John Arbuthnot Fisher, *Memories and Records* (New York, 1920), vol. 2, pp. 178, 204.

72. Howarth, *Ships of the Rising Sun*, p. 139.

73. Letter Fiske to Dewey, 7 April 1911, no. 449, General Board Papers.

74. Bradley Fiske, *From Midshipman to Rear Admiral* (New York, 1919), p. 481.

75. Ibid., p. 503.

76. Richard Hough, *The Great War at Sea: 1914–1919* (Oxford, 1983), p. 317; John Keegan, *The Price of Admiralty* (New York, 1988), p. 158.

77. Letter Daniels to Fiske, 20 May 1918, cited in Fiske, *From Midshipman to Rear Admiral*, p. 676.

78. Statement of Admiral W. F. Fullam, Proceedings of the Special Board and Records of Evidence (Eberle Board), National Archives.

79. Morison, *Sims*, p. 504.

80. Letter Sims to Fiske, 6 January 1921, Sims Papers.

81. Speech by W. F. Fullam, *Aviation*, November 1921, Fullam Papers.

82. Letter Fiske to Fullam, November 1921, Fullam Papers.

83. "Notes on General Policy of Air Service Organization Recommended by William Mitchell," 11 April 1919, Mitchell Papers.

84. Emile Gauvreau and Lester Cohen, *Billy Mitchell* (New York, 1942), p. 41.

85. Alfred F. Hurley, *Billy Mitchell: Crusader for Air Power* (New York, 1964), pp. 59–60.

86. *Literary Digest*, 19 February 1921, pp. 14–15; Gauvreau and Cohen, *Billy Mitchell*, p. 48; Hurley, *Billy Mitchell*, p. 64.

87. Gauvreau and Cohen, *Billy Mitchell*, p. 42.

88. Hoag, *Preface to Preparedness*, pp. 90, 95.

89. Ibid., pp. 37–38; Braisted, *Navy in the Pacific, 1909–1922*, p. 493.

90. *Philadelphia Public Ledger*, 22 December 1920.

91. Letter Borah to Fullam, 20 January 1921, Fullam Papers.

92. *Congressional Record* 60, pp. 2112–2116.

93. *New York Times*, 31 January 1921, p. 8.

94. U.S. Congress, House Committee on Naval Affairs, *Hearings on Naval Policy of the United States* (Washington, 1921), pp. 655–662, 697–699, 712–713.

95. Ibid., pp. 763–764.

96. W. G. Harding to H. C. Lodge, 20 February 1921, Henry Cabot Lodge Papers; *New York Times*, 1 January 1921; Adelphia D. Bowen, "The Disarmament Movement, 1918–1935" (Ph.D. Dissertation, Columbia University, 1956), p. 23; Merlo J. Pusey, *Charles Evans Hughes* (New York, 1951), p. 455.

97. Braisted, *Navy in the Pacific, 1909–1922*, p. 502.

98. Gauvreau and Cohen, *Billy Mitchell*, p. 53.

99. Hurley, *Billy Mitchell*, p. 66.

100. Ibid., p. 66; Isaac Don Levine, *Mitchell: Pioneer of Air Power* (New York, 1943), pp. 226–227.

101. Archibald D. Turnbull and Clifford L. Lord, *History of United States Aviation* (New Haven, 1949), pp. 196–197.

102. *New York Times*, 21 July 1921, p. 1; Levine, *Mitchell*, p. 240.

103. Letter Denby to Hughes, 9 June 1921; Letter Hughes to Denby, 11 June 1921, Charles Evans Hughes Papers.

104. Turnbull and Lord, *History of United States Aviation*, p. 195.

105. *New York Times*, 21 July 1921, p. 1.

106. Richard Hough, *The Death of the Battleship* (New York, 1963), p. 32.

107. Burke Davis, *The Billy Mitchell Affair* (New York, 1967), p. 103.

108. Gauvreau and Cohen, *Billy Mitchell*, p. 61.

109. "Report of Reconnaissance by Brigade Commander of Operations by the 14th Heavy Bombardment Squadron, Langley Field against the ex-German Battleship *Ostfriesland* with 2000-pound Bombs," William Mitchell Papers.

110. *New York Herald*, 22 July 1921; Hough, *Death of the Battleship*, p. 34.

111. Levine, *Mitchell*, p. 254.

112. A Japanese guest on the *Henderson*, a Mr. Katsuda, had timed the attack with a stopwatch.

113. W. F. Fullam, "Bombing Tests in Review," 7 August 1921, *New York Tribune*, Fullam Papers.

114. Davis, *The Billy Mitchell Affair*, p. 108; Levine, *Mitchell*, p. 256.

Chapter Ten

1. See letter E. A. Silsby to the General Board, Study File 420-2, General Board Papers.

2. Betty Glad, *Charles Evans Hughes and the Illusion of Innocence* (Urbana, 1966), pp. 521–527.

3. Roosevelt to General Board, 27 July 1921, Classified Board of the Secretary of the Navy 1919–1926, P.D. 138–9, NA RG 30, National Archives.

4. Letter Charles E. Hughes to Secretary of the Navy Denby, 1 September 1921, folder labeled General Board and the Conference on the Limitation of Armaments, General Board Papers.

5. See Memorandum General Board to Secretary of the Navy, 5 November 1921, GB 436 (Serial 1066v), Charles Evans Hughes Papers.

6. Chairman of the General Board to Secretary of the Navy, 12 September 1921, 3 October 1921, 8 October 1921, File 438-1 (Serial 1088) General Board Papers.

7. William Howard Gardiner, "Memorandum on Naval Matters Connected with the Washington Conference on the Limitation of Armaments, 1921," 25 October 1924, Max L. Bristol Papers, Library of Congress.

8. Chairman of the General Board (Rodgers) to Secretary of the Navy Denby, 14 October 1921, File 438-1, General Board Papers.

9. Gardiner, "Memorandum."

10. Letter Hughes to Denby, 25 October 1921, cited in full in ibid.

11. Memorandum for the Secretary of the Navy, 26 October 1921, Washington Conference Advisory Committee, File No. 438, General Board Papers.

12. Letter 26 October 1921, cited in Gardiner, "Memorandum."

13. Theodore Roosevelt, Jr., Diary, 10 November 1921, Theodore Roosevelt, Jr., Papers.

14. Mark Sullivan, *The Great Adventure at Washington* (Garden City, 1922), pp. 3–4.

15. Roosevelt, Jr., Diary, 12 November 1921.

16. Ernest Andrade, "United States Naval Policy in the Disarmament Era: 1921–1937" (Ph.D. Dissertation, Michigan State University, 1966), p. 26.

17. Sullivan, *The Great Adventure at Washington*, pp. 21–22.

18. Ibid., pp. 26–27.

19. William R. Braisted, *The United States Navy in the Pacific, 1909–1922* (Austin, Tex., 1971), p. 599.

20. Sadao Asada, "Japanese Admirals and the Politics of Naval Limitation: Kato Tomosaburo vs. Kato Kanjii," in *Naval Warfare in the Twentieth Century, 1900–1945: Essays in Honour of Arthur Marder*, ed. Gerald Jordan (London, 1977), pp. 151, 155–156.

21. Roosevelt, Jr., Diary, 1 November, 15 November 1921.

22. Asada, "Japanese Admirals and the Politics of Naval Limitation," p. 144.

23. Braisted, *Navy in the Pacific, 1909-1922*, p. 603; Stephen Howarth, *The Fighting Ships of the Rising Sun: The Drama of the Imperial Japanese Navy, 1895–1945* (New York, 1983), p. 160.

24. Roosevelt, Jr., Diary, 15 November 1921.

25. Ibid., 18 November 1921.

26. Ibid., 20 November 1921.

27. Ibid., 27 November 1921.

28. Cable Kato Tomosaburo to Uchida, 23 November 1921, Japanese Foreign Ministry Papers, Special Studies 16, Library of Congress Microfilms.

29. Asada, "Japanese Admirals and the Politics of Naval Limitation," pp. 146–147.

30. Ibid., p. 159.

31. Howarth, *Ships of the Rising Sun*, pp. 134–140.

32. Asada, "Japanese Admirals and the Politics of Naval Limitation," pp. 157–158.

33. Roosevelt, Jr., Diary, 12 December 1921; Braisted, *Navy in the Pacific, 1909–1922*, p. 615; L. Ethan Ellis, *Republican Foreign Policy, 1921-1933* (New Brunswick, 1968), pp. 114–116; Harold and Margaret Sprout, *Toward a New Order of Sea Power* (Princeton, 1943), pp. 176–180.

34. Sprout and Sprout, *Toward a New Order of Sea Power*, p. 185.

35. Roosevelt, Jr., Diary, 15 December 1921.

36. Letter Hughes to Harvey, 16 December 1921, *Foreign Relations of the United States* (Washington, 1922), vol. 2, pp. 132–133; Letter Briand to Hughes, 18 December 1921, in ibid., vol. 2, pp. 135–136.

37. Roosevelt, Jr., Diary, 29 December 1921.

38. "Report of the Subcommittee on Aircraft, 30 December 1921," in *Conference on the Limitation of Armament: Subcommittees* (Washington, 1922), p. 196.

39. Alfred F. Hurley, *Billy Mitchell: Crusader for Air Power* (New York, 1964), p. 71; Ellis, *Republican Foreign Policy, 1921-1923*, p. 120.

40. Roosevelt, Jr., Diary, 30 December 1921.

41. Ibid., 3 January 1921.

42. Ibid., 4 January 1922.

43. Arthur Hezlet, *Aircraft and Seapower* (New York, 1970), p. 111; Braisted, *Navy in the Pacific, 1909-1922*, p. 637.

44. C. L. Hoag, *Preface to Preparedness: The Washington Conference and Public Opinion* (Washington, 1941), p. 134.

45. *Foreign Relations of the United States* (Washington, 1921), vol. 1, pp. 69–80; *Conference on the Limitation of Armaments* (Washington, 1922), p. 86.

46. *Conference on the Limitation of Armaments*, p. 102.

47. Ibid., p. 476.

48. Ibid., p. 490.

49. Ibid., p. 488.

50. Ibid., p. 492.

51. Ibid., pp. 570–578.

52. Richard Dean Burns, "Regulating Submarine Warfare, 1921–41: A Case Study in Arms Control and Limited War," *Military Affairs* 35, no. 2 (April 1971), p. 57.

53. Ernest Andrade, "Submarine Policy in the United States Navy, 1919–1941," *Military Affairs* 35, no. 2 (April 1971), p. 55.

54. Conference on the Limitation of Armaments, Senate Document, 67th Congress, No. 126, p. 812.

55. See Memorandum 9 April 1930, Bristol Papers; Albert Gleaves, "Aviation in Relation to Seapower," Gleaves Papers; Memorandum 29 March 1922, 1108/GB, Study File 420-2, General Board Papers; Dudley Knox, *The Eclipse of American Sea Power* (New York, 1922), pp. 46–59.

56. Letter Fullam to Sims, 9 June 1923, Sims Papers.

Chapter Eleven

1. See for example, Rear Admiral Albert Gleaves, "Aviation and the Fleet: An Address Delivered Before the Rotary Club, Washington, DC," June 1925, Gleaves Papers; J. K. Taussig, "A Balanced Fleet for the United States Navy," *USNIP* 51, no. 7 (July 1925), p. 1114; Archibald D. Turnbull and Clifford L. Lord, *History of United States Aviation* (New Haven, 1949), pp. 199–200.

2. "Statement of Rear Admiral W. F. Fullam to the Aircraft Investigating Committee of Congress," 1924, Fullam Papers.

3. Ibid.

4. William D. Leahy, Diary, 15 and 23 March 1923, Leahy Papers; William V. Pratt, "Autobiography" (unpublished), chap. 17, p. 7, Pratt Papers; Robert E. Coontz, *From Mississippi to the Sea* (Philadelphia, 1930), pp. 424–429.

5. "Statement of Fullam to Aircraft Investigating Committee."

6. Turnbull and Lord, *United States Aviation*, pp. 253–254.

7. Stephen W. Roskill, *Naval Policy Between the Wars* (London, 1968), vol. 1, pp. 468–469; Thadius V. Tuleja, *Statesmen and Admirals: Quest for a Far Eastern Policy* (New York, 1968), p. 30.

8. Roskill, *Naval Policy Between the Wars*, vol. 1, pp. 56–57; cited in Turnbull and Lord, *United States Aviation*, p. 243; "Report of Special Board (on) Results of Development of Aviation on the Development of the Navy," 17 January 1925, in Navy

Department, *Information Concerning the U.S. Navy and Other Navies* (Washington, 1925).

9. Turnbull and Lord, *United States Aviation*, p. 243.

10. "The Special Board Appointed by an Order of the Secretary of the Navy Dated September 23, 1924," Office of the Secretary of the Navy, Secret and Confidential Correspondence 1919–26 109-14:3 to 111-I, Boxes 23-24, Modern Military Records, U.S. National Archives, pp. 449, 470; 965–966; 495–496, 510; 428.

11. Ibid., pp. 714–738.

12. Turnbull and Lord, *United States Aviation*, p. 244.

13. C. F. Hughes, "Testimony Before Special Board," p. 965.

14. Gerald Wheeler, *Prelude to Pearl Harbor: The United States Navy in the Far East* (Columbus, Mo., 1963), p. 116.

15. Letter Calvin Coolidge to Secretary of the Navy, 28 January 1925, Study File 420-2, General Board Papers; Memorandum from Senior Member of the Special Board to Secretary of the Navy, 31 January 1925, General Board Papers, 30 3809-1237 GB, No. 420.

16. Roskill, *Naval Policy Between the Wars*, vol. 1, pp. 115, 223–224, 533; Stephen Roskill, *Naval Policy Between the Wars*, vol. 2 (London, 1976), pp. 22, 340; Stephen E. Pelz, *Race to Pearl Harbor: The Failure of the Second London Naval Conference and the Onset of World War II* (Cambridge, Mass., 1974), pp. 30, 31.

17. Ernest Andrade, "Submarine Policy in the United States Navy, 1919–1941," *Military Affairs*, 35, no. 2 (April 1971), p. 50.

18. Ibid., pp. 51–52.

19. See "Notes for Use of Senior Member, General Board, Panama, 27 February 1931, Mark L. Bristol Papers; Andrade, "Submarine Policy in the United States Navy, 1919–1941," p. 53; C. E. Lockwood, *Down to the Sea in Subs* (New York, 1967), pp. 199–200.

20. See Letter Senior Member to Secretary of the Navy, 5 April 1927, GB Study File 420-2 (Serial 1345), General Board Papers.

21. C. F. Hughes, "Draft of Opening Statement Geneva Conference May 27, 1927," Hilary Jones Papers.

22. Letter 5 April 1927, GB 420-2 (Serial 1345); Ernest Andrade, "United States Naval Policy in the Disarmament Era: 1921–1937" (Ph.D. Dissertation, Michigan State University, 1966), p. 193.

23. Arthur Hezlet, *The Submarine and Sea Power* (New York, 1967), pp. 75, 116.

24. Ibid., pp. 108–109, 112–113.

25. Pelz, *Race to Pearl Harbor*, p. 30; Roskill, *Naval Policy Between the Wars*, vol. 2, p. 180.

26. Turnbull and Lord, *United States Aviation*, p. 189; Yates Stirling, *Sea Duty: The Memoirs of a Fighting Admiral* (New York, 1939), p. 184; J. J. Clark and Clark G. Reynolds, *Carrier Admiral* (New York, 1967), pp. 16–17.

27. Turnbull and Lord, *United States Aviation*, p. 260.

28. Letter 5 November 1927, Senior Member to Secretary of the Navy, cited in "Characteristics of Aircraft Carriers," GB 420-7 (Serial 1623), 16 March 1928, General Board Papers; Robert Gordon Kaufman, *Arms Control During the Pre-Nuclear Era: The United States and Naval Limitation Between the Two World Wars* (New York, 1990), p. 85; E. B. Potter et al., *The United States and World Sea Power* (Englewood Cliffs, N.J., 1955), p. 592.

29. Roskill, *Naval Policy Between the Wars*, vol. 2, p. 46; Clark and Reynolds, *Carrier Admiral*, p. 45.

30. Roskill, *Naval Policy Between the Wars*, vol. 1, p. 62.

31. Thadius V. Tuleja, *Statesmen and Admirals: Quest for a Far Eastern Policy* (New York, 1968), pp. 70–71; Pratt, "Autobiography," chap. 21, pp. 2–3.

32. See Fleet Problems I–VII, Office of Secretary (Including CNO) Correspondence 1919–1926, 198-35, pp. 1-7, Modern Military Records, U.S. National Archives; Theodore Roscoe, *On the Seas and in the Air* (New York, 1970), p. 234.

33. "Black Remarks," Critique, Fleet Problem IX, Office of the Secretary, Confidential Correspondence 1927–1939, A16-2 (5-VIII) to A 16-3 (5-IX), Modern Military Records, U.S. National Archives.

34. "Remarks by the Chief of Staff, Battle Fleet (Hepburn) at Critique"; "Statement on Fleet Problem IX by Rear Admiral J. M. Reeves, Commander Aircraft Squadrons, Battle Fleet," Fleet Problem IX, Office of the Secretary, Confidential Correspondence 1927–1939, Modern Military Records, U.S. National Archives; John D. Hayes, "W. V. Pratt," *Shipmate: U.S. Naval Academy Alumni Association* 26, no. 6-7 (June 1963).

35. "Remarks by Commander Black Fleet, W. V. Pratt," Fleet Problem IX, Office of the Secretary, Confidential Correspondence 1927–1939, Modern Military Records, U.S. National Archives.

36. "Remarks of Captain Berrien," "Blue Critique," Fleet Problem IX.

37. Edward Arpee, *From Frigate to Flat-tops* (private publication, 1953), p. 155.

38. Clark G. Reynolds, *The Fast Carriers: The Forging of an Air Navy* (New York, 1968), p. 17.

39. Pratt, "Autobiography," chap. 20, pp. 25–26.

40. Letter Chief of Naval Operations (Pratt) to Fleet (SC), 28 November 1930, Office of the Secretary Confidential Correspondence 1927–1939, Modern Military Records, U.S. National Archives.

41. "Admiral Reeves' Comments," Fleet Problem XII, Office of the Secretary, Confidential Correspondence, Modern Military Records, U.S. National Archives.

42. Letter Andrew T. Long to Mark L. Bristol, 20 July 1931, Bristol Papers.

43. "Remarks of Admiral W. V. Pratt . . . at the Critique of Fleet Problem XII," Bristol Papers.

44. Letter OFNAV to Admiral Pratt, 22 February 1931; Letter Pratt to Secretary of the Navy, 22 February 1931, Bristol Papers.

45. Andrade, "Naval Policy in the Disarmament Era," p. 93; Taussig, "A Balanced Fleet for the United States Navy," p. 1118; see for example letter Senior Member of General Board to Secretary of the Navy, 31 May 1922, GB 420-2 (Serial 1130); letter Senior Member GB to Secretary of the Navy, 30 March 1926, GB 420-2 (Serial 1313), General Board Papers.

46. W. D. Puleston, "Modernizing the USS *Mississippi*," *Scientific American* 150, no. 6 (June 1934), pp. 298–299; Roskill, *Naval Policy Between the Wars*, vol. 1, p. 343, n. 6.

47. See for example letter Senior Member of General Board to Secretary of the Navy, 19 December 1922, GB 420-2 (Serial 1155), General Board Papers.

48. Roskill, *Naval Policy Between the Wars*, vol. 2, pp. 332–333, 420–421; Stephen Howarth, *The Fighting Ships of the Rising Sun: The Drama of the Imperial Japanese Navy, 1895–1945* (New York, 1983), pp. 217–218.

49. Puleston, "Modernizing the USS *Mississippi*," p. 300.

50. Pelz, *Race to Pearl Harbor*, pp. 218–219.

51. Andrade, "Naval Policy in the Disarmament Era," p. 91, cited in Clark and Reynolds, *Carrier Admiral*, p. 19.

52. Letter Senior Member GB to Secretary of the Navy, 19 December 1922, GB 420-2 (Serial 1155); Kaufman, *Arms Control During the Pre-Nuclear Era*, pp. 96–97.

53. Letter Geddes to Hughes, 5 March 1923, *Foreign Relations of the United States*, (Washington, 1923), vol. 1, pp. 25–28; Telegram Charles E. Hughes to U.S. Embassy UK, 20 March 1923, General Board Papers; British Embassy, Washington to Secretary of State, 14 February 1924, General Board Papers; Andrade, "Naval Policy in the Disarmament Era," p. 95.

54. Kaufman, *Arms Control During the Pre-Nuclear Era*, pp. 97–98.

55. Wheeler, *Prelude to Pearl Harbor*, pp. 111–112; Peter Hodges, *The Big Gun: Battleship Main Armament: 1860–1945* (Annapolis, Md., 1981), pp. 66, 79.

56. W. F. Fullam, *Philadelphia Public Ledger*, 25 March 1923, Fullam Papers.

57. Andrade, "Naval Policy in the Disarmament Era," p. 92.

58. Charles A. Beard, *The Navy: Defense or Portent?* (New York, 1932), p. 88.

59. Andrade, "Naval Policy in the Disarmament Era," pp. 97–98.

60. Kaufman, *Arms Control During the Pre-Nuclear Era*, p. 87.

61. Andrade, "Naval Policy in the Disarmament Era," p. 119.

62. U.S. Senate, "Hearings: Building up the United States Navy to the Strength Permitted by the Washington and London Naval Treaties," 1932, 72nd Congress, 1st Session, p. 3.

63. Kaufman, *Arms Control During the Pre-Nuclear Era*, p. 79.

64. Ibid., p. 108.

65. Ibid., p. 109; Roskill, *Naval Policy Between the Wars*, vol. 1, p. 515.

66. Andrade, "Naval Policy in the Disarmament Era," pp. 139–140.

67. Roskill, *Naval Policy Between the Wars* vol. 1, p. 514; Kaufman, *Arms Control During the Pre-Nuclear Era*, p. 110.

68. *Congressional Record* 69, 68th Congress, 2nd Session, p. 95.

69. Roskill, *Naval Policy Between the Wars*, vol. 1, p. 549.

70. Kaufman, *Arms Control During the Pre-Nuclear Era*, pp. 114–115.

71. Ibid., p. 125.

72. Roskill, *Naval Policy Between the Wars*, vol. 1, p. 506; Kaufman, *Arms Control During the Pre-Nuclear Era*, pp. 116–117.

73. Raymond O'Connor, *Perilous Equilibrium: The United States and the London Conference of 1930* (Lawrence, Kan., 1959), pp. 33–34, 43–44; Kaufman, *Arms Control During the Pre-Nuclear Era*, pp. 118–123.

74. Roskill, *Naval Policy Between the Wars* vol. 1, pp. 61–62; Tulja, *Statesmen and Admirals*, p. 47.

75. O'Connor, *Perilous Equilibrium*, pp. 47, 62; Kaufman, *Arms Control During the Pre-Nuclear Era*, p. 125.

76. Letter Senior Member (A. T. Long) to the Secretary of the Navy, 11 August 1928; memorandum 28 February 1929, No. 438-1 (Serial 1408), Naval Records Group 80, U.S. National Archives; memorandum 6 June 1930, GB 420-2, pp. 31–36.

77. Andrade, "Submarine Policy," p. 53; for a slightly different view of the board's motives, see Richard Dean Burns, "Regulating Submarine Warfare, 1921–41: A Case Study in Arms Control and Limited War," *Military Affairs* 35, no. 2 (April 1971), pp. 57–58.

78. Pelz, *Race to Pearl Harbor*, pp. 1–17; Howarth, *Ships of the Rising Sun*, pp. 166–181; Sadao Asada, "Japanese Admirals and the Politics of Naval Limitation: Kato Tomosabvuro vs. Kato Kanjii," in *Naval Warfare in the Twentieth Century, 1900–1945: Essays in Honour of Arthur Marder*, ed. Gerald Jordan (London, 1977), p. 161.

79. Kaufman, *Arms Control During the Pre-Nuclear Era*, pp. 126–127.

80. Ibid., p. 129; Henry Stimson and McGeorge Bundy, *On Active Service in Peace and War* (New York, 1948), pp. 167–168.

81. Wheeler, *Prelude to Pearl Harbor*, pp. 173–174; Kaufman, *Arms Control During the Pre-Nuclear Era*, p. 135.

82. Tuleja, *Statesmen and Admirals*, pp. 50–51; O'Connor, *Perilous Equilibrium*, p. 105.

83. Andrade, "Naval Policy in the Disarmament Era," pp. 210–211.

84. O'Connor, *Perilous Equilibrium*, p. 84.

85. Ibid.

86. Andrade, "Naval Policy in the Disarmament Era," p. 193.

87. Ibid., p. 233.

88. Ibid., pp. 211–212; Burns, "Regulating Submarine Warfare," pp. 57–58.

89. Kaufman, *Arms Control During the Pre-Nuclear Era*, p. 140; *Hearings on the London Naval Treaty of 1930*, 71st Congress, 2nd Session (Washington, 1930), p. 63.

90. Pratt, "Autobiography," chap. 20, p. 24.

91. Robert L. O'Connell, *Of Arms and Men: A History of War, Weapons and Aggression* (New York, 1989), p. 275.

92. Pelz, *Race to Pearl Harbor*, p. 19.

93. James Crowley, *Japan's Quest for Autonomy: 1930–1938* (Princeton, 1966), p. 199.

94. Pelz, *Race to Pearl Harbor*, pp. 62–63.

95. George V. Fagan, "FDR and Naval Limitation," *USNIP* 81, no. 4 (April 1955), p. 415.

96. Pelz, *Race to Pearl Harbor*, p. 75; Kaufman, *Arms Control During the Pre-Nuclear Era*, p. 177.

97. Pelz, *Race to Pearl Harbor*, pp. 128–129; Andrade, "Naval Policy in the Disarmament Era," pp. 363–364; memorandum 1 October 1939, GB 438-1 (Serial 1640/6B), General Board Papers.

98. Robin Rudoff, "The Influence of the German Navy on the British Search for Naval Arms Control, 1928–1935" (Ph.D. Dissertation, Tulane University, 1964), pp. 220–274.

99. Pelz, *Race to Pearl Harbor*, pp. 114–122.

100. Ibid., p. 139.

101. Kaufman, *Arms Control During the Pre-Nuclear Era*, p. 179.

102. Meredith Berg, "The United States and the Breakdown of Naval Limitation, 1934–1939" (Ph.D. Dissertation, Tulane University, 1966), pp. 174–175, 200; Andrade, "Naval Policy in the Disarmament Era," pp. 396–397.

103. Pelz, *Race to Pearl Harbor*, pp. 34–39, 198–199, 224; Louis Morton, "War Plan ORANGE: Evolution of a Strategy," *World Politics* 11, no. 2 (January 1959), pp. 240–250. The Japanese apparently obtained a purloined copy of the ORANGE plan in the mid-1930s, though their own plan had been in effect well before that acquisition. Howarth, *Ships of the Rising Sun*, p. 201.

104. Morton, "War Plan ORANGE," pp. 235, 243.

105. Ibid., pp. 232–237.

106. Hector Bywater, *Sea Power in the Pacific* (Boston, 1921), pp. 256–257.

107. Hector Bywater, *The Great Pacific War* (New York, 1925), p. 295.

108. Sutherland Denlinger and Charles B. Gary, *War in the Pacific: A Study of Peoples and Battle Problems* (New York, 1936), pp. 317, 320.

109. Pelz, *Race to Pearl Harbor,* pp. 34–36.

110. Ibid., p. 39.

111. See for example Samuel Elliot Morison, *History of the United States Naval Operations in World War II,* vol. 3 (Boston, 1948), p. 23.

112. Berg, "The United States and the Breakdown of Naval Limitation," pp. 239–240.

113. Estimates of the exact tonnage range from Pelz (62,000), to Howarth (70,000+), to Berg (72,809), to Reynolds (75,000).

114. Howarth, *Ships of the Rising Sun,* pp. 245–246.

115. Pelz, *Race to Pearl Harbor,* p. 34.

116. Samuel Elliot Morison, *History of the United States Naval Operations in World War II,* vol. 1 (Boston, 1947), p. viii.

117. Andrade, "Naval Policy in the Disarmament Era," p. 253.

118. Armin Rappaport, *The Navy League of the United States* (Detroit, 1962), pp. 157–158.

119. Tuleja, *Statesmen and Admirals,* p. 93.

120. Roskill, *Naval Policy Between the Wars,* vol. 1, p. 65; Andrade, "Naval Policy in the Disarmament Era," pp. 336–337.

121. Letter Bureau of Construction and Repair to General Board, 23 September 1935, Study File 420-6, General Board Papers.

122. Letter Chairman of the General Board to the Secretary of the Navy, 11 August 1937, Study File 420-6 (Serial 1749), General Board Papers; letter Harold Stark to Claude Bloch, 12 July 1937, Bloch Papers.

123. Letter Commander Battleships, Battle Force, to Chairman of the General Board, 13 July 1937, Study File 420-5, General Board Papers.

124. Letter Chairman of General Board to Secretary of the Navy, 11 August 1937, General Board Papers.

125. Richard Hough, *The History of the Modern Battleship: Dreadnought* (New York, 1964), pp. 241, 250–251, 255–256.

126. Letter J. Taussig to H. E. Yarnell, 3 May 1939, Yarnell Papers.

127. Letter Franklin Roosevelt to W. D. Leahy, 30 December 1937; William D. Leahy, Diary, Leahy Papers.

128. Hough, *Dreadnought,* pp. 212–220.

129. Letter Chairman of the General Board to Secretary of the Navy, 27 December 1939, Study File 420-6 (Serial 1911), General Board Papers; letter Secretary of the Navy to Rep. Scrugham, 16 January 1940, Study File 420-6 (Serial 0513), General Board Papers.

130. Letter Commander-in-Chief of U.S. Fleet to Chief of Naval Operations, 31 January 1940, Study File 420-6, General Board Papers; letter Admiral C. C. Bloch to Chairman of the General Board, 14 February 1940; letter Commander-in-Chief of the U.S. Fleet to Chairman of the General Board, 7 March 1440; letter President of the Naval War College to Chairman of the General Board, 28 February 1940, letter Commander Atlantic Squadron to Chairman of the General Board, 25 February 1940, Study File 420-6, General Board Papers.

131. Report no. 231, Japan, 11 October 1939, Naval Intelligence, GB Study File 420-6; "Characteristics of Battleships, 1941 Building Program, 28 June 1939, Study File 420-6, General Board Papers.

132. Letter President of Naval War College to Chairman of General Board, 28 February 1940, General Board Papers.

133. Bureau of Construction and Repair to Secretary of the Navy, 5 April 1938, GB 420-2, General Board Papers.

134. Memorandum for Admiral Stark from Chairman of the General Board (Sexton), 3 June 1440, GB 420-2 (Serial 1972), General Board Papers.

135. This included fifteen old battleships plus the seventeen new ones.

136. Letter E. C. Kalbfus to Chairman of the General Board, 1 October 1935, Study File 420-6, NC3/XTA (1935–42), General Board Papers.

137. Memorandum for Chief of Naval Operations from Chairman of the General Board (Sexton), 7 October 1939, 420-2 (Serial 1885-A), General Board Papers.

138. Letter Chairman of the General Board to the Secretary of the Navy, 11 April 1940, 420-6 (Serial 1942), General Board Papers.

139. Letter Admiral Harry E. Yarnell to Rear Admiral C. P. Snyder, President of the Naval War College, 10 January 1939, Yarnell Papers.

140. Stirling, *Sea Duty,* pp. 301–302.

141. Roskill, *Naval Policy Between the Wars,* vol. 2, p. 206.

142. Ibid., pp. 218, 415; Andrade, "Naval Policy in the Disarmament Era," p. 409.

143. Andrade, "Naval Policy in the Disarmament Era," p. 160.

144. Memorandum, 3 May 1938, 420-2 (Serial 1790), General Board Papers.

145. Ibid.

146. Memorandum Chairman of the General Board, 31 January 1940, 420-5 (Serial 1861), General Board Papers.

147. John Major, "The Navy Plans for War," in *In Peace and War: Interpretations of American Naval History, 1775–1978,* ed. Kenneth J. Hagan (Westport, Conn., 1978), p. 251.

148. Andrade, "Submarine Policy," p. 55.

149. Ibid., pp. 54–55.

150. Michael Gannon, *Operation Drumbeat: The Dramatic True Story of Germany's First U-Boat Attacks Along the American Coast in World War II* (New York,

1990), see esp. chaps. 6–9; quotation in Theodore Roscoe, *United States Submarine Operations in World War II* (Annapolis, 1949), p. 5.

151. Morton, "War Plan ORANGE," p. 247.

152. Letter Yarnell to Leahy, 15 October 1937; Letter Yarnell to C. C. Bloch, 21 January 1938, Yarnell Papers.

153. Letter Yarnell to C. F. Snyder, 9 January 1937, Yarnell Papers.

154. Reynolds, *Carrier Admiral*, p. 44.

155. Ernest J. King and Walter M. Whitehall, *Fleet Admiral King: A Naval Record* (New York, 1952), p. 281.

156. Ibid.

157. Major, "The Navy Plans for War," p. 246.

158. Ibid., p. 249.

159. Memorandum prepared by Rear Admiral Rowcliffe, 26 August 1944, Bloch Papers.

160. R. J. Quinlan, "The United States Fleet: Diplomacy, Strategy, and the Allocation of Ships (1940–1941)," in *American Civil-Military Decisions: A Book of Case Studies*, ed. H. Stein (New York, 1963), pp. 158, 161; Major, "The Navy Plans for War," pp. 258–259; Morison, *History of United States Naval Operations in World War II*, vol. 1, p. 57.

161. Major, "The Navy Plans for War," pp. 258–259; Morison, *History of United States Naval Operations in World War II*, vol. 1, p. 57.

162. Major, "The Navy Plans for War," p. 259.

163. Pelz, *Race to Pearl Harbor*, pp. 205, 221; Kaufman, *Arms Control During the Pre-Nuclear Era*, p. 186.

164. O'Connell, *Of Arms and Men*, pp. 273–274.

165. Jiro Horikoshi, *Eagles of Mitsubishi: The Story of the Zero Fighter* (Seattle, 1980, trans. from 1970 Japanese ed.), pp. 93–100.

166. See for example Howarth, *Ships of the Rising Sun*, p. 199; Morison, *History of United States Naval Operations in World War II*, vol. 1, pp. 129–130.

167. Reynolds, *The Fast Carriers*, p. 6.

168. Howarth, *Ships of the Rising Sun*, p. 242.

169. Ibid., p. 243.

170. See for example Pelz, *Race to Pearl Harbor*, p. 134; Kaufman, *Arms Control During the Pre-Nuclear Era*, pp. 160, 191; or Howarth, *Ships of the Rising Sun*, p. 179.

171. Ibid., p. 167.

172. Ibid., p. 218.

173. Memorandum "On New Armaments and Plans," Aviation Section of the Navy General Staff to Navy Minister, 30 January 1941, cited in Howarth, *Ships of the Rising Sun*, p. 245; Pelz, *Race to Pearl Harbor*, p. 224.

174. John Toland, *The Rising Sun in the Pacific: The Decline and Fall of the Japanese Empire 1936–1945* (New York, 1970), p. 151.

175. Ibid.

176. Morison, *History of U.S. Naval Operations in World War II*, vol. 1, pp. 113–114.

177. Ibid.

178. George Sanson, "Japan's Fatal Blunder," in *The Use of Force*, ed. Robert Art and Kenneth Waltz (Boston, 1971), pp. 209–210.

179. Memorandum Admiral Rowcliffe to Admiral Sexton, 27 December 1941, GB 420-6, General Board Papers.

180. Memorandum from Admiral King to Chairman of the General Board, 30 July 1942, GB 420-2, General Board Papers.

Chapter Twelve

1. William R. Nichols, "Battleships 1991: An Assessment," *USNIP*, June 1991, p. 75.

About the Book
and Author

Sacred Vessels is an irreverent account of the modern battleship and its place in American naval history from the sinking of the coal-fired *Maine* in Havana Harbor in 1898 to the deployment of the cruise missile–armed *Missouri* in the Persian Gulf in 1991.

With provocative insight and wit, Robert O'Connell conclusively demonstrates that the vaunted battleship was in fact never an effective weapon of war, even before developments in aircraft and submarine technology sealed its doom. The world's navies failed to recognize the full implications of rapid technological change at the turn of the century but were enthralled by the revolutionary design of the HMS *Dreadnought*, launched in 1903. Nations raced to build and deploy the biggest, the fastest, and the greatest possible number of battleships, usually at the expense of much more effective forms of naval force. Dreadnoughts became the international currency of great power status, subject to the same anxious accountancy as nuclear weapons today. Their awesome beauty captured the public's imagination and won the unquestioning devotion of naval officers everywhere.

When war came in 1914, the world held its breath in anticipation of a modern-day Trafalgar, but dreadnoughts everywhere avoided battle, and when they were forced to fight, the results were inconclusive or irrelevant. In spite of this display of impotence, the world's shipyards continued to turn out the great vessels. The sinking of the heart of the U.S. battlefleet at Pearl Harbor—an event that finally forced the United States into World War II—ironically also began to shake the U.S. Navy free from its infatuation with the dreadnought in favor of the more practical charms of the aircraft carrier. Still, sheer faith in the battleship ensured that it would live to fight again, this time with even more questionable results. In fact, says O'Connell, battleships have never played an important role in the outcome of any modern war, but they have continued to be resurrected and refurbished—even garnished with nuclear weapons—right up to the present day.

Television images of the *Missouri* and the *Wisconsin* firing on the shores of Iraq in 1991 were not just a glimpse of an anachronism: We were witnessing, with a lingering sense of awe, the last gasp of a fire-breathing behemoth that in actuality was all but toothless from the moment of its conception. *Sacred Vessels* is more than the unmasking of a false idol of naval history. It is a cautionary tale about the often unacknowledged influence of human faith, culture, and tradition on the exceedingly important, costly, and supposedly rational process of nations arming themselves for war.

Robert L. O'Connell is Senior Analyst at the U.S. Army Intelligence Agency's Foreign Science and Technology Center. He was a member of the U.S. delegation to the Conference on Disarmament in Geneva. He has a Ph.D. in history from the University of Virginia.

Dr. O'Connell's first book was *Of Arms and Men: A History of War, Weapons, and Aggression.* He is a contributing editor to *MHQ: The Quarterly Journal of Military History,* for which he has written numerous articles and essays.

Index